Introduction to Computational Economics Using Fortran

Introduction to Computational Economics Using Fortran

Exercise and Solutions Manual

Hans Fehr

Maurice Hofmann

Fabian Kindermann

OXFORD
UNIVERSITY PRESS

OXFORD
UNIVERSITY PRESS

Great Clarendon Street, Oxford, OX2 6DP,
United Kingdom

Oxford University Press is a department of the University of Oxford.
It furthers the University's objective of excellence in research, scholarship,
and education by publishing worldwide. Oxford is a registered trade mark of
Oxford University Press in the UK and in certain other countries

First Edition published in 2020
Impression: 1

Published in the United States of America by Oxford University Press
198 Madison Avenue, New York, NY 10016, United States of America

British Library Cataloguing in Publication Data
Data available

Library of Congress Control Number: 2019909884

ISBN 978–0–19–885037–3

Printed and bound by
CPI Group (UK) Ltd, Croydon, CR0 4YY

CONTENTS

1 Fortran 90: A simple programming language

Exercise 1.1

(a) In Program 1.1 the error message for unreadable input is implemented by adding the **iostat** argument to the usual **read**(*,*) command. The variable `ios` is assigned a value of zero if the input was read in correctly, but carries a non-zero error-code otherwise. After reading in each number, we check whether the variable `ios` is equal to zero and stop the program otherwise, so that the computation process of the sum, difference, product, and quotient of `x` and `y` is not executed in this case.

(b) If the variables are declared all as **integer**, subtraction, addition, and multiplication (and exponentiation) will prove no problem. However, division works differently from division with variables of type **real***8. Integer division ignores the remainder, so that any decimal places are truncated.

Exercise 1.2

By default the compiler interprets integer literals in our source code (see Program 1.2) to be of type **integer**. However as we assign the result of adding 55555553 and 10000001 in the first case to a variable of type **real** and in the other case to a variable of type **real***8, it will be converted to the respective data type. While the data type **real** uses only 32 bit (4 byte) of memory to store a value in a variable, the data type **real***8 reserves 64 bit (8 byte) for a variable. The memory that is allocated to a specific variable decides over the range of values that can be stored in it and the precision at which a value is stored. The lower memory that is reserved for variables of type **real** leads to a precision of seven digits, which is referred to as *single precision*, whereas the variables of type **real***8 have a precision of fifteen digits, which is known as *double precision*. This explains why we can observe a slightly different result for variable `sum1` compared to variable `sum2` when we print the output to the screen, despite having initially assigned the same value to both variables.

Program 1.1 Read, write, and basic arithmetic operations in Fortran

```
program Calculation

    implicit none

    ! declaration of variables
    integer :: ios
    real*8 :: x, y
    real*8 :: addit, diffit, prodit, quotit

    ! read the first number
    write(*,*)'Type in the 1. real number: '
    read(*,*, iostat = ios)x

    ! check whether input is readable
    if(ios /= 0)stop 'Error: number is not readable'

    ! read the second number
    write(*,*)'Type in the 2. real number: '
    read(*,*, iostat = ios)y

    ! check whether number is readable
    if(ios /= 0)stop 'Error: number is not readable'

    ! perform arithmetic operations
    addit = x + y
    diffit = x - y
    prodit = x*y
    quotit = x/y

    ! print output
    write(*,'(a, f14.6)')'Sum        =', addit
    write(*,'(a, f14.6)')'Difference =', diffit
    write(*,'(a, f14.6)')'Product    =', prodit
    write(*,'(a, f14.6)')'Quotient   =', quotit

end program
```

Program 1.2 Variable types `real` and `real*8` in Fortran

```
program RealAndStar8

    implicit none

    ! declaration of variables
    real :: sum1
    real*8 :: sum2

    ! calculation of the sums
    sum1 = 55555553 + 10000001
    sum2 = 55555553 + 10000001

    ! print output
    write(*,'(a, f15.2)')'Using real   =', sum1
    write(*,'(a, f15.2)')'Using real*8 =', sum2

end program
```

Exercise 1.3

Similar to integer literals, the compiler interprets real literals by default to be of type **real**, so that the respective real number is only handled with *single precision*. To indicate that a numerical literal should be interpreted to be of type **real***8 and treated with *double precision*, we have to make sure in our source code that the letter `d` is embedded in the respective literal. This letter represents the exponent of 10 if *double precision* literals are used, ie `5d0` $= 5$, `5d-1` $= 0.5$, and `5d1` $= 50$.

(a) In the first expression that is suggested in Program 1.3 both the base and exponent of the value 10^9 are interpreted as **integer** literals. Before actually writing the result into the first entry of the array `rvar1`, the computer will perform the arithmetic operation and obtains a result that is itself of type **integer**. It is then implicitly converted into the **real***8 data type when it is written into the first entry of the array `rvar1`. If, however, at least base or exponent are of type **real***8, we obtain results that are already of type **real***8 and hence do not need to convert the values when we write them into the second and third entry of our array `rvar1`. As the type **integer** can handle values in the range from $-2^{31}+1$ to $2^{31}-1$, we fail to compute the value 10^{10} with the first expression suggested in the exercise. Our compiler will make us aware of this problem with an error message upon compilation. The second and third method to assign the value 10^{10} don't cause any problems, as we are able to deal with values in the range of approximately -10^{308} to $+10^{308}$ if numerical literals are interpreted to be of type **real***8. Finally, note the shortcut we used to print all entries of our arrays `rvar1` and `rvar2` to the screen.

(b) If the letter `d` is not embedded in the literal of a real number it is handled with *single precision*, which guarantees, as discussed in Exercise 1.2 above precision usually only for the first seven digits, while with *double precision* the level of precision is increased to the first fifteen digits. It is important to note that a computer is only able to approximate the majority of real numbers as it is working in the binary system instead of the decimal system and hence has to convert each real number we use from base ten to base two. Only

Program 1.3 *Single* and *double precision* literals

```
! assign 10**9 to rvar1
rvar1(1) = 10**9
rvar1(2) = 10d0**9
rvar1(3) = 10**9d0

! assign 10**10 to rvar2
!rvar2(1) = 10**10
rvar2(2) = 10d0**10
rvar2(3) = 10**10d0

! print output
write(*,'(a)')'                                  Without d0
With base d0              With expo d0'
write(*,'(a, 3f22.2)')'Exp  9', (rvar1(i), i = 1, 3)
write(*,'(a, 3f22.2)')'Exp 10', (rvar2(i), i = 1, 3)
```

numbers that can be written in the form of m/n where m and n are integers and n is an integral power of 2 are representable with a finite number of digits in the binary system. If we assign the real number 0.000000000003 in single precision to the first entry of the array `x` this yields 0.000000000002999999880126 when printing the result to the screen. The conversion error thus occurs when the first decimal places are different from zero. Assigning the same number in *double precision* to the second entry of array `x` makes the conversion error not occur before the twenty-ninth decimal place.

(c) The compiler rounds off the value to be of *single precision* without the letter `d` in the literal. The number `3.1415926535` is not precise after the seventh digit under *single precision*, while `3.1415926535d0` would be stored with all the digits intact. If we specify values in *single precision* in our source code, it thus does not make sense to declare more than six decimal places.

Exercise 1.4

The `T` we print to the screen when running the code in Program 1.4 means that our logical expression holds **`.true.`** for the values $x = 4$, $y = 6$, and $z = 8$. The computer will proceed as follows when evaluating the statement: At first, it checks whether each of the individual logical statements we connected in our expression are **`.true.`** and then moves on to operate logical operators. The most binding logical operator is **`.and.`**, which means that all **`.and.`** operators will be evaluated before the **`.or.`** operator. The result of the logical operator **`.and.`** will be **`.true.`** if both statements we link to each other are **`.true.`**. However, in the case of the logical operator **`.or.`** only one of the statements has to be **`.true.`** to make this expression hold and obtain the result **`.true.`**. For our second parameter combination $x = 4$, $y = 6$, and $z = 2$, the result we print to the screen is `F`, indicating that our logical expression does not hold for this combination of parameters.

Program 1.4 Evaluating logical statements in Fortran

```
program Logicals

    implicit none

    ! declare variables
    integer :: x, y, z

    ! assign values
    x = 4
    y = 6
    z = 8

    ! print output
    write(*,*) (x >= 3 .and. y <= 4 .and. z == 5 &
                  .or. x <= y .and. y < z)

end program
```

Exercise 1.5

Before we proceed with the numerical implementation, we have to take the derivatives of our tax function with respect to taxable income y by hand. Table 1.1 summarizes the actual tax burden $T(y)$, marginal tax rate $\frac{\partial T(y)}{\partial y}$, and average tax rate $\frac{T(y)}{y}$ for a given income y in €.

The marginal tax rate tells us what is the tax rate on an additional € earned, while the average tax rate tells us which fraction of total taxable income y is paid as taxes. In our numerical implementation (see Program 1.5), we first of all read in a value for the taxable income y and then use an if-statement to separate our tax brackets. Note the \$ sign in the formatter of our **write** statement, which is used to avoid a line-break and to write the value we assign to y in the same line as the text string that asked us to type in an income.

Table 1.1 The German income tax function

y	$T(y)$	$\frac{\partial T(y)}{\partial y}$
$y < 8131$	0	0
$8131 < y < 13469$	$(933.70x + 1400)x$	$(1867.4x + 1400)/10000$
$13470 < y < 52881$	$(228.74z + 2397)z + 1014$	$(457.48z + 2397)/10000$
$52882 < y < 250730$	$0.42y - 8196$	0.42
$y > 250731$	$0.45y - 15718$	0.45

$x = (y - 8130)/10000, z = (y - 13469)/10000$

Program 1.5 Numerical implementation of the German tax function

```
program TaxFunction
    [......]
    ! read the income from console
    write(*,'(a,$)')'Type in the income: '
    read(*,*)y

    x = (y - 8130d0)/10000d0
    z = (y - 13469d0)/10000d0

    if(y < 8131d0)then
        T = 0d0
        average = 0d0
        marginal = 0d0
    elseif(y < 13470d0)then
        T = (933.70d0*x + 1400d0)*x
        average = T/y
        marginal = (1867.4d0*x + 1400d0)/10000d0
    elseif(y < 52882d0)then
        [......]
    endif

    ! print output
    write(*,'(a, f14.6)')'tax burden:          ', T
    write(*,'(a, f14.6)')'average tax:         ', average*100d0
    write(*,'(a, f14.6)')'marginal tax rate:', marginal*100d0

end program
```

At the end of the program, we then print our results to the screen and see that both the average as well as the marginal tax rate are increasing with income.

Exercise 1.6

(a) The algorithm to compute a certain element of the Fibonacci series is stored in the function `fib` after the **`contains`** statement in program `sol_prog01_06`. As the first two elements of the Fibonacci series need to be equal to one and all the following elements are the sum of the two previous elements of the series, we use an if statement to separate the computation process for the first two elements from that of all further elements of the series. In the main program itself, we then only read in the element-number of our Fibonacci series and print the result to the screen. In Program 1.6, we define the variables `a0, a1, a2`, and `fib` to be of type **`real`**`*8` instead of **`integer`**, despite every single element of the Fibonacci series having to be by definition an integer number. This is because using variables of type **`integer`** would only provide enough memory to compute up to the forty-sixth element of the Fibonacci series.

Program 1.6 Function to evaluate the Fibonacci series

```
function fib(n)

    implicit none

    ! input variables
    integer, intent(in) :: n
    integer:: j
    real*8 :: a0, a1, a2, fib

    ! Calculation of the result
    if(n <= 2)then
        a0 = 1
    else

        ! initialize the first two elements
        a1 = 1
        a2 = 1

        ! calculate the n-th element
        do j = 3, n
            a0 = a1 + a2
            a2 = a1
            a1 = a0
        enddo
    endif

    fib = a0

end function
```

(b) Binet's formula is the closed-form solution to the Fibonacci series and is implemented in function `Binform(n)` in the source code shown in Program 1.6.a. The advantage of this closed-form solution is that we don't have to compute the value of a certain element of the Fibonacci series iteratively by adding up all previous elements, but only have to evaluate a single formula.

(c) However, evaluating this formula comes with imprecisions, as computers only work with approximations for real numbers (see Exercise 1.3 (b) for a more detailed discussion). These imprecisions are negligible for lower elements of the Fibonacci series, but become more relevant for elements $n > 90$. Plotting the difference between the iterative solution from (a) and the closed-form solution from (b) with the GNUplot interface from the toolbox shows how this difference is increasing in n. The subroutines and functions from the toolbox are made available in our main program through `use toolbox` at the very beginning of our code (see Program 1.6.b).

Program 1.6.a Binet's formula

```
function Binform(n)

    implicit none

    ! input variables
    integer, intent(in) :: n
    real*8:: Binform
    real*8:: golden_ratio

    golden_ratio = (1d0 + sqrt(5d0))/2d0

    Binform = (golden_ratio**(n) - &
                  (1d0 - golden_ratio)**(n))/sqrt(5d0)

end function
```

Program 1.6.b Plot approximation error of Binet's formula

```
program Fibonacci

    use toolbox
    [......]
    do i = 1, plotmax
        x(i) = i
        diff(i) = abs(fib(i) - Binform(i))
    enddo

    call plot(x, diff, legend='Diff')
    call execplot()

contains
    [......]
end program
```

Exercise 1.7

There are n dice, each with k sides. Then the sum of numbers is always in the interval $[n, n+1, \ldots, n \cdot k - 1, n \cdot k]$. Since the total number of pairs is k^n, the probability of the first and the last sum (n and $n \cdot k$) is always $1/k^n$, the probability of the second and the next-to-last sum ($n+1$ and $n \cdot k - 1$) is always n/k^n. However, as deriving a general analytical solution for the probability that a certain sum occurs is quite involved, obtaining the probability distribution through simulation is an attractive alternative.

After declaring the variables as usual, calling the subroutine `init_random_seed` as in Program 1.7 ensures that the random number generator is initialized at some arbitrary value that depends on the time and date at which the program is executed. Otherwise, it is possible that the sequence of random numbers drawn by the subroutine **`random_number`**`(x)` is the same every time your program is restarted.

The subroutine **`random_number`**`(x)` returns a single random number x from the uniform distribution over the interval $[0, 1]$ for each roll of the n dice. A roll of a k-sided dice is then derived by multiplying this number x with the number of sides k and converting it into an integer number through **`int`**`(k*x)`. Since this conversion simply truncates the decimal places of `k*x`, one has to add a one to this number if we assume that the lowest number of dots on a dice is one. Next, the sum of dots for n dice is derived using the **`sum`** command and the respective element of the array `Dsum` is increased by 1 in each iteration step. After `iter` draws of the n dice, the array elements of `Dsum` tell us how many times the different sums have occurred. In order to derive the simulated probabilities, we have to divide this number by the total number of iterations. One can check whether the first and second probabilities as well as the last and the next-to-last probabilities are $1/k^n$ and n/k^n, respectively.

Program 1.7 Simulate dice roll

```
[......]
! set random seed
call init_random_seed()

dice = 0
Dsum = 0d0
do i = 1, iter
    do j = 1, n
        call random_number(x)
        dice(j) = int(k*x) + 1
    enddo
    Dsum(sum(dice)) = Dsum(sum(dice)) + 1d0
enddo
SimProb = Dsum/iter*100d0
[......]
```

Exercise 1.8

In the previous exercise it was (at least in some parameter combinations) possible to derive the probability for certain events through analytical reasoning. In this exercise, it is an even more complex task to derive a closed-form solution, which again makes simulation a very helpful tool for us. Similar to the previous exercise, we call the subroutine `init_random_seed` to ensure that the random number generator is again initialized at some arbitrary value. We then simulate in each iteration step n dice, which are rolled `mroll` times (see Program 1.8). First, the two conditions x and y, which would end the game, are defined and the required count variable is initialized, then the iteration do-loop is set up and the new subroutine `random_int(dice(k),intl,inth)` is called once for each dice in any roll.

If the sum of all dice is x, we increase the count variable `count_x` by one, check whether the number of rolls it took us to end the game is higher than the current maximum number of rolls from all previous iterations, and leave the j-loop. If the sum of all n dice

Program 1.8 Approximate distribution through simulation

```
program RollDiceEndCondition
    [......]
    x = 4
    y = 10
    count_x = 0d0
    max_roll = 0
    do i = 1, iter
        do j = 1, mroll
            do k = 1, n
                call random_int(dice(k), 1, 6)
            enddo

            if (sum(dice) == x) then
                count_x = count_x + 1d0
                max_roll = max(max_roll, j)
                exit
            elseif (sum(dice) == y) then
                max_roll = max(max_roll, j)
                exit
            endif
        enddo
    enddo
    [......]
contains

    subroutine random_int(result, intl, inth)
    [......]
    end subroutine

end program
```

is y, the number of rolls is compared to the current maximum number of rolls and the j-loop is left. In all other cases, the n dice are rolled again. After we reach the maximum number of iterations, we compute the percentage of how often the game will be stopped by the first condition instead of the second, and vice versa, to finally print our results to the screen. Note that the subroutine `random_int` is defined after the **`contains`** statement.

From Exercise 1.7 we know that for $n = 2$ the probabilities for the sums of 4, 7, and 10 are 3/36, 6/36, and 3/36, respectively. Hence, if the sum of dots of all n, the dice has to be either $x = 4$ or $y = 10$ to end the game, both events are equally likely, and thus the probability that either x or y occurs first is 50% each. For $x = 4$ and $y = 7$, the probability that the game is stopped by the first condition is 33.33% and the probablity that the game is stopped by the second condition is 66.66%, as it is twice as likely that the sum of all dots is equal to $y = 7$ instead of $x = 4$.

Similarly, we know in the case of $n = 3$ from Exercise 1.7 that the probabilities for the sums of 4, 5, and 17 are 3/216, 5/216, and 3/216, respectively. Applying the same reasoning as for $n = 2$, this yields again a computed probability of 50% for both conditions if we set $x = 4$ and $y = 17$, while for $x = 4$ and $y = 5$ the probability that x would occur first is 33.33% and the probability that y would occur first is 66.66%. Increasing the number of iterations helps us to increase the precision of our results and makes us converge towards the actual analytical solution.

Exercise 1.9

The code for the solution of this problem is stored in two separate files, `sol_prog01_09` and `sol_prog_01_09m`. The first file contains the main program (which is shown as well in Program 1.9), while the second is used to store the module `globals` with parameter definitions and the function `utility`. Similar to the toolbox, we make the parameters and the function `utility`, which are stored in the module `globals`, accessible in the main program with the **`use`** statement.

(a) Our consumption level is read into the variable `c_read` and the utility is computed for different values of γ. The function `utility` expects with `c_local` and `gamma_local` two variables from the main program as input. The flag `_local` to these variables indicates that these variables are local to the function itself, ie that they can only be accessed in the function `utility`. At the beginning of the function, we first of all check whether the consumption level it received from the main program is greater than zero. If this is the case, we proceed to computing the utility for this level of consumption for an assigned parameter `gamma_local`. Note again the `$` sign in the formatter of our **`write`** statement, which is used to avoid a line-break and write the number we chose in the same line as the message that asked us to type in a number.

(b) In order to plot the utility function for different values of γ, we have to use the GNUPlot interface from the toolbox. To do so, we set up an equidistant grid with `NC` gridpoints for $c \in [0.1, 1]$ and compute the respective utility values $u(c)$ for specific values

Program 1.9 Evaluate and plot utility function

```
include "sol_prog01_09m.f90"

program CalcUtil

    use globals
    use toolbox
    [......]
    ! read in consumption value
    write(*,'(a, $)')'Type in a consumption level: '
    read(*,*)c_read

    ! print output
    write(*,*)
    do ig = 1, NG
        write(*,'(3(a,f8.2,2x))')'c = ', c_read, ' U = ', &
            utility(c_read, gamma_array(ig)), &
            ' gamma = ', gamma_array(ig)
    enddo

    ! set up equidistant grid to plot utility to the screen
    do ic = 1, NC
        c(ic) = dble(ic)/dble(NC)
    enddo

    ! calculate and plot utility for
    ! different consumption levels
    do ig = 1, NG
        do ic = 1, NC
            u(ic) = utility(c(ic), gamma_array(ig))
        enddo

        ! print output
        write(label(ig),'(a,f6.4)')'gamma = ', gamma_array(ig)
        call plot(c, u, legend=label(ig))
        call execplot()
    enddo

end program
```

of γ. As we want to plot the graph with a legend that displays the respective γ values, we have to store this value in the variable `label`, which is set up to be of the same shape as the array `gamma_array`. Calling the subroutine `plot` provides the data for GNUPlot and receives the arrays `c` and `u` as input, together with the optional character string that is used to store the legend for our plot. Finally, the plot is executed for each value of γ by calling the subroutine `execplot`.

Exercise 1.10

The program to solve this problem is set up very similar to the one in Exercise 1.9. It again uses a separate file aside from the main program to define the module `globals` in which the functions `utility` and `utility_int` are stored. However, the function `utility` now only receives consumption as input argument, since the parameter γ is set to a fixed value.

Module 1.10m Subroutine to evaluate utility function

```
subroutine utility_int(a_local, b_local, u_local)

    implicit none

    ! input variables
    real*8, intent(in) :: a_local, b_local
    real*8, intent(out) :: u_local(:)
    real*8 :: c_local(size(u_local))
    integer :: n, j

    ! check whether 0 <= a < b:
    if(a_local <= 0d0 .or. b_local < a_local)then
        stop 'Error: a <= 0 or b < a: subroutine can't be used'
    endif

    ! size of the array u_local
    n = size(u_local)

    ! calculation of consumption level and utilities
    do j = 1, n
        c_local(j) = a_local + dble(j-1)/dble(n-1)*&
                     (b_local - a_local)
        u_local(j) = utility(c_local(j))
    enddo

end subroutine
```

(a) Subroutine `utility_int` is called in total with three arguments, ie interval boundaries `a` and `b`, as well as the array `u` that is used to store the function values. The **`intent(out)`** argument next to the declaration of the `u_local` array indicates that this argument of the subroutine is used to give back a result whenever it is called. The subroutine first of all checks whether the values set for a and b suffice the condition $0 < a < b$.

(b) If the condition holds for the values a and b, the subroutine proceeds to determining the size of the array `u_local` that was handed to the subroutine. This is done with the Fortran intrinsic function **`size`** to set up the array `c_local` with points at which the function should be evaluated. The full subroutine `utility_int` is shown in Module 1.10m.

(c) These points are set up on an equidistant grid, with $n - 1$ equally spaced intervals between the lower bound a and the upper bound b, according to:

$$c_j = a + \frac{(j-1)}{n-1}(b-a) \quad \text{for} \quad j = 1, \ldots, n$$

where we cast the integer values `j-1` and `n-1` in our program explicitly with the **`dble`** command to *double precision*. After having computed the values of the function `utility` for each of these points, we print them to the screen in the main program.

2 Numerical solution methods

Exercise 2.1

LU-factorization decomposes a matrix A with the help of the Gaussian elimination method into the product of a lower triangular matrix L and an upper triangular matrix U, for which:

$$LU = A$$

holds. This equality obviously is true if we initially set L equal to the identity matrix and U equal to A. Applying the Gaussian elimination algorithm to bring the matrix U into the desired upper triangular shape requires us to iteratively swap rows, multiply rows by non-zero numbers or add the multiple of one row to another. However, performing these operations to obtain a zero in a certain cell makes it necessary to undo these operations by adding the same multiple to the same cell in L as otherwise the above equality would no longer hold.

(a) We start with initializing the matrix L to be equal to the identity matrix and U to be equal to our matrix A:

$$L = \begin{bmatrix} 1 & 0 & 0 & 0 \\ 0 & 1 & 0 & 0 \\ 0 & 0 & 1 & 0 \\ 0 & 0 & 0 & 1 \end{bmatrix} \qquad U = \begin{bmatrix} 1 & 5 & 2 & 3 \\ 1 & 6 & 8 & 6 \\ 1 & 6 & 11 & 2 \\ 1 & 7 & 17 & 4 \end{bmatrix}.$$

In the first step, we subtract the first row of the matrix U from the second, third, and fourth row of U and hence add a one in the first column of the respective row in matrix L:

$$L = \begin{bmatrix} 1 & 0 & 0 & 0 \\ 1 & 1 & 0 & 0 \\ 1 & 0 & 1 & 0 \\ 1 & 0 & 0 & 1 \end{bmatrix} \qquad U = \begin{bmatrix} 1 & 5 & 2 & 3 \\ 0 & 1 & 6 & 3 \\ 0 & 1 & 9 & -1 \\ 0 & 2 & 15 & 1 \end{bmatrix}.$$

Next, we subtract the second row of U from the third row and two times from the fourth row. Undoing these operations in the matrix L yields a one in the second column of row three and a two in the second column of row four:

$$L = \begin{bmatrix} 1 & 0 & 0 & 0 \\ 1 & 1 & 0 & 0 \\ 1 & 1 & 1 & 0 \\ 1 & 2 & 0 & 1 \end{bmatrix} \qquad U = \begin{bmatrix} 1 & 5 & 2 & 3 \\ 0 & 1 & 6 & 3 \\ 0 & 0 & 3 & -4 \\ 0 & 0 & 3 & -5 \end{bmatrix}.$$

Finally, we subtract the third row of U from the fourth row and hence add a one to the third column in L:

$$L = \begin{bmatrix} 1 & 0 & 0 & 0 \\ 1 & 1 & 0 & 0 \\ 1 & 1 & 1 & 0 \\ 1 & 2 & 1 & 1 \end{bmatrix} \qquad U = \begin{bmatrix} 1 & 5 & 2 & 3 \\ 0 & 1 & 6 & 3 \\ 0 & 0 & 3 & -4 \\ 0 & 0 & 0 & -1 \end{bmatrix}.$$

This gives us the final decomposition of our matrix A into the lower triangular matrix L and the upper triangular matrix U.

LU-factorization is implemented numerically in the subroutine `lu_dec(A, L, U)` from the toolbox. Its first argument is an array `A`, which stores the matrix that should be decomposed, while the other arguments `L` and `U` are arrays for the resulting lower and upper triangular matrix. After using the subroutine `lu_dec` to decompose the matrix A, we multiply the matrices L and U and see that we obtain the initial matrix A again. Note the syntax in Program 2.1 we use to print the matrices. Nesting the shortcut we used to print the arrays in Exercise 1.3 (a) in itself is equivalent to setting up a nested do-loop and hence is a very convenient method for us to print matrices.

(b) With the lower triangular matrix L and the upper triangular matrix U at hand, we can now compute the solution to the linear equation system:

$$\underbrace{\begin{bmatrix} 1 & 5 & 2 & 3 \\ 1 & 6 & 8 & 6 \\ 1 & 6 & 11 & 2 \\ 1 & 7 & 17 & 4 \end{bmatrix}}_{A} \underbrace{\begin{bmatrix} x_1 \\ x_2 \\ x_3 \\ x_4 \end{bmatrix}}_{x} = \underbrace{\begin{bmatrix} 1 \\ 2 \\ 1 \\ 1 \end{bmatrix}}_{b}$$

by rewriting our equation system in the form:

$$Ax = (LU)x = L(Ux) = Ly = b$$

Program 2.1 Numerical implementation of LU-factorization

```
! print matrix A to the screen
write(*, '(a)')'A = '
write(*, '(4f7.1)')((A(j, i),i=1,4),j=1,4)

! decompose matrix A
call lu_dec(A, L, U)

! check the result from lu_dec
A_test = matmul(L, U)
```

and then solving the linear equation system $Ly = b$ for y using forward substitution in the first step and $Ux = y$ for x using backward substitution in the second step. Here we obtain when solving the equation system $Ly = b$ for y,

$$\begin{aligned} y_1 &= 1 \\ y_2 &= (2-1)/1 = 1 \\ y_3 &= (1-1-1)/1 = -1 \quad \text{and} \\ y_4 &= (1-1-2\cdot 1+1)/1 = -1, \end{aligned}$$

which is equivalent to:

$$y = \begin{bmatrix} 1 \\ 1 \\ -1 \\ -1 \end{bmatrix}.$$

Using that to solve the equation system $Ux = y$ with backward substitution, we obtain:

$$\begin{aligned} x_4 &= 1 \\ x_3 &= (-1+4)/3 = 1 \\ x_2 &= (1-6\cdot 1-3\cdot 1)/1 = -8 \quad \text{and} \\ x_1 &= (1-5\cdot(-8)-2\cdot 1-3\cdot 1)/1 = 36, \end{aligned}$$

which is:

$$x = \begin{bmatrix} 36 \\ -8 \\ 1 \\ 1 \end{bmatrix}.$$

Alternatively, we can use the subroutine `lu_solve(A, b)` from the toolbox which directly solves an equation system with LU-factorization (see Program 2.1.a). It stores the solution x to the linear equation system in the array `b` and yields the same result for x as our calculations above.

Exercise 2.2

(a) The intertemporal maximation problem of the household is:

$$\max_{c_1,c_2} \; U(c_1,c_2) = \frac{c_1^{1-\frac{1}{\gamma}}}{1-\frac{1}{\gamma}} + \beta\frac{c_2^{1-\frac{1}{\gamma}}}{1-\frac{1}{\gamma}} \qquad \text{s.t.} \quad c_1 + \frac{c_2}{1+r} = w$$

Program 2.1.a Solving a linear equation sytem using LU-factorization

```
! solve the linear equation system
call lu_solve(A, b)

! check the result from lu_solve
b_test = matmul(A, b)

! print output
write(*,'(a)')'b = '
write(*,'(4f7.1)')(b(i),i=1,4)
write(*,'(/a)')'b_test = '
write(*,'(4f7.1)')(b_test(i),i=1,4)
```

and yields the following Lagrangian:

$$\mathcal{L} = \frac{c_1^{1-\frac{1}{\gamma}}}{1-\frac{1}{\gamma}} + \beta\frac{c_2^{1-\frac{1}{\gamma}}}{1-\frac{1}{\gamma}} + \lambda\left(w - c_1 - \frac{c_2}{1+r}\right).$$

Taking derivatives with respect to c_1, c_2, and λ allows us to set up the following equation system:

$$\frac{\partial\mathcal{L}}{\partial c_1} = c_1^{-\frac{1}{\gamma}} - \lambda = 0$$
$$\frac{\partial\mathcal{L}}{\partial c_2} = \beta c_2^{-\frac{1}{\gamma}} - \frac{\lambda}{1+r} = 0$$
$$\frac{\partial\mathcal{L}}{\partial\lambda} = w - c_1 - \frac{c_2}{1+r} = 0.$$

From the first two equations we get:

$$c_1 = [\beta(1+r)]^{-\gamma}c_2$$

as the intertemporal optimality condition. Substituting this into our third equation and using the given parameter values yields $c_1 = c_2 = 0.5$ for the optimal consumption path. The individual will smooth out consumption perfectly over two periods as she discounts future utility at the market interest rate (ie $\beta = 1/(1+r)) = 1$). Plugging this result either into the first or second equation yields $\lambda = 4$. The Lagrange-multiplier λ can be interpreted as the marginal change in utility resulting from a marginal increase of income.

(b) In this exercise we apply `fzero` to solve the nonlinear equation system from (a) we obtained by taking the first-order derivatives of our Lagrangian. We therefore declare a logical variable `check` and initialize a one-dimensional array `x_root` of length 3 with a guess of starting values for the iteration process. The actual equation system from (a) is stored in the function `foc` in our module `globals` and handed over to `fzero` when it is called by the main program (see Module 2.2m). There are two important points to note here: first, the function `foc` needs to be stored in a separate module, which means that it cannot be an element of the contains statement in the main program; and second, despite knowing the number of unknowns of our equation system, the function itself and the array it expects as input always has to be of assumed-size type if we want to solve multidimensional problems.

The subroutine `fzero` will then start the numerical iteration procedure to solve the equation system. If convergence is reached in less than the maximum number of iteration steps, the value **`.false.`** is assigned to the variable `check`. If, on the other hand, `fzero` did not converge, `check` will carry the value **`.true.`** and we print an error message to the screen before we stop the program (see Program 2.2). After `fzero` was executed, correctly we proceed to print the results to the screen and see that we indeed obtained a good approximation to the analytical solution.

(c) In order to solve the intertemporal optimization problem using the subroutine `fminsearch`, one way is to rearrange the household's budget constraint:

$$c_2 = (w - c_1)(1 + r)$$

Module 2.2m First-order conditions from the Lagrangian

```
function foc(x_in)

    implicit none

    real*8, intent(in) :: x_in(:)
    real*8 :: foc(size(x_in, 1))

    ! set up equation system to solve
    foc(1) = x_in(1)**(-1d0/gamma) - x_in(3)
    foc(2) = beta*x_in(2)**(-1d0/gamma) - x_in(3)/(1d0+r)
    foc(3) = w - x_in(1) - x_in(2)/(1d0+r)

end function
```

Program 2.2 Solving the non-linear equation system with `fzero`

```
! initialize x_root
x_root = 0.1d0

! call subroutine fzero
call fzero(x_root, foc, check)

! check whether fzero was executed correctly
if(check)stop 'Error: fzero did not converge'
```

and substitute into household's utility function:

$$\widetilde{U}(c_1) = \frac{c_1^{1-\frac{1}{\gamma}}}{1-\frac{1}{\gamma}} + \beta\,\frac{[(w-c_1)(1+r)]^{1-\frac{1}{\gamma}}}{1-\frac{1}{\gamma}}.$$

We now only have to optimize this function in one dimension over c_1 and can recover c_2 through the rearranged budget constraint from above. Since `fminsearch` is minimizing the objective function, we have to multiply it by -1 and restate our optimization problem as:

$$\min_{c_1} \widetilde{U}(c_1) = (-1)\left[\frac{c_1^{1-\frac{1}{\gamma}}}{1-\frac{1}{\gamma}} + \beta\,\frac{[(w-c_1)(1+r)]^{1-\frac{1}{\gamma}}}{1-\frac{1}{\gamma}}\right].$$

$\widetilde{U}(c_1)$ is stored in the function `utility` in the module `globals` (see Module 2.2m.a).

We initialize the upper bound `b` of our searching interval by setting c_2 to zero and derive the lower bound `a` from the assumption of non-negative consumption. For the starting value stored in `x_minimize`, it is sufficient to use any value within this interval $[a, b]$. `x_minimize` is now only a scalar, since we iterate only over c_1 and make use of the fact that c_2 is implicitly determined through the budget constraint. Program 2.2.a shows how to call the subroutine `fminsearch` in our code.

The subroutine `fminsearch` will perform a maximum of 150 iteration steps, store the solution in the variable `x_minimize`, and write the respective function value into the variable `fret` after convergence is reached. It will print an error message if the maximum number of iterations is reached without convergence. When printing the solution to the screen, c_2^* is recovered from the budget constraint for a given c_1^*.

Module 2.2m.a Utility function to be maximized

```
function utility(x_in)

    implicit none

    real*8, intent(in) :: x_in
    real*8 :: utility

    ! set up utility we want to maximize
    utility = -(x_in**egam/egam &
                + beta*((w - x_in)*(1d0+r))**egam/egam)

end function
```

Program 2.2.a Solve optimization problem using `fminsearch`

```
! initialize interval for fminsearch and x_minimize
a = 0d0
b = w
x_minimize = w/2d0

! call subroutine fminsearch
call fminsearch(x_minimize, fret, a, b, utility)
```

Exercise 2.3

Before we proceed to discuss the solution to this exercise, it is useful to explain the computation of the weights ω_j, which are used to derive the two subintervals in each iteration i. Consider Figure 2.1, where we divide the interval $[a_i, b_i]$ using points $x_{i,1}$ and $x_{i,2}$. The distances $x_{i,2} - a_i$ and $b_i - x_{i,1}$ define the two possible next bracketing segments. For these bracketing segments, the two conditions:

$$x_{i,2} - a_i = b_i - x_{i,1} \quad \text{and} \quad \frac{x_{i,1} - a_i}{b_i - a_i} = \frac{x_{i,2} - x_{i,1}}{b_i - x_{i,1}}$$

should hold. The first condition requires that both segments are of equal length and the second condition induces *scale similarity*, which implies that $x_{i,2}$ divides the interval $[x_{i,1}, b_i]$ in the same fraction as $x_{i,1}$ divides the interval $[a_i, b_i]$.

From the definitions in Figure 2.1, the two conditions can be reformulated as:

$$\omega_1 + z = 1 - \omega_1$$
$$\omega_1 = \frac{z}{1 - \omega_1}.$$

These two equations give the quadratic equation:

$$\omega_1^2 - 3\omega_1 + 1 = 0, \qquad \text{which yields} \quad \omega_1 = \frac{3 - \sqrt{5}}{2}$$

when solving for ω_1.

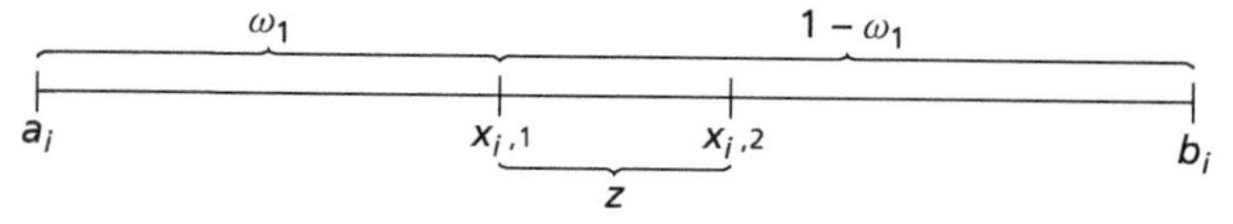

Figure 2.1 Optimal subintervals for Golden-Search

Now we can proceed to computing the global minimum of the function $f(x) = x \cdot cos(x^2)$ using Golden-Search. As explained in Section 2.3.1 of the book, the basic idea of this algorithm is to divide in each iteration i the interval $[a_i, b_i]$ into two new segments $[a_i, x_{i,1}]$ and $[x_{i,2}, b_i]$, for which we test whether $f(x_{i,1}) \lesseqgtr f(x_{i,2})$. If $f(x_{i,1}) < f(x_{i,2})$, then the new interval borders is set to:

$$a_{i+1} = a_i \quad \text{and} \quad b_{i+1} = x_{i,2}$$

since the minimum is implicitly assumed to be closer to the interval in which we observe the lower function value during an iteration step. Vice versa, this yields for $f(x_{i,1}) > f(x_{i,2})$:

$$a_{i+1} = x_{i,1} \quad \text{and} \quad b_{i+1} = b_i.$$

(a) The function `minimize(a, b)` in the module `globals` contains the numerical implementation of the Golden-Search algorithm and receives two arguments `a` and `b`. These variables store the initial interval borders for our iteration procedure and are **`real`**`*8` scalars of type **`intent(in)`**, which means that they cannot be modified throughout the function. However, as we want to update our interval borders in any iteration step, we pass `a` and `b` over to local variables `a1` and `b1`, which we can then update with the new interval borders in each iteration step, as shown Module 2.3m.

We obtain the new interval borders by comparing the function values at the two potential candidates $x_{i,1}$ and $x_{i,2}$ and adjust either the lower or the upper bound according to the rule above. The intuition behind Golden-Search is that the minimum we are looking for is closer to the smaller of these two function values, and thus narrowing down our interval in this way will make us converge to the actual minimum. We set up a do-loop with 200 iterations for our Golden-Search algorithm and iterate until the convergence criterion:

$$|b_i - a_i| < 10^{-6}$$

Module 2.3m Function `minimize` with Golden-Search algorithm

```
function minimize(a, b)

    implicit none

    ! declaration of variables
    real*8, intent(in) :: a
    real*8, intent(in) :: b
    integer :: iter
    real*8 :: minimize
    real*8 :: a1, b1, x1, x2, f1, f2

    ! set starting values for the iteration
    a1 = a
    b1 = b
    [......]
end function
```

is met. After the convergence is reached, we compute two further function values at $x_{i,1}$ as well as $x_{i,2}$, and return the smaller of the two values as the minimum of our function.

(b) Golden-Search is only working reliably if there is one unique minimum in the interval $[a, b]$. Otherwise, we would run the risk of being stuck in a local minimum instead of finding the actual global minimum. One way around this problem is to split the interval $[a, b]$ into a set of subintervals and to perform Golden-Search on each of these subintervals. Program 2.3 shows how we use the subroutine `grid_Cons_Equi` from the toolbox to split the interval $[a, b]$ into n subintervals of equal length and compute the respective minimum for each subinterval with the function `minimize` from (a). We write these minima for the different subintervals to the array `minimum_x`.

(c) In the next step, we compute the function values for each of these minima in `minimum_x` and assign them to the array `fmin`. The **`minloc`** command allows us to locate the position of the minimum in the array `fmin`. If we set n high enough, so that each subinterval contains only one minimum, this minimum should coincide with the global minimum of our function (see Program 2.3.a). Trying out different values for n shows that $n \geq 4$ intervals are necessary in our case to find the global minimum of $f(x) = x \cdot cos(x^2)$ at $x = 4.691893$ in the interval $[0, 5]$, see Figure 2.2.

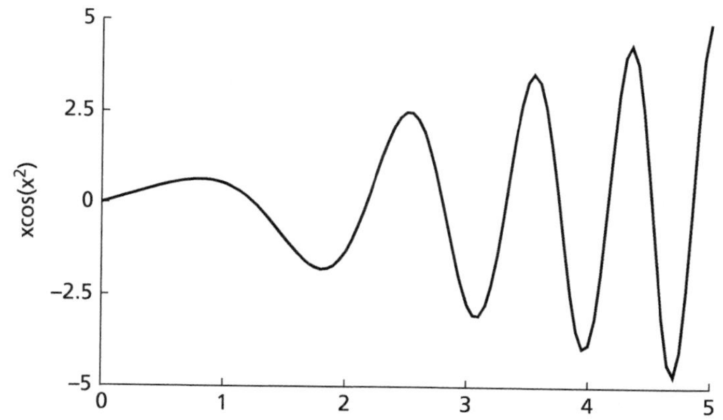

Figure 2.2 Plot of $xcos(x^2)$

Program 2.3 Search for local minima in subintervals

```
! set up n subintervals
call grid_Cons_Equi(x, x_l, x_u)

! find minimum value in each interval
do i = 1, n
    minimum_x(i) = minimize(x(i-1), x(i))
enddo
```

Program 2.3.a Locate minimum of all subintervals

```
! calculate function values
fmin = minimum_x*cos(minimum_x**2d0)

! locate global minimum
i_global = minloc(fmin, 1)
min_global = minimum_x(i_global)
fmin_global = min_global*cos(min_global**2d0)
```

Exercise 2.4

This intertemporal optimization problem differs from Exercise 2.2 only with respect to the time horizon. While the household before lived for two periods and received labour income in the first period, the optimization problem is now extented to three periods, with labour income in the first two periods. We restrict ourselves in the solution to numerical optimization with the subroutine `fminsearch` from the toolbox, but point out that this problem is still analytically tractable and thus could either be solved by hand or using the subroutine `fzero` with respect to the equation system resulting from the Lagrangian.

(a) Similar to above, it is possible to reduce the dimension of our optimization problem by reformulating our intertemporal budget constraint, so that:

$$c_1 = w + \frac{w - c_2}{1+r} - \frac{c_3}{(1+r)^2}.$$

Substituting the new constraint into our objective function thus makes our problem a two-dimensional optimization problem, ie:

$$\widetilde{U}(c_2, c_3) = \frac{1}{1-\frac{1}{\gamma}}\left[w + \frac{w - c_2}{1+r} - \frac{c_3}{(1+r)^2}\right]^{1-\frac{1}{\gamma}} + \beta\frac{c_2^{1-\frac{1}{\gamma}}}{1-\frac{1}{\gamma}} + \beta^2\frac{c_3^{1-\frac{1}{\gamma}}}{1-\frac{1}{\gamma}}.$$

(b) Restating the utility maximization in the form:

$$\min_{c_2, c_3} \; -\widetilde{U}(c_2, c_3)$$

then allows us to use the subroutine `fminsearch` from the toolbox as before. However, as the subroutine will now iterate over c_2 and c_3, we have to set the initial guess `x_in` as well as the interval boundaries `a` and `b` we provide to `fminsearch` in two dimensions. As shown in Program 2.4, the lower bound `a` is 0 in both dimensions in order to ensure non-negativity of consumption, while the upper bound `b` is set to the maximum possible consumption in the second and third periods, respectively. Note that the starting values we provide to `fminsearch` are no longer as irrelevant for the result we obtain as was the case in Exercise 2.2 (c) and that we should particularly avoid setting them close to the interval bounds.

The objective function $-\widetilde{U}(c_2, c_3)$ is stored again in the separate module `globals` within the function `utility`. Most importantly, the function `utility` has to expect an array of assumed-size type as input (see Module 2.4m). Otherwise, `fminsearch` will not accept it.

(c) Given the optimal solutions c_2^* and c_3^*, it is possible to compute c_1^* from the budget constraint and print the results to the screen, see Table 2.1.

In the initial calibration, the lifetime labour income is split equally over all periods and consumption is perfectly smooth over the household's lifecycle. This is, as in Exercise 2.2,

Program 2.4 Solve the three-period intertemporal optimization problem

```
program Intertemporal2dim
    [......]
    ! declaration of variables
    real*8 :: x_in(2), a(2), b(2), fret

    ! initialize interval for fminsearch and x_minimize
    a = (/0d0, 0d0/)
    b = (/(w + w*(1d0+r)), (w*(1d0+r) + w*(1d0+r)**2d0)/)
    x_in = w/2d0

    ! call subroutine fminsearch
    call fminsearch(x_in, fret, a, b, utility)
    [......]
end program
```

Module 2.4m Utility function to be maximized

```
function utility(x_in)

    implicit none

    ! declaration of variables
    real*8, intent(in) :: x_in(:)
    real*8 :: utility
    real*8 :: c(3)
    [......]
end function
```

Table 2.1 Sensitivity analysis

w	r	c_1	c_2	c_3
1.0	0.0	0.66	0.66	0.66
2.0	0.0	1.33	1.33	1.33
1.0	0.1	0.66	0.69	0.73

because the household discounts future utitilty in his intertemporal optimization problem at the market interest rate, ie:

$$\beta = \frac{1}{(1+r)}$$

holds. An increase in wages will not change the intertemporal allocation, but only comes with an income effect that leads to an even rise in consumption over all periods. On the other hand, a change in the interest rate alters the intertemporal allocation, as the above equality no longer holds if β is left unchanged. Changing β and holding everything else constant has a similar effect as changing the interest rate.

Exercise 2.5

(a) The analytical solution of the integral is given by:

$$\int_{-1}^{1} \exp(-x)\mathrm{d}x = \left[\ \exp(-x)(-1)\ \right]_{-1}^{1} = \exp(1) - \exp(-1) \approx 2.350402.$$

Trapezoid rule: the numerical implementation of the trapezoid rule computes the weights and stores them in the array `w_trapez`, as shown in Program 2.5. We approximate the integral by summing up the weighted function values of our function $\exp(-x)$ at each node of the grid in the integration range. For $n = 10$, the difference to the analytical solution is $\Delta_{\text{Trapezoid}} = 0.007829456$, ie the approximated result differs from the third decimal place on from the analytical solution. In order to increase the precision of our result from the trapezoid rule, we need to raise the number of nodes on our grid. However, even setting $n = 30$ only allows us to match the first three decimal places.

Simpson rule: as deriving weights ω_i for all nodes in our grid for the Simpson rule is very complicated, we carry out the summation explicitly, see Program 2.5.a. The approximation of the integral is then given by the sum of the areas under

Program 2.5 Trapezoid rule to compute integral numerically

```
! compute weights for trapezoid rule
w_trapez(0) = h/2d0
w_trapez(n) = h/2d0
w_trapez(1:n-1) = h

! use trapezoid rule for integral of exp(-x)
f_trapez_exp = exp(-x_int)
trapez_exp = sum(w_trapez*f_trapez_exp,1)
```

the second-order polynomial in each subinterval within the integration range. For $n = 10$, the Simpson rule already matches the analytical result by five decimal places ($\Delta_{\text{Simpson}} = 0.000001304$), which is a result of the better fit when using a second-order polynomial to approximate our integrand. Increasing the number of quadrature nodes to $n = 20$ raises the precision even by two further decimal places.

Gauss–Legendre quadrature: in the case of Gauss–Legendre quadrature, which is shown in Program 2.5.b, our quadrature nodes and weights are computed by the subroutine `legendre` from the toolbox and are written into the arrays `x_gauss` and `w_gauss`, respectively. Similar to the trapezoid rule, the integral is approximated by summing up the weighted function values of our function $\exp(-x)$ at each node of the grid in the integration range. Compared to the other integration methods, Gauss–Legendre quadrature achieves by far the best results. As it allows the most flexibility in approximating the underlying function, it matches the first twelve decimal places of the analytical solution already for $n = 10$.

Table 2.2 summarizes the results.

Program 2.5.a Simpson rule to compute integral numerically

```
simpson_exp = exp(-a) + exp(-b)

do i = 1, n-1
   simpson_exp = simpson_exp + 2d0*exp(-x_int(i))
enddo

do i = 0, n-1
   simpson_exp = simpson_exp + 4d0*exp(-(x_int(i) &
                       + x_int(i+1))/2d0)
enddo

simpson_exp = simpson_exp*h/6d0
```

Program 2.5.b Gauss–Legendre quadrature to compute integral numerically

```
call legendre(a, b, x_gauss, w_gauss)

! gauss-legendre for integral of exp(-x)
f_gauss_exp = exp(-x_gauss)
gauss_exp = sum(w_gauss*f_gauss_exp, 1)
```

Table 2.2 Alternative approximations of $\int_{-1}^{1} \exp(-x)dx$

n	$\Delta_{\text{Trapezoid}}$	Δ_{Simpson}	Δ_{GL}
10	0.007829456	0.000001304	0.000000000
20	0.001958342	0.000000082	0.000000000
30	0.000870455	0.000000016	0.000000000

(b) In this case, the analytical solution for the integral is given by:

$$\int_{-1}^{1} |x|^{0.5} \mathrm{d}x = \int_{0}^{1} x^{0.5} \mathrm{d}x + \int_{-1}^{0} (-x)^{0.5} \mathrm{d}x$$
$$= \left[\frac{x^{3/2}}{3/2}\right]_0^1 + \left[-\frac{(-x)^{3/2}}{3/2}\right]_{-1}^0 = \frac{2}{3} + \frac{2}{3} = \frac{4}{3}.$$

Similar to (a), Table 2.3 summarizes the approximation error of all three integration methods. The pattern we observe is different from (a). The integral is now best approximated by the Simpson rule, while Gauss–Legendre quadrature yields even less precise results than the trapezoid rule. This results from the fact that Gauss–Legendre quadrature uses only a single high-order polynomial to approximate the integrand over the whole integration range, which results in very accurate results as long as the integrand is smooth, but performs poorly for less nicely behaved integrands. Here, it is the kink at $x = 0$ (see Figure 2.3) which makes approximation with a single polynomial difficult and leads Gauss–Legendre quadrature to be inferior to summed Newton-Cotes methods.

However, if we make use of the symmetry property of $|x|^{0.5}$ and rewrite the integral as:

$$\int_{-1}^{1} |x|^{0.5} \mathrm{d}x = 2 \int_{0}^{1} x^{0.5} \mathrm{d}x$$

Table 2.3 Alternative approximations of $\int_{-1}^{1} |x|^{0.5} \mathrm{d}x$

n	$\Delta_{\text{Trapezoid}}$	Δ_{Simpson}	Δ_{GL}
10	−0.033856137	−0.005134153	−0.059387875
20	−0.012314649	−0.001815317	−0.023225694
30	−0.006786449	−0.000988143	−0.013095918

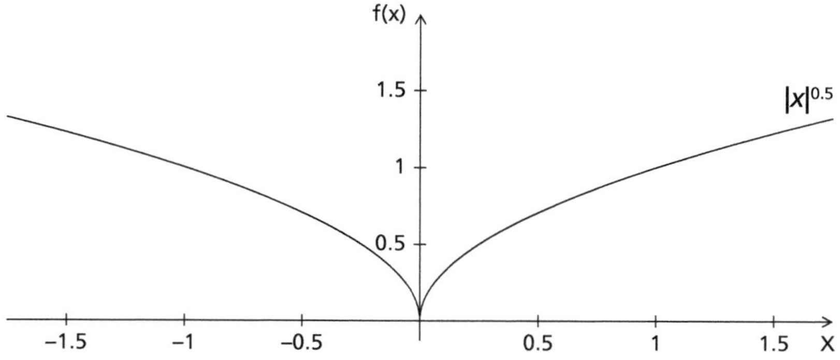

Figure 2.3 Non-differentiability of $|x|^{0.5}$ at 0

to avoid having to deal with the kink of our integrand at 0, then Gauss–Legendre quadrature will again yield the most accurate approximations to the analytical solution. Since the actual integration is now only performed over half of the initial interval, we use $n = 5, 10$, and 15 quadrature nodes to obtain an approximation that is comparable to previous results.

In Program 2.5.c, we use the logical variable `symmetry` as a switch to decide whether to make use of this symmetry property in the computation of the integral or not. If this variable takes the value **`.true.`**, we reset the integration interval to compute the weights for each of our new equidistant quadrature nodes for trapezoid rule and to obtain Gauss–Legendre nodes and weights from the subroutine `legendre`. Similar to above, the integral is approximated for the trapezoid rule and Gauss–Legendre integration by the weighted sum of the function values at the new quadrature nodes. For the Simpson rule, we explicitly carry out the summation of the areas under the approximated integrand. We obtain the value for the integral over the full integration range $[-1, 1]$ by simply multiplying by two (see Program 2.5.d). While Newton-Cotes methods hardly increase in precision compared to the results without making use of the symmetry, Table 2.4 shows that Gauss–Legendre quadrature is a lot more accurate than before and again yields the most precise results.

Program 2.5.c Compute new weights if symmetry is used

```
if(symmetry)then

    ! set lower and upper bound for interval
    a = 0d0
    b = 1d0

    ! compute interval length
    h = (b-a)/dble(n)

    ! get equidistant nodes
    call grid_Cons_Equi(x_int, a, b)

    ! compute weights for trapezoid rule
    w_trapez(0)  = h/2d0
    w_trapez(n)  = h/2d0
    w_trapez(1:n-1)  = h

    ! gauss-legendre nodes and weights
    call legendre(a, b, x_gauss, w_gauss)

endif
```

Program 2.5.d Compute new integrals with symmetry property

```
if(symmetry)then
   trapez_sqrtabs  = 2d0*trapez_sqrtabs
   simpson_sqrtabs  = 2d0*simpson_sqrtabs
   gauss_sqrtabs  = 2d0*gauss_sqrtabs
endif
```

Table 2.4 Alternative approximations of $\int_{-1}^{1} |x|^{0.5} dx$ with symmetry

n	$\Delta_{\text{Trapezoid}}$	Δ_{Simpson}	Δ_{GL}
5	−0.033856138	−0.005134154	0.000759542
10	−0.012314650	−0.001815317	0.000135947
15	−0.006786449	−0.000988143	0.000045930

Exercise 2.6

Consumer surplus is a measure of consumer benefit, which indicates how far the consumers' willingness to pay is above the market price. It is defined as the surface between the inverse demand curve $p(d)$ and the actual market price p.

Given the initial price $p = 3$, the consumer surplus is thus the small area under the inverse demand curve that lies above the market price $p = 3$. A fall in the market price to $p = 1$ then simply increases the consumer surplus to the area under the inverse demand curve and above $p = 1$ (see Figure 2.4). Determining the relative change in consumer surplus:

$$\Delta CS = \frac{CS(1) - CS(3)}{CS(3)}$$

thus requires us to compute the following integrals:

$$CS(3) = \int_0^{d(3)} (p(x) - 3)\mathrm{d}x = \int_0^{d(3)} p(x)\mathrm{d}x - 3 \cdot d(3)$$

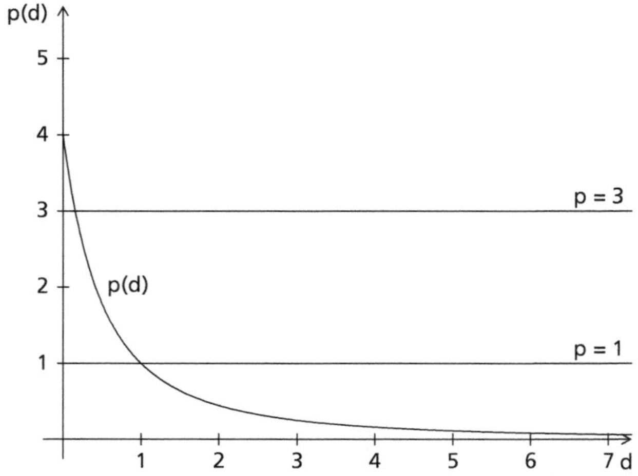

Figure 2.4 Market equilibrium for $p = 1$ and $p = 3$

and

$$CS(1) = \int_0^{d(1)} (p(x) - 1)dx = \int_0^{d(1)} p(x)dx - 1 \cdot d(1),$$

where $d(p)$ is the demand function and can simply be obtained by inverting $p(d)$, ie:

$$d(p) = \frac{2}{\sqrt{p}} - 1.$$

Computing the consumer surplus for $p = 3$ and $p = 1$ analytically, yields:

$$CS(3) = \int_0^{d(3)} p(x)dx - 3 \cdot d(3) = \left[\frac{-4}{(d+1)^{-1}}\right]_0^{\frac{2}{\sqrt{3}}-1} - 3\left(\frac{2}{\sqrt{3}} - 1\right)$$
$$= -2\sqrt{3} + 4 - \frac{6}{\sqrt{3}} + 3 \approx 0.071797$$

and:

$$CS(1) = \int_0^{d(1)} p(x)dx - 1d(1) = \left[\frac{-4}{(d+1)^{-1}}\right]_0^1 - 1 = -2 + 4 - 1 = 1,$$

so that the relative change after the fall in price from $p = 3$ to $p = 1$ is:

$$\Delta CS = \frac{1 - 0.071797}{0.071797} \approx 12.928203.$$

The numerical implementation shown in Program 2.6 builds up on `sol_prog02_05`. It only differs in that we now store the inverse demand function $p(d)$ in a separate function `p_func` and set up a do-loop to compute the consumer surplus for the two cases separately. The reason for using the function `p_func` is simply to make our life easier and to avoid having to write out the actual function $p(d)$ each time we use it in our program. The input argument `d` of this function is assumed to be a scalar of type `real*8`. We let the do-loop iterate exactly two times in order to distinguish the two cases we want to compute the consumer surplus for. In the first iteration step of the do-loop, we set the market price equal to the old market price, and in the second iteration step we set it to the new one.

The computed consumer surplus is then stored in the array `cs`, where the first dimension indicates the integration method we used and the second dimension whether it is the consumer surplus for the old price $p = 3$ or the new price $p = 1$. Table 2.5 summarizes the results and compares them to the analytical solution. A decrease in the price p leads to an increase in the consumer surplus. In line with our results from Exercise 2.5 we find that Gauss–Legendre quadrature yields the best approximation, followed by Simpson's rule, while trapezoid rule integration performs poorly for $n = 10$.

Program 2.6 Compute consumer surplus

```
a = 0d0

! set up loop to compute the required intervals
do i = 1, 2

    ! set p equal to the old market price
    if(i == 1)p = p_1

    ! set p equal to the new market price
    if(i == 2)p = p_2

    ! compute the upper bound for integral
    b = 2d0*p**(-0.5d0) - 1d0
    [......]
    ! compute consumer surplus
    CS(1, i) = trapez - b*p
    CS(2, i) = simpson - b*p
    CS(3, i) = gauss - b*p

enddo
```

Table 2.5 Comparison of the results of different integration methods

	Analytical	Trapezoid rule	Simpson's rule	Gauss–Legendre quadrature
ΔCS(in %)	1292.8203	1299.8370	1292.8247	1292.8203

Exercise 2.7

This exercise illustrates how interpolation techniques can be a very helpful tool in numerical optimization. We use a second-order polynomial:

$$p(\tau) = c_o + c_1\tau + c_2\tau^2$$

to interpolate the tax function $T(\tau)$ from which we only know for three realizations of τ the generated tax revenue $T(\tau)$. In order to determine the coefficients c_0, c_1, and c_2 we thus have to solve the following equation system:

$$\begin{aligned} c_0 + c_1\tau_0 + c_2\tau_0^2 &= T(\tau_0) \\ c_0 + c_1\tau_1 + c_2\tau_1^2 &= T(\tau_1) \\ c_0 + c_1\tau + c_2\tau_2^2 &= T(\tau_2). \end{aligned}$$

With the values from the table in the exercise, we obtain in matrix notation:

$$\underbrace{\begin{bmatrix} 1 & 37 & 37^2 \\ 1 & 42 & 42^2 \\ 1 & 45 & 45^2 \end{bmatrix}}_{\Phi} \underbrace{\begin{bmatrix} c_0 \\ c_1 \\ c_2 \end{bmatrix}}_{c} = \underbrace{\begin{bmatrix} 198.875 \\ 199.500 \\ 196.875 \end{bmatrix}}_{y}.$$

We can easily solve for the coefficients $c = [0, 10, -0.125]^T$ as in Exercise 2.1, using LU-decomposition. With these coefficients, we can write our polynomial to approximate the tax function as:

$$p(\tau) = 0 + 10\tau - 0.125\tau^2 = 10\tau - 0.125\tau^2$$

and would obtain the revenue-maximizing tax rate by taking the derivative through the first-order condition:

$$p'(\tau) = 10 - 0.2\tau = 0 \quad \Rightarrow \quad \tau^* = 40.$$

In our numerical implementation, we use the function `poly_interpol` from the toolbox to perform the interpolation. This function receives three input arguments, `x`, `xi`, and `yi`, where the first argument denotes the point at which the approximated function should be evaluated and the remaining two arguments are the sets of points that are used to set up the equation system for computing the coefficients of our polynomial.

Before proceeding to determining the revenue-maximizing tax rate numerically, we plot the tax function in the range $[35, 45]$ to the screen using the GNUPlot interface from the toolbox (see Figure 2.5). Similiar to before, we do this by setting up an equidistant grid over this range with the help of the subroutine `grid_Cons_Equi` and evaluate the interpolated tax function at each of these gridpoints. We can also use the values at these

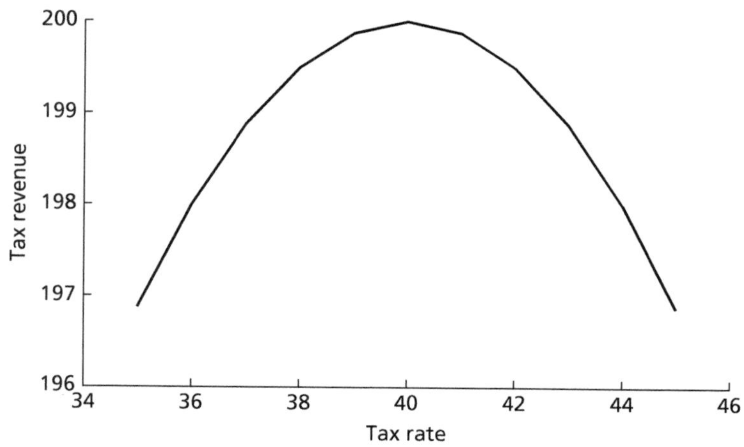

Figure 2.5 Second-order polynomial interpolated tax-function $T(\tau)$

Program 2.7 Compute revenue-maximizing tax-rate τ^*

```
call grid_Cons_Equi(tau_plot, tau_l, tau_u)
t_plot = poly_interpol(tau_plot, tau_data, t_data)
[......]
! find maximum tax-rate using the maxloc command
i_max = maxloc(t_plot, 1) - 1
tau_opt = tau_plot(i_max)
t_opt = t_plot(i_max)
[......]
! initialize initial guess for tau_in
tau_in = 37.5d0

! call subroutine fminsearch
call fminsearch(tau_in, fret, tau_l, tau_u, tax_func)
```

gridpoints to determine the revenue-maximizing tax rate τ. We simply locate the index of the highest tax revenue in the array `t_plot` by using the **`maxloc`** command. Beware of the fact that the **`maxloc`** command starts counting the entries of an array from one, which means that we have to subtract one from the value the **`maxloc`** command returns for the array `t_plot` as this array's first entry is at position zero. With this index at hand we get the optimal tax rate `tau_opt` by plugging it into the array `tau_plot`. While this method is particularly attractive because of its intuition and simplicity, one should keep in mind that it will only yield good results if the equidistant grid we use is dense enough. Another way to obtain the revenue-maximizing tax rate is simply to set up the subroutine `fminsearch` over the interval $[35, 45]$. In each iteration step and for each new guess `x_in`, the polynomial interpolation with the subroutine `poly_interpol` is performed in the function `tax_func`. The major advantage of using the polynomial interpolation function `poly_interpol` from the toolbox in this exercise is that it can perform interpolation with an arbitrary set of gridpoints. Both methods are illustrated in Program 2.7. We cannot apply spline interpolation from the toolbox, since it would require the gridpoints to be allocated either equidistant or with a distance that is growing at a fixed rate. The toolbox provides us with a subroutine to perform piecewise linear interpolation on an arbitrary grid; however, piecewise linear interpolation performs in general poorly for few gridpoints.

Exercise 2.8

In this exercise, we approximate the function $cos(x)$ on the interval $[0, 2\pi]$ through linear as well as spline interpolation and compare our results to the actual function values of the cosine function. As we cannot handle continuous functions on a computer, we simply sample the true cosine function as a reference on a grid with a very high density of points in the interval $[0, 2\pi]$. As before, we set up this grid to be equidistant with the subroutine `grid_Cons_Equi` from the toolbox and store it in the array `x_plot`, while the true function values for the cosine function are stored in the array `y_real`.

Similarly, we use an equidistant grid to obtain the nodes for interpolation of the cosine function with linear and spline interpolation. This grid covers the same range $[0, 2\pi]$ and is stored in the array `x`, whereas the corresponding function values are kept in the array `y`. For each of the subintervals between two interpolation nodes, we can then compute the slope and the intercept of the linear function to interpolate $cos(x)$ as:

$$m_i = \frac{f(x_i) - f(x_{i-1})}{x_i - x_{i-1}} \quad \text{and} \quad t_i = f(x_{i-1}) - m_i x_{i-1} \quad \text{for} \quad i = 1, ..., n.$$

Evaluating the linearly interpolated function:

$$f(x) = m_i x + t_i$$

between two gridpoints then simply requires us to make sure that we choose the slope m_i and intercept t_i appropriately for the interval the value x lies in. We identify this interval as shown in Program 2.8, with the help of the function `grid_Inv_Equi` from the toolbox, which inverts the formula of an equidistant grid with $n+1$ nodes over an interval $[a, b]$ to

$$j = \frac{x - a}{b - a} n.$$

If x lies in between two gridpoints, the function will return a value in between the two integer indices of the gridpoints according to this formula. Rounding this value down to

Program 2.8 Manual implementation of piecewise linear interpolation

```
! compute slope and intercept for each subinterval
do i = 1, n

    m(i) = (y(i) - y(i-1))/(x(i) - x(i-1))
    t(i) = y(i) - m(i)*x(i)

enddo

! manual piecewise linear interpolation
do j = 0, n_plot

    ! get the subinterval for a certain entry from xplot
    i = int(grid_Inv_Equi(x_plot(j), 0d0, 2d0*pi, n)) + 1

    ! k should be smaller than the maximum
    ! number of subintervals n
    i = min(i, n)

    ! interpolate function value
    y_plot(1, j) = m(i)*x_plot(j) + t(i)

enddo
```

Table 2.6 Maximum approximation errors of the different approaches

	Piecewise linear (linear EQ)	Piecewise linear (toolbox)	Cubic spline
n = 10	0.046561	0.046561	0.004154
n = 20	0.01216	0.01216	0.000345
n = 30	0.005445	0.005445	0.000072

the lower integer with the help of the **int** command tells us the index of the gridpoint left to a certain value x. Increasing the value of this gridpoint by one then gives the index i of the subinterval we are interested in.

Before proceeding to piecewise linear interpolation of the cosine function at the gridpoints in the array `x_plot`, we ensure that the index i we derived is not above the maximum number of subintervals n. We then use the linear interpolation subroutine `linint_Equi` and the piecewise spline interpolation function from the toolbox to interpolate the cosine function and evaluate it on the same grid that is stored in the array `x_plot`. The maximum approximation errors of all three interpolation methods are summarized in Table 2.6, where we evaluated our interpolated functions on a grid with $n_{plot} = 1000$. We see that our own implementation of piecewise linear interpolation yields the same result as the subroutine `linint_Equi`, but performs worse than the spline interpolation approach.

Plotting the interpolated and the actual cosine function for $n = 10$ (see Figure 2.6) shows that piecewise linear interpolation performs particularly poorly for few gridpoints, while spline interpolation already yields a very good fit in this case. Note that using the spline interpolation approach requires us to declare the array `coeff` to be of length $n+3$, as we need $n + 3$ coefficients to define the cubic spline.

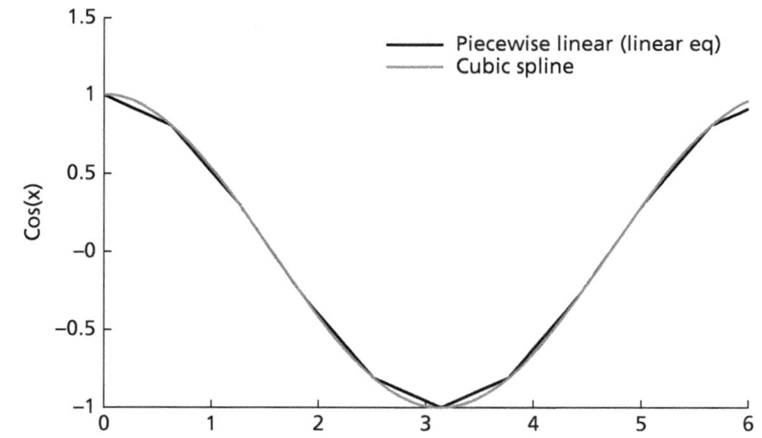

Figure 2.6 Linear and spline interpolation of *cos*(*x*)

Exercise 2.9

The first-order condition of one of the m Cournot oligopolists in the market is given by:

$$FOC(q) = P - q\frac{P^{1+\eta}}{\eta} - \alpha\sqrt{q} - q^2.$$

As there is no closed-form solution to this first-order condition, numerical optimization together with spline interpolation will once again prove to be a useful tool.

(a) As illustrated in Program 2.9, we at first discretize the interval $[0.1, 3.0]$ for our price p using the subroutine `grid_Cons_Equi` and initialize the array `coeff_q` that will store the coefficients for spline interpolation to zero. In the second step, we set up a do-loop that iterates over all gridpoints in the price interval and computes the optimal quantity q^{opt}, which is supplied by one firm. This is done by calling the subroutine `fzero` in each iteration step and providing the function `foc` from the module `globals` that stores the first-order condition to it. These optimal quantities are stored in the array `q` and then printed to the screen, together with the corresponding price p.

As the first-order condition is only defined for values $q \geq 0$, it is important to avoid setting the starting value `q_in` for the subroutine `fzero` too close to zero to ensure that Newton's method will never provide a negative quantity q as a guess when iterating. If we want to completely avoid the problem of ending up outside the defined domain of our first-order condition, we could use bisection search instead to find the root for the above first-order condition and set the interval in which bisection search should iterate over q to be non-negative.

Program 2.9 Compute optimal solution at each gridpoint

```
! initialize coefficients for interpolation to zero
coeff_q = 0d0

! initialize grid for interpolation
call grid_Cons_Equi(p, p_l, p_u)

! calculate quantities q at each gridpoint
do ip = 0, N
    ! set initial guess
    q_in = 1d0

    ! set communicatation variable
    ip_com = ip

    ! call fzero
    call fzero(q_in, foc, check)
    if(check)stop 'Error: fzero did not converge'

    ! copy solution at gridpoint
    q(ip) = q_in

enddo
```

Instead of calling the subroutine fzero for each gridpoint separately, it would be conceivable to interpret the set of first-order conditions of all gridpoints as a nonlinear-equation system. Instead of using Newton's method, the subroutine fzero would then apply Broyden's method to solve for the optimal quantities q^{opt}. However, this is a bad idea as Broyden's method performs poorly if the equations in the equation system are independent, as is obviously the case here.

(b) The subroutine spline_interp allows us to compute the interpolation coefficients coeff_q for spline interpolation. After having computed these coefficients, we set up a grid with a high density of points and store it in the array p_plot. We use it to plot the individual supply of the m Cournot oligopolists, the aggregate supply, and the aggregate demand. As we assume that each of the competitors does not react to the decisions of the other firms, aggregate demand is simply m times individual supply. Note that adding the additional argument legend to the subroutine plot allows us to assign a legend to the curve we plot. Similarly, as is illustrated in Program 2.9.a, the arguments xlabel and ylabel for the subroutine execplot allow us to assign labels to the respective axis, while xlim and ylim restrict the range we are plotting.

We see in Figure 2.7 that demand is falling with increasing prices and the trade-off an individual firm faces: an increase in the price P will, on the one hand, increase revenue, but, on the other hand, crowd out demand.

(c) In order to derive the equilibrium price p_equi we again use the subroutine fzero, which now receives the function market with the market equilibrium condition as argument (see Module 2.9m). In each iteration step that is performed by fzero, the spline_eval command that is used in our function market will evaluate the interpolated supply function at the respective guess in the current iteration step. When using fzero, we should again be careful with setting the initial guess, as both the demand function as well as the interpolated supply function are only defined for non-negative values.

Program 2.9.a Plot individual supply, market supply and demand

```
call grid_Cons_Equi(p_plot, p_l, p_u)

! interpolate supply for plot
q_s_plot = (/ (spline_eval(p_plot(ip), &
                coeff_q, p_l, p_u), ip = 0, NP) /)

! compute demand
q_d_plot = p_plot**(-eta)

! initialize plot
call plot(p_plot, q_d_plot, legend='Market Demand')
call plot(p_plot, q_s_plot, legend='Individual Supply')
call plot(p_plot, m*q_s_plot, legend='Aggregate Supply')

! execute plot
call execplot(xlim=(/0.1d0, 3d0/), ylim=(/0d0, 2d0/), &
                xlabel='Demand/Quantity', ylabel='Price')
```

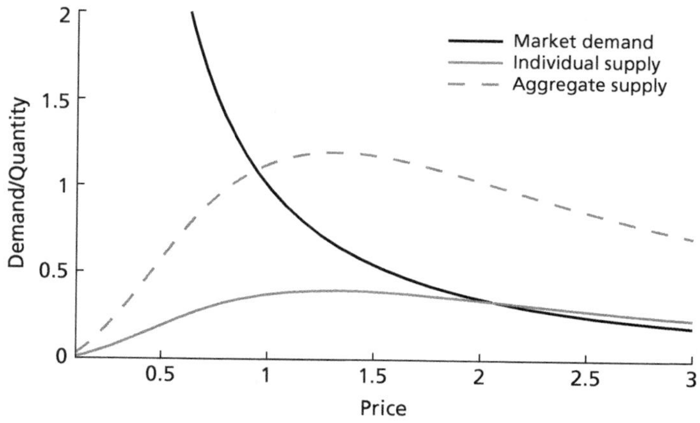

Figure 2.7 Market equilibrium for $m = 3$ firms

Module 2.9m Market equilibrium condition

```
function market(p_in)

    use toolbox

    real*8, intent(in) :: p_in
    real*8 :: market

    market = p_in**(-eta) - m*spline_eval(p_in, coeff_q, &
                p_l, p_u)

end function
```

After `fzero` converges, we print our results to the screen and obtain under the initial parameterization a market equilibrium price $p^* = 0.9443$ and an equilibrium quantity $q^* = 1.0897$.

(d) An increase in the number of competitors m makes the market price, p^* in equilibrium decrease and increases the quantity traded q^*. On the other hand, fewer competitors decrease competition and let the market price p^* increase and the quantity q^* decrease.

Increasing the price elasticity makes the demand curve steeper, so that already small changes in price yield considerable changes in demand. Firms take this change in demand into account in their optimization problem, which leads to a lower equilibrium price p^* and higher equilibrium quantity q^*.

The cost parameter α only affects the individual supply curve. A lower (higher) value for α increases (decreases) individual supply, which will then reduce (increase) the equilibrium price. Table 2.7 summarizes the results.

Table 2.7 Sensitivity analysis Cournot model

	$m = 2$	$m = 4$	$\eta = 0.5$	$\eta = 2.5$	$\alpha = 0.5$	$\alpha = 1.5$
p^*	1.1733	0.8253	1.7097	0.9245	0.7675	1.1222
q^*	0.7868	1.3334	0.7648	1.2168	1.4872	0.8411

Exercise 2.10

Given the set of price realizations and profits from the exercise, we are searching for the profit-maximizing set of prices (p_R^*, p_A^*) using the numerical implementation of spline interpolation in the toolbox.

(a) We begin in Program 2.10 with initializing the two-dimensional array `G` with the profit matrix from the exercise and the coefficients `coeff_G` to zero. We then follow the steps as suggested in the exercise and set up equidistant grids on the interval [0.5, 12.5] using the subroutine `grid_Cons_Equi` from the toolbox for the prices p_R and p_A in order to obtain the same set of prices as in the table from the exercise.

Similarly, we use the grid constructor `grid_Cons_Equi` to set up a dense, two-dimensional equidistant grid in the same interval for both dimensions p_R and p_A, which we will use to evaluate the spline that interpolates the profit function. We store these grids in the arrays `pr_plot` and `pa_plot`, respectively, and write the function values at each point of the resulting two-dimensional grid into the array `G_plot`, which we can use to plot the profit function to the screen and locate the profit-maximizing set of prices p_R^* and p_A^*.

For three-dimensional plots we use the subroutine `plot3d` from the toolbox. It receives in the most basic set-up three arrays of same length as arguments which provide it with the data for the three dimensions. Here, these arrays are `pr_plot`, `pa_plot`, and `G_plot`. In contrast to the two-dimensional plotting interface for GNUPlot, `plot3d` will provide the data to GNUPlot and execute the plot in one step.

Program 2.10 Plot of the profit-maximizing price combination

```
call spline_interp(G, coeff_G)

! two-dimensional interpolation for profit functions
do ir = 0, Nplot
    do ia = 0, Nplot
        G_plot(ir, ia) = spline_eval((/pr_plot(ir), &
        pa_plot(ia)/), coeff_G, &
                  (/p_min, p_min/), (/p_max, p_max/))
    enddo
enddo

! plot the profit function using spline interpolation
call plot3d(pr_plot, pa_plot, G_plot)

! locate maximum of the interpolated profit function
ix = maxloc(G_plot) - 1
```

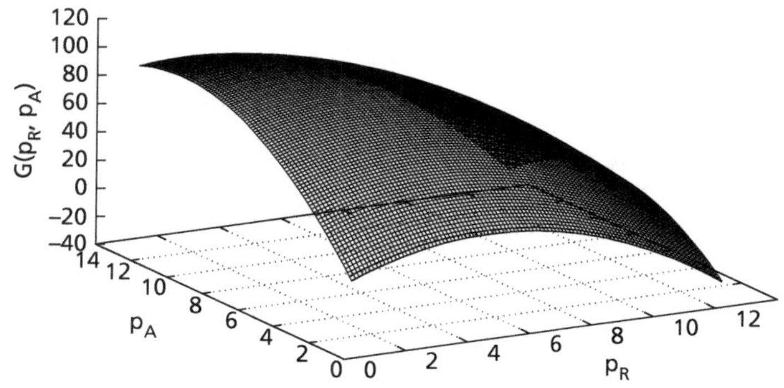

Figure 2.8 Spline interpolated profit function

The plot in Figure 2.8 illustrates that there is one unique maximum in the interval we are looking at. As in the one-dimensional optimization problem from Exercise 2.7., where we needed to find the revenue-maximizing tax rate, we can use the **maxloc** command as well in two dimensions to locate the profit-maximizing set of prices (p_A^*, p_B^*).

Note that we now need to assign the result **maxloc** to get us back to an array of length two. Again, we have to subtract one from the indices the **maxloc** command provides for us to obtain the actually optimal indices. As already explained, **maxloc** starts numbering the arrays, starting with one. Plugging these indices into the arrays `pr_plot` and `pa_plot` gives us the optimal set of prices $P_R^* = 2.7800$ and $P_A^* = 9.3800$, which yield a profit of $G = 105.0040$ if we use 100 gridpoints.

(b) For given demand functions, the profit function $G(p_R, p_A)$ is defined as:

$$
\begin{aligned}
G(p_R, p_A) &= (p_R - c)x_R + (p_A - c)x_A \\
&= (p_R - c)(10 - p_R) + (p_A - c)(20 - p_A - 0.5p_R).
\end{aligned}
$$

In order to maximize this profit function with `fminsearch`, we provide it with the array `x_minimize` that contains starting values for the set of prices (P_R, P_A) and the function `profit` that stores the above profit function $G(p_R, p_A)$. We then iterate in both price dimensions over the interval [0.5, 12.5] from (a) and print our result to the screen. With the actual 'true' demand functions at hand, profits are maximized for $c = 0.1$ with the combination of prices $p_R^* = 2.7333$ and $p_A^* = 9.3666$ at $G = 105.0066$.

Alternatively, using the subroutine `fzero` to maximize profit requires us to take the derivatives of the profit function with respect to the prices p_R^* and p_A^* and to solve the following equation system:

$$
\frac{\partial G}{\partial p_R} = 10 - 2p_R - 0.5p_A + 1.5c = 0
$$

$$
\frac{\partial G}{\partial p_A} = 20 - 2p_A - 0.5p_R + c = 0.
$$

Table 2.8 Comparison between approximated and actual solution

	p_R^*	p_A^*	$G(p_R^*, p_A^*)$
max G()	2.7333	9.3666	105.0066
`Nplot= 100`	2.7800	9.3800	105.0040
`Nplot= 1000`	2.7320	9.3678	105.0066
`Nplot= 10000`	2.7332	9.3668	105.0066

These first-order conditions are stored in the function `foc` in the module `globals`. The solution `fzero` yields with this function `foc` is the same we obtain for $c = 0.1$ with `fminsearch`.

(c) The different grid sizes yield the results reported in Table 2.8 for the 'true' and the approximated optimum.

Simply using the **`maxloc`** command from (a) with 100 gridpoints already yields solutions fairly close to the results we obtained using `fminsearch` and `fzero`.

Exercise 2.11

We have $n = 3$ gravel pits and $m = 4$ building sites. Define the vector $c = [c_1, \ldots, c_{n\times m}]$ as cost vector for the different transport combinations, ie c_1 is the transport from gravel pit A_1 to building site B_1, etc. Similarly, define vector $x = [x_1, \ldots, x_{n\times m}]$ as the vector of tons which are transported from gravel pit A_i to building site B_j. The optimization problem is then to minimize the total cost of transport given the quantity restrictions of the gravel pits and the orders of the building sites. Consequently, we have:

$$\min_{x_1,\ldots,x_{12}} \quad 10x_1 + 70x_2 + 100x_3 + 80x_4 + 130x_5 + 90x_6$$

$$+120x_7 + 110x_8 + 50x_9 + 50x_9 + 30x_{10} + 80x_{11} + 10x_{12},$$

subject to:

$$x_1, \ldots, x_{12} \geq 0$$

and:

$$
\begin{array}{cccccccccccccl}
x_1+ & x_2+ & x_3+ & x_4 & & & & & & & & & \le 11\\
 & & & & x_5+ & x_6+ & x_7+ & x_8 & & & & & \le 13\\
 & & & & & & & & x_9+ & x_{10}+ & x_{11}+ & x_{12} & \le 10\\
x_1+ & & & & x_5+ & & & & x_9 & & & & = 5\\
 & x_2+ & & & & x_6+ & & & & x_{10} & & & = 7\\
 & & x_3+ & & & & x_7+ & & & & x_{11} & & = 13\\
 & & & x_4+ & & & & x_8+ & & & & x_{12} & = 6.
\end{array}
$$

In matrix notation, this can be formulated as:

$$\min_x c^T x \quad s.t. \quad x \geq 0 \quad \text{and} \quad Ax \leq b,$$

where the matrix A is of dimension $(n + m, n \times m)$ and contains only ones or zeros. Vector $b = [11, 13, \ldots, 6]$ contains the maximum quantities. Note that the constraints have to be sorted in such a way as to start with the lower-than or equality constraints and then add the greater-than or equality constraints.

Given the matrix A and the vectors x, c, and b, subroutine `solve_lin(x, c, A, b, 3, 0, 0)` is used in Program 2.11 to solve this equation system. This procedure yields the following results for transport tons x and cost, as shown in Table 2.9.

The costs, for example, for A_1 can be simply computed using `sum(x(1: 4)*c(1: 4))`, where the * literal multiplies the first four entries of array x with the first four entries of array c. The slack variables are not explicitly handed back by the subroutine, but they can be calculated easily by including the variable `y`, which has then a value $y = Ax - b$. In the present example, the second constraint is not binding.

Table 2.9 Solution from the simplex algorithm

	B_1	B_2	B_3	B_4	Σ	Costs
A_1	5	3	3	0	11	560
A_2	0	0	10	0	10	1200
A_3	0	4	0	6	10	1180
Σ	5	7	13	6	31	1940

Program 2.11 Simplex algorithm for transportation cost

```
program Transport
    [......]
    ! declaration of variables
    real*8 :: c(n*m), x(n*m)
    real*8 :: A(n+m, n*m), b(n+m)

    ! set up transportation costs
    c(:) = (/10d0, 70d0, 100d0, 80d0, & ! gravel-pit 1
            130d0, 90d0, 120d0, 110d0, & ! gravel-pit 2
            50d0, 30d0, 80d0, 10d0/)  ! gravel-pit 3

    ! set up matrix for restriction
    A(1, :) = (/1d0, 1d0, 1d0, 1d0, 0d0, 0d0, 0d0, 0d0, &
                        0d0, 0d0, 0d0, 0d0/) ! gravel-pit 1
    [......]

    ! set up target vector for restriction
    b(:) = (/11d0, 13d0, 10d0, 5d0, 7d0, 13d0, 6d0/)

    ! solve the linear problem
    call solve_lin(x, c, A, b, 3, 0, 4)

    ! print output
    write(*,'(a)')'building site  :    1    2    3    4    &
                                             Sum      costs'
    write(*,'(a,4f5.1,2f10.1)')'gravel-pit 1   :', x(1:4), &
                              sum(x(1:4)), sum(x(1:4)*c(1:4))
    [......]
end program
```

3 The static general equilibrium model

Exercise 3.1

Given the CES function:

$$\left[\alpha X^{1-1/\epsilon} + (1-\alpha)Y^{1-1/\epsilon}\right]^{\frac{1}{1-1/\epsilon}},$$

we first define $\sigma = 1 - \frac{1}{\epsilon}$ for notational convenience. Then we have:

$$\begin{aligned}\lim_{\sigma\to 0}\left[\alpha X^{\sigma} + (1-\alpha)Y^{\sigma}\right]^{\frac{1}{\sigma}} &= \lim_{\sigma\to 0}\exp\left(\log\left(\left[\alpha X^{\sigma} + (1-\alpha)Y^{\sigma}\right]^{\frac{1}{\sigma}}\right)\right)\\ &= \exp\left(\lim_{\sigma\to 0}\log\left(\left[\alpha X^{\sigma} + (1-\alpha)Y^{\sigma}\right]^{\frac{1}{\sigma}}\right)\right).\end{aligned}$$

Note that we can move the limit around here because the exponential function is continuous and strictly monotonically increasing. For the limit of the inner part we have:

$$\lim_{\sigma\to 0}\log\left(\left[\alpha X^{\sigma} + (1-\alpha)Y^{\sigma}\right]^{\frac{1}{\sigma}}\right) = \lim_{\sigma\to 0}\frac{\log\left(\alpha X^{\sigma} + (1-\alpha)Y^{\sigma}\right)}{\sigma}.$$

For the denominator, we obviously have $\lim_{\sigma\to 0}\sigma = 0$. For the numerator, we get:

$$\begin{aligned}\lim_{\sigma\to 0}\log\left(\alpha X^{\sigma} + (1-\alpha)Y^{\sigma}\right) &= \log\left(\lim_{\sigma\to 0}\left(\alpha X^{\sigma} + (1-\alpha)Y^{\sigma}\right)\right)\\ &= \log[\alpha + (1-\alpha)] = \log(1) = 0.\end{aligned}$$

Consequently, both the numerator and the denominator have a limit of zero. Therefore we can apply l'Hopital's rule. The derivative of the numerator is:

$$\frac{d}{d\sigma}\log\left(\alpha X^{\sigma} + (1-\alpha)Y^{\sigma}\right) = \frac{\alpha\log(X)\cdot X^{\sigma} + (1-\alpha)\log(Y)\cdot Y^{\sigma}}{\alpha X^{\sigma} + (1-\alpha)Y^{\sigma}}.$$

As the derivative of the denominator is equal to 1, we get:

$$\lim_{\sigma\to 0} \frac{\log\left(\alpha X^{\sigma} + (1-\alpha)Y^{\sigma}\right)}{\sigma} = \lim_{\sigma\to 0} \frac{\alpha \log(X)\cdot X^{\sigma} + (1-\alpha)\log(Y)\cdot Y^{\sigma}}{\alpha X^{\sigma} + (1-\alpha)Y^{\sigma}}.$$

Note that $\lim_{\sigma\to 0} X^{\sigma} = \lim_{\sigma\to 0} Y^{\sigma} = 1$, so that we obtain:

$$\begin{aligned}\lim_{\sigma\to 0} \frac{\alpha \log(X)\cdot X^{\sigma} + (1-\alpha)\log(Y)\cdot Y^{\sigma}}{\alpha X^{\sigma} + (1-\alpha)Y^{\sigma}} &= \frac{\alpha\log(X) + (1-\alpha)\log(Y)}{\alpha + (1-\alpha)}\\ &= \alpha\log(X) + (1-\alpha)\log(Y)\\ &= \log\left[X^{\alpha}Y^{1-\alpha}\right].\end{aligned}$$

Summing up, we have:

$$\lim_{\epsilon\to 1}\left[\alpha X^{1-1/\epsilon} + (1-\alpha)Y^{1-1/\epsilon}\right]^{\frac{1}{1-1/\epsilon}} = \exp\left(\log\left[X^{\alpha}Y^{1-\alpha}\right]\right) = X^{\alpha}Y^{1-\alpha}.$$

Exercise 3.2

(a) Demand functions are derived from solving the maximization problem:

$$\max_{X_1,X_2}\; U(\cdot) = \left(\alpha^{\frac{1}{\nu}}X_1^{1-\frac{1}{\nu}} + (1-\alpha)^{\frac{1}{\nu}}X_2^{1-\frac{1}{\nu}}\right)^{\frac{1}{1-\frac{1}{\nu}}} \quad \text{s.t. } p_1X_1 + p_2X_2 = \bar{Y}.$$

The resulting Lagrange function is:

$$\mathcal{L}(X_1, X_2, \lambda) = \left(\alpha^{\frac{1}{\nu}}X_1^{1-\frac{1}{\nu}} + (1-\alpha)^{\frac{1}{\nu}}X_2^{1-\frac{1}{\nu}}\right)^{\frac{1}{1-\frac{1}{\nu}}} - \lambda(p_1X_1 + p_2X_2 - \bar{Y}),$$

yielding the optimality conditions:

$$\frac{\partial\mathcal{L}}{\partial X_1} = \alpha^{\frac{1}{\nu}}X_1^{-\frac{1}{\nu}}\left(\alpha^{\frac{1}{\nu}}X_1^{1-\frac{1}{\nu}} + (1-\alpha)^{\frac{1}{\nu}}X_2^{1-\frac{1}{\nu}}\right)^{\frac{1}{\nu-1}} - \lambda p_1 \stackrel{!}{=} 0$$

$$\frac{\partial\mathcal{L}}{\partial X_2} = (1-\alpha)^{\frac{1}{\nu}}X_2^{-\frac{1}{\nu}}\left(\alpha^{\frac{1}{\nu}}X_1^{1-\frac{1}{\nu}} + (1-\alpha)^{\frac{1}{\nu}}X_2^{1-\frac{1}{\nu}}\right)^{\frac{1}{\nu-1}} - \lambda p_2 \stackrel{!}{=} 0$$

$$\frac{\partial\mathcal{L}}{\partial \lambda} = p_1X_1 + p_2X_2 - \bar{Y} \stackrel{!}{=} 0.$$

By dividing the first two optimality conditions, we get:

$$\frac{\alpha^{\frac{1}{\nu}} X_1^{-\frac{1}{\nu}} \left(\alpha^{\frac{1}{\nu}} X_1^{1-\frac{1}{\nu}} + (1-\alpha)^{\frac{1}{\nu}} X_2^{1-\frac{1}{\nu}} \right)^{\frac{1}{\nu-1}}}{(1-\alpha)^{\frac{1}{\nu}} X_2^{-\frac{1}{\nu}} \left(\alpha^{\frac{1}{\nu}} X_1^{1-\frac{1}{\nu}} + (1-\alpha)^{\frac{1}{\nu}} X_2^{1-\frac{1}{\nu}} \right)^{\frac{1}{\nu-1}}} = \frac{p_1}{p_2},$$

so that:

$$X_1 = \left(\frac{p_2}{p_1}\right)^{\nu} \frac{\alpha}{(1-\alpha)} X_2.$$

Plugging this demand equation into the budget constraint yields:

$$\begin{aligned} p_1 \left(\frac{p_2}{p_1}\right)^{\nu} \frac{\alpha}{(1-\alpha)} X_2 + p_2 X_2 &= \bar{Y} \\ X_2 \left(p_1^{1-\nu} p_2^{\nu} \frac{\alpha}{1-\alpha} + p_2 \right) &= \bar{Y}, \end{aligned}$$

so that:

$$X_2 = \frac{(1-\alpha)}{p_2^{\nu}} \left(\alpha p_1^{1-\nu} + (1-\alpha) p_2^{1-\nu} \right)^{-1} \bar{Y} = \frac{(1-\alpha)\bar{Y}}{p_2^{\nu} P}.$$

Substituting this demand into the optimality condition above yields:

$$X_1 = \frac{\alpha \bar{Y}}{p_1^{\nu} P}.$$

(b) Besides defining ν and computing the price index P, only the labour market equation has to change in function `markets`. While the labour demand does not change, consumption (and therefore output) does change, so that we now get:

$$\frac{\beta_1}{w} \frac{\alpha \bar{Y}}{p_1^{\nu-1} P} + \frac{\beta_2}{w} \frac{(1-\alpha)\bar{Y}}{p_2^{\nu-1} P} - \bar{L} = 0.$$

Consequently, the program code of module `sol_prog03_02m` now changes, as shown in Module 3.2m.

We have normalized $p_1 = 1.0$ and always get $p_1 > p_2$. Consequently, the higher the elasticity of substitution ν, the more the household will substitute consumption demand from X_1 towards X_2 in the initial equilibrium. The shift in demand shifts production and, since the second good is more labour-intensive ($\beta_2 > \beta_1$), demand for labour increases,

Module 3.2m Market solution with CES utility

```
function markets(x)
    [......]
    ! calculate total income
    Ybar = w*Lbar+r*Kbar
    PP   = alpha*p(1)**(1d0-nu)+(1d0-alpha)*p(2)**(1d0-nu)

    ! get market equations
    [......]
    markets(3)  = beta(1)*alpha*Ybar/(w*p(1)**(nu-1d0)*PP)+ &
    beta(2)*(1-alpha)*Ybar/(w*p(2)**(nu-1d0)*PP)-Lbar

end function
```

so that the wage will rises relative to the interest rate. Note, however, that the factor price change is very modest.

Exercise 3.3

(a) In order to derive the demand for aggregate consumption of goods C and leisure ℓ, we again formulate the Lagrange function:

$$\mathcal{L}(C,\ell,\lambda) = \left[(1-\alpha)^{\frac{1}{\nu}}C^{1-\frac{1}{\nu}} + \alpha^{\frac{1}{\nu}}\ell^{1-\frac{1}{\nu}}\right]^{\frac{1}{1-\frac{1}{\nu}}} + \lambda(PC + w\ell - \bar{Y}),$$

from where we derive the optimality conditions:

$$\frac{\partial \mathcal{L}}{\partial C} = (1-\alpha)^{\frac{1}{\nu}}C^{-\frac{1}{\nu}}\left[(1-\alpha)^{\frac{1}{\nu}}C^{1-\frac{1}{\nu}} + \alpha^{\frac{1}{\nu}}\ell^{1-\frac{1}{\nu}}\right]^{\frac{1}{\nu-1}} + \lambda P \overset{!}{=} 0$$

$$\frac{\partial \mathcal{L}}{\partial \ell} = \alpha^{\frac{1}{\nu}}\ell^{-\frac{1}{\nu}}\left[(1-\alpha)^{\frac{1}{\nu}}C^{1-\frac{1}{\nu}} + \alpha^{\frac{1}{\nu}}\ell^{1-\frac{1}{\nu}}\right]^{\frac{1}{\nu-1}} + \lambda w \overset{!}{=} 0$$

$$\frac{\partial \mathcal{L}}{\partial \lambda} = PC + w\ell - \bar{Y} \overset{!}{=} 0.$$

Dividing the first two optimality conditions yields:

$$\frac{P}{w} = \frac{(1-\alpha)^{\frac{1}{\nu}}C^{-\frac{1}{\nu}}}{\alpha^{\frac{1}{\nu}}\ell^{-\frac{1}{\nu}}} = \left(\frac{(1-\alpha)\ell}{\alpha C}\right)^{\frac{1}{\nu}} \quad \Rightarrow \quad C = \frac{(1-\alpha)}{\alpha}\left(\frac{w}{P}\right)^{\nu}\ell.$$

Plugging this into the budget constraint yields:

$$P\frac{1-\alpha}{\alpha}\left(\frac{w}{P}\right)^{\nu}\ell + w\ell = \bar{Y} \Rightarrow \frac{w^{\nu}\ell}{\alpha}\left((1-\alpha)P^{1-\nu} + \alpha w^{1-\nu}\right) = \bar{Y}.$$

Using $\Omega = (1-\alpha)P^{1-\nu} + \alpha w^{1-\nu}$, we get $\ell = \frac{\alpha \bar{Y}}{w^\nu \Omega}$. Plugging this function in the equation for consumption yields $C = \frac{(1-\alpha)\bar{Y}}{P^\nu \Omega}$.

The solution for the demand of goods X_1, X_2 is the same as in Exercise 3.2 using $\alpha = \alpha_1$, $1-\alpha = \alpha_2$, $\nu = \nu_x$ and available resources $Y_D = \bar{Y} - w\ell$.

(b) As in the previous exercise, the main adjustment has to be made in the function `markets`. On the one side, we have to redefine $\bar{Y}$ and P, as well as to specify Ω. The labour market equilibrium condition $L_1 + L_2 + \ell - \bar{T} = 0$ now can be rearranged as:

$$\frac{\beta_1}{w}\frac{\alpha_x Y_D}{p_1^{\nu_x - 1}P} + \frac{\beta_2}{w}\frac{(1-\alpha_x)Y_D}{p_2^{\nu_x - 1}P} + \frac{\alpha \bar{Y}}{w^\nu \Omega} - \bar{T} = 0$$

$$\left[\frac{\beta_1 \alpha_x}{p_1^{\nu_x - 1}} + \frac{\beta_2(1-\alpha_x)}{p_2^{\nu_x - 1}}\right]\frac{w^{\nu-1}\Omega - \alpha}{w^\nu \Omega P}\bar{Y} + \frac{\alpha \bar{Y}}{w^\nu \Omega} - \bar{T} = 0,$$

where we have used the definition $Y_D = \bar{Y} - w\ell = \bar{Y} - \frac{\alpha \bar{Y}}{w^{\nu-1}\Omega}$. The function `markets` now changes, as shown in Module 3.3m.

Of course, we still have to compute C, ℓ, Y_i, and U in the main program, as shown in Program 3.3. When we increase the elasticity of substitution from $\nu_x = 0.5$ towards $\nu_x = 1.5$, we observe the same economic adjustments as in the previous exercise. Consequently, there is a shift in demand towards the second sector, so that the wage rises and the interest rate declines. When, in addition, the elasticity of substitution is increased

Module 3.3m Market solution with two-stage utility function

```
function markets(x)
    [......]
    ! calculate total income
    Ybar = w*Tbar+r*Kbar
    PP = alphax*p(1)**(1-nux) + (1d0-alphax)*p(2)**(1d0-nux)
    Omega = (1-alpha)*PP**(1-nu) + alpha*w**(1-nu)

    ! get market equations
    [......]
    markets(3) = (beta(1)*alphax/p(1)**(nux-1d0)+beta(2)*&
      1d0-alphax)/p(2)**(nux-1d0))*(w**(nu-1d0)*Omega-alpha)&
      /(w**nu*Omega*PP)*Ybar+alpha*Ybar/w**nu/Omega-Tbar
end function
```

Program 3.3 Market solution with two-stage utility function

```
C     = (1d0-alpha)*Ybar/PP**nu/Omega
ell   = alpha*Ybar/(w**nu*Omega)
YD    = Ybar-w*ell
Y(1)  = alphax*YD/p(1)**nux/PP
Y(2)  = (1d0-alphax)*YD/p(2)**nux/PP
[......]
U     = ((1d0-alpha)**(1d0/nu)*C**mu+alpha**(1d0/nu)*ell**mu)&
        **(1d0/mu)
```

from $\nu = 0.5$ to $\nu = 1.5$, households shift from consumption towards leisure demand more strongly, since wages are much lower than the price for consumption goods. Consequently, on the labour market, wages increase much more strongly and the production of both goods is reduced significantly. Lower demand for capital reduces the interest rate.

In the current set up, whether we actually find a solution depends heavily on the initial guess x. For the present parameter selection, we always get a runtime error if we start outside the range $[0.2, 0.4]$. Therefore we will implement an alternative solution technique in the next exercise.

Exercise 3.4

(a) In order to derive per-unit demands, we define the profit function (which already includes the technology constraint):

$$\max_{L_i,K_i} \Pi = q_i \left[\beta_i L_i^{1-\frac{1}{\sigma_i}} + (1-\beta_i) K_i^{1-\frac{1}{\sigma_i}}\right]^{\frac{1}{1-\frac{1}{\sigma_i}}} - wL_i - rK_i,$$

which yields the optimality conditions:

$$\begin{aligned}
\frac{\partial \Pi}{\partial L_i} &= \beta_i L_i^{-\frac{1}{\sigma_i}} \left[\beta_i L_i^{1-\frac{1}{\sigma_i}} + (1-\beta_i) K_i^{1-\frac{1}{\sigma_i}}\right]^{\frac{1}{\sigma_i - 1}} - w = 0 \\
\frac{\partial \Pi}{\partial K_i} &= (1-\beta_i) K_i^{-\frac{1}{\sigma_i}} \left[\beta_i L_i^{1-\frac{1}{\sigma_i}} + (1-\beta_i) K_i^{1-\frac{1}{\sigma_i}}\right]^{\frac{1}{\sigma_i - 1}} - r = 0.
\end{aligned}$$

Dividing the two conditions, we obtain:

$$\frac{w}{r} = \frac{\beta_i}{1-\beta_i}\left(\frac{K_i}{L_i}\right)^{\frac{1}{\sigma_i}} \quad \Rightarrow \quad K_i = \left[\frac{w(1-\beta_i)}{r\beta_i}\right]^{\sigma_i} L_i.$$

Plugging this into the production function, we get:

$$\begin{aligned}
Y_i &= \left\{\beta_i L_i^{1-\frac{1}{\sigma_i}} + (1-\beta_i)\left[\left(\frac{w(1-\beta_i)}{r\beta_i}\right)^{\sigma_i} L_i\right]^{1-\frac{1}{\sigma_i}}\right\}^{\frac{1}{1-\frac{1}{\sigma_i}}} \\
&= L_i \left\{\beta_i + (1-\beta_i)\left[\frac{w(1-\beta_i)}{r\beta_i}\right]^{\sigma_i - 1}\right\}^{\frac{1}{1-\frac{1}{\sigma_i}}},
\end{aligned}$$

so that:

$$l_i = \frac{L_i}{Y_i} = \left\{\beta_i + (1-\beta_i)\left[\frac{r\beta_i}{w(1-\beta_i)}\right]^{1-\sigma_i}\right\}^{-\frac{1}{1-\frac{1}{\sigma_i}}}.$$

Similarly, we substitute $L_i = \left[\frac{r\beta_i}{w(1-\beta_i)}\right]^{\sigma_i} K_i$ into the production function in order to derive k_i.

(b) Assuming CES production functions make it complicated to derive the equilibrium price vector as in the Exercise 3.3, since the factor demand functions are now more complicated. Consequently, we use a different approach, where we normalize $w = 1.0$ and search for the equilibrium interest rate r only. In order to implement these steps, we mainly have to adjust module `prog03_03m` from the book, as shown in Module 3.4m. Given a factor price vector (w, r), we first derive the per-unit demand l_i and k_i from the function derived above and then compute the consumer prices $p_i = l_i w + k_i r$. Given consumer prices, we compute the price indices P and Ω, as well as the total income $\bar{Y}$. Next, optimal consumption and leisure demand can be derived from the demand equations. Then we compute disposable income Y_D and derive the goods demand X_i, which must be equal to output Y_i. Finally, we use the per-unit demand functions to derive total factor demand $K = kY$ and $L = lY$, so that we can check the capital market equilibrium $K_1 + K_2 - \bar{K} = 0$.

Note that with this solution method, we normalize the wage rate to one and solve for producer prices directly using optimal per-unit factor demands. Consequently, we only

Module 3.4m Market solution with CES production function

```
function markets(x)
    [......]
    ! calculate prices
    w = 1d0
    r = x
    ly =  (beta + (1d0-beta)*(beta*r/((1d0-beta)*w))**(1d0-sigma))&
        **(-1d0/rho)
    ky =  ((1d0-beta) + beta*((1d0-beta)*w/(beta*r))**(1d0-sigma))&
        **(-1d0/rho)
    p = ly*w + ky*r
    [......]
    ell   = alpha*Ybar/w**nu/Omega
    YD    = Ybar-w*ell
    Y(1)  = alphax*YD/p(1)**nux/PP
    Y(2)  = (1d0-alphax)*YD/p(2)**nux/PP
    L     = ly*Y
    K     = ky*Y

    ! get market equations
    markets = K(1)+K(2)-Kbar

end function
```

have to search for the equilibrium interest rate, which means that we only have to balance the capital market. As a result, this solution algorithm can be started with a wider range of initial guesses.

(c) The initial equilibrium with $\sigma_i = 0.5$ features $w < r$. Consequently, when we increase the elasticity of substitution of the two production factors, both firms will demand more labour input instead of capital input. As a consequence, the interest rate falls (since wages cannot increase) and labour input (supply of households) rises. The fall in interest rates with constant wages will reduce both consumer prices, so that goods demand increases on the household side, which triggers higher production output.

Exercise 3.5

This exercise is a straightforward extension of Exercise 3.4. We mainly have to adjust module `prog03_04m` from the book, as shown in Module 3.5m. First, we have to introduce the government variables G, τ_i, τ_w, and τ_r as well as net-of-tax prices q_i, w^n, and r^n. Besides the capital market equilibrium, we also have to make sure that the government budget is balanced. Consequently, we now solve a two-dimensional equation system:

$$K_1 + K_2 - \bar{K} = 0$$

$$q_1 G - \sum_{i=1}^{2} \tau_i q_i X_i - \tau_w w(\bar{T} - \ell) - \tau_r r \bar{K} = 0.$$

As in Exercise 3.4, we again normalize $w = 1.0$ and search for the equilibrium interest rate r and the budget-balancing consumption tax $\tau = \tau_1 = \tau_2$. Now we first derive producer prices q_i from the per-unit demand and then compute the consumer prices $p_i = q_i(1+\tau)$, as well as net wage $w^n = w(1 - \tau_w)$ and net interest rate $r^n = r(1 - \tau_r)$. From the price indices P and Ω optimal consumption and leisure demand can be derived. Next, given disposable income Y_D, the goods demand X_i is computed. Note that now government consumption G (which only consists of good one) has to be added to private demand in order to derive equilibrium output Y_i. Finally, we get total factor demand using the per-unit demand functions, so that we can check the two equilibrium conditions specified above.

When we simulate the same policies as in Table 3.1 in the book, we do not get the equivalence results because now the producer price of government consumption q_1 is not normalized to 1.0 any more. Therefore, while we keep the output G fixed, government expenditures $q_1 G$ (and the required tax revenues) are different in every simulation.

Module 3.5m Model with government activity

```
function markets(x)
    [......]
    ! calculate prices
    w          = 1d0
    r          = x(1)
    tauc(1)  = x(2)
    tauc(2)  = tauc(1)
    ly =  (beta + (1d0-beta)*(beta*r/((1d0-beta)*w))**(1d0-sigma))&
            **(-1d0/rho)
    ky =  ((1d0-beta) + beta*((1d0-beta)*w/(beta*r))**(1d0-sigma))&
            **(-1d0/rho)
    q   = ly*w + ky*r
    p   = q*(1d0+tauc)
    wn  = w*(1d0-tauw)
    [......]
    ! calculate other economic variables
    Ybarn  = wn*Tbar+rn*Kbar
    C      = (1d0-alpha)*Ybarn/PP**nu/Omega
    ell    = alpha*Ybarn/w**nu/Omega
    YD     = Ybarn-wn*ell
    Xd(1)  = alphax*YD/p(1)**nux/PP
    Xd(2)  =  (1d0-alphax)*YD/p(2)**nux/PP
    Y(1)   = Xd(1) + G
    Y(2)   = Xd(2)
    L      = ly*Y
    K      = ky*Y

    ! get market equations
    markets(1)=K(1)+K(2)-Kbar
    markets(2)=q(1)*G-sum(tauc*q*Xd)-tauw*w* &
                (Tbar-ell)-taur*r*Kbar
end function
```

Exercise 3.6

We now introduce intermediate goods. The module `prog03_06m` from the book has to be adjusted as shown in Module 3.6m. Most importantly, we have to introduce the input coefficient matrix and solve for optimal production quantities using subroutine `lu_solve`.

Simulating the model with $\nu = \nu_x = \sigma_i = 0.5$ gives an equilibrium where $r > w = 1.0 > q_1 > q_2$. Consequently, when ν increases from 0.5 to $\nu = 1.5$, households substitute leisure demand for goods demand (since labour is more expensive than goods). As a consequence, producer prices increase as well as the output of both goods. In order to balance the increase in labour supply, the interest rate has to increase, so that companies substitute capital input for labour input.

When (in addition) ν_x increases to 1.5, households substitute consumption of good X_1 for consumption of good X_2 (note that we still have $q_2 < q_1$). Since the latter is labour intensive, the interest rate decreases, which reduces both producer prices in turn

Module 3.6m Market solution with intermediate goods

```
function markets(x)
    [......]
    q = w*ly + r*ky
    call lu_solve(ID-transpose(a), q)

    p = q*(1d0+tauc)
    [......]
    Y(2) = Xd(2)
    call lu_solve(ID-a, Y)

    K = ky*Y
    L = ly*Y
    [......]
end function
```

and reduces available income. As a consequence, the production of good 1 (good 2) falls (increases) compared to the previous simulation. However, because of less available income, households consume much less consumption goods than before.

Finally, when the elasticity in the production function is increased to 1.5, labour demand rises and capital demand falls (since $w < r$). The interest rate therefore falls, reducing producer prices (and available income) much further. Consequently, consumption and leisure demand fall compared to the previous simulation.

Exercise 3.7

In the smopec model, the function `market` from module `prog03_06m` in the book has to be adjusted, as shown in Module 3.7m. Since the producer price for good 2 is now fixed, we need to compute the price q_1 from the zero profit condition of sector 1, so that we get:

$$q_1 Y_1 = q_1 X_{11} + q_2 X_{21} + wL_1 + rK_1 \quad \Rightarrow \quad q_1 = \frac{a_{21}q_2 + wl_1 + rk_1}{1 - a_{11}}.$$

Given producer prices, it is no problem to compute consumer prices and net-of-tax factor prices and derive the household demands for goods and leisure. In order to derive the output quantities of both sectors, we use the equilibrium condition of the goods market for the first good and the labour market equilibrium condition:

$$\begin{aligned} Y_1 &= X_{11} + X_{12} + X_1 + G \\ L_1 + L_2 &= \bar{T} - \ell, \end{aligned}$$

Module 3.7m Market solution in smopec model

```
function markets(x)
    [......]
    r          = 1d0
    q(2)       = 1d0
    w          = x(1)
    tauc(1)    = x(2)
    tauc(2)    = tauc(1)

    ky = a0*((1d0-beta)/beta*w/r)**beta
    ly = a0*(beta/(1d0-beta)*r/w)**(1d0-beta)
    q(1) =  (a(2,1)*q(2)+w*ly(1)+r*ky(1))/(1d0-a(1,1))
    [......]
    Xd = alpha/p*Ybarn
    ell   =  (1d0-alpha(1)-alpha(2))/wn*Ybarn

    Y(1)  = Xd(1)+G
    Y(2)  = Tbar-ell
    mat(1, :) = (/1d0-a(1,1), -a(1,2)/)
    mat(2, :) = (/ly(1), ly(2)/)
    call lu_solve(mat, Y)
    K = ky*Y
    L = ly*Y

    markets(1)=(1d0-a(2,2))*q(2)-a(1,2)*q(1)-w*ly(2)-r*ky(2)
    markets(2)=q(1)*G-sum(tauc*q*Xd)-tauw*w*&
                          (Tbar-ell)-taur*r*Kbar

end function markets
```

which can be transformed into:

$$\begin{bmatrix} 1-a_{11} & -a_{12} \\ l_1 & l_2 \end{bmatrix}\begin{bmatrix} Y_1 \\ Y_2 \end{bmatrix} = \begin{bmatrix} X_1 + G \\ \bar{T} - \ell \end{bmatrix}.$$

We can solve for the output quantities using subroutine `lu_solve`. Given the output quantities, we can derive factor demands and check whether markets are in equilibrium. Since we have already applied the equilibrium condition for the first good market and the labour market, we now check the equilibrium on the market for the second good and the government budget. The capital market is then automatically balanced.

(a) When the model is solved with uniform consumption taxes, the equilibrium tax rate is 18% and the economy exports 56.8 units of good 2 to the world market and imports capital in the same amount.

(b) When the tax structure changes such that the second good is taxed five times as much as the first good, household demand shifts from the second to the first good. Consequently, production of the second good decreases and exports increase up to 57.88 units. At the same time, welfare decreases from 24.95 to 24.86 because of the higher tax distortions.

Module 3.8m Market solution with factor input taxes

```
function markets(x)
    [......]
    w         = 1d0
    r         = x(1)
    tauc(1)   = x(2)
    tauc(2)   = tauc(1)
    rg =  (1d0+tauk)*r
    wg =  (1d0+taul)*w

    ky=a0*(((1d0-beta)*wg)/(beta*rg))**beta
    ly=a0*((beta*rg)/((1d0-beta)*wg))**(1d0-beta)
    q = wg*ly + rg*ky
    [......]
    markets(1)  = K(1)+K(2)-Kbar
    markets(2)  = q(1)*G-sum(tauc*q*Xd)-tauw*w*(Tbar-ell)-&
                  taur*r*Kbar-sum(taul*w*L)-sum(tauk*r*K)

end function markets
```

Exercise 3.8

We define `tauk(2)` and `taul(2)` in the variable definition section and then set these taxes at the respective values in the main program. Module `prog03_06m` of the book has to be adjusted, as shown in Module 3.8m, where we define the gross factor prices `rg` and `wg`, which include factor taxes.

(a) Compared to the equilibrium with a pure consumption tax, a tax on capital input in sector 1 induces a substitution of capital inputs by labour inputs in sector 1. The producer price increases. The consumer price rises much less since the consumption tax rate can be reduced significantly from 7 to roughly 1 per cent. Private demand for consumer good 1 falls only slightly, while the demand for consumer good 2 increases significantly (due to lower consumer price). Consequently, intermediate input demand from sector 2 rises, while intermediate input demand from sector 1 decreases slightly. Overall, utility decreases only slightly from 19.98 to 19.97.

(b) A tax on labour input in sector 2 induces a substitution of labour input by capital in this sector. Now prices in sector 2 increase compared to the initial equilibrium and demand for goods from sector 2 falls. The consumption tax rate could be again reduced from 7 to 1 per cent. Note that welfare falls more strongly, from 19.98 to 19.95. The reason is that the input tax now further distorts labour supply, while in Exercise 3.7 the input tax reduced labour supply distortions.

Exercise 3.9

(a) With $\tau_2 = 0$ and $T_2 = 0$, the zero profit condition of sector 2 is:

$$q_2 Y_2 = q_1(1+\tau_1)X_{12} + q_2 X_{22} + wL_2 + rK_2.$$

Module 3.9m Market solution with zero rating

```
function markets(x)
   [......]
   q = w*ly+r*ky
   a(1,2) = a(1,2)*(1d0+lambda*tau(1))
   call lu_solve(ID-transpose(a), q)
   [......]
   Y(1) = Xd(1)+G
   Y(2) = Xd(2)
   a(1,2) = a(1,2)/(1d0+lambda*tau(1))
   call lu_solve(ID-a, Y)
   [......]
   T(1)=tau(1)*q(1)*Y(1)-sum(tau*q*a(:,1))*Y(1)
   T(2)=tau(2)*q(2)*Y(2)-(1d0-lambda)*sum(tau*q*a(:,2))*Y(2)

   markets(1) = K(1)+K(2)-Kbar
   markets(2) = p(1)*G-sum(T)-tauw*w*(Tbar-ell)-taur*r*Kbar

end function markets
```

Consequently, the tax rate now appears in the equation system that defines producer prices:

$$\begin{bmatrix} 1-a_{11} & -a_{21} \\ -a_{12}(1+\tau_1) & 1-a_{22} \end{bmatrix} \begin{bmatrix} q_1 \\ q_2 \end{bmatrix} = \begin{bmatrix} wl_1 + rk_1 \\ wl_2 + rk_2 \end{bmatrix}.$$

(b) In order to implement the difference between zero rating and exemption, we introduce the parameter `lambda`, which is set in the main program to a value of 0 (zero rating) or 1 (exemption). The parameter is only used in Module 3.9m to define the matrix `A` used for the computation of producer prices and to calculate sector-specific tax revenues. When the government substitutes zero rating in sector 2 by exemption, tax revenues increase, so that the consumption tax for sector 1 can be reduced from 18 to 12 per cent. At the same time, producer (and consumer) prices in sector 2 increase, which reduces demand for sector 2 goods and increases demand for sector 1 goods. When the exemption system is introduced, welfare increases from 19.94 to 19.97. The reason is that the system dampens the distortion caused by the differentiated consumption tax, since it induces a shift in demand towards sector 1 goods.

Exercise 3.10

(a) When both countries switch from the destination principle (DP) towards the origin principle (OP), the zero profit condition of sector i changes to:

$$p_i Y_i = \sum_{j=1}^{2} p_j X_{ji} + (wL_i + rK_i)(1+\tau_i).$$

Module 3.10m Market solution with international trade

```
function markets(x)
    [......]
    q(:,1)  =  (w(1)*ly(:,1)+r*ky(:,1))*(1d0+lambda*tauc(:,1))
    call lu_solve(ID-transpose(a), q(:,1))
    q(1,2)  =  (a(2,1)*q(2,1)+(w(2)*ly(1,2)+r*ky(1,2))* &
                   (1d0+lambda*tauc(1,2)))/(1d0-a(1,1))
    q(2,2)  =  q(2,1)

    do i = 1, 2
        p(:,i)  =  q(:,i)*(1d0+(1d0-lambda)*tauc(:,i))
        [......]
    enddo
    [......]
    wh(:,1)  =  w(1)
    wh(:,2)  =  w(2)
    if (lambda == 0) then
        T = tauc*q*Xd
    else
        T = tauc*(wh*L+r*K)
    endif
    [......]
    markets(3)  =  q(1,1)*G-sum(T(:,1))-&
         tauw(1)*w(1)*(Tbar(1)-ell(1))-taur(1)*r*Kbar(1)
    markets(4)  =  q(1,2)*G-sum(T(:,2))-&
         tauw(2)*w(2)*(Tbar(2)-ell(2))-taur(2)*r*Kbar(2)

end function markets
```

Consequently, consumer prices in the home country can now be computed directly from:

$$\begin{bmatrix} 1-a_{11} & -a_{21} \\ -a_{12} & 1-a_{22} \end{bmatrix} \begin{bmatrix} p_1 \\ p_2 \end{bmatrix} = \begin{bmatrix} (wl_1 + rk_1)(1+\tau_1) \\ (wl_2 + rk_2)(1+\tau_2) \end{bmatrix}.$$

In addition, the computation of consumption tax revenues has to be adjusted to:

$$T = \sum_{i=1}^{2} \tau_i (wL_i + rK_i).$$

(b) We again introduce a parameter `lambda`, which is set to 0 (DP) or 1 (OP) in the main program. The module `prog03_07m` of the book then needs to be adjusted to Module 3.10m.

A switch from DP towards OP induces a reduction of the tax rate in the home country A, and vice versa for country B. Indeed, the tax rate rises in country B from 6 to 24 per cent. Nevertheless, the welfare change is modest, since prices mostly adjust in the opposite direction. Welfare falls in country B from 17.38 to 17.00, while it rises in country A from 23.02 to 23.37. In special cases (that is all goods traded, fixed labour supply), such a reform produces no real changes at all, since only prices adjust.

4 Topics in finance and risk management

Exercise 4.1

The general structure for the program for the optimal portfolio weights both with and without a risk-free asset is the same as in program `prog04_02` from Chapter 4 of the book. Again, the stock data is initialized in the first step within the subroutine `returns`, which is then used to compute the expected value of the stocks and to set up the corresponding variance–covariance matrix. However, the optimization problem itself is now solved by using the subroutine `fminsearch` from the toolbox instead of using either the rootfinding routine `fzero` or a Monte Carlo approach. Similar to the Monte Carlo approach in Section 4.1.4 of the book, the subroutine `fminsearch` does not require taking derivatives to find a solution to the investor's optimization problem and is able to solve it directly subject to the respective constraints (see Chapter 2 in the book). The crucial advantage of using `fminsearch` compared to a simple Monte Carlo approach is its higher computational efficiency for a given level of numerical precision.

With a risk-free asset, the optimization problem without a short-selling constraint is given by:

$$\max_{\omega_f,\omega} \ \omega_f r_f + \omega^T \mu - \frac{\gamma}{2}\omega^T \Sigma \omega \quad s.t. \ \omega_f + \omega^T I = 1,$$

which yields, after plugging the constraint into the utility function:

$$\max_{\omega} \ \omega^T(\mu - r_f I) - \frac{\gamma}{2}\omega^T \Sigma \omega.$$

This function is stored within the function `utility_rf` in the module `globals`. The optimization problem can be solved directly by using the subroutine `fminsearch`, which iterates in three dimensions to find the optimal portfolio weights for the investor's preferences. As illustrated in Program 4.1, the subroutine `fminsearch` again receives five arguments: an initial guess `x_in` of the optimal portfolio weights; a variable `fret` that gives back the investor's utility in the optimum; an array for the lower bound `x_l`; and an array for the upper bound `x_u` of the interval, in which it should search for the optimum, as well as the function itself that should be optimized.

Program 4.1 Subroutine `fminsearch` with a risk-free asset

```
! initial guess for portfolio shares
x_in(1:NN) = 0.2d0

! initialize boundaries for portfolio weights
x_l = -1d0
x_u =  1d0

! maximize utility
call fminsearch(x_in(1:NN), fret, x_l, x_u, utility_rf)
```

The first guess is to set `x_in = 0.2d0` in all three dimensions. All entries of the array for the lower bound are set to `x_l = -1d0` and all elements in the array for the upper bound are initialized as `x_u = 1d0`. Finally, the function `utility_rf` is handed to the subroutine `fminsearch`. Note that `utility_rf` stores the negative of the investor's actual utility function, as `fminsearch` is constructed such as to find the minima of optimization problems. In the absence of a short-selling constraint, the program yields the same optimal portfolio weights $\omega_f = -0.111$, $\omega_1 = 0.335$, $\omega_2 = 0.571$, and $\omega_3 = 0.205$, as in the fifth column of Table 4.3 in the book.

In the scenario without a risk-free asset, the optimization problem is given by:

$$\max_{\omega} \ \omega^T \mu - \frac{\gamma}{2} \omega^T \Sigma \omega \quad s.t. \ \omega^T I = 1,$$

and is stored within the function `utility` in the module `globals`. The constraint:

$$\omega^T I = \omega_1 + \omega_2 + \omega_3 = 1$$

is hereby reformulated to:

$$\omega_3 = 1 - \omega_1 - \omega_2$$

and plugged into the optimization problem, so that the subroutine `fminsearch` only has to optimize over two dimensions. This subroutine again receives the same arguments as

Program 4.1.a Subroutine `fminsearch` without a risk-free asset

```
! initial guess for portfolio shares
x_in(1:NN-1) = 0.2d0

! initialize boundaries for portfolio weights
x_l =  0d0
x_u =  1d0

! maximize utility
call fminsearch(x_in(1:NN-1), fret, x_l(1:NN-1), &
     x_u(1:NN-1), utility)
```

above; however, the initial guess for the optimum as well as the interval bounds now use only the first two (ie $N - 1$) entries of the respective arrays (see Program 4.1.a).

Running the program yields $\omega_1 = 0.262$, $\omega_2 = 0.535$, and $\omega_3 = 0.203$ as optimal portfolio shares.

Exercise 4.2

The solution of this problem is set up so as to search for the root of the equation:

$$S_0\Phi(d_1) - e^{-r\Delta T}K\Phi(d_2) - c^E = 0,$$

with:

$$d_1 = \frac{\log\left(\frac{S_0}{K}\right) + \left(r + \frac{\sigma^2}{2}\right)\Delta T}{\sigma\sqrt{\Delta T}} \quad \text{and} \quad d_2 = d_1 - \sigma\sqrt{\Delta T}$$

and c^E as the exogenously given price of the European call option and σ as the unknown (ie the implied volatility). The problem has to be solved with numerical methods, as there is no closed-form solution for the cumulative density function of the normal distribution. This is done in Program 4.2 using the subroutine `fzero` from the toolbox. The main program only sets up the initial guess for the unknown, calls the subroutine `fzero`, and prints the solution to the screen. The equation itself has to be stored in the module `globals`, together with the required parameters to initialize the Black-Scholes formula (see Module 4.2m). The subroutine `fzero` receives this function, together with the initial guess `sigma` and a logical variable `check` as input. The computed implied volatility of the option is $\sigma^{impl} = 10.1\%$ and is only slightly different from its actual value of $\sigma = 10\%$.

Program 4.2 Subroutine `fzero` to compute the implicit volatility

```
! set up initial guess
sigma = 0.5d0

! call subroutine fzero
call fzero(sigma, DIFF, check)

! check for convergence
if(check)stop 'Error: fzero did not converge'

! print output to the screen
write(*,'(a,f10.1)')'Implied Volatility (in %): ', &
                                             sigma*100
```

Module 4.2m The equation solved to obtain the implicit volatility

```
function DIFF(sigma)

    implicit none
    real*8, intent(in) :: sigma
    real*8 :: DIFF, d_1, d_2

    d_1 = (log(S_0/KK) + (r+sigma**2/2d0)*Del_TT)/&
            sigma/sqrt(Del_TT)
    d_2 = d_1 - sigma*sqrt(Del_TT)
    DIFF = S_0*normalCDF(d_1, 0d0, 1d0) - &
           KK*exp(-r*Del_TT)*normalCDF(d_2, 0d0, 1d0) - c_E

end function
```

Exercise 4.3

Program 4.3 is structured similar to program `prog04_05` in Chapter 4 of the book, in which the price of Asian-type options is determined. However, as standard European options are not path-dependent, the Monte Carlo simulation will only simulate the stock prices at maturity, and not the whole path itself. In the first part of this program, the prices of the European call option and the European put option are computed analytically through the Black-Scholes formula. The results are stored in all entries of the arrays `c_E` and `p_E`, which both have the same length `JJ` as the arrays `c_EMC` and `p_EMC` used for the results of the Monte Carlo simulation. This is done to allow comparison of the results from the analytical solution to simulated results in a common plot at the end of the program. The variable `JJ` in Program 4.3 defines the maximum number of simulated

Program 4.3 Fair value of European options with Monte Carlo simulation

```
! set up monte carlo algorithm
do ij = 1, JJ

    ! simulate stock-prices at maturity
    call simulate_normal(z, 0d0, 1d0)
    S_T = S_0*exp((r-sigma**2/2d0)*Del_TT + &
            sigma*sqrt(Del_TT)*z)

    ! calculate payoff at maturity
    pi_c(ij) = max(S_T - KK, 0d0)
    pi_p(ij) = max(KK - S_T, 0d0)

enddo

! use different number of paths to compute premium
do ij = 1, JJ
    c_EMC(ij) = exp(-r*Del_TT)*sum(pi_c(1:ij))/dble(ij)
    p_EMC(ij) = exp(-r*Del_TT)*sum(pi_p(1:ij))/dble(ij)
    npaths(ij) = dble(ij)
enddo
```

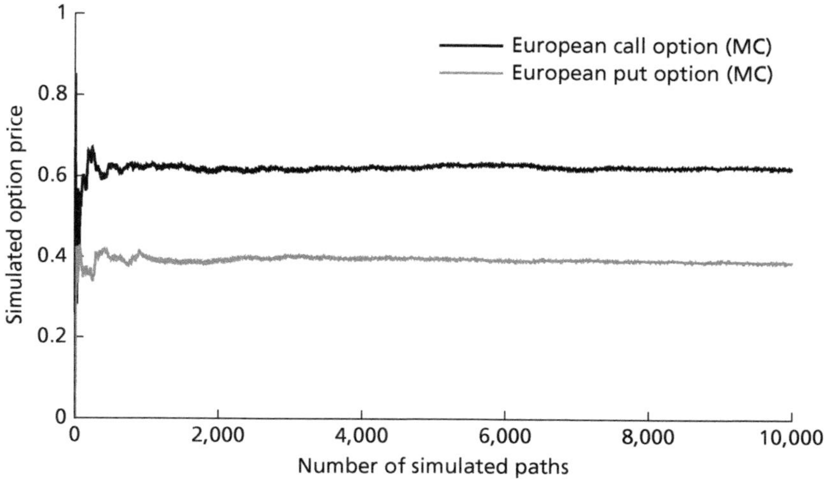

Figure 4.1 Convergence of the Monte Carlo algorithm

stock prices at maturity and is set to 20,000 in this program. For each number `ij` of simulated stock prices at maturity, the fair value of the European call option and of the European put option are then computed in the Monte Carlo simulation as the discounted average pay-off at maturity.

As illustrated in Figure 4.1, the solution of the Monte Carlo simulation is converging with an increasing number of simulations to the analytical solution from the Black-Scholes formula. Already, 10,000 simulations yield a good approximation for the analytical solution.

Exercise 4.4

(a) This problem is solved again with a similar algorithm as the one used in Exercise 4.3, with the difference that the pay-off of the option is now conditioned on whether the underlying's price was at least once below the barrier $H = 24$ until maturity. The number of simulated paths in the Monte Carlo algorithm is initialized to `JJ = 20000`. For each of these paths, it is checked on a daily basis whether the barrier is hit or not (ie `TT = 62`).

If the barrier is hit for one of the simulated paths, the logical variable `active` is set to `.true.`, indicating that the option is activated and has a pay-off equal to a standard European option. Otherwise, the logical variable `active` remains at the value `.false.` and the pay-off of the option is equal to zero (see Program 4.4). With these pay-offs at maturity at hand, the price of the European barrier call option and of the European barrier put option can be computed by discounting the respective expected pay-off for a European call option and a European put option to the date of issue. The simulated

Program 4.4 Monte Carlo approach for European barrier options

```
! simulate price paths and corresponding profits
do ij = 1, JJ

    ! reset barrier
    active = .false.

    ! generate a price path
    call simulate_normal(z, 0d0, 1d0)
    S(0) = S_0
    do it = 1, TT
        S(it) = S(it - 1)*exp((r-sigma**2/2d0)*del_t &
                + sigma*sqrt(del_t)*z(it))

        ! check wether barrier is hit at all
        if(S(it) < H)active(1) = .true.
        [......]
    enddo

    pi_C(:, ij) = 0d0
    pi_P(:, ij) = 0d0

    ! compute payoff at maturity conditional on whether
    ! barrier is hit
    if (active(1)) then
        pi_C(1, ij) = max(S(TT) - KK, 0d0)
        pi_P(1, ij) = max(KK - S(TT), 0d0)
    endif
    [......]
enddo
```

fair value is equal to $c^{EB} = 0.022$ for a European call option and to $p^{EB} = 0.321$ for a European put option. It should be obvious that this result depends crucially on the position of the barrier and how often it is checked whether the barrier is hit over the lifetime of an option. With the values from Table 4.4, and a barrier below S_0, this makes the European call option almost worthless, and affects the fair price of the put option only very slightly. The reason for this is that the call option is only profitable for those paths for which the underlyings price first falls below the barrier $H = 24$ but then rises again and finishes above the strike price $K = S_0 = 25$. Figure 4.2 shows the convergence of the Monte Carlo algorithm.

(b) In order to determine the price of European barrier call options and European barrier put options for which the barrier is active only in a certain timeframe, the code in Program 4.4 from Part (a) has to be modified only slightly. Program 4.4.a shows the respective activation condition for the case that the barrier has to be hit within the first ten days after the option is issued or the last ten days before maturity. In the first scenario, the price of a European barrier call option falls to (roughly) $c^{EB} = 0.003$, while the price of a European barrier put option decreases even more drastically, to about $p^{EB} = 0.019$. This can simply be explained through the fact that there exist only few paths for which the price of the underlying falls during the first ten days below the barrier $H = 24$.

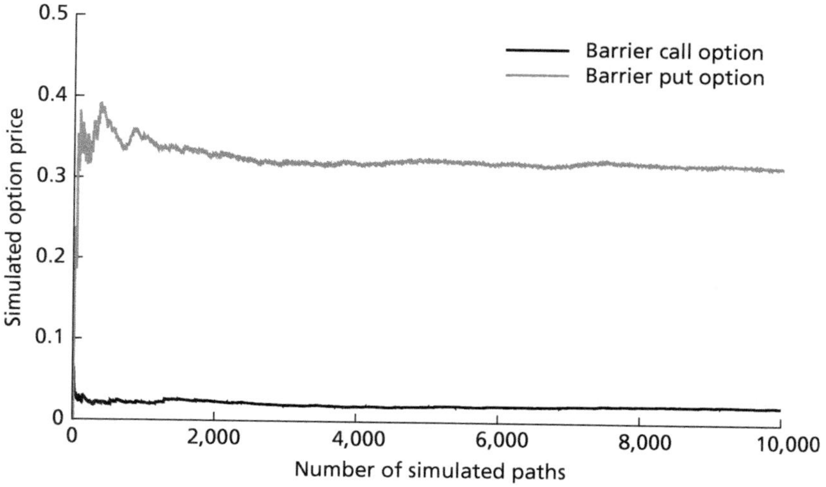

Figure 4.2 Monte Carlo algorithm with increasing number of simulations

Program 4.4.a Monte Carlo approach for European barrier options

```
! check wether barrier is hit at all
if(S(it) < H .and. it < TT_B)active(2) = .true.
if(S(it) < H .and. it > TT - TT_B)active(3) = .true.
```

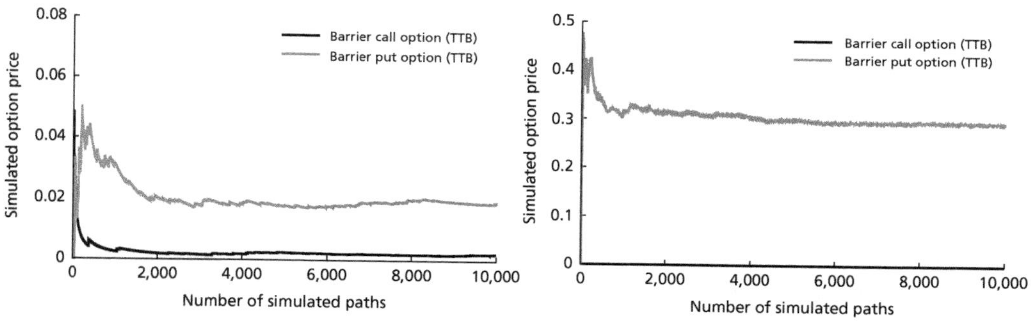

Figure 4.3 Monte Carlo simulation for prices of European barrier options

The second scenario, in which the option can only become active in the last ten days before maturity affects in particular the call option. The call option is now worthless, ie $c^{EB} = 0$, as there exist no paths which would activate the option during the last ten days before maturity and still finish above the strike price $K = S_0 = 25$. The fair value of the put option, on the other hand, falls only slightly, to $p^{EB} = 0.295$. If the value of the underlying finishes below the strike price K, it is very likely that the option has been activated in the last ten days, as the difference between H and K is small. These results are summarized in Figure 4.3.

Program 4.5 Closed-form solution for the price of a Binary option

```
! compute price of Binary call and put
d_2 = (log(S_0/KK) + (r-sigma**2/2d0)*Del_TT)/&
      sigma/sqrt(Del_TT)
c_BI = q*normalCDF(d_2, 0d0, 1d0)
p_BI = q*normalCDF(-d_2, 0d0, 1d0)
```

Exercise 4.5

Under the assumption of continuous stock prices according to Equation (4.13) in the book, the probability that the spot price $S_{\Delta T}$ for the underlying will finish above or below the strike price K at maturity can be derived in a similar way to the Black-Scholes formula. The values of Binary call options and Binary put options are then the expected pay-offs of this option at maturity discounted to the date of issue, ie:

$$\begin{aligned} c^{BI} &= e^{-r\Delta T} q \int_K^\infty f(S_{\Delta T})\, dS_{\Delta T} \\ &= e^{-r\Delta T} q \left(1 - \Phi\left(\frac{\ln K - \ln S_0 - (r - \frac{\sigma^2}{2})\Delta T}{\sigma\sqrt{\Delta T}}\right)\right) \\ &= e^{-r\Delta T} q\Phi(d_2) \end{aligned}$$

for a Binary call option, and:

$$p^{BI} = e^{-r\Delta T} q\Phi(-d_2)$$

as the price of a Binary put option, where we used the same definition for d_2 as in Section 4.2 of the book The numerical implementation in Program 4.5 of the model requires only the computation of this formula and yields, with the values from Table 4.4 in the book:

$$c^{BI} = 17.08 \quad \text{and} \quad p^{BI} = 12.92.$$

Exercise 4.6

(a) The concept of Lookback options is close to Asian options, so that only small changes in program `prog04_05` are necessary. The number of simulated paths is left unchanged at 20,000 and the stock price is evaluated again on a daily basis. However, the strike price has to be replaced by the minimum price of the underlying realized during the lifetime of the option for a call in the pay-off at maturity and by the realized maximum price for a put. The price of the Floating Strike Lookback call option and of the Floating Strike Lookback put option can then be computed by discounting the respective expected pay-off to the date of issue. Both the price for the European Lookback call option (roughly $c^{LB} = 1.05$) and the European Lookback put option (roughly $p^{LB} = 0.84$) are above the respective prices of standard European options.

(b) Computing the price of a European Fixed Strike Lookback option is similar to Part (a), but the spot price of the underlying at maturity in the pay-off is now replaced by the maximum realized spot price of the underlying during the option's lifetime for a call option. For a European Fixed Strike Lookback put option, on the other hand, the spot price at maturity is replaced by the minimum spot price for the underlying realized over the option's lifetime. The numerical implementation of both the Monte Carlo simulation for the Floating Strike Lookback option from Part (a) and the European Fixed Strike Lookback option is shown in Program 4.6. The price of a Fixed Strike Lookback call is now given by $c^{LB} = 1.07$ and for a Fixed Strike Lookback put by $p^{LB} = 0.82$.

Program 4.6 Monte Carlo simulation for European Lookback options

```
do ij = 1, JJ

    ! generate a price path
    call simulate_normal(z, 0d0, 1d0)
    S(0) = S_0
    do it = 1, TT
        S(it) = S(it - 1)*exp((r-sigma**2/2d0)*del_t + &
                sigma*sqrt(del_t)*z(it))
    enddo

    ! calculate payoff at maturity for
    ! a floating strike option
    pi_c(1, ij) = max(S(TT) - minval(S(:)), 0d0)
    pi_p(1, ij) = max(maxval(S(:)) - S(TT), 0d0)

    ! calculate payoff at maturity for
    ! a fixed strike option
    pi_c(2, ij) = max(maxval(S(:)) - KK, 0d0)
    pi_p(2, ij) = max(KK - minval(S(:)), 0d0)
enddo

! compute price for lookback options from simulated paths
do ij = 1, JJ
    do in = 1, NN
        c_LB(in, ij) = exp(-r*Del_TT)*&
                       sum(pi_c(in, 1:ij))/dble(ij)
        p_LB(in, ij) = exp(-r*Del_TT)*&
                       sum(pi_p(in, 1:ij))/dble(ij)
        npaths(ij) = dble(ij)
    enddo
enddo
```

Exercise 4.7

(a) The price of the Chooser option can be derived analytically as:

$$\begin{aligned}
p^{CH} &= e^{-r\Delta T_1} \max\left[\, c^E(S_{\Delta T_1}, K, \Delta T_2 - \Delta T_1); p^E(S_{\Delta T_1}, K, \Delta T_2 - \Delta T_1)\,\right] \\
&= e^{-r\Delta T_1} \max\left[\, c^E(S_{\Delta T_1}, K, \Delta T_2 - \Delta T_1); c^E(S_{\Delta T_1}, K, \Delta T_2 - \Delta T_1)\right. \\
&\quad \left. + Ke^{-r(\Delta T_2 - \Delta T_1)} - S_{\Delta T_1}\,\right] \\
&= c^E(S_0, K, \Delta T_2) + e^{-r\Delta T_1} \max[Ke^{-r(\Delta T_2 - \Delta T_1)} - S_{\Delta T_1}; 0] \\
&= c^E(S_0, K, \Delta T_2) + p^E(S_0, Ke^{-r(\Delta T_2 - \Delta T_1)}, \Delta T_1).
\end{aligned}$$

In the first step, we use the put-call-parity in order to substitute out the price of a European call $c^E(S_{\Delta T_1}, K, \Delta T_2 - \Delta T_1)$. The final step is to note that the second term is the price of a European put option with an adjusted strike price that can be exercised at T_1. Consequently, the price of a Chooser option is equivalent to the price of a European call option with strike price K and maturity ΔT_2 plus the price of a European put option with an adjusted strike price $Ke^{-r\Delta(T_2 - T_1)}$ and maturity T_1.

Using the values from Table 4.3 and with the decision date $T_1 = 31$, the price of the Chooser option is given by $p^{CH} = 0.92$. The numerical implementation thus requires only to set the computation of the Black-Scholes formula for the respective call and put as illustrated in Program 4.7.

(b) The Monte Carlo approach is implemented in Program 4.7.a. We again simulate 20,000 paths for S_j until date T_1, then compute for each path the resulting prices for the call, as well as the put options at date T_1 and compute the maximum price. Finally, we take

Program 4.7 Closed-form solution of a Chooser option

```
! compute parameters for Black-Scholes
! formula with maturity T2
d_1 = (log(S_0/KK) + (r+sigma**2/2d0)* &
      Del_TT_2)/sigma/sqrt(Del_TT_2)
d_2 = d_1 - sigma*sqrt(Del_TT_2)
c_E = S_0*normalCDF(d_1, 0d0, 1d0) &
      - KK*exp(-r*Del_TT_2)*normalCDF(d_2, 0d0, 1d0)

! compute parameters for Black-Scholes
! formula with maturity T1
Dis_KK = KK*exp(-r*(Del_TT_2-Del_TT_1))
d_1 = (log(S_0/Dis_KK) + (r+sigma**2/2d0)* &
      Del_TT_1)/sigma/sqrt(Del_TT_1)
d_2 = d_1 - sigma*sqrt(Del_TT_1)
p_E = -S_0*normalCDF(-d_1, 0d0, 1d0) &
      + KK*exp(-r*Del_TT_1)*normalCDF(-d_2, 0d0, 1d0)

! compute the price of a Chooser option
p_CH = c_E + p_E
```

Program 4.7.a Monte Carlo simulation of a Chooser option

```
do ij = 1, JJ

    ! generate a price path
    call simulate_normal(z, 0d0, 1d0)
    S(0) = S_0
    ! simulate paths of stock prices until T1
    do it = 1, TT_1
        S(it) = S(it - 1)*exp((r-sigma**2/2d0)*del_t &
                        + sigma*sqrt(del_t)*z(it))
    enddo
    d_1 = (log(S(TT_1)/KK) + (r+sigma**2/2d0)*&
          (Del_TT_2 - Del_TT_1)) &
          /sigma/sqrt(Del_TT_2-Del_TT_1)
    d_2 = d_1 - sigma*sqrt(Del_TT_2-Del_TT_1)
    c_E = S(TT_1)*normalCDF(d_1, 0d0, 1d0) &
          - KK*exp(-r*(Del_TT_2-Del_TT_1))*&
            normalCDF(d_2, 0d0, 1d0)
    p_E = -S(TT_1)*normalCDF(-d_1, 0d0, 1d0) &
          + KK*exp(-r*(Del_TT_2-Del_TT_1))*&
            normalCDF(-d_2, 0d0, 1d0)

    ! compute max price at T1
    pi(ij) = max(c_E, p_E)

enddo

! compute price for lookback options from simulated paths
do ij = 1, JJ
    p_CHMC(ij) = exp(-r*Del_TT_1)*sum(pi(1:ij))/dble(ij)
    npaths(ij) = dble(ij)
enddo
```

the average maximum price, discount it to the initial period, and obtain with $p^{CH} = 0.87$ a good approximation for the analytical solution.

Exercise 4.8

The solution algorithm for a Bermuda option builds upon the computation of the price of an American option in program `prog04_04` of the book. It is again necessary to find the point of time prior to maturity at which it is optimal to exercise the option, with the restriction that the option can only be exercised at a certain number of pre-specified dates. These pre-specified dates have to be explicitly considered in the numerical implementation of the algorithm (see Program 4.8). At days at which the execution of the option is allowed, we have to take into account that it is worthwhile executing the option whenever the difference between underlying and strike price is larger than the continuation value.

Program 4.8 Binomial tree to compute Bermuda option

```
! work recursively through the binomial tree
do it = TT_3 - 1, 1, -1
    do n = 0, it

        ! check whether to exercise the
        ! option prior to maturity
        if(it == TT_1 .or. it == TT_2)then
            c_B(it, n) = max(S_tn(it, n) - KK, &
                         exp(-r*del_t) &
                         *(p*c_B(it+1, n+1) &
                         + (1d0-p)*c_B(it+1, n)))
            p_B(it, n) = max(KK - S_tn(it, n), &
                         exp(-r*del_t) &
                         *(p*p_B(it+1, n+1) &
                         + (1d0-p)*p_B(it+1, n)))
        else
            c_B(it, n) = exp(-r*del_t)&
                         *(p*c_B(it+1, n+1) &
                          + (1d0-p)*c_B(it+1, n))
            p_B(it, n) = exp(-r*del_t)&
                         *(p*p_B(it+1, n+1) &
                         + (1d0-p)*p_B(it+1, n))
        endif
    enddo
enddo
```

For the same reason as for an American call option, it is never profitable to exercise a Bermuda call option prior to maturity. The fair value of a Bermuda call option is thus again equal to the price of a European call option. This is, however, different for a put option. Here, it can indeed be profitable to exercise the option prior to maturity. Intuitively, it is clear that the value of a Bermuda put option lies between the values of a European put option and an American put option.

Exercise 4.9

The code to compute these sensitivities is structured such that the main program is only used to print the output and execute the plot, while the respective difference quotients to approximate the partial derivatives of the option price are computed within subroutines that are stored in the module `globals`. The Delta (Δ) and the Gamma (Γ) of an option are approximated by difference quotients that assume a marginal increase of the spot price at the date of issue for the underlying, while the difference quotient used to approximate the Vega ($\mathcal{V}$) and the Rho (ρ) of an option are computed under the assumption of a percentual increase in the volatility of the underlying σ and the risk-free interest rate r, respectively. Finally, Theta (θ) is computed as a decrease of the time to maturity in days.

The structure of the different subroutines to approximate the respective partial derivatives through difference quotients is similar in all cases. For instance, the difference quotients to approximate the Δ of a European call and a European put are given by:

$$\Delta_c = \frac{\partial c}{\partial S} = \frac{c^E(S_0 + \delta, K, \Delta T) - c^E(S_0, K, \Delta T)}{\delta}$$
$$\Delta_p = \frac{\partial c}{\partial S} = \frac{p^E(S_0 + \delta, K, \Delta T) - p^E(S_0, K, \Delta T)}{\delta}.$$

The value δ is crucial for the precision of the approximation and set to 10^{-5}. Program 4.9 shows the corresponding numerical implementation. The values $c^E(S_0, K, \Delta T)$, $c^E(S_0 + \delta, K, \Delta T)$, $p^E(S_0, K, \Delta T)$, and $p^E(S_0 + \delta, K, \Delta T)$ used to compute the above difference coefficients are determined in the subroutine `black_scholes`. The difference quotients are then handed over to the main program and printed to the screen. In order to obtain a plot of the difference quotients for different spot prices S_0 at the date of issue, a grid of spot prices S_0 is set up over the interval $[20, 30]$ and stored in the array `S_plot` with, in total, `nplot` entries.

The grid is an equidistant grid and the variable `nplot` gives the number of points at which the difference quotients are computed. A higher density of gridpoints results in a smoother plot, however requires at the same time a higher computational effort. Similar to the array `S_plot`, in which the spot prices S_0 are stored, the corresponding difference quotients are now written in the main program into local arrays with a flag `plot` and the same length `0:nplot`.

Note that the code can be easily adopted to compute the sensitivities for American or other types of exotic options, simply by modifying/replacing the subroutine `black_scholes`. The Black-Scholes formula used to compute the price of European options might, for instance, be replaced by a binomial approach or a Monte Carlo simulation. Table 4.1 summarizes the sensitivities of a European option with respect to

Program 4.9 Delta of a European call and put option

```
subroutine approx_delta(S_in, r_in, sigma_in, Del_TT_in, &
            KK_in, delta_c_out, delta_p_out)
    [......]
    ! compute delta of an option
    call black_scholes(S_in, r_in, &
            sigma_in, Del_TT_in, &
            KK_in, c_temp(1), p_temp(1))
    call black_scholes(S_in + delta, r_in, &
            sigma_in, Del_TT_in, &
            KK_in, c_temp(2), p_temp(2))

    delta_c_out = (c_temp(2) - c_temp(1))/delta
    delta_p_out = (p_temp(2) - p_temp(1))/delta

end subroutine
```

Table 4.1 Sensitivity analysis for a European call and put

	Price	Δ	Γ	$\mathcal{V}$	θ	ρ
Call	0.62733	0.58866	0.31250	0.04844	−0.00616	0.03494
Put	0.38056	−0.41134	0.31250	0.04844	−0.00220	−0.02645

the spot price at the date of issue S_0 of the underlying, the volatility σ, time to maturity T, and the risk-free interest rate r.

Delta (Δ): if the spot price S_0 of the underlying at the date of issue is marginally increased by € 1 and all other parameters held constant, the price of a European call option will increase by $\Delta_c = 0.58866$, whereas the price of a European put option will decrease by $\Delta_p = -0.41134$. The positive sign for Δ_c results from the fact that an increased spot price S_0 at the date of issue makes a call more likely to be exercised at maturity and thus more expensive. On the other hand, the same increase in the spot price S_0 makes the exercise of the European put at maturity less likely and the option consequently less valuable, which is reflected in the negative sign for Δ_p. As illustrated in Figure 4.4, there exists a threshold for the spot price $S_0 > K$, from which the execution of the call at maturity is certain, and the put expires worthless. A further increase in the spot price S_0 at the date of issue will thus increase the price of the call directly proportional to the increase in S_0. However, it will have no impact on the price of a put. Similarly, there exists an opposite threshold for $S_0 < K$, from which the call will expire worthless and the fair value of the put will increase directly proportional to a further decrease in S_0, as the execution of the put at maturity becomes certain.

Gamma (Γ): This factor measures how the Delta of an option changes for an increase of the spot price S_0 of the underlying at the date of issue. It can be shown with the help of the put-call-parity that as long as the assumptions made to the financial market in

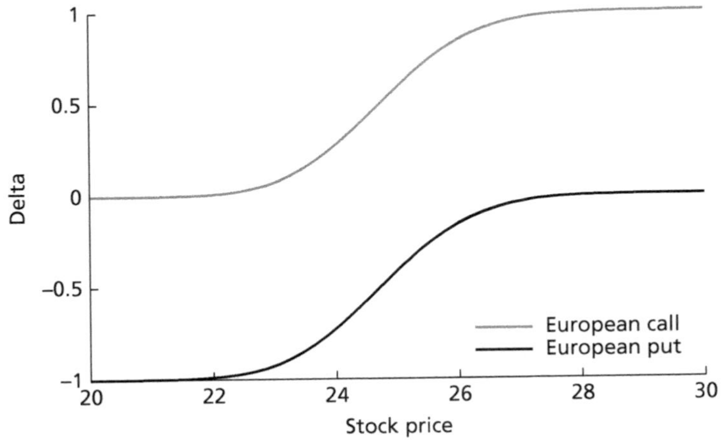

Figure 4.4 Delta of European call and put options around S_0

Section 4.2 of the book hold true, Gamma has to have the same value for both a European call and a European put. Computing the difference quotient for the values from Table 4.4 of the book yields $\Gamma_c = \Gamma_p = 0.31250$. This means that the price of a European call option will increase with a rising slope for a given spot price, while the price of a European put option will decrease with a falling slope. Figure 4.5 shows that Delta is most sensitive for spot prices S_0 smaller than, but close to the strike price K, and that Gamma approaches a value of zero as soon as the exercise of either the call or the put becomes certain at maturity.

Vega ($\mathcal{V}$): Similar to the Gamma of an option, it can be shown by using the put-call-parity that Vega must be the same for a European call and a European put. For the parameters from Table 4.4 in the book, the Vega of a European option is given by $\mathcal{V}_c = \mathcal{V}_p = 0.04844$. A marginal increase in the volatility of the underlying by 1 per cent thus implies a rise in the price of both the call as well as the put. Figure 4.6 shows that the price of a European option is most sensitive to the volatility σ of its underlying for spot prices S_0 close to the strike price K.

Theta (θ): The Theta of an option measures the sensitivity of the option value with respect to the remaining time to maturity. The parameters specified in Table 4.4 of the book yield the value $\theta_c = -0.00616$ for a European call and the value $\theta_p = -0.00220$ for a European put. The price for the call as well as for the put will thus decrease if the time to maturity is reduced (see Figure 4.7).

Rho (ρ): The Rho of an option is positive for a call option $\rho_c = 0.03494$ and negative for a put option $\rho_p = -0.02645$, as it increases the expected spot price at maturity. According to equation (4.13) in the book, this makes it more likely that the European call is executed at maturity and at the same time increases the pay-off upon execution. The opposite holds for the European put. Figure 4.8 illustrates that Rho is positive for a call as long as the initial stock price is large enough. If the initial price of the underlying is too small, the likelihood that the call is executed becomes almost zero, and hence the expected pay-off

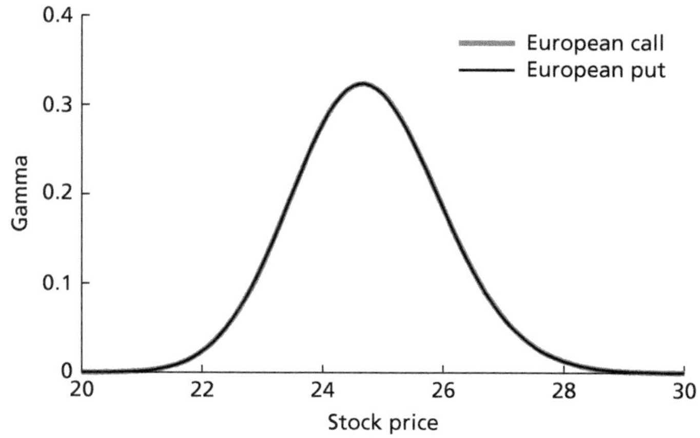

Figure 4.5 Gamma of European call and put options around S_0

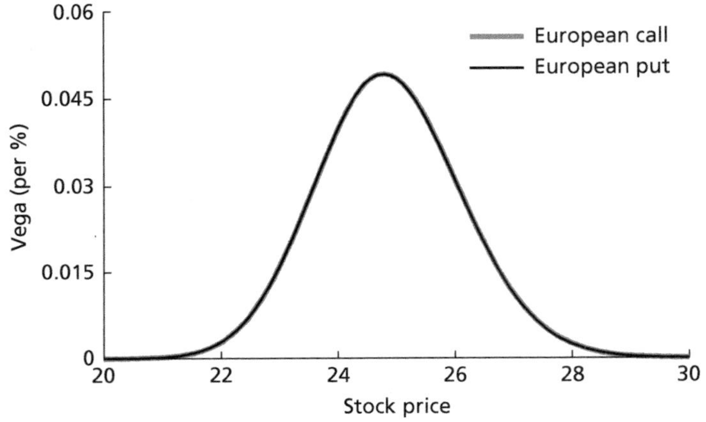

Figure 4.6 Vega of European call and put options around S_0

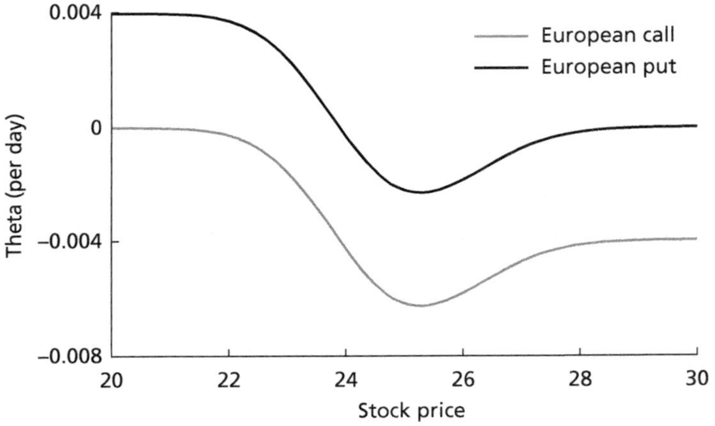

Figure 4.7 Theta of European call and put options around S_0

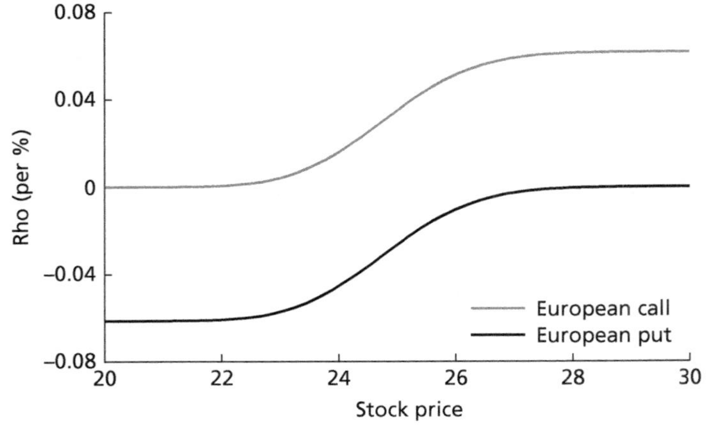

Figure 4.8 Rho of European call and put options around S_0

of the option is zero regardless of the size of the interest rate. Consequently, for such levels of S_0, Rho needs to be zero.

Exercise 4.10

(a) The price of a Straddle is given by the fair value of a portfolio consisting of a European call option c^E and a European put option p^E, which can be computed through the Black-Scholes formula and is equal to $V^{Straddle} = 9.23$. The pay-off of a Straddle is close to zero if the spot price at maturity of the underlying S_T finishes close to the strike price K (see Figure 4.9). The bigger the difference between the spot and the strike price, the higher the pay-off. An investor will thus purchase a Straddle if he expects that the spot price at maturity of the underlying is significantly different from the strike price.

(b) The price of a Strangle is given by the fair value of a portfolio consisting of a European call option and a European put option with the respective strike prices $K_1 = 105$ and $K_2 = 95$. The fair value of a Strangle $V^{Strangle} = 5.11$ is below the fair value of a Straddle, as this position will expire worthless if the spot price finishes within the interval $S_T \in [K_2, K_1]$. Buying a Strangle is thus the appropriate strategy if the investor expects strong changes in the spot price of the underlying (see Figure 4.10).

(c) The fair value of a Butterfly Spread can again be computed through the fair value of the equivalent portfolio using the Black-Scholes formula. In contrast to the Straddle and Strangle from above, an investor holding a Butterfly Spread would thus expect that the spot price of the underlying will be close to the strike price at maturity. The fair value is now given by $V^{Butterfly} = 5.80$. Figure 4.11 shows the pay-off for different realizations of the stock price S_T.

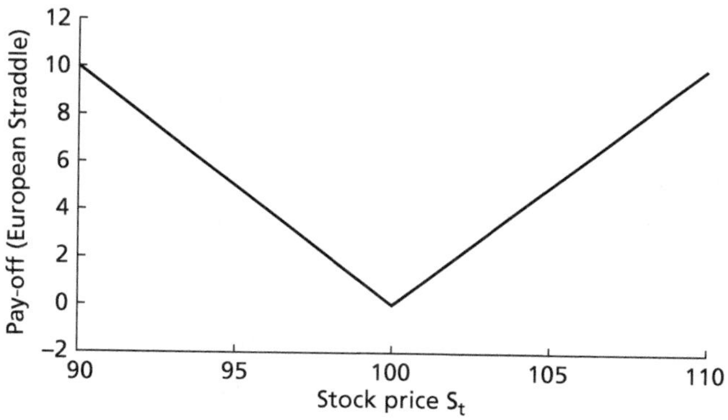

Figure 4.9 Pay-off diagram of a Straddle

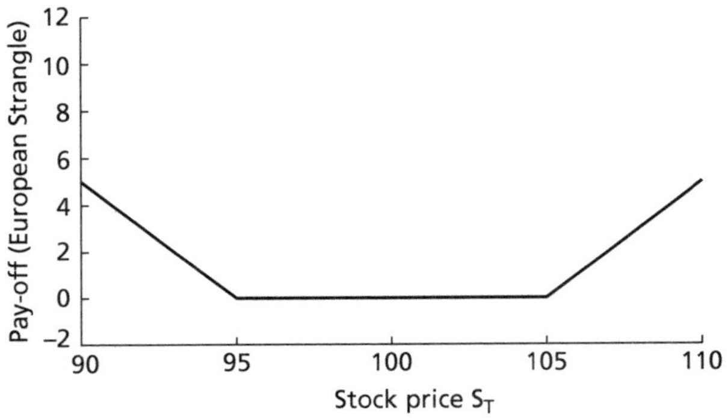

Figure 4.10 Pay-off diagram of a Strangle

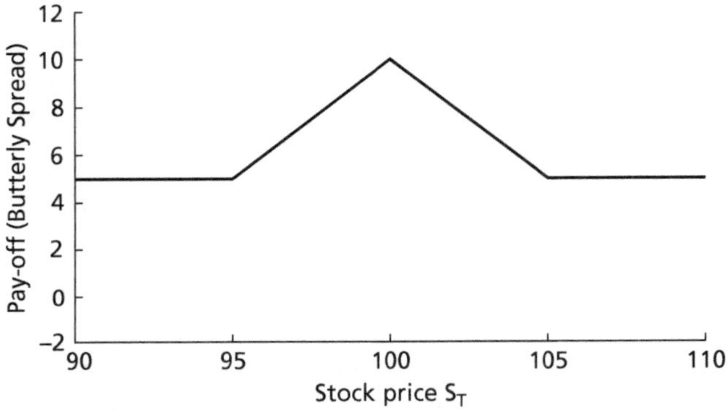

Figure 4.11 Pay-off diagram of a Butterfly Spread

Exercise 4.11

(a) The solution of this exercise is based on program `prog04_09` of the book. As before, we first compute the first two moments μ_i and σ_{ij} for all policies of Table 4.13 in the book, as well as the expected benefit–price ratio and the variance of the portfolio. In addition, we now also introduce the third and fourth centered moments of the distribution—the skewness and the excess kurtosis or simply excess—of the benefit–price ratio in order to better describe the risk in an insurer's portfolio (see Program 4.11).

The resulting values are summarized in Table 4.2. It is important to note that these values change for each set of simulated mortality paths, ie any run of the program.

For both annuity insurances (ie policies $i = 1, 2$) the skewness is negative. This means that the benefit–price ratios are slightly left-leaning and hence tend to have a comparably low-risk exposure. This is especially the case with a slightly positive excess for both polices, indicating that the majority of benefit–price ratios are located close to the respective expected value. All three life insurance contracts have a positive expected skewness, which indicates that the distributions of the benefit–price ratios are rather

Program 4.11 Skewness and excess

```
! compute skewness and excess for portfolio
do ii = 1, NN
    skew(ii)   = sum((l(ii, :)-mu(ii))**3)/ &
                 sig(ii, ii)**1.5d0/dble(KK)
    excess(ii) = sum((l(ii, :)-mu(ii))**4)/ &
                 sig(ii, ii)**2/dble(KK) - 3d0
enddo

! compute skewness and excess for portfolio
skew_p = sum((l_p(:)-mu_p)**3)/sig_p**1.5d0/dble(KK)
excess_p = sum((l_p(:)-mu_p)**4)/sig_p**2/dble(KK) - 3d0
```

Table 4.2 Skewness and excess for policies in Table 4.13

i	1	2	3	4	5
$skew_i$	−0.1278	−0.1016	0.3547	0.1432	0.1528
$excess_i$	0.0337	0.0269	0.2519	0.0003	0.0357

Table 4.3 Skewness and excess for portfolios in Table 4.14

	Skewness	Excess
Initial	0.2482	0.0948
Optimized		
$\gamma = 10.0$	0.3670	0.2678
$\gamma = 15.0$	0.3946	0.3056
$\gamma = 20.0$	0.4214	0.3448

right-leaning for these policies. However, the excess of policy 3 is significantly above the excess of the two other life insurances 4 and 5, indicating that the probability mass for the price–benefit ratio is concentrated close to its expected value $\mu_i = 0.888$. The variance thus results rather from rare but extreme events. While the additional risk of the right skewness for the insurance policy 4 is limited with its expected price–benefit ratio of $\mu_4 = 0.933$, it implies additional downward risk for policy 5, which already comes with expected deficits for the insurer. Table 4.3 shows how the skewness and the excess of the portfolio change with a decrease in an individual's risk aversion, if an individual chooses the optimal portfolio. The results show that insurers accept a higher skewness and a higher excess in their portfolio with a decreasing risk aversion. This implies that the variance of the price–benefit ratios of portfolios is in particular due to rare but adverse and extreme developments in the forecasted mortalities.

As illustrated in Program 4.11.a, we determine the optimal insurer portfolio for different values of the risk aversion γ within one program. This is realized with a do-loop

Program 4.11.a Skewness and excess for different risk aversions γ

```
do ig = 1, 3

    ! initialize communication variable for risk aversion
    gamma_com = gamma(ig)
    [......]
    ! solve first oder conditions
    call fzero(x_in, focs, check)
    [......]
    !#############################################################
    ! GET PROPERTIES OF OPTIMAL PORTFOLIO
    !#############################################################
    [......]
    ! print results
    write(*, '(/a/)')'OPTIMAL PORTFOLIO'
    [......]
enddo
```

that calls the rootfinding subroutine `fzero` to solve the system of first-order conditions stored in the function `focs` for different values of risk aversion. By following this approach, we ensure that we are using the same simulated mortality paths to determine each of the optimal portfolios.

(b) The location of the minimum variance portfolios for given expected values μ_p (ie the efficiency curve) can be computed similar to the portfolio selection problem without a risk-free asset in the first section of Chapter 4 of the book by solving the following optimization problem:

$$\min_{\omega} \ \frac{1}{2}\omega^T \Sigma \omega \quad \text{s.t.} \quad I^T \omega = 1 \text{ and } \mu^T \omega = \mu_p.$$

This yields the parabola:

$$\sigma_p^2(\mu_p) = \frac{a\mu_p^2 - 2b\mu_p + c}{ac - b^2},$$

with $a = I^T \Sigma^{-1} I$, $b = I^T \Sigma^{-1} \mu$ and $c = \mu^T \Sigma^{-1} \mu$ as the analytical solution for the location of these portfolios. These values are computed in the numerical implementation (Program 4.11.b) of the model and the plot is set up so that the minimum variance portfolios are computed for $\mu_p \in [0.8, 1.2]$.

Figure 4.12 shows that the initial portfolio of selling $n_i = 1000$ contracts for each policy is inefficient, since there exists a portfolio that has the same variance but yields a lower benefit–price ratio.

(c) The weights ω_i of an efficient portfolio with an expected benefit–price ratio of $\mu_p = 0.969$ can be computed with the first-order conditions from the respective Lagrangean of the above optimization problem, ie

Program 4.11.b Location of minimum variance portfolios for a given μ_p

```
IID(:) = 1.0d0

! invert variance-covariance matrix
siginv = lu_invert(sig)

! derive parameters
a_mv = dot_product(matmul(IID, siginv), IID)
b_mv = dot_product(matmul(IID, siginv), mu)
c_mv = dot_product(matmul(mu, siginv), mu)

! create plot data for efficient portfolios
do ii = 0, 1000
    x1(ii) = 1d0/1000d0*dble(ii+500)
enddo
y1 = (a_mv*x1**2 - 2d0*b_mv*x1+c_mv)/(a_mv*c_mv - b_mv**2)

call plot(y1, x1)
```

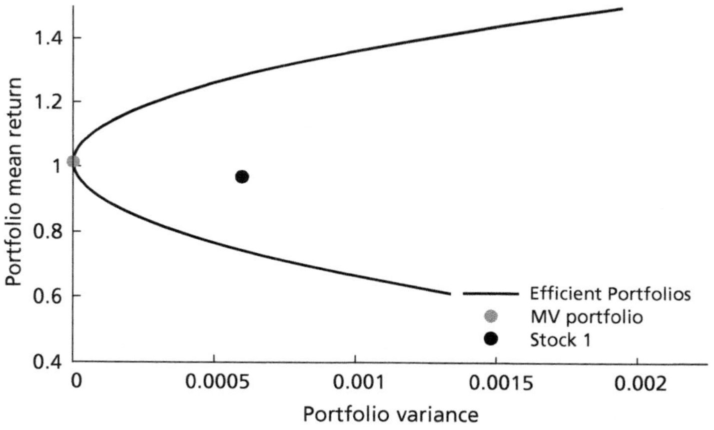

Figure 4.12 Location of the minimum variance portfolios for a given μ_p

$$\omega = \Sigma^{-1}(\lambda_1 I + \lambda_2 \mu)$$

with:

$$\lambda_1 = \frac{c - b\mu_p}{ac - b^2} \quad \text{and} \quad \lambda_2 = \frac{a\mu_p - b}{ac - b^2}.$$

This yields:

$$\omega = [1.905, -1.126, 0.426, -0.191, -0.015]$$

for the optimal portfolio weights and implies that the insurer's portfolio should consist to 190.5 per cent of its initial balance out of policy 1 and to 42.6 per cent of policy 3, which is

Table 4.4 Minimum variance portfolios

	Mean	Variance	Skew.	Excess	VaR_{95}	$CVaR_{95}$
$\omega(\mu_p)$	0.9691279	0.0000163	0.5748	1.5704	0.976	0.979
ω^{mv}	1.0135576	0.0000001	0.1549	0.1801	1.015	1.015

financed through short-selling policies 2, 4, and 5. The respective sample statistics of the benefit–price ratios for the simulated mortality paths of this portfolio are summarized in Table 4.4. For the same mean $\mu_p = 0.969$ as realized in the initial portfolio, the variance $\sigma_p^2 = 0.0000163$ of this portfolio is now significantly lower than in the initial portfolio from Chapter 4. The excess of the portfolio indicates a very centered distribution of the benefit–price ratios, which is reflected as well in the VaR_{95} and the $CVaR_{95}$ being close to the mean μ_p.

(d) A closed-form solution for the global minimum variance portfolio was derived in Section 4.1 of the book as:

$$\omega^{mv} = \frac{\Sigma^{-1} I}{I^T \Sigma^{-1} I},$$

which yields the weights:

$$\omega^{mv} = [0.425, -0.038, -0.020, -0.092, 0.726].$$

The minimum variance portfolio of an insurer should thus consist of 42.5 per cent of its initial balance of the policy 1, 72.6 per cent of the initial balance of the policy 5, with the other portfolios sold short. The sample statistics for the distribution of the benefit–price ratios for the global minimum variance portfolio are summarized in the second line of Table 4.4. Choosing the global minimum variance portfolio is not necessarily a good strategy for the insurer, as it comes with an expected loss.

Exercise 4.12

(a) The principle idea of this exercise is to test whether the number n_i of contracts sold for policy 5 is high enough to be robust against unsystematic individual mortality risk. This is done by simulating for all n_i insured people their remaining life expectancy as a random draw from the underlying distribution. At the beginning of program `sol_prog04_12` we initialize mortality rates for the base year $q_{x,0}$ by calling subroutine `init_data`. As in program `prog04_09` of the book, the parameters of the insurance policy 5 from Table 4.13, the maximum number of insured people N and the interest rate r are defined at the beginning of the module `globals`.

(b) After the variables are initialized, the subroutine `init_borders` is called, which sets up the interval borders k_j used to simulate the remaining lifetime of each insured individual (see Module 4.12m). The underlying idea of this simulation is the same as in `prog04_08` from Section 4.3.2 of the book: we divide the unit interval proportional to the probability distribution $q_{x,0}$ into $T - x$ sub-intervals. We then make a draw from the uniform distribution and select the remaining lifetime according to the sub-interval the draw falls into.

(c) In Program 4.12, we draw $n_i = 1, ..., N$ random numbers from the unit interval using the subroutine `simulate_uniform` from the toolbox. We obtain the corresponding remaining lifetime of an insured person in the subroutine `get_LI` and use it to compute the discounted payment per one € benefit for the respective insurance contract. Averaging over all draws n_i, and taking the discount factor ξ_2 into account yields the corresponding expected cost of the insurer per € of benefit for an insurance contract. This should be equal to the market price $p^m = 0.41$ from Table 4.13 in the book, if a

Module 4.12m Projection to the death probability distribution

```
subroutine init_borders()

    implicit none
    real*8 :: PP
    integer :: ij

    ! Compute right borders of intervals
    k(0) = 0d0
    PP = 1.0d0
    do ij = 1, TT-x+1
        k(ij) = k(ij-1) + q(x+ij-1)*PP
        PP = PP*(1.0d0-q(x+ij-1))
    enddo

end subroutine
```

Program 4.12 Simulation of individual mortality risk

```
! simulate individual mortality
do in = 1, NN

    ! draw random number
    call simulate_uniform(rand, 0d0, 1d0)

    ! compute individual payout
    ! and averaging over all contracts
    ind_LI(in) = get_LI(rand)
    agg_LI(in) = (1d0-xi_2)*sum(ind_LI(1:in))/dble(in)

enddo
```

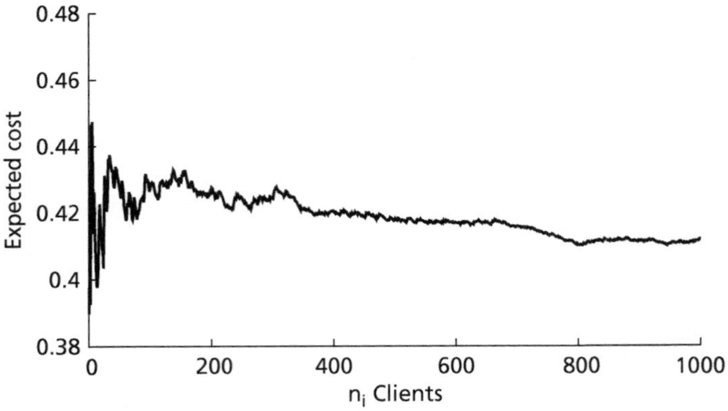

Figure 4.13 Convergence to $p_m = 0.41$ with increasing contracts n_i

sufficiently high number of contracts is sold. This is an application of the law of large numbers, which tells us that the life expectancy of the insured approximately equals the life expectancy of the total population whenever the number of clients is large enough. Figure 4.13 illustrates that $n_i = 200$ contracts still yield a considerable approximation error, while a total number of contracts $n_i = 1000$ already comes close to $p^m = 0.41$.

5 The life-cycle model and intertemporal choice

Exercise 5.1

With a durable consumption good, households maximize the utility function:

$$U(c_1, c_2, c_3, a_h) = u(c_1, a_h) + \beta u(c_2, a_h) + \beta^2 u(c_3, a_h) \quad \text{with}$$
$$u(c_j, a_h) = \frac{[\theta c_j^\nu + (1-\theta) a_h^\nu]^{\frac{1-1/\gamma}{\nu}}}{1 - 1/\gamma},$$

subject to the intertemporal budget constraint:

$$c_1 + a_h + \frac{c_2 + \delta_h a_h}{R} + \frac{c_3 + p_h a_h}{R^2} = w + \frac{w}{R} + \frac{(1-\delta_h) a_h}{R^2}.$$

The respective Lagrangean is:

$$\mathcal{L} = u(c_1, a_h) + \beta u(c_2, a_h) + \beta^2 u(c_3, a_h) - \lambda \left(c_1 + a_h + \frac{c_2 + \delta_h a_h}{R} + \frac{c_3 + p_h a_h}{R^2} - w - \frac{w}{R} - \frac{(1-\delta_h) a_h}{R^2}\right).$$

The resulting first-order conditions read:

$$\frac{\partial \mathcal{L}}{\partial c_1} = u_{c_1}(c_1, a_h) - \lambda = 0 \quad \Rightarrow \quad u_{c_1}(c_1, a_h) = \lambda$$
$$\frac{\partial \mathcal{L}}{\partial c_2} = \beta u_{c_2}(c_2, a_h) - \lambda/R = 0 \quad \Rightarrow \quad R\beta u_{c_2}(c_2, a_h) = \lambda$$
$$\frac{\partial \mathcal{L}}{\partial c_3} = \beta^2 u_{c_3}(c_3, a_h) - \lambda/R^2 = 0 \quad \Rightarrow \quad (R\beta)^2 u_{c_3}(c_3, a_h) = \lambda$$
$$\frac{\partial \mathcal{L}}{\partial a_h} = \sum_{j=1}^{3} \beta^{j-1} u_{a_h}(c_j, a_h) - \lambda \left(1 + \frac{\delta_h}{R} + \frac{r + 2\delta_h - 1}{R^2}\right) = 0,$$

where we already substituted $p_h = r + \delta_h$. In our simulations, we set $R\beta = 1$ so that we get $u_{c_j}(c_j, a_h) = u_c$, which implies $c_j = c$ for all $j = 1, 2, 3$. This, in turn, means that the marginal utility of the durable good has to be identical across periods, ie $u_{a_h}(c, a_h) = u_{a_h}$. The last first-order condition therefore implies:

$$(1 + \beta + \beta^2)u_{a_h} = u_c \left(1 + \frac{\delta_h}{R} + \frac{r + 2\delta_h - 1}{R^2}\right).$$

This condition can be used to explain the numerical results in this exercise.

The implementation of the durable goods model is based on program `prog_05_01` of the book. In order to incorporate durable goods consumption into this program, we have to change both the function `utility` and the minimization process. The new function `utility` is shown in Module 5.1m. In addition to the two savings levels a_2 and a_3, this function also receives durable consumption a_h. Note that a_h enters both the budget constraint and the instantaneous utility levels `u` in any of the three periods. In the main program, we need to first set the upper and lower bounds for the additional choice variable a_h and account for the maximum debt level `a_low` (see Program 5.1). Afterwards, we can solve for the optimum of `utility` using the subroutine `fminsearch` from the toolbox.

(a) The results of our simulations are summarized in Table 5.1. In case $\delta_h = 1.0$, the durable good has the same properties as the ordinary consumption good in the sense that it requires the same expenditure in every period. As already explained, the simplifying assumption $R\beta = 1$ implies that—without any further restrictions—regular

Module 5.1m Utility function with durable goods

```
function utility(x)
    [......]
    a(1) = 0d0
    ah = x(1)
    a(2) = x(2)
    a(3) = x(3)

    ph = R - 1d0 + delh

    ! consumption (insure consumption > 0)
    c(1) = w - a(2) - ah
    c(2) = R*a(2) + w - a(3) - delh*ah
    c(3) = R*a(3) + (1d0-ph-delh)*ah
    c = max(c, 1d-10)
    ah = max(ah, 1d-10)

    u(1) = (theta*c(1)**nu+(1d0-theta)*ah**nu)**(egam/nu)/egam
    u(2) = (theta*c(2)**nu+(1d0-theta)*ah**nu)**(egam/nu)/egam
    u(3) = (theta*c(3)**nu+(1d0-theta)*ah**nu)**(egam/nu)/egam

    utility = -(u(1) + beta*u(2) + beta**2*u(3))

end function
```

Program 5.1 Upper and lower bounds for `fminsearch`

```
low = (/0d0, -a_low, -a_low/)
up = (/w + a_low, w, R*w + w/)
x = up/3d0

! minimization routine
call fminsearch(x, fret, low, up, utility)
```

Table 5.1 Savings with a durable good

R	θ	δ_h	a_h	c_1	a_2	c_2	a_3	c_3
1.0	0.5	1.0	0.33	0.33	0.33	0.33	0.33	0.33
1.0	0.7	1.0	0.10	0.56	0.33	0.56	0.67	0.56
1.2	0.5	1.0	0.33	0.37	0.29	0.37	0.64	0.37
1.0	0.5	0.5	0.89	0.22	−0.11	0.22	0.22	0.22
(1.0	0.5	0.3	1.35	0.15	−0.50	0.36	−0.27	0.27)
1.0	0.5	0.3	1.32	0.18	−0.50	0.32	−0.21	0.32

$R\beta = w = 1$; $\gamma = 0.5$; $\nu = 0.5$; a_low = 0.5.

consumption is identical in all periods. Since $R = 1$ also implies $\beta = 1$, the last optimality condition boils down to:

$$u_{a_h} = u_c \quad \text{so that} \quad (1-\theta)a_h^{\nu-1} = \theta c^{\nu-1}.$$

Consequently, when households weigh both consumption types equally in the utility function ($\theta = 0.5$), we get $a_h = c$, as shown in the first line of Table 5.1. Note that this result is independent of ν.

(b) When the weight of ordinary consumption c increases to $\theta = 0.7$, we still get identical consumption c in all periods, but now we have $c > a_h$. From the last optimality condition, it should be clear that in this case ν does affect the optimal allocation. The higher is ν, the more an increase in θ shifts demand towards ordinary consumption c. Increasing the interest rate to $R = 1.2$ (while reducing the discount factor to $\beta = 1/1.2$) drives up the price of durable goods in the last period. Consequently, it shifts demand towards ordinary consumption goods. This can also be derived from the first-order condition, which in this case implies that $u_{a_h} > u_c$, so that ordinary goods consumption increases relative to the consumption of the durable good. A fall in δ_h reduces the cost of durable goods consumption and therefore works in the other direction. The first-order condition now implies that $u_{a_h} < u_c$, so that we get $a_h > c$. When depreciation is sufficiently low, it is even optimal to finance the durable good with debt, since the proceeds from selling it again will finance consumption in the last period. If the maximum debt level is hit in the first period, it could happen that `fminsearch` does not generate the optimal solution with one call (see the line in parentheses in Table 5.1). At least in the second and third periods, the ordinary consumption levels should be equal.

We therefore need to call `fminsearch` a second time, as shown in Program 5.1, with the new starting values derived from the previous solution. The resulting optimal solution is shown in the last line of Table 5.1 and again features identical consumption in the last two periods of the agent's life.

(c) When wages in the second period are uncertain, savings in the durable good become less attractive because of its low liquidity. Households build precautionary savings, which especially increases (liquid) financial assets. Therefore, durable and non-durable consumption have to decline in the first period.

Exercise 5.2

The program for this exercise is based on `prog05_02` of the book. Wages and consumption in the first two periods are certain, while consumption in the third period is uncertain owing to risky health expenditures. The potential realizations of health expenditure are calculated in the main program `sol_prog05_02` using the subroutine `grid_Cons_Equi(hc, mu-sigma, mu+sigma)`. This subroutine spans an equidistant set of points between `mu-sigma` and `mu+sigma` and stores them in the array `hc`. We attach identical weighs to each of these discrete points, ie `weight_h = 1d0/NH`. The function `utility` takes into account the uncertainty over third-period consumption. To this end, we define a separate array `c3`, which stores the resulting last period consumption for all possible health expenditures (see Module 5.2m). We calculate expected utility using the weights `weight_h`.

Table 5.2 shows the optimal consumption and savings decisions for different parameter specifications. With certain health expenditure, consumption is perfectly smoothed over

Module 5.2m Utility function with uncertain health

```
function utility(x)
    [......]
    c(1) = w - a(2)
    c(2) = R*a(2) + w - a(3)
    c3 = R*a(3) - hc
    c = max(c, 1d-10)
    c3 = max(c3, 1d-10)

    utility = 0d0
    do ih = 1, NH
        utility = utility + weight_h(ih)*c3(ih)**egam
    enddo

    ! utility function
    utility = -(c(1)**egam + beta*c(2)**egam + &
                beta**2*utility)/egam

end function utility
```

Table 5.2 Savings with uncertain health

σ	c_1	a_2	c_2	a_3	$E[c_3]$	$Std[c_3]$	$Std[hc]$
0.0	0.50	0.50	0.50	1.00	0.50	0.00	0.00
0.3	0.47	0.53	0.47	1.06	0.56	0.18	0.18
0.5	0.42	0.58	0.42	1.17	0.67	0.50	0.50

$R = \beta = w = 1$; $\gamma = 0.5$; $E[hc] = \mu = 0.5$; $NH = 20$.

the life cycle and third-period savings suffice to finance $hc = \mu = 0.5$. When health expenditures become uncertain, the household reduces consumption in the first and the second period in order to increase precautionary savings. Note that consumption is identical in the first two periods, but expected consumption increases in the third period under the presence of uncertainty. The more the uncertainty σ in the last period, the higher are precautionary savings a_3. Note that if the number of health expenditure nodes `NH` is reduced to `NH=5`, for example, the uniform distribution is only badly approximated and results change. A larger number of nodes reduces this approximation error, and with `NH=20` it is already very small, meaning that a further increase in nodes only leads to minor changes in results.

Exercise 5.3

The solution of this exercise is again based on program `prog05_02` from the book. Yet this time the second-period wage is not log-normally distributed. Instead, second-period labour income has only two possible realizations, 0 or 1, with attached probabilities `weight_w`. Hence, we define second-period wage realizations and probabilities as shown in Program 5.3. In addition, we set $n_w = 2$ in the module `globals` and keep everything else unchanged.

Table 5.3 shows the optimal consumption and savings decisions for different parameter specifications. With `weight_w(1)=0.0d0` we are in the deterministic model and households have perfectly smooth consumption, ie $c_j = 0.67$ for all $j = 1, 2, 3$. When disability risk rises, consumption in the first period decreases significantly in order to make room for precautionary savings. Available resources in the second period are then consumed with equal shares in periods 2 and 3, as all uncertainty has been released

Program 5.3 Wages with disability risk

```
! discretize w
w = (/0d0, 1d0/)
weight_w(1)  = 0.5d0
weight_w(2)  = 1d0 - weight_w(1)
```

Table 5.3 Savings with disability risk

ω	c_1	a_2	$E[c_2]$	$Std[c_2]$	$E[c_3]$	$Std[a_3]$
0.00	0.67	0.33	0.67	0.00	0.67	0.00
0.01	0.64	0.36	0.68	0.05	0.68	0.05
0.10	0.53	0.47	0.68	0.15	0.68	0.15
0.50	0.40	0.60	0.55	0.25	0.55	0.25

$R = \beta = w = 1;\ \gamma = 0.5.$

once the household has entered period 2. For example, when the disability probability increases to 0.5 (ie expected income in period 2 is 0.5), households only consume 0.4 in the first period and save 0.6. Expected consumption in the two remaining periods is then 0.55.

Exercise 5.4

The solution of this exercise is based on program `prog05_04` from the book. With entry cost $F < w$, one has to compute the optimal behaviour with and without stock market participation. Program 5.4 therefore defines adjusted input variables for two calls of `fminsearch`. In the case of stock market participation, the function `utility_st` is almost identical to the function `utility` in module `prog05_04m` from the book, except that we need to subtract the entry cost F in period 1. In the case without stock market participation, we simply set `omega=0d0`. In this case, uncertainty only exists with respect to wage risk. Therefore, in the function `utility_b`, all variables are assigned the same values for different interest rate realizations. As shown in Module 5.4m, the function `utility_b` without participation is much simpler than `utility_st`, since we do not need

Program 5.4 Utilities with stock market participation cost

```
real*8 :: x1(2*(1+n_w*n_R)), x2(1+n_w*n_R)
real*8 :: fret1, low1(2*(1+n_w*n_R)), up1(2*(1+n_w*n_R))
real*8 :: fret2, low2(1+n_w*n_R), up2(1+n_w*n_R)
[......]
call fminsearch(x1, fret1, low1, up1, utility_st)

! lower and upper border and initial guess for bond investment
[......]
call fminsearch(x2, fret2, low2, up2, utility_b)
omega = 0d0

! check whether market entry is optimal
if(-fret1 > -fret2)then
    fret1 = utility_st(x1)
endif
```

Module 5.4m Utility without stock market participation

```
function utility_b(x)
    [......]
    a(1, :) = 0d0
    a(2, :) = x(1)
    ic = 2
    iwR = 1
    do iw = 1, n_w
        do ir2 = 1, n_R
            a(3, iwR) = x(ic)
            ic = ic + 1
            iwR = iwR + 1
        enddo
    enddo

    ! consumption
    c(1,:,:) = mu_w - a(2, 1)
    iwR = 1
    do iw = 1, n_w
        do ir2 = 1, n_R
            c(2, iwR, :) = Rf*a(2, 1) + wR(iwR, 1) - a(3, iwR)
            c(3, iwR, :) = Rf*a(3, iwR)
            iwR = iwR + 1
        enddo
    enddo
    c = max(c, 1d-10)
    [......]
end function
```

to take into account the different interest rate realizations and do not need to optimize over `omega`. If utility with stock market participation is higher than without stock market participation, we have to call `utility_st` again using the optimal decision stored in `x1` in order to recalculate all variables for the case of stock market participation (see Program 5.4).[1]

Table 5.4 reports the main findings of this exercise. It can be directly compared with Table 5.3 from the book. In the deterministic case, investors would accept fixed cost up to about 16 per cent of annual income in order to participate in the stock market. As in the first line of Table 5.3 in the book, it is then optimal to invest all their resources in stocks in both periods. However, as they have to pay the entry costs, consumption is now lower in all periods compared to the respective solution in the book. When entry cost is too high, so that investors decide not to buy stocks any more, they smooth their consumption perfectly over the life cycle. Yet, the lower return reduces consumption. When wages and interest rates are uncertain, investors are more sensitive to entry cost. The lower part of Table 5.4 shows that for the chosen wage and return risk combination, they only accept an entry cost up to 4 per cent of annual income in order to participate in the stock market.

[1] Note that in this exercise, the subroutine `fminsearch` is again very sensitive to the initial guess of `x` (see the discussion in Exercise 5.1).

Table 5.4 Portfolio choice with entry cost

σ_R^2	σ_w^2	F	c_1	a_2	ω_1	$E(c_2)$	$E(a_3)$	$E(\omega_2)$	$E(c_3)$
0.00	0.00	0.16	0.60	0.24	1.00	0.68	0.62	1.00	0.75
		0.17	0.67	0.33	0.00	0.67	0.67	0.00	0.67
0.50	0.50	0.04	0.56	0.40	0.77	0.74	0.73	0.33	0.78
		0.05	0.57	0.43	0.00	0.72	0.72	0.00	0.72

$w = \mu_w = R_f = \beta = 1$; $\mu_R = 1.22$; $\rho = 0.0$; $\gamma = 0.5$; $n_w = n_R = 5$.

Exercise 5.5

We implement the utility function with constant average risk aversion (CARA) into module `prog_05_04m` of the book. In the variable definition part, we specify a new variable `u(3,n_w*n_R,n_R)` that stores period-specific utilities in order to make our life a little easier. Using this variable, total utility is then computed in the function `utility`, as shown in Module 5.5m.

Constructing a graphical representation of the correlation between equity share and available resources (ie income from working and saving) in the main program is more tricky. After computing the possible income realizations in the second period, we have to sort this array as well as the array `omega(2, :)` in order to plot a suitable graph. Program 5.5 shows how to implement this task. We first record the different income realizations of period 2 in an array `income` and the corresponding equity shares in an array `shares`. In addition to sorting the array `income` in ascending order, the subroutine `sort` from the toolbox returns an **`integer`** array `ind(n_w*n_R)` that contains the information on how the array was sorted. Using this information, we can redefine the array `shares` with the same structure. Now it is possible to print and store a graph of income and

Module 5.5m Utility with CARA preferences

```
utility = 0d0
iwR = 1
do iw = 1, n_w
    do ir2 = 1, n_R
        do ir3 = 1, n_R
            prob = weight_wR(iwR)*weight_R(ir3)
            u(2, iwR, :) = 1d0 - exp(-c(2, iwR, 1)/gamma)
            u(3, iwR, ir3) = 1d0 - exp(-c(3, iwR, ir3)/gamma)
            utility = utility + &
                      prob*(u(2, iwR, 1)+beta*u(3, iwR, ir3))
        enddo
        iwR = iwR + 1
    enddo
enddo
u(1, :, :) = 1d0-exp(-c(1, 1, 1)/gamma)
utility  = -(u(1, 1, 1) + beta*utility)
```

Program 5.5 Sorting and plotting income and equity shares

```
income(:) = wR(:, 1) + (Rf+omega(1, 1)*(wR(:, 2)-Rf))*a(2, 1)
share(:) = omega(2, :)
call sort(income, ind)
share(:) = share(ind)
call plot(income(:), share)
call execplot(xlabel='Income', ylabel='Equity share')
```

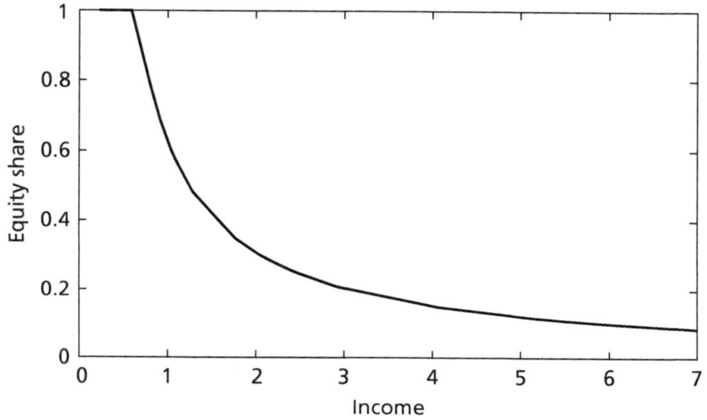

Figure 5.1 Correlation of equity share and income

investment behaviour using the subroutines `plot` and `execplot`. The resulting graph in Figure 5.1 shows a clear negative relationship between equity share and income.

Exercise 5.6

Bequest motives are independent of lifespan uncertainty. Even without lifespan uncertainty, households might want to bequeath something to their heirs when they die. When lifespan is uncertain, intended and unintended bequest can arise, when households decease before reaching their maximum lifetime. We implement a bequest motive into program `prog05_05` from the book. In the variable declaration part, we define an array `b(2:4,n_w)`, which stores bequests at different ages for all possible realizations of wages. In order to allow for households to leave aggregate savings at the end of their maximum lifespan, we also define `a(4, n_w)`. Owing to the partial equilibrium nature of the problem, we do not consider bequest received from testators. Consequently, only the budget constraint in the last period of life is altered by subtracting possible assets left to the descendants. The utility derived from period-specific inheritable wealth has to be added to the utility function, as shown in Module 5.6m.

Module 5.6m Model with bequest utility

```
b(2, :) = R*(1d0 - omega(1, 1))*a(2, 1)
b(3, :) = R*(1d0 - omega(2, :))*a(3, :)
b(4, :) = R*a(4, :)
b = max(b, 1d-10)

! expected utility of period 3
utility = 0d0
do iw = 1, n_w
    utility = utility + weight_w(iw)*beta**2*psi(2)*psi(3)* &
                       (c(3, iw)**egam+beta*nu*b(4, iw)**egam)
enddo

! expected utility of period 2
do iw = 1, n_w
    utility = utility + weight_w(iw)*beta*psi(2)*(c(2,iw) &
              **egam + beta*(1d0-psi(3))*nu*b(3, iw)**egam)
enddo

! add first period utility
utility = -(c(1, 1)**egam + beta*(1d0-psi(2))*nu*b(2, 1)**egam &
              + utility)/egam
```

Table 5.5 Annuity choice with bequest motives and pensions

σ_w^2	*pen*	ν	c_1	a_2	a_2^a	c_2	a_3	a_3^a	c_3	a_4
0.90	1.00	0.00	0.80	0.17	0.03	1.08	0.00	0.12	1.27	0.00
	0.00	0.00	0.67	0.00	0.33	0.94	0.00	0.33	0.94	0.00
	0.00	0.05	0.61	0.14	0.25	0.84	0.19	0.32	0.84	0.19
	1.00	0.05	0.73	0.27	0.00	0.97	0.20	0.10	1.14	0.25

$R = \beta = w = \mu_w =$; $\underline{a} = 0.0$; $\gamma = 0.5$; $\psi_2 = 0.8$; $\psi_3 = 0.5$; $n_w = 5$.

(a) In order to analyse the impact of bequest motives and pensions on annuity choice, the first line of Table 5.5 replicates the results from a simulation without bequest motives from Table 5.4 of the book. Since households receive pension benefits in the last period of life, it is optimal for them to only partially annuitize their savings in the first period of life. This damps the impact of wage shocks. When pension benefits are eliminated in the next step, households annuitize all their savings, since longevity insurance becomes more important than the insurance against income shocks. The optimal allocation implies that surviving households always consume identical amounts in the last two periods of life, which, of course, depends on the survival rates.

(b) When a bequest motive is introduced, households again reduce annuitized savings in both periods. As a consequence, consumption declines throughout the entire life, since the return on regular assets is lower than the return on annuitized assets. Expected consumption of surviving households is again perfectly smoothed over the last two periods. The introduction of pension benefits shifts all savings towards regular accounts. As in the situation without bequest motives, perfect consumption smoothing is not possible any more. This is due to the fact that some households who receive a negative wage shock in period 2 would like to finance higher consumption using debt, which they cannot do.

Exercise 5.7

In this exercise, we introduce uncertain lifespan and annuity demand into the portfolio choice model `prog_05_04` from the book. We distinguish between equity, bonds, and annuities. Hence, the shares ω_e and ω_a are optimized in the first two periods of life. Given these shares, we define:

$$sh_e = \omega_e, \quad sh_a = (1-\omega_e)\omega_a, \quad \text{and} \quad sh_b = (1-\omega_e)(1-\omega_a)$$

as the fractions of total assets saved in equity, annuities, and bonds. These fractions are deterministic in the first period, but become stochastic in the second period, where they depend on the realization of the wage and the interest rate.

(a) With these definitions at hand, the budget constraints in the three periods read:

$$\begin{aligned} c_1 &= w - a_2 \\ \tilde{c}_2 &= \tilde{w} + \left[sh_{b,1}R_f + sh_{e,1}\tilde{R}_2 + \frac{sh_{a,1}}{p_{a,1}}\right]a_2 - \tilde{a}_3 \\ \tilde{c}_3 &= pen + \left[\widetilde{sh}_{b,2}R_f + \widetilde{sh}_{e,2}\tilde{R}_3 + \frac{\widetilde{sh}_{a,2}}{p_{a,2}}\right]\tilde{a}_3 + \frac{sh_{a,1}}{p_{a,1}}a_2. \end{aligned}$$

In order to implement the model numerically, we specify new variables `omega_e`, `omega_a` and `sh` in the definition part of module `sol_prog05_07m`. Module 5.7m shows how the portfolio shares ω_e and ω_a feature into the function `utility`, which is optimized by `fminsearch`. Of course, the vector `x` as well as the lower and upper boundaries have to be adjusted in the main program in order for `fminsearch` to work correctly. The fractions `sh` and the consumption values in each possible state are derived from the budget constraints, as shown in Module 5.7m.a.

(b) The results of the different simulations are reported in Table 5.6. Since there is no bequest motive and we abstract from pension income, there is a strong incentive to invest into annuities in order to insure life-span risk, especially in the second period. For all parametrization, bond and equity investments are zero in period 2. In the first period, households might save in equity, but never in bonds. In the deterministic benchmark, households save a small amount in equity in the first period, but mostly in annuities. On the one side, the (certain) return on equity investment is higher than the return on bonds.

Module 5.7m Definition of portfolio shares

```
a(1, :) = 0d0
a(2, :) = x(1)
omega_e(1, :) = x(2)
omega_a(1, :) = x(3)
ic = 4
iwR = 1
do iw = 1, n_w
    do ir2 = 1, n_R
        a(3, iwR) = x(ic)
        omega_e(2, iwR) = x(ic + 1)
        omega_a(2, iwR) = x(ic + 2)
        ic = ic + 3
        iwR = iwR + 1
    enddo
enddo
```

Module 5.7m.a Budget constraints with bonds, equity, and annuities

```
c(1, :, :) = mu_w - a(2, 1)
iwR = 1
do iw = 1, n_w
    do ir2 = 1, n_R
        sh(1) = (1d0-omega_e(1, 1))*(1d0-omega_a(1, 1))
        sh(2) = omega_e(1,1)
        sh(3) = (1d0-omega_e(1, 1))*omega_a(1, 1)
        c(2,iwR, :) = (sh(1)*Rf + sh(2)*wR(iwR, 2) + &
                      sh(3)/pa(1))*a(2, 1) + wR(iwR, 1)-a(3, iwR)
        do ir3 = 1, n_R
            sh(1) = (1d0-omega_e(2, iwR))*(1d0-omega_a(2, iwR))
            sh(2) = omega_e(2, iwR)
            sh(3) = (1d0-omega_e(2, iwR))*omega_a(2, iwR)
            c(3, iwR, ir3) = pen + (sh(1)*Rf+sh(2)*R(ir3) +  &
                           sh(3)/pa(2))*a(3, iwR) + (1d0 -  &
                      omega_e(1, 1))*omega_a(1, 1)*a(2, 1)/pa(1)
        enddo
        iwR = iwR + 1
    enddo
enddo
```

Table 5.6 Savings with annuities, bonds, and equity

σ_w^2	σ_R^2	ρ	ξ	$\hat{R}$	c_1	a_2^e	a_2^a	$E(c_2)$	a_3^a	$E(c_3)$
0.00	0.00	0.00	0.00	1.00	0.82	0.02	0.16	0.82	0.34	0.82
0.50					0.70	0.00	0.30	0.91	0.33	0.91
	0.50				0.69	0.00	0.31	0.93	0.33	0.93
		0.50			0.70	0.00	0.30	0.91	0.33	0.91
			0.20		0.70	0.00	0.30	0.86	0.35	0.79
				0.90	0.69	0.00	0.31	0.83	0.36	0.72

$pen = 0$; $R_f = \beta = w = \mu_w = 1$; $\mu_R = 1.22$; $\gamma = 0.5$; $\psi_2 = 0.8$; $\psi_3 = 0.5$; $n_w = 5$.

In addition, fair priced annuities are better than equity, since they insure against longevity risk. Equity is only used to smooth consumption over the life cycle. With a stochastic wage in the second period, it is optimal to increase precautionary savings and save only in annuities. Now consumption is only smoothed over the last two periods, when all uncertainty regarding income has been revealed. Adding stochastic equity returns (either uncorrelated or correlated with wage risk) changes overall uncertainty only slightly, since households hardly save in equity under the present parametrization. The introduction of overhead costs or lower returns on the annuity fund reduces the attractiveness of annuities. For the parametrization shown in Table 5.6, households still save only in annuities, but now consumption smoothing is not optimal any more. If we set $\xi > 0.5$ and/or $\hat{R} < 0.9$, it even becomes interesting to buy bonds and equity instead of annuities.

6 The overlapping generation model

Exercise 6.1

We first need to introduce subroutine initialize, which is shown below in Module 6.1m. This subroutine specifies the main policy parameters in the initial equilibrium, as well as along the reform path. As in program prog06_02 of the book, we also determine aggregate labour supply, as well as the budget-balancing contribution rate of the pension system.

The subroutine get_SteadyState shown in Module 6.1m.a has a very similar structure to the subroutine get_Transition. However, we only need to compute prices, decisions, and quantities for one particular year, $t = 0$. Note that we have to provide an initial guess for the capital stock KK, which we need together with aggregate labour input LL to compute factor prices.

Module 6.1m Policy parameters for OLG model

```
subroutine initialize

    ! set baseline parameters
    g(1:3)        = (/0.12d0, 0.12d0, 0.0d0/)
    by(0:TT)      = 0d0
    kappa(0:TT)   = 0d0
    n_p(0:TT)     = 0.2d0
    tax(0:TT)     = 1
    lsra_on       = .false.

    ! set reform values
    tax(1:TT) = 2
    [......]
    ! get labour  supply and pension payments
    LL =  (2d0+n_p)/(1d0+n_p)
    taup = kappa/((2d0+n_p)*(1d0+n_p))
    [......]
end subroutine
```

Module 6.1m.a Subroutine for calculation of steady state

```
subroutine get_SteadyState
    [......]
    ! initial guess for capital stock
    KK(0) = 1d0

    do iter = 1, itermax

        ! get prices, decisions and quantities
        call factor_prices(0)
        call decisions(0)
        call quantities(0)
        call government(0)
        [......]
        ! check whether goods market is in equilibrium
        if(abs(YY(0) - CC(0) - II(0) - GG(0))/YY(0) < tol) &
                exit

    enddo
    [......]
end subroutine
```

Exercise 6.2

(a) In order to simulate a small, open economy (smopec), we introduce the logical variable `smopec` (which indicates whether the program should assume a closed or an open economy), net foreign assets `BF(0:TT)`, and the trade balance `TB(0:TT)`. The subroutines `factor_prices` and `quantities` have to be adjusted, as shown in Modules 6.2m and 6.2m.a, in order to account for the different structure of capital markets.

Finally, we also need to adjust the goods market equilibrium condition to incorporate the trade balance. We use this condition both in the subroutine `get_SteadyState` and `get_Transition` to check for convergence of the simulation process.

(b) Simulation results for the small, open economy are reported in Table 6.1. Compared to the case of a closed economy, consumption of future households does not seem to change too much. The capital stock as well as factor prices remain constant throughout the transition, since the reduction in domestic savings is balanced by an inflow of foreign assets. Due to constant wages and interest rates, middle-aged and younger households in

Module 6.2m Factor prices in the smopec model

```
subroutine factor_prices(it)
    [......]
    if(smopec .and. it > 0)then
        r(it) = r(0)
    else
        r(it) = alpha*(KK(it)/LL(it))**(alpha-1d0)-delta
    endif
    [......]
end subroutine
```

Module 6.2m.a Aggregate variables in the smopec model

```
subroutine quantities(it)
    [......]
    if(smopec .and. it > 0)then
        KK(it) = LL(it)*((r(it)+delta)/alpha) &
                 **(1d0/(alpha-1d0))
        BF(it) = AA(it) - KK(it) - BA(it) - BB(it)
        TB(it) = (1d0+n_p(itp))*BF(itp) - (1d0+r(it))*BF(it)
    else
        KK(it) = damp*(AA(it)-BB(it)-BA(it))+(1d0-damp)*KK(it)
    endif
    [......]
end subroutine
```

Table 6.1 From consumption to income taxation in smopec

t	τ^w, τ^r	τ^c	c_1	c_2	c_3	K	TB	r	HEV
−1									14.33
0	0.00	0.29	0.22	0.30	0.42	0.27	0.00	1.15	1.15
1	0.21	0.00	0.22	0.31	0.48	0.27	−0.05	1.15	−4.12
2	0.22	0.00	0.22	0.28	0.41	0.27	0.02	1.15	−5.21
3	0.23	0.00	0.21	0.28	0.37	0.27	0.05	1.15	−5.56
⋮	⋮	⋮	⋮	⋮	⋮	⋮	⋮	⋮	⋮
∞	0.23	0.00	0.21	0.28	0.36	0.27	0.06	1.15	−5.64
Δ*									−0.28

$g_1 = g_2 = 0.12$; $g_3 = 0$; $b_y = 0$; $\kappa = 0$; $n_p = 0.2$.

the reform year are hurt (compared to the closed economy reported in Table 6.2 of the book), while future households lose much less now. The negative net foreign assets have to be balanced by future trade surpluses. In terms of aggregate efficiency, on the other hand, we can hardly see any difference between the two economies.

Exercise 6.3

In order to implement a corporate tax, we define the arrays `tauk(0:TT)` and `eps(0:TT)`, which store the tax rate τ^k and the allowance factor ϵ, respectively. Starting with program `sol_prog06_02` from the previous exercise, we only need to make three minor adjustments. First, the subroutine `factor_prices` needs to be adapted such that the corporate tax system is taken into account when calculating the competitive market interest rate (see Module 6.3m). Second, the subroutine `quantities` now requires an adjustment of the capital stock calculation in the case of a smopec model (see Module 6.3m.a). Finally, subroutine `government` needs to account for corporate tax revenue in the government's

Module 6.3m Corporate taxes in factor price equation

```
subroutine factor_prices(it)
    [......]
    if(smopec .and. it > 0)then
        r(it) = r(0)
    else
        r(it) = (1d0-tauk(it))/(1d0-eps(it)*tauk(it))* &
                (alpha*(KK(it)/LL(it))**(alpha-1d0)-delta)
    endif
    [......]
end subroutine
```

Module 6.3m.a Corporate taxes for capital stock in smopec model

```
if(smopec .and. it > 0)then
    KK(it) = LL(it)*((r(it)*(1d0-eps(it)*tauk(it))/ &
             (1d0-tauk(it))+delta)/alpha)**(1d0/(alpha-1d0))
    BF(it) = AA(it) - KK(it) - BA(it) - BB(it)
    TB(it) = (1d0+n_p(itp))*BF(itp) - (1d0+r(it))*BF(it)
else
    KK(it) = damp*(AA(it)-BB(it)-BA(it)) + (1d0-damp)*KK(it)
endif
```

budget constraint. We could also make the corporate tax rate endogenous by adding an additional element to the tax indicator `tax`. However, in order to keep things simple, we leave this to the interested programmer.

(a) Table 6.2 compares the results when the corporate tax rate is introduced in the closed economy and in the small, open economy. In the closed economy, the consumption tax rate can be reduced immediately from 29 to 21 per cent. At the same time, there is a one-time adjustment of the interest rate. All other variables, especially wages, remain constant, so that the whole tax incidence falls on capital owners. Consequently, older cohorts are hurt by lower asset returns, which overcompensate the lower consumption tax burdens. Younger cohorts benefit from lower tax burdens, since the tax payments are implicitly shifted towards later ages. Overall, a move from consumption towards corporate taxation induces an efficiency loss of 0.2 per cent of remaining resources, as the corporate tax rate mainly distorts asset accumulation.

When the same policy is simulated in a small, open economy, the outcome is completely different. Again, the consumption tax rate can be reduced as before. But now capital has to be invested abroad, so that the capital stock falls on impact in order to keep interest payments at their internationally competitive level. Consequently, wages have to fall significantly. As a result, the incidence of the tax now falls on workers instead of capital owners. Older cohorts, hence, benefit from lower-consumption tax burdens, while younger cohorts are hurt by lower wages. The latter induce long-run welfare losses of 4.34 per cent of available resources. Because productive capital moves abroad, the efficiency loss induced by the policy reform increases to 2.15 per cent of resources, ie it is about ten times higher in the small, open than in the closed economy.

Table 6.2 Introduction of corporate taxes

t	τ^k	τ^c	c_1	c_2	c_3	K	w	r	HEV
Closed economy									
−1									−4.63
0	0.00	0.29	0.22	0.30	0.42	0.27	0.39	1.15	−2.13
1	0.20	0.21	0.23	0.30	0.40	0.27	0.39	0.92	1.96
2	0.20	0.21	0.23	0.30	0.40	0.27	0.39	0.92	1.93
⋮	⋮	⋮	⋮	⋮	⋮	⋮	⋮	⋮	⋮
∞	0.20	0.21	0.23	0.30	0.40	0.27	0.39	0.92	2.00
Δ^*									−0.20
Small open economy									
−1									6.39
0	0.00	0.29	0.22	0.30	0.42	0.27	0.39	1.15	−0.13
1	0.20	0.21	0.21	0.30	0.45	0.20	0.36	1.15	−3.73
2	0.20	0.22	0.21	0.29	0.42	0.20	0.36	1.15	−4.17
⋮	⋮	⋮	⋮	⋮	⋮	⋮	⋮	⋮	⋮
∞	0.20	0.23	0.21	0.29	0.40	0.20	0.36	1.15	−4.34
Δ^*									−2.15

$g_1 = g_2 = 0.12$; $g_3 = 0$; $b_y = 0$; $\kappa = 0$; $n_p = 0.2$.

(b) As Table 6.3 shows, an allowance for imputed interest cost works in the same way as an elimination of corporate taxation, meaning the inverse to what we studied in Part (a). Effectively, taxable profits become zero and the corporate tax rate disappears from the optimality condition for capital investment. Consequently, in the closed economy, the interest rate immediately increases upon the date of reform and the economy again converges to the situation without corporate taxes and higher consumption taxes in the long run. Older cohorts benefit, since higher interest payments dominate the increase in consumption taxes. Younger cohorts are hurt mostly from higher-consumption tax burdens. The efficiency gain is now roughly 0.2 per cent, meaning of the same (absolute) size as the efficiency loss in Part (a).

Consumption taxes also have to increase in the small, open economy, but now capital inflows immediately increase the capital stock. The interest rate remains constant and the wage rate increases upwards. Consequently, older cohorts are hurt and younger cohorts benefit significantly. The aggregate efficiency gain now is 2.13 per cent.

Exercise 6.4

Implementing lags or announcements in fiscal policies is straightforward. We simply have to set `tax(2:TT)=3`. This is done in program `sol_prog06_04`, which is not shown here. In our model, households have perfect foresight. Hence, they already know in period 1 of the transition that the government will conduct the tax reform in period 2. This anticipation causes a reaction in the period before the reform, as shown in Table 6.4. Since the youngest cohort knows that their tax burden will rise in the future, c_1 falls slightly in period 1. On the other hand, the middle cohort knows that their tax burden will fall in the future, so that they increase their consumption c_2 even before the reform. Overall, aggregate consumption rises slightly, so that the consumption tax rate can be reduced slightly in period 1 of the transition (not shown in Table 6.4). As a result, older cohorts experience a slight utility gain. When the tax reform actually hits in period 2, the economic reactions are similar to those in Table 6.4 of the book. Most

Table 6.3 Introduction of an allowance for imputed interest cost

t	ϵ	τ^c	c_1	c_2	c_3	K	w	r	HEV
Closed economy									
−1									4.85
0	0.00	0.21	0.23	0.30	0.40	0.27	0.39	0.92	2.19
1	1.00	0.29	0.22	0.30	0.42	0.27	0.39	1.14	−1.93
2	1.00	0.29	0.22	0.30	0.42	0.27	0.39	1.14	−1.89
⋮	⋮	⋮	⋮	⋮	⋮	⋮	⋮	⋮	⋮
∞	1.00	0.29	0.22	0.30	0.42	0.27	0.39	1.15	−1.97
Δ^*									0.19
Small open economy									
−1									−6.70
0	0.00	0.21	0.23	0.30	0.40	0.27	0.39	0.92	−0.35
1	1.00	0.30	0.24	0.30	0.37	0.37	0.43	0.92	3.22
2	1.00	0.28	0.24	0.31	0.40	0.37	0.43	0.92	3.76
⋮	⋮	⋮	⋮	⋮	⋮	⋮	⋮	⋮	⋮
∞	1.00	0.28	0.24	0.31	0.41	0.37	0.43	0.92	3.96
Δ^*									2.13

$g_1 = g_2 = 0.12;\ g_3 = 0;\ b_y = 0;\ \kappa = 0;\ \tau^k = 0.2;\ n_p = 0.2.$

Table 6.4 From consumption to labour income taxation with announcement

t	τ^w	τ^c	c_1	c_2	c_3	K	w	r	HEV
−1									0.22
0	0.00	0.29	0.22	0.30	0.42	0.27	0.39	1.15	10.62
1	0.00	0.29	0.21	0.32	0.42	0.27	0.39	1.15	4.53
2	0.31	0.00	0.19	0.33	0.50	0.26	0.39	1.17	−8.97
3	0.33	0.00	0.17	0.28	0.49	0.21	0.37	1.36	−15.17
⋮	⋮	⋮	⋮	⋮	⋮	⋮	⋮	⋮	⋮
∞	0.37	0.00	0.15	0.23	0.37	0.14	0.32	1.83	−26.20
Δ^*									−0.32

$g_1 = g_2 = 0.12, g_3 = 0.0, b_y = 0.0, \kappa = 0.0, n_p = 0.2.$

importantly, the long-run equilibria are identical. Note, however, that the distortions of the initial consumption decision induced by the policy pre-announcement reduces aggregate efficiency by 0.32 per cent of resources, while the reform was neutral in terms of efficiency without pre-announcement.

Exercise 6.5

Program `sol_prog06_05`, which is not shown here, simulates a permanent fertility decline with the different structure of government expenditure. Table 6.5 shows the results. As in Table 6.8 of the book, the change in the population structure increases the per-capita capital stock, so that wages increase and the interest rate falls. The former is to the benefit of the younger cohorts, while the latter hurts older cohorts. However, now the change in the population structure does not change the demand for public goods in the short run, but only decreases the number of people who have to finance it. Consequently, the consumption tax rate increases throughout the transition. This hurts all cohorts, so that the economy experiences an overall dramatic efficiency loss of almost 5 per cent of resources.

Exercise 6.6

(a) A household born in period t which lives for J years maximizes the utility function:

$$U_t = U(c_{1,t}, \ldots, c_{J,s}) = \sum_{j=1}^{J} \beta^{j-1} u(c_{j,s}) \qquad \text{with} \quad u(c) = \frac{c^{1-\frac{1}{\gamma}}}{1-\frac{1}{\gamma}}$$

Table 6.5 Permanent fertility decline with consumption taxation

t	n_p	τ^c	c_1	c_2	c_3	K	w	r	HEV
−1									−4.68
0	0.20	0.21	0.23	0.32	0.45	0.27	0.39	1.15	−5.16
1	0.00	0.27	0.23	0.30	0.41	0.32	0.41	1.07	−1.81
2	0.00	0.25	0.24	0.31	0.41	0.37	0.42	0.98	0.19
⋮	⋮	⋮	⋮	⋮	⋮	⋮	⋮	⋮	⋮
∞	0.00	0.24	0.25	0.32	0.43	0.40	0.43	0.92	1.95
Δ^*									−4.97

$g_1 = g_2 = 0.0$; $g_3 = 0.24$; $b_y = \kappa = 0.0$.

with $s = t + j - 1$. The *intertemporal budget constraint* reads:

$$\sum_{j=1}^{J} \frac{p_s c_{j,s}}{R_s^n} = \sum_{j=1}^{J} \frac{w_s^n h_j + pen_{j,s}}{R_s^n} =: W_{1,t} \quad \text{with} \quad R_s^n = \Pi_{i=t+1}^{s}(1 + r_i^n),$$

where w_s^n, r_i^n define the net wage and interest rate in year s and i, respectively. The variable h_j indicates individual labour productivity at age j. For now, we set it to a value of one during employment years and let it fall to zero at retirement j_r. During retirement years, agents receive a pension that is a constant fraction κ of the net wage in a given year. We therefore have:

$$h_j = \begin{cases} 1 & \text{if } j < j_r \text{ and} \\ 0 & \text{otherwise} \end{cases} \quad \text{and} \quad pen_{j,s} = \begin{cases} 0 & \text{if } j < j_r \text{ and} \\ \kappa w_s^n & \text{otherwise.} \end{cases}$$

The first-order conditions are:

$$c_{j+1,s+1} = \left(\beta R_{s+1}^n \frac{p_s}{p_{s+1}}\right)^{\gamma} c_{j,s} \quad \text{for } j = 1, \ldots, J-1.$$

Recursive substitution of these first-order conditions gives the optimal consumption path over the life cycle:

$$c_{j,s} = \beta^{(j-1)\gamma} \left(R_s^n \cdot \frac{p_t}{p_s}\right)^{\gamma} c_{1,t} \quad \text{with} \quad s = t + j - 1.$$

Substituting this into the above budget constraint yields:

$$\sum_{j=1}^{J} \frac{p_s}{R_s^n} \left[\beta^{(j-1)\gamma} \left(R_s^n \frac{p_t}{p_s}\right)^{\gamma} c_{1,t}\right] = p_t c_{1,t} \sum_{j=1}^{J} \beta^{(j-1)\gamma} \left(\frac{1}{R_s^n} \frac{p_s}{p_t}\right)^{1-\gamma} \stackrel{!}{=} W_{1,t},$$

which can be rearranged to:

$$c_{1,t} = \Psi_{1,t} W_{1,t} \qquad \text{with} \quad \Psi_{1,t} = \frac{1}{p_t} \left\{\sum_{j=1}^{J} \beta^{(j-1)\gamma} \left(\frac{1}{R_s^n} \frac{p_s}{p_t}\right)^{1-\gamma}\right\}^{-1}.$$

In order to aggregate individual variables to economy-wide quantities, we define the normalized population size of a cohort of age j at time t as $m_{j,t} = m_{j-1,t-1}/(1+n_{p,t})$, with normalization $m_{1,t} = 1$. The aggregate variables in period t are then computed from:

$$C_t = \sum_{j=1}^{J} c_{j,t} m_{j,t} \qquad A_t = \sum_{j=1}^{J} a_{j,t} m_{j,t} \qquad L_t = \sum_{j=1}^{J} h_j m_{j,t}.$$

(b) In order to make the program more flexible, we let the maximum age `JJ` and the retirement age `JR` be parameters, as shown in Module 6.6m. The array variables have to be adjusted accordingly. The main adjustment is then made in subroutine `decisions`, which simplifies to what is shown in Module 6.6m.a. The functions `get_W` and `get_Psi` compute the remaining present value of resources and the propensity to consume out of available resources for a specific cohort aged `ij` in a year `it`, respectively. The function `get_W` is shown in Module 6.6m.b. We start out by recording current income $w_j^n h_j + pen_{j,t}$. Next, we have to account for the fact that old households along the transition might already have accumulated some wealth and that all generations along the transition might receive LSRA payments `v`. Finally, we iterate over the remaining life cycle of the household and add up discounted income streams. The propensity to consume out of life-time resources $\Psi_{j,t}$ is calculated in Module 6.6m.c. This function simply applies the formula stated above, allowing for an arbitrary starting age `ij`. Given an initial consumption level $c_{j,t}$, the subroutine `get_path` derives the future consumption path using the first-order condition of the household (see Module 6.6m.d). Note that, owing to the new structure of the subroutine `decisions`, we now have to initialize assets in the first year of the transition. This is done in subroutine `get_Transition`, where we set $a(:,1) = a(:,0)$.

Finally, we can use the function `get_W` also in the subroutine `lsra`, when we calculate transfers to the old cohorts and determine aggregate available resources. The new aggregation method (using cohort weights $m_{j,t}$) is used in subroutine `quantities`, as

Module 6.6m Definition of variables in OLG model

```
integer, parameter :: TT = 25
integer, parameter :: JJ = 3
integer, parameter :: JR = 3
[......]
real*8 :: Tpen(0:TT), TXR(0:TT), h(JJ), m(JJ,0:TT)
real*8 :: a(JJ,0:TT), c(JJ,0:TT), util(JJ,0:TT), v(-JJ+2:TT)
```

Module 6.6m.a Subroutine `decisions` in flexible OLG model

```
subroutine decisions(it)
    [......]
    ! solve cohort that just entered the economy
    c(1, it) = get_Psi(1, it)*get_W(1, it)
    call get_path(1, it)

    ! derive behaviour for all other cohorts in year 1
    if(it == 1)then
        do ij = 2, JJ
            c(ij, it) = get_Psi(ij, it)*get_W(ij, it)
            call get_path(ij, it)
        enddo
    endif

end subroutine
```

Module 6.6m.b Computation of individual resources

```
function get_W(ij,it)
    [......]
    ! get current value of resources
    get_W = wn(it)*h(ij) + pen(ij, it)
    if(it == 1 .and. ij > 1)get_W = get_W + &
                            Rn(it)*a(ij, it) + v(-ij+2)
    if(it >= 1 .and. ij == 1)get_W = get_W + v(it)

    ! iterate over remainder of life span
    PRn = 1d0
    do ijp = ij+1, JJ
        itp = year(it, ij, ijp)
        PRn = PRn*Rn(itp)
        get_W = get_W + (wn(itp)*h(ijp) + pen(ijp, itp))/PRn
    enddo

end function
```

Module 6.6m.c Computation of marginal consumption

```
function get_Psi(ij,it)
    [......]
    get_Psi = 1d0
    PRn = 1d0

    do ijp = ij+1, JJ
        itp = year(it, ij, ijp)
        PRn = PRn*Rn(itp)
        get_Psi = get_Psi + beta**((ijp-ij)*gamma)* &
                  (p(itp)/PRn/p(it))**(1d0-gamma)
    enddo
    get_Psi = 1d0/p(it)/get_Psi

end function
```

shown in Module 6.6m.e. Note that we now also compute `LL` in this subroutine. The reason for this will become clear in Chapter 7. Of course, we also have to adjust the output routines and the computation of the utilities accordingly.

(c) When we increase life span from three to twelve periods, this implies that one model period covers roughly five real years instead of twenty years. Consequently, the population growth rate and the depreciation rate have to be adjusted accordingly and the length of the transition path has to be extended. We can convert the three-period model population growth rate of 0.20 into a J-period model population growth rate n_p by requiring that:

$$(1 + n_p)^J \overset{!}{=} (1.20)^3 \quad \text{or} \quad n_p = (1.2)^{3/J} - 1.$$

This yields $n_p \approx 0.05$ for $J = 12$. We furthermore set `TT=100`. When we increase life span to fifty-five periods (ie one period is one real year), we set `TT=200` and obtain $n_p \approx 0.01$.

Module 6.6m.d Computation of consumption path

```
subroutine getpath(ij,it)
    [......]
    PRn = 1d0
    ! determine consumption path
    do ijp = ij+1, JJ

        ! get future and previous year and interest factor
        itp = year(it, ij, ijp)
        itm = year(it, ij, ijp-1)
        PRn = PRn*Rn(itp)

        ! get consumption and assets
        c(ijp, itp) = beta**((ijp-ij)*gamma)*&
            (PRn*p(it)/p(itp))**gamma*c(ij,it)
        a(ijp, itp) = wn(itm)*h(ijp-1) + pen(ijp-1, itm) +  &
            Rn(itm)*a(ijp-1, itm) - p(itm)*c(ijp-1, itm)
        if(itp == 2)a(ijp, itp) = a(ijp, itp) + v(-ijp+3)
        if(itp > 2 .and. ijp == 2)a(ijp, itp) = &
            a(ijp, itp) + v(itm)
    enddo

end subroutine
```

Module 6.6m.e Aggregation of individual variables

```
CC(it) = 0d0
AA(it) = 0d0
LL(it) = 0d0
do ij = 1, JJ
    CC(it) = CC(it) + c(ij, it)*m(ij, it)
    AA(it) = AA(it) + a(ij, it)*m(ij, it)
    LL(it) = LL(it) + h(ij)*m(ij, it)
enddo
```

Table 6.6 From consumption to income taxation

t	τ^w, τ^r	τ^c	C	K	Y	w	r	HEV
−53								24.98
−52								23.67
⋮	⋮	⋮	⋮	⋮	⋮	⋮	⋮	⋮
0	0.00	0.28	37.1	118.5	48.6	1.03	0.12	−5.21
1	0.21	0.00	40.2	118.5	48.6	1.03	0.12	−5.31
2	0.21	0.00	39.6	115.4	48.2	1.02	0.13	−5.92
⋮	⋮	⋮	⋮	⋮	⋮	⋮	⋮	⋮
∞	0.24	0.00	32.1	80.1	43.2	0.91	0.16	−13.50
Δ*								−2.50

$g_y = 0.2132$; $b_y = 0.0$; $\kappa = 0.0$; $n_p = 0.01$; $J = 55$; $j_r = 41$.

Table 6.6 shows the results of a switch from consumption to income taxation for a life span of fifty-five years. Qualitatively, the simulated effects are the same as in the three-period model reported in Table 6.3 of the book. However, the taxation of capital income now causes a distortion of individual behaviour in many more periods. As a result, the negative efficiency consequences of the reform weigh much stronger. If, in addition, we change the labour productivity profile of households to:

$$h_j = 1 + 0.05j - 0.001j^2,$$

the negative efficiency effect is enforced, and declines to -3.19. The hump shape of the labour productivity profile makes savings an even more important measure for consumption smoothing, and its distortion consequently creates higher efficiency losses.

7 Extending the OLG model

Exercise 7.1

Different preferences change the household decision process and the computation of utilities. Consequently, the adjustments to program `prog07_01` are in the subroutines `decisions`, `shadw`, `getpath`, and `utility`, and the function `get_Psi`. In subroutine `decisions`, the shadow wage subroutine is now as shown in Program 7.1. In function `get_Psi`, we compute marginal propensities to consume out of total wealth for different preference functions, as shown in Program 7.1.a. The respective marginal consumption formula for Cobb-Douglas utility is derived on pages 262ff. of the book. The remaining subroutines are adjusted in a quite similar way.

Comparing the results of a policy reform with different preference functions is difficult, since we cannot generate the same initial equilibrium. If we give consumption and leisure identical (relative) weights in the CES and the CD function,[1] then the aggregate efficiency loss rises with the CD function for both policies considered. When consumption taxes are substituted by wage taxes, aggregate efficiency losses increase from 0.50 (reported in Table 7.2 of the book) to 0.79 per cent of resources. When the pay-as-you-go pension

Program 7.1 Call of shadow wage subroutine

```
call get_path(ij, it)
if(CES .or. CD)call shadw(ij, it)
```

Program 7.1.a Case structure for marginal consumption calculation

```
if(CES)then
    get_Psi = get_Psi + beta**((ijp-ij)*gamma)*(p(ik)/&
              PRn/p(it))**(1d0-gamma)*vv(ijp)**((1d0-gamma)/&
              (rho-gamma))
elseif(CD)then
    get_Psi = get_Psi + beta**((ijp-ij)*gamma)*((p(ik)/p(it))&
              **nu/PRn)**(1d0-gamma)*(wn(ijp,ik)/wn(ij,it))&
              **((1d0-nu)*(1d0-gamma))
else
    get_Psi = get_Psi + beta**((ijp-ij)*gamma)*(p(ik)/&
              PRn/p(it))**(1d0-gamma)
endif
```

[1] Assuming $\nu = 1.5$ with CES utility implies relative weights of $\frac{1}{1+1.5} = 0.4$ and $\frac{1.5}{1+1.5} = 0.6$ for consumption and leisure, respectively. Setting $\nu = 0.4$ with CD utility implies weights of 0.4 and 0.6.

system is introduced, efficiency losses increase from 1.33 (reported in Table 7.3 of the book) to 3.21 per cent of resources. In both cases, efficiency losses are only due to labour supply distortions. Consequently, a higher intratemporal elasticity of substitution increases economic distortions and efficiency losses.

Exercise 7.2

(a) All individual variables now need an additional dimension, which identifies their skill class (see Program 7.2). Prices are the same for all skills; consequently, they don't need to be adjusted. Yet, labour supply behaviour typically differs across agents of different skill types, so that the shadow wage rates `mu` and net wages `wn` have to be skill specific. We also allow for skill-specific pension benefits (although strictly speaking we wouldn't need it in the present simulation). All aggregate variables and government parameters don't need a skill index.

(b) Since we have all calculations for both skill classes, all functions and subroutines in `decisions` now include the skill variable `ik` as an input. This way, we can omit additional loops within the different functions and subroutines. Program 7.2.a shows the subroutine `decisions`, which is adjusted for skill types. The aggregation of variables then requires an additional loop. Yet, with a properly defined aggregation variable `m`, this is not a

Program 7.2 Individual variables of model with skill classes

```
real*8 :: mu(JJ, SS, 0:TT), wn(JJ, SS, 0:TT), h(JJ, SS), &
          m(JJ, SS, 0:TT)
real*8 :: a(JJ, SS, 0:TT), c(JJ, SS, 0:TT), &
          util(JJ, SS, 0:TT), v(SS, -JJ+2:TT)
real*8 :: l(JJ, SS, 0:TT), pen(JJ, SS, 0:TT)
```

Program 7.2.a Individual decisions with skill classes

```
do ik = 1, SS
    c(1, ik, it) = get_Psi(1, ik, it)*get_W(1, ik, it)
    call getpath(1, ik, it)
    if(nu /= 0)call shadw(1, ik, it)
enddo

if(it == 1)then
    do ij = 2, JJ
        do ik = 1, SS
            c(ij, ik, it) = get_Psi(ij, ik, it)*get_W(ij, ik, it)
            call getpath(ij,ik,it)
            if(nu /= 0)call shadw(ij, ik, it)
        enddo
    enddo
endif
```

Program 7.2.b Aggregation of variables with skill classes

```
do ij = 1, JJ
   do ik = 1, SS
      CC(it) = CC(it) + c(ij, ik, it)*m(ij, ik, it)
      AA(it) = AA(it) + a(ij, ik, it)*m(ij, ik, it)
      LL(it) = LL(it) + h(ij, ik)*(1d0-l(ij, ik, it))&
                        *m(ij, ik, it)
   enddo
enddo
```

problem, as shown in Program 7.2.b. Note that by setting initial values to the measure `m` in the subroutine `initialize`, we already specify the fraction of low- and high-skilled households in the population. Finally, the compensation scheme in subroutine `lsra` could be designed in different ways. In order to derive a measure of aggregate efficiency, we need a reference value for utility in the initial equilibrium. In principle, this could be the utility of a household from any skill class. This means that not only existing cohorts in the reform year are compensated, but also future cohorts of specific skill classes. The cost (or benefits) of the remaining skill class are then computed endogenously from the Lump-Sum Redistribution Authority (LSRA) budget constraint. In the following simulations, we assume that the low-skilled households along the transition path are compensated to have a zero welfare effect, and the high-skilled are burdened with the resulting cost (or gain from the benefits).

(c) With a very small share of low-skilled households, for example 0.01, the results from Table 7.3 in the book can be replicated. Increasing the share of low-skilled households in the population changes the macroeconomic and welfare results quite significantly. Since the pension is flat, ie independent of former contributions, it is a very redistributive instrument, and labour supply distortions rise dramatically when the share of low-skilled population increases. For example, when the low-skilled are 50 per cent and 80 per cent of the population, the efficiency loss increases from 1.33 to 2.93 per cent and to 8.08 per cent, respectively.

Exercise 7.3

(a) Besides individual variables, prices, government parameters, and aggregate variables now need to be denoted with an additional dimension which identifies their country of origin. Since we assume an international goods market and free international mobility of capital, the goods price can still be normalized to a value of one, and the world interest rate only differs across periods, and not across countries. Labour input, on the other hand, is completely immobile across countries, so that we need to distinguish country-specific gross wage rates `w(ik, it)`.

Program 7.3 Factor price computation in two-country model

```
r(it) = (1d0-tauk(1, it))/(1d0-eps(1, it)*tauk(1, it))*        &
        (alpha*(KK(1, it)/LL(1, it))**(alpha-1d0)-delta)

do ik = 1, SS
    w(ik, it) = (1d0-alpha)*(KK(ik, it)/LL(ik, it))**alpha
    do ij = 1, JJ
        wn(ik, ij, it) = (h(ik, j)*w(ik, it)+mu(ik, ij, it))&
                            *(1d0-tauw(ik, it)-taup(ik, it))
    enddo
    Rn(ik, it) = 1d0 + r(it)*(1d0-taur(ik, it))
    p(ik, it) = 1d0 + tauc(ik, it)
enddo
```

Program 7.3.a Aggregation of variables in two-country model

```
do ik = 1, SS
    do ij = 1,JJ
        CC(ik, it) = CC(ik, it) + c(ik, ij, it)*m(ik, ij, it)
        AA(ik, it) = AA(ik, it) + a(ik, ij, it)*m(ik, ij, it)
        LL(ik, it) = LL(ik, it) + h(ik, ij)*(1d0-l(ik, ij, it)) &
                        *m(ik, ij, it)
    enddo
    YY(ik, it) = KK(ik, it)**alpha*LL(ik, it)**(1d0-alpha)
    BB(ik, it) = by(ik, it)*YY(ik, it)
    if(ik > 1)KK(ik, it) = LL(ik, it)*((r(it)*(1d0-eps(ik, it)&
                            *tauk(ik, it))/(1d0-tauk(ik, it))+ &
                            delta)/alpha)**(1d0/(alpha-1d0))
enddo
KK(1, it) = damp*(sum(AA(:, it))-sum(BB(:, it))-sum(BA(:, it))&
            -sum(KK(2:SS, it)))+(1d0-damp)*KK(1, it)

do ik = 1, SS
    II(ik, it) = (1d0+n_p(itp))*KK(ik, itp) - (1d0-delta)*KK(ik, it)
    if(ik < SS)TB(ik, it) = YY(ik, it) - CC(ik, it) - &
                            II(ik, it) - GG(ik, it)
    if(ik == SS)TB(SS, it) = -sum(TB(1:SS-1, it))
enddo
```

(b) Compared to the program in Exercise 7.2., the price calculations in subroutine `factor_prices` also have to be carried out for each of the two countries as shown in Program 7.3. We derive the world interest rate from the optimality condition in the first country, and later on treat the second country as a small, open economy that faces the world interest rate. Given factor and consumer prices, the derivation of individual decisions is fairly similar to all previous programs. Yet, government parameters and prices are country-specific. Consumption, assets, and labour supply are aggregated separately for the two countries in the subroutine `quantities` (see Program 7.3.a). As already explained, we treat the second country as a small, open economy, so that its capital stock is derived from the first-order condition with a fixed world-market interest rate. The first country's capital stock can then be derived from the equilibrium condition of the world capital market. Similarly, we derive the trade balance of the first country from the

Program 7.3.b Computation of tax revenues in two-country model

```
do ik = 1, SS
    taxrev(ik, 1) = tauc(ik, it)*CC(ik, it)
    [......]
    taup(ik, it) = Tpen(ik, it)/w(ik, it)/LL(ik, it)
enddo
```

national goods market equilibrium condition. The trade balance of the second country then has to simply be the negative value of this. Note that in this set-up, we cannot define net foreign assets without further assumptions about the domestic private investment shares in foreign capital. However, since we don't need net foreign assets in the following calculations, we just do not compute them. Finally, we calculate the budget-balancing tax rates separately for each country in subroutine `government`, as shown in Program 7.3.b.

(c) If countries differ only with respect to their relative size, the resulting solution always is an autarky equilibrium. If trade arose in such a model, it must be the consequence of differences in preferences, technologies, government parameters, or population dynamics.

(d) A switch from consumption towards income taxation in one country negatively affects the other country in the long run, through the international capital market. The reduction of savings in the reform country leads to an increase in the interest rate there, inducing capital inflows from the other (non-reforming) country in order to equalize prices on the international capital market. In the short run, older cohorts benefit from higher returns. Yet, future cohorts are hurt, since the lower capital stock reduces wages and drives up consumption tax rates. Of course, these negative spill-over effects are of second order, meaning that the long-run welfare losses are always higher in the reform country. Note that the present model completely abstracts from terms-of-trade effects, since countries are trading a homogenous good.

Exercise 7.4

(a) This program is based on program `prog07_02` of the book. With additional periods and human capital depreciation, individual productivity at age $j > 1$ is now defined by:

$$h_{j,s}(e_t) = h_1(1 + \xi e_t^{\upsilon})(1 - \delta_h)^{j-2}.$$

The education decision of the household who enters the labour market in period t therefore changes to:

$$\max_{e_t} \; W_{1,t} = [1 - (1 - \tau_t^s)e_t]w_t^n h_1 + \sum_{j=2}^{j_r-1} \frac{w_s^n h_{j,s}(e_t)}{R_{t,s}^n} + \sum_{j_r}^{J} \frac{pen_{j,s}}{R_{t,s}^n},$$

where $w_s^n = w_s(1 - \tau_s^w - \tau_s^p)$ defines the net wage (per efficiency unit) of a j-year old worker in period $s = t + j - 1$. Households work until they retire at age j_r, while $R_{t,s}^n = \Pi_{k=t+1}^{s} R_k^n$ denotes the discount factor for future periods. From the resulting first-order condition, we now derive the optimal eduction time as:

$$e_t = \left(\frac{\xi \upsilon \sum_{j=2}^{j_r-1} w_s^n (1 - \delta_h)^{j-2} (R_{t,s}^n)^{-1}}{w_t^n (1 - \tau_t^s)} \right)^{\frac{1}{1-\upsilon}}. \tag{7.1}$$

Given optimal education time, the future human capital stock can be computed as in the original program `prog07_02` of the book, but now we include depreciation. Subroutine `getedu` that derives the optimal education investment as well as the path of human capital is shown in Program 7.4. In subroutine `quantities`, aggregate labour supply needs to be computed from:

$$L_t = \sum_{j=1}^{j_r-1} h_{j,t} m_{j,t} - h_1 e_t.$$

(b) Table 7.1 shows the initial equilibrium without and with depreciation of human capital. Without depreciation, education investment in the first period is quite high (0.38 relative to 0.13 in Table 7.4 of the book) due to the dramatic increase in returns, meaning

Program 7.4 Computation of optimal education time

```
subroutine getedu(it)
    [......]
    ! Compute pv of net wage
    pvw = 0d0
    PRn = 1d0
    do ij = 2, JR-1
        itp = year(it, ij-1)
        PRn = PRn*Rn(itp)
        pvw = pvw + w(itp)*(1d0-tauw(itp)-taup(itp))* &
                                   (1d0-delh)**(ij-2)/PRn
    enddo

    e(it) =(xi*upsi*pvw/(wn(1, it)*(1d0-taus(it))))**(1d0/(1d0-upsi))
    if(e(it) > 0.99d0)e(it) = 0.99d0

    do ij = 2, JR-1
        itp = year(it, 1, ij)
        h(ij, itp) = (1d0+xi*e(it)**upsi)*(1d0-delh)**(ij-2)
    enddo

end subroutine
```

a higher income in three periods. Additional human capital increases labour input and at the same time reduces savings, since households borrow at young ages to finance their educational investment. Wages are therefore fairly low and the interest rate is high. When human capital depreciates, education decreases, owing to a lower return. Labour input falls due to lower human capital. Yet, assets and the capital stock are higher, since people save more at younger ages. Despite higher wages, utility is lower with depreciation than without it.

(c) Table 7.2 reports the transition path when a flat pension system is introduced into the model economy with endogenous human capital. The initial equilibrium is the same as in Table 7.1 in the case with depreciation. Hence, we do not report it again. The introduction of a flat pension system has similar economic effects as the move towards income taxation in Table 7.4 of the book. On impact, education investment declines, as higher contribution rates reduce the return on education, despite the fall in the opportunity cost of education. Lower education leads to a higher labour input in the reform year, as households who would have otherwise spent their time building human capital flow into the labour market. In the following years, however, aggregate human capital, and therefore labour input, again falls back to the original level. Owing to lower savings (and corresponding capital), future wages fall significantly, so that consumption tax rates increase along the transition path. Note that there are no distortions of the education decision because the contribution rates cancel out in equation (7.1).

Table 7.1 Equilibrium without and with human capital depreciation

δ_h	τ^c	C	e	L	K	w	r	U
0.00	0.28	2.03	0.38	4.29	1.05	0.46	0.80	−10.30
0.50	0.30	1.58	0.33	2.91	1.41	0.56	0.50	−12.21

$g_y = 0.205$; $n_p = 0.2$; $\xi = 1.2$; $\upsilon = 0.5$; $J = 6$; $j_r = 5$.

Table 7.2 Pensions with endogenous human capital

t	τ^p	τ^c	C	e	L	K	w	r	HEV
−4									40.58
−3									43.95
⋮	⋮	⋮	⋮	⋮	⋮	⋮	⋮	⋮	⋮
1	0.15	0.26	1.83	0.27	2.98	1.41	0.56	0.51	−7.23
2	0.15	0.28	1.70	0.26	2.93	1.23	0.54	0.55	−10.52
⋮	⋮	⋮	⋮	⋮	⋮	⋮	⋮	⋮	⋮
∞	0.15	0.35	1.37	0.25	2.87	0.90	0.49	0.68	−17.18
Δ*									0.00

$g_y = 0.205$; $n_p = 0.2$; $\xi = 1.2$; $\upsilon = 0.5$; $\delta_h = 0.5$; $J = 6$; $j_r = 5$.

Exercise 7.5

With variable labour supply, households who enter the labour market in period t maximize the utility function:

$$U(c_{1,t}, \ell_{1,t}, \dots) = \sum_{j=1}^{J} \beta^{j-1} u(c_{j,s}, \ell_{j,s}),$$

subject to the intertemporal budget constraint:

$$\sum_{j=1}^{J} \frac{p_s c_{j,s} + w^n_{j,s}\ell_{j,s}}{R^n_{t,s}} = (1-e_t)w^n_{1,t} + \tau^s_t e_t w_t + \sum_{j=2}^{j_r-1} \frac{w^n_{j,s}}{R^n_{t,s}} + \sum_{j=j_r}^{J} \frac{pen_{j,s}}{R^n_{t,s}},$$

where we now define:

$$w^n_{j,s} = \left[\, w_s h_{j,s}(e_t) + \mu_{j,s} \,\right](1 - \tau^w_s - \tau^p_s).$$

The shadow wage $\mu_{j,s}$ ensures that leisure demand plus education investment do not exceed the time endowment, ie

$$\begin{aligned} e_t + \ell_{1,t} &\leq 1, \quad \mu_{1,t} \geq 0, \quad \text{and} \quad \mu_{1,t}(1 - e_t - \ell_{1,t}) = 0 \\ \ell_{j,s} &\leq 1, \quad \mu_{j,s} \geq 0, \quad \text{and} \quad \mu_{j,s}(1 - \ell_{j,s}) = 0 \quad \forall\, j > 1. \end{aligned}$$

As before, we set $R^n_{t,s} = \Pi^s_{k=t+1} R^n_k$. Now the education decision depends on the labour supply decision, since the household maximizes net income:

$$\max_{e_t} \; (1-e_t)w^n_{1,t} + \tau^s_t e_t w_t + \sum_{j=2}^{j_r-1} \frac{w^n_{j,s}(1-\ell_{j,s})}{R^n_{t,s}}.$$

From the respective first-order condition, education investment is given by:

$$e_t = \left(\frac{\xi \upsilon \sum_{j=2}^{j_r-1} w^n_s (1-\delta_h)^{j-2}(1-\ell_{j,s})(R^n_{t,s})^{-1}}{w^n_{1,t} - \tau^s_t w_t} \right)^{\frac{1}{1-\upsilon}}.$$

Consequently, labour supply is taken into account in the calculation of education investment in subroutine `getedu`.[2] At the same time, the education decision affects labour

[2] For technical reasons, we restrict maximal education investment to 0.9.

supply and savings. In principle, maximum wealth $W_{1,t}$, as well as the first-order conditions for consumption and leisure demand, can be derived, as in Section 7.1 of the book. However, the net wage is now measured in human capital units, which in turn depend on the previous education decision.

(a) The subroutines `get_W`, `get_Psi` and `get_path` can be taken from program `prog07_01` of the book. Only subroutine `get_path` has to be adjusted in order to account for education investments in the calculation of assets. The calculation of shadow wages in subroutine `shadw` needs to be adjusted, too, since the time restriction in the first period is $\ell_{1,t} + e_t \leq 1$. Hence, the shadow wage at age $j = 1$ is computed from:

$$\mu_{1,t} = \frac{\nu p_t}{1 - \tau_t^w - \tau_t^p} \left(\frac{c_{1,t}}{1 - e_t}\right)^{1/\rho} - w_t h_{1,t}.$$

At higher ages, there is hardly any change (see subroutine `shadw` in Program 7.5). Besides subroutine `shadw`, we also have to adjust the aggregation of labour supply in subroutine `quantities` and the computation of subsidy payments in subroutine `government`.

(b) Table 7.3 reports the transition path after the introduction of education subsidies in the model with variable labour supply. In the initial equilibrium, households only spend 16 per cent of their time endowment on education. As the education subsidy distorts labour supply, households increase education investment and work less in their first year on the labour market. As a consequence, aggregate labour input and consumption fall on impact. In order to finance the subsidy, the consumption tax rate increases from 30 to 33 per cent, which explains the welfare losses of the elderly. Younger cohorts in the reform year benefit from the subsidy, so that they experience welfare gains.

Program 7.5 Shadow wages with endogenous human capital

```
do ijp = ij, JJ
   itp = year(it, ij, ijp)
   if(ijp == 1)then
      if(l(1,itp) + e(itp) > 1d0-5d-2)then
         mu(1, itp) = (1d0-damp)*mu(1, itp)+ damp*( &
                      (c(1, itp)/(1d0-e(itp)))**(1d0/rho) &
                      *nu*p(itp)/(1d0-tauw(itp)-taup(itp))&
                      - h(1, itp)*w(itp))
         if(mu(1, itp) < 0d0)mu(1, itp) = 0d0
      else
         mu(1, itp) = (1d0-damp)*mu(1, itp)
      endif
   else
      if(l(ijp, itp) > 1d0-5d-2)then
         [......]
      endif
   endif
enddo
```

Table 7.3 Education subsidies with variable labour supply

t	τ^s	τ^c	C	e	L	K	w	r	HEV
−4									−1.91
−3									−1.85
⋮	⋮	⋮	⋮	⋮	⋮	⋮	⋮	⋮	⋮
0	0.00	0.30	1.01	0.16	1.88	0.84	0.55	0.53	0.47
1	0.20	0.33	0.99	0.24	1.81	0.84	0.56	0.51	0.64
2	0.20	0.33	0.99	0.24	1.86	0.82	0.55	0.53	0.32
⋮	⋮	⋮	⋮	⋮	⋮	⋮	⋮	⋮	⋮
∞	0.20	0.32	1.02	0.25	1.92	0.82	0.54	0.55	0.22
Δ*									−0.31

$g_y = 0.205$; $n_p = 0.2$; $\xi = 1.2$; $\upsilon = 0.5$; $\delta_h = 0.2$; $J = 6$; $j_r = 5$.

Table 7.4 Pensions with variable labour supply

t	τ^p	τ^c	C	e	L	K	w	r	HEV
−4									27.11
−3									29.96
⋮	⋮	⋮	⋮	⋮	⋮	⋮	⋮	⋮	⋮
1	0.25	0.26	1.16	0.10	1.80	0.84	0.56	0.51	−8.16
2	0.24	0.29	1.04	0.09	1.82	0.67	0.52	0.60	−11.06
⋮	⋮	⋮	⋮	⋮	⋮	⋮	⋮	⋮	⋮
∞	0.24	0.38	0.80	0.09	1.81	0.45	0.46	0.79	−15.53
Δ*									−2.60

$g_y = 0.205$; $n_p = 0.2$; $\xi = 1.2$; $\upsilon = 0.5$; $\delta_h = 0.2$; $J = 6$; $j_r = 5$.

Throughout the transition, labour input increases again owing to the higher human capital. Yet, lower savings decrease the capital stock and wages slightly, so that welfare gains of future cohorts decrease. Overall, efficiency losses from distorted labour supply sum up to 0.31 per cent of aggregate resources.

(c) The introduction of a pay-as-you-go financed pension system is shown in Table 7.4. We again start from the same initial equilibrium as in the previous simulation. The introduction of pensions has quite different macroeconomic and welfare effects compared to education subsidies. Pension contributions reduce the return on education, due to the fall of future net wages. Consequently, optimal education investment falls on impact from 16 per cent to roughly 10 per cent of time endowment. However, households also consume more leisure, so that savings as well as wages fall during the transition. The elderly are now gaining significantly, at the cost of younger and future cohorts. Again, the policy generates aggregate efficiency losses, which now amount to about 2.6 per cent of aggregate resources.

Exercise 7.6

(a) We maximize the utility function:

$$U(c_{1,t},\ldots,\ell_{t+4}) = \sum_{j=1}^{4} \beta^{j-1} u(c_{j,s}) + \beta^4 u(c_{5,t+4},\ell_{t+4}) + \beta^5 u(c_{6,t+5})$$

with:

$$u(c) = \frac{c^{1-1/\gamma}}{1-1/\gamma} \quad \text{and} \quad u(c,\ell) = \frac{1}{1-\frac{1}{\gamma}}\left[c^{1-1/\rho} + \nu\ell^{1-1/\rho}\right]^{\frac{1-1/\gamma}{1-1/\rho}},$$

subject to the intertemporal budget constraint:

$$\sum_{j=1}^{6} \frac{p_s c_{j,s}}{R^n_{t,s}} + \frac{(w^n_{5,t+4} - pen_{t+4})\ell_{t+4}}{R^n_{t,t+4}} =$$

$$(1-(1-\tau^s_t)e_t)w^n_{1,t} + \sum_{j=2}^{j_r} \frac{w^n_{j,s}}{R^n_{t,s}} + \frac{pen_{t+5}}{R^n_{t,t+5}} =: W_{1,t},$$

where we have now set:

$$w^n_{j,s} = \left[\, w_s h_{j,s}(e_t) + \mu_{j,s} \,\right](1-\tau^w_s - \tau^p_s) \quad \text{with:} \quad h_{j,s}(e_t) = e_j h_1(1+\xi e^{\upsilon}_t)(1-\delta_h)^{j-2}$$

and $\mu_{j,s} = 0 \;\forall j \neq j_r$. Compared to Exercise 7.5, we include the age-productivity profile e_j and compute a shadow wage only in the retirement period. Aggregate resources are computed as if the household would work full-time at age j_r. The education decision now depends on the retirement decision, since the household maximizes net income:

$$\max_{e_t}\; (1-(1-\tau^s_t)e_t)w^n_{1,t} + \sum_{j=2}^{j_r-1} \frac{w^n_{j,s}}{R^n_{t,s}} + \frac{w^n_{5,t+4}(1-\ell_{t+4})}{R^n_{t,t+4}}.$$

From the respective first-order condition, education investment is given by:

$$e_t = \left(\frac{\xi\upsilon\left[\sum_{j=2}^{j_r-1} \frac{w^n_s e_j (1-\delta_h)^{j-2}}{R^n_{t,s}} + \frac{w^n_{t+4} e_5 (1-\delta_h)^3 (1-\ell_{t+4})}{R^n_{t,t+4}}\right]}{(1-\tau^s_t)w^n_{1,t}}\right)^{\frac{1}{1-\upsilon}}.$$

Consequently, the retirement decision has to be included for the calculation of education investment in subroutine `getedu`.

The derivatives of the Lagrange function with respect to $c_{j,s}$, $c_{5,t+4}$ and ℓ_{t+4} give the first-order conditions:

$$\beta^{j-1} c_{j,s}^{-1/\gamma} = \lambda \frac{p_s}{R^n_{t,s}} \qquad \forall \; j = 1, \ldots, 4, 6$$

$$\beta^4 \left[c_{5,t+4}^{1-1/\rho} + \nu \ell_{t+4}^{1-1/\rho} \right]^{\frac{1/\rho - 1/\gamma}{1-1/\rho}} c_{5,t+4}^{-1/\rho} = \lambda \frac{p_{t+4}}{R^n_{t,t+4}}$$

$$\beta^4 \left[c_{5,t+4}^{1-1/\rho} + \nu \ell_{t+4}^{1-1/\rho} \right]^{\frac{1/\rho - 1/\gamma}{1-1/\rho}} \nu \ell_{t+4}^{-1/\rho} = \lambda \frac{w^n_{5,t+4} - pen_{t+4}}{R^n_{t,t+4}}.$$

Combining the last two conditions gives:

$$\ell_{t+4} = \left(\frac{w^n_{5,t+4} - pen_{t+4}}{\nu p_{t+4}} \right)^{-\rho} c_{5,t+4},$$

which is substituted back into the second condition so that:

$$\beta^4 \left[1 + \nu^\rho \left(\frac{w^n_{5,t+4} - pen_{t+4}}{p_{t+4}} \right)^{1-\rho} \right]^{\frac{\rho-\gamma}{\gamma(1-\rho)}} c_{5,t+4}^{-1/\gamma} = \lambda \frac{p_{t+4}}{R^n_{t,t+4}}.$$

Dividing both sides with the optimality condition for $c_{1,t}^{-1/\gamma} = \lambda p_t$ gives, after rearranging:

$$c_{5,t+4} = \nu_{t+4} \left[\beta^4 \frac{p_t}{p_{t+4}} R^n_{t,t+4} \right]^\gamma c_{1,t}$$

with $\nu_{t+4} = \left[1 + \nu^\rho \left(\frac{w^n_{5,t+4} - pen_{t+4}}{p_{t+4}} \right)^{1-\rho} \right]^{\frac{\rho-\gamma}{1-\rho}}$. In a similar way, we can derive:

$$c_{j,s} = \left[\beta^{j-1} \frac{p_t}{p_s} R^n_{t,s} \right]^\gamma c_{1,t} \qquad \forall \; j = 2, 3, 4, 6.$$

Substituting back into the budget constraint yields:

$$\sum_{j \neq 5} \frac{p_s}{R^n_{t,s}} \left[\beta^{j-1} \frac{p_t}{p_s} R^n_{t,s} \right]^\gamma c_{1,t} + \frac{p_{t+4}}{R^n_{t,t+4}} \nu_{t+4} \left[\beta^4 \frac{p_t}{p_{t+4}} R^n_{t,t+4} \right]^\gamma c_{1,t} +$$

$$\frac{p_{t+4}}{R^n_{t,t+4}} \nu^\rho \left(\frac{w^n_{5,t+4} - pen_{t+4}}{p_{t+4}} \right)^{1-\rho} c_{5,t+4} := W_{1,t}.$$

Finally, after substituting the above condition for $c_{5,t+4}$ and rearranging we get $c_{1,t} = \Psi_{1,t} W_{1,t}$ with:

$$\Psi_{1,t} = \frac{1}{p_t}\left\{\sum_{j\neq 5} \beta^{\gamma(j-1)} \left[\frac{p_s}{p_t}(R^n_{t,s})^{-1}\right]^{1-\gamma} + \beta^{4\gamma}\left[\frac{p_{t+4}}{p_t}(R^n_{t,t+4})^{-1}\right]^{1-\gamma} v_{t+4}^{\frac{1-\gamma}{\rho-\gamma}}\right\}^{-1}.$$

Given $c_{1,t}$, the optimal path for consumption, $c_{j,s}$ and leisure ℓ_{t+4} is derived using the above first-order conditions.

The problem is now that this approach does not exactly apply when we re-optimize for a $j = j_r$ old household in period t. To see this, we maximize:

$$\max \mathcal{L} = u(c_{5,t}, \ell_t) + \beta u(c_{6,t+1}) - \lambda\left\{p_t c_{5,t} + (w^n_{5,t} - pen_t)\ell_t + \frac{p_{t+1}c_{6,t+1}}{R^n_{t,t+1}} - W_{5,t}\right\},$$

which gives the first-order conditions:

$$\left[c_{5,t}^{1-1/\rho} + v\ell_t^{1-1/\rho}\right]^{\frac{1/\rho-1/\gamma}{1-1/\rho}} c_{5,t}^{-1/\rho} = \lambda p_t$$

$$\left[c_{5,t}^{1-1/\rho} + v\ell_t^{1-1/\rho}\right]^{\frac{1/\rho-1/\gamma}{1-1/\rho}} v\ell_t^{-1/\rho} = \lambda(w^n_{5,t} - pen_t),$$

$$\beta c_{6,t+1}^{-1/\gamma} = \lambda\frac{p_{t+1}}{R^n_{t,t+1}},$$

from which we derive:

$$\ell_t = \left(\frac{w^n_{5,t} - pen_t}{vp_t}\right)^{-\rho} c_{5,t},$$

which is substituted back to give:

$$v_t^{1/\gamma} c_{5,t}^{-1/\gamma} = \lambda p_t.$$

Substituting now $\lambda = \beta c_{6,t+1}^{-1/\gamma}\frac{R^n_{t,t+1}}{p_{t+1}}$ gives, after rearranging:

$$c_{6,t+1} = v_t^{-1}\left[\beta\frac{p_t}{p_{t+1}}R^n_{t,t+1}\right]^{\gamma} c_{5,t}.$$

Substituting into the budget constraint gives:

$$p_t c_{5,t} + \nu^\rho \left(\frac{w^n_{5,t} - pen_t}{p_t}\right)^{1-\rho} p_t c_{5,t} + \frac{p_{t+1}}{R^n_{t,t+1}} \nu_t^{-1} \left[\beta \frac{p_t}{p_{t+1}} R^n_{t,t+1}\right]^\gamma c_{5,t} = W_{5,t}$$

or:

$$p_t c_{5,t} \nu_t^{\frac{1-\rho}{\rho-\gamma}} + \nu_t^{-1} \beta^\gamma \left[\frac{p_{t+1}}{p_t}(R^n_{t,t+1})^{-1}\right]^{1-\gamma} p_t c_{5,t} = W_{5,t},$$

so that we finally get $c_{5,t} = \Psi_{5,t} W_{5,t}$ with:

$$\Psi_{5,t} = \frac{\nu_t}{p_t}\left\{\beta^\gamma \left[\frac{p_{t+1}}{p_t}(R^n_{t,t+1})^{-1}\right]^{1-\gamma} + \nu_t^{\frac{1-\gamma}{\rho-\gamma}}\right\}^{-1}.$$

Note that marginal consumption of a j_r-year old household in period t is not consistent with $\Psi_{1,t}$ above. The optimal consumption path is similarly modified to neutralize the adjustment in marginal consumption.

(b) Besides the changes in subroutine `getedu`, the main adjustments compared to program `sol_prog07_04` are in function `get_Psi` and subroutine `get_path`. Both have to take into account the difference of the consumption functions in the retirement age j_r when households immediately retire in the reform year and when they retire in the future. Program 7.6 shows these adjustments in the marginal consumption function and Program 7.6.a shows the adjustment with respect to the optimal consumption path. Of

Program 7.6 Marginal consumption with endogenous retirement

```
function get_Psi(ij,it)
    [......]
    get_Psi = 0d0
    PRn = 1d0
    do ijp = ij, JJ
        itp = year(it, ij, ijp)
        itm = year(it, ij, ijp+1)
        if(ijp /= JR)then
            get_Psi = get_Psi + beta**((ijp-ij)*gamma)*&
                     (p(itp)/PRn/p(it))**(1d0-gamma)
        else
            vv = (1d0+nu**rho*((wn(ijp, itp)-pen(ijp, itp))/ &
                   p(itp))**(1d0-rho))**((rho-gamma)/(1d0-rho))
            get_Psi = get_Psi + beta**((ijp-ij)*gamma)* &
                     (p(itp)/PRn/p(it))**(1d0-gamma)* &
                     vv**((1d0-gamma)/(rho-gamma))
        endif
        PRn = PRn*Rn(itm)
    enddo
    get_Psi = 1d0/get_Psi/p(it)
    if(ij == JR)get_Psi = get_Psi*vv

end function
```

Program 7.6.a Optimal consumption path with endogenous retirement

```
subroutine get_path(ij, it)
    [......]
    PRn = 1d0
    do ijp = ij+1, JJ
        itp = year(it, ij, ijp)
        itm = year(it, ij, ijp-1)
        PRn = PRn*Rn(itp)
        if(ijp /= JR)then
            c(ijp, itp) = (beta**(ijp-ij)*PRn*p(it)/ &
                              p(itp))**gamma*c(ij, it)
        else
            vv = (1d0+nu**rho*((wn(ijp, itp)-pen(ijp, itp))/&
                    p(itp))**(1d0-rho))**((rho-gamma)/(1d0-rho))
            c(ijp, itp)=vv*(beta**(ijp-ij)*PRn*p(it)/&
                              p(itp))**gamma*c(ij, it)
            l(itp) = ((wn(ijp, itp)-pen(ijp, itp))/&
                              nu/p(itp))**(-rho)*c(ijp, itp)
        endif

        if(ij == JR)then
            vv = (1d0 + nu**rho*((wn(ij, it)-pen(ij, it))/p(it)) &
                    **(1d0-rho))**((rho-gamma)/(1d0-rho))
            l(it) = ((wn(ij, it)-pen(ij, it))/nu/ &
                           p(it))**(-rho)*c(ij, it)
            c(6, it+1) = (beta*Rn(it+1)*p(it)/ &
                           p(it+1))**gamma/vv*c(ij, it)
        endif
        [......]
    enddo

end subroutine
```

course, in subroutines `quantities` and `government` the aggregation of labour supply and pensions needs to be adjusted to account for variable labour supply in the year of retirement j_r.

(c) The introduction of a productivity profile which reflects training on the job induces households to delay retirement and work longer, even with positive human capital depreciation. As shown in Table 7.5, households only work 17 per cent of their time endowment in the period of retirement with the present calibration. The introduction of a subsidy of 10 per cent increases education time substantially from 30 to 36 per cent of time endowment. At the same time, the consumption tax rate rises by 1 per cent in order to finance the subsidy. Since retirement is only indirectly affected, labour supply is mainly reduced because of higher education investments. Along the transition, higher consumption taxes slightly reduce savings and capital accumulation. Wages remain almost constant, while the interest rate increases slightly. Older households are hurt by the reform because of higher consumption taxes, while younger and future households benefit slightly. The efficiency loss is very modest, at roughly 0.2 per cent of resources.

(d) The introduction of a pay-as-you-go financed pension system is shown in Table 7.6. Since we start from the same initial equilibrium as in the previous Table 7.5,

Table 7.5 Education subsidies with endogenous retirement

t	τ^S	τ^C	C	e	ℓ	L	K	w	r	HEV
−4										−1.33
−3										−0.93
⋮	⋮	⋮	⋮	⋮	⋮	⋮	⋮	⋮	⋮	⋮
0	0.00	0.29	1.85	0.30	0.82	3.71	1.17	0.49	0.67	−0.27
1	0.10	0.30	1.84	0.36	0.82	3.65	1.17	0.50	0.67	0.75
2	0.10	0.30	1.84	0.36	0.83	3.69	1.16	0.49	0.68	0.48
⋮	⋮	⋮	⋮	⋮	⋮	⋮	⋮	⋮	⋮	⋮
∞	0.10	0.30	1.87	0.36	0.82	3.75	1.15	0.49	0.69	0.39
Δ^*										−0.18

$g_y = 0.205$; $n_p = 0.2$; $\xi = 1.0$; $\upsilon = 0.5$; $\delta_h = 0.2$; $J = 6$; $j_r = 5$.

Table 7.6 Pensions with endogenous retirement

t	τ^p	τ^C	C	e	ℓ	L	K	w	r	HEV
−4										25.62
−3										21.44
⋮	⋮	⋮	⋮	⋮	⋮	⋮	⋮	⋮	⋮	⋮
1	0.12	0.27	1.97	0.24	1.00	3.68	1.17	0.50	0.67	−8.19
2	0.12	0.29	1.85	0.23	1.00	3.64	1.05	0.48	0.71	−10.53
⋮	⋮	⋮	⋮	⋮	⋮	⋮	⋮	⋮	⋮	⋮
∞	0.12	0.33	1.62	0.23	1.00	3.56	0.87	0.46	0.81	−14.53
Δ^*										−1.66

$g_y = 0.205$; $n_p = 0.2$; $\xi = 1.0$; $\upsilon = 0.5$; $\delta_h = 0.2$; $J = 6$; $j_r = 5$.

we do not report it again. The introduction of the pension reduces net wages and therefore the returns to education. Consequently, education investment of younger cohorts falls significantly, while at the same time elderly households retire earlier. On impact, both effects almost neutralize each other, so that labour supply hardly changes. During the transition, lower education investments further reduce labour supply, while lower savings dampens capital accumulation and wages. Of course, older cohorts are benefiting from the reform, while younger and future cohorts are losing significantly. Overall, the aggregate efficiency loss amounts to 1.7 per cent of resources.

Exercise 7.7

The simulated impact of an increase in life expectancy is shown in Table 7.7. On impact, rising life expectancy increases the return to education, which induces more investment in education. Hence, human capital and (effective) labour supply increase significantly.

Table 7.7 Rising life expectancy, endogenous education, and retirement

t	$\psi_{2,t}$	$\psi_{3,t}$	$\psi_{6,t}$	$E[T]$	C	e	ℓ	L	K	BQ
0	0.85	0.85	0.85	4.15	1.62	0.17	0.92	2.86	0.53	0.16
1	0.85	0.85	0.85	4.34	1.61	0.17	0.92	2.86	0.53	0.16
2	0.90	0.85	0.85	4.48	1.62	0.18	0.92	2.92	0.53	0.16
3	0.90	0.85	0.85	4.59	1.64	0.19	0.92	2.95	0.55	0.16
⋮	⋮	⋮	⋮	⋮	⋮	⋮	⋮	⋮	⋮	⋮
∞	0.90	0.90	0.90	4.69	1.85	0.21	0.87	3.12	0.70	0.13

$g_y = \kappa = 0.0$; $\omega_{b,4} = \omega_{b,5} = 0.5$; $\nu = 0.4$; $n_p = 0.2$.

While higher life expectancy induces a delay in retirement, higher available resources increase the demand for leisure. Consequently, households retire only slightly later in the long run. On the other hand, they save significantly more, so that the capital stock rises substantially. Nevertheless bequests fall in the long run, since households consume their higher savings in old age.

Exercise 7.8

In this exercise, we extend the endogenous growth model in program `prog_07_03` of the book from three to six periods. The main adjustments are the computation of the optimal education time e_t and the calculation of aggregate labour supply.

(a) Households now work for four periods and need to take into account human capital depreciation. Consequently, human capital during working periods is defined by:

$$h_{2,t+1} = h_{1,t}(1+\xi e_t^{\upsilon}) \quad h_{3,t+2} = h_{2,t+1}(1-\delta_h) \quad h_{4,t+3} = h_{2,t+1}(1-\delta_h)^2.$$

As before, we assume $h_{1,t} = \mu h_{2,t}$, so that we get:

$$h_{1,t+1} = \mu h_{2,t+1} = h_{1,t}(1+\xi e_t^{\upsilon})\mu = h_{1,t}(1+n_{e,t+1}).$$

Available resources are given by:

$$\widetilde{W}_{1,t} = [1-(1-\tau_t^s)e_t]w_t^n h_{1,t} + \sum_{j=2}^{j_r-1} \frac{w_s^n h_{j,s}}{R_{t,s}^n} + \sum_{j=j_r}^{J} \frac{\widetilde{pen}_{j,s}}{R_{t,s}^n},$$

with $s=t+j-1$. The household chooses optimal education investment from maximizing normalized resources:

$$\max_{e_t} W_{1,t} = \frac{\widetilde{W}_{1,t}}{h_{1,t}} = [1 - (1 - \tau_t^s)e_t]w_t^n + \sum_{j=2}^{j_r-1} \frac{w_s^n(1-\delta_h)^{j-2}(1+\xi e_t^{\upsilon})}{R_{t,s}^n} + \sum_{j=j_r}^{J} \frac{pen_{j,s}}{R_{t,s}^n}.$$

This yields the optimal education investment as:

$$e_t = \left(\frac{\xi\upsilon\sum_{j=2}^{j_r-1} w_s^n(1-\delta_h)^{j-2}(R_{t,s}^n)^{-1}}{w_t^n(1-\tau_t^s)}\right)^{\frac{1}{1-\upsilon}}.$$

Aggregate labour input can be derived from:

$$\tilde{L}_t = (1-e_t)h_{1,t}N_t + h_{2,t}N_{t-1} + h_{3,t}N_{t-2} + h_{4,t}N_{t-3}$$

so that normalized labour input is given by:

$$L_t = \frac{\tilde{L}_t}{h_{1,t}N_t} = (1-e_t) + \sum_{j=2}^{j_r-1} \frac{(1-\delta_h)^{j-2}(1+n_{e,t+j-2})\hat{m}_{j,t}}{\mu}.$$

(b) In Table 7.8, we show the consequences of higher human capital depreciation rates for education time and growth. Higher human capital depreciation directly reduces the incentive to invest in education. However, at the same time labour supply is reduced, so that wages increase. This in turn improves the incentive to invest in education. Table 7.8 shows that for low depreciation rates, the wage effect dominates, so that education time and the growth rate of the economy rises. However, when depreciation rises further, the direct effect dominates and education time falls back to the original level. Note that aggregate consumption and utility fall with higher depreciation.

(c) The appropriate base for the replacement rate is net income just before retirement, which is given by $w_s^n(1-\delta_h)^2(1+n_{e,s-2})$.

Table 7.8 Equilibrium with rising human capital depreciation

δ_h	C	e	n_e	L	K	w	r	U
0.00	0.95	0.25	1.01	2.49	0.18	0.32	1.90	−8.59
0.50	0.82	0.27	1.04	2.03	0.27	0.36	1.40	−9.21
1.00	0.73	0.25	1.00	1.75	0.32	0.42	0.99	−10.43

$g_y = n_p = 0.0$; $\xi = 2.0$; $\upsilon = 0.5$; $\mu = 1.0$; $J = 6$; $j_r = 5$.

Exercise 7.9

In this exercise, the human-capital production function also depends on public infrastructure X_t, ie schools, universities, etc.

(a) Given the new human-capital production function, optimal education investment can be computed from:

$$e_t = \left(\frac{\xi \upsilon_1 X_t^{\upsilon_2} \sum_{j=2}^{jr-1} w_s^n (1-\delta_h)^{j-2} (R_{t,s}^n)^{-1}}{w_t^n (1-\tau_t^s)} \right)^{\frac{1}{1-\upsilon_1}}.$$

To implement this numerically, we mainly have to adjust the formula for the optimal education decision in the subroutine `getedu`, as shown in Program 7.9. In the subroutine `government`, we need to account for public infrastructure costs, which are a fraction of GDP. In addition, the goods market equation needs to include X_t on the demand side in the same way as public goods consumption.

(b) With low investment in public infrastructure, the return to education is small, so that households rather work than spend time in education. When public infrastructure increases, time spent in education also rises, as does the endogenous growth rate n_e. This reduces aggregate labour supply (measured in human-capital units of the young cohort), savings, and wages. Higher outlays for infrastructure need to be financed by rising consumption taxes. When public infrastructure increases further, the negative wage effects dominates at some point, and utility starts to decrease. With the present parametrization, optimal infrastructure investment is roughly 2 per cent of GDP, as shown in the Table 7.9.

(c) The macroeconomic adjustment and the welfare effects of a rise in public infrastructure are reported in Table 7.10. When public infrastructure investment rises from 0.5 to 2 per cent of GDP, consumption taxes have to increase by two percentage points. This has a negative impact on already retired cohorts. Middle-aged cohorts, who are still working in the reform period, benefit from the increase in interest rates. The youngest cohort experience the largest positive welfare effects, because they still receive higher wages. However, higher education investment reduces savings over time, so that along

Program 7.9 Optimal education with public infrastructure

```
subroutine getedu(it)
    [......]
    e(it) = (upsi1*xi*XX(it)**upsi2*pvw/(wn(it)*&
             (1d0-taus(it))))**(1d0/(1d0-upsi1))
    if(e(it) > 0.99d0)e(it)=0.99d0

    itp = year(it, 1, 2)
    ne(itp) = mu*(1d0+xi*e(it)**upsi1*XX(it)**upsi2)-1d0
    [......]
end subroutine
```

the transition the capital stock declines and wages fall again. This causes a reduction in welfare of future cohorts relative to the young generations in period 1. Overall, however, they still gain in terms of welfare.

(d) In a small, open economy, there are no factor price reactions. Consequently, all households who were born before the reform period loose, since they have to pay higher-consumption taxes. The youngest cohort in the reform year again benefits the most. Yet, as education time hardly falls along the transition, future cohorts benefit much more than before.

Exercise 7.10

(a) This exercise is a straightforward extension of program `prog_07_04` from the book. Besides defining survival rates and the human capital profile, we also need to specify the bequest distribution scheme:

$$\Gamma_{j,s} = \frac{\omega_{b,j}}{\sum_{i=1}^{J} \omega_{b,i} m_{i,s}},$$

Table 7.9 Optimal infrastructure investment with endogenous growth

X/Y	C	τ^c	e	n_e	L	w	U
0.005	2.63	0.01	0.04	0.13	3.63	0.55	−8.530
0.010	2.26	0.01	0.05	0.21	3.45	0.52	−8.505
0.015	2.03	0.02	0.06	0.28	3.33	0.49	−8.493
0.020	**1.86**	**0.02**	**0.07**	**0.33**	**3.24**	**0.48**	**−8.489**
0.025	1.73	0.03	0.08	0.38	3.17	0.46	−8.493
0.030	1.63	0.04	0.08	0.42	3.11	0.45	−8.503

$n_p = g_y = 0.0$; $\xi = 5.0$; $\upsilon_1 = 0.2$; $\upsilon_2 = 0.7$; $\mu = 1.0$.

Table 7.10 Increasing public infrastructure with endogenous growth

t	X/Y	τ^c	e	n_e	L	K	w	r	HEV
−4									−1.96
−3									−0.31
−2									2.59
−1									3.46
0	0.005	0.01	0.04	0.13	3.63	1.65	0.55	0.52	2.80
1	0.020	0.02	0.10	0.13	3.57	1.65	0.55	0.52	12.88
2	0.020	0.02	0.08	0.42	3.25	1.26	0.53	0.58	7.22
3	0.020	0.02	0.07	0.36	3.18	1.05	0.50	0.65	3.51
⋮	⋮	⋮	⋮	⋮	⋮	⋮	⋮	⋮	⋮
∞	0.020	0.02	0.07	0.33	3.24	0.90	0.48	0.74	0.48
Δ^*									5.91

$g_y = n_p = 0.0$; $\xi = 5.0$; $\upsilon_1 = 0.2$; $\upsilon_2 = 0.7$; $\mu = 1.0$.

Program 7.10 Computing the bequest distribution

```
do it = 0, TT
    m(1, it) = 1d0
    GAM(1, it) = omebeq(1)
    itm = year(it, 2, 1)
    do ij = 2, JJ
        m(ij, it) = m(ij-1, itm)*psi(ij, it)/(1d0+n_p(it))
        GAM(1, it) = GAM(1, it) + omebeq(ij)*m(ij, it)
    enddo
    do ij = JJ, 1, -1
        GAM(ij, it) = omebeq(ij)/GAM(1, it)
    enddo
enddo
```

which is derived in subroutine `initialize`, Program 7.10. We set $\omega_{b,1} = \omega_{b,2} = 0.5$ and $\omega_{b,3} = \omega_{b,4} = 0.25$. The simulation results are not reported, since they are qualitatively similar, as in all previous pension reforms reported here and in the book.

(b) The main problem is that households have less incentives to save when they know they will die with some positive probability. When aggregate savings become too low, the interest rate rises dramatically, generating income effects that further reduce savings. In this case, it is not possible to compute an equilibrium any more. In order to stabilize the system, human capital, the population growth rate, or the survival rates have to be increased. All these measures increase aggregate savings in the economy.

Exercise 7.11

(a) We maximize the Lagrangean:

$$\mathcal{L} = \sum_{j=1}^{J} \beta^{j-1}\Psi_{1,j}\left[u(c_{j,s}) + \beta\nu(1-\psi_{j+1,s+1})u(R^n_{s+1}a_{j+1,s+1})\right]$$
$$+\sum_{j=1}^{J}\lambda_j\left[\, R^n_s a_{j,s} + w^n_{j,s} + b_{j,s} + pen_{j,s} - p_s c_{j,s} - a_{j+1,s+1}\,\right]$$

where $s = t + j - 1$ and $\Psi_{1,j} = \Pi_{i=1}^{j}\psi_{i,m}$, with $m = t + i - 1$, as in the book. From the derivatives with respect to $c_{j,s}$ and a_{j+1}, we get:

$$\beta^{j-1}\Psi_{1,j}u'(c_{j,s}) = \lambda_j p_s$$
$$\beta^{j-1}\Psi_{1,j}\beta\nu(1-\psi_{j+1,s+1})R^n_{s+1}u'(R^n_{s+1}a_{j+1,s+1}) = \lambda_j - R^n_{s+1}\lambda_{j+1}.$$

Substituting out the Lagrange multipliers and rearranging, we get:

$$\frac{u'(c_{j,s})}{p_s} = \beta R^n_{s+1}\left[\nu(1-\psi_{j+1,s+1})u'(R^n_{s+1}a_{j+1,s+1}) + \psi_{j+1,s+1}\frac{u'(c_{j+1,s+1})}{p_{s+1}}\right],$$

which implies for our CRRA utility function:

$$\frac{c_{j,s}^{-\frac{1}{\gamma}}}{p_s} = \beta R^n_{s+1}\left[\nu(1-\psi_{j+1,s+1})\left(R^n_{s+1}a_{j+1,s+1}\right)^{-\frac{1}{\gamma}} + \psi_{j+1,s+1}\frac{c_{j+1,s+1}^{-\frac{1}{\gamma}}}{p_{s+1}}\right].$$

Note that for $\nu = 0$ we can derive the same optimality conditions as in Section 7.3.1 of the book. With $\nu > 0$, the above optimality condition can be interpreted in a straightforward manner. The left-hand side shows the marginal utility cost of one unit of additional savings, while the right-hand side shows the expected marginal utility gains from additional bequest or additional consumption in the future, discounted to the present period.

(b) Given these optimality conditions, we cannot apply our usual solution procedure. The reason is that we have J non-linear equations that cannot be substituted into the intertemporal budget constraint. Consequently, we need to solve the system together

Program 7.11 Consumption path computation with bequest motives

```
subroutine get_path(ij, it)
    [......]
    real*8 :: x(JJ-ij+1), vh

    it_com = it
    ij_com = ij

    x = 0.2d0
    call fzero(x, foc, check)

    if(check) stop 'fzero did not converge'

    do ijp = ij, JJ

        vh = 0d0
        if(it == 1 .and. ij > 1)vh = v(2-ij)
        if(it >= 1 .and. ij == 1)vh = v(it)

        itp = year(it, ij, ijp)
        itm = year(it, ij, ijp+1)
        c(ijp, itp) = x(ijp-ij+1)
        a(ijp+1, itm) = Rn(itp)*a(ijp, itp) + wn(itp)*h(ijp)+ &
                        beq(ijp, itp) + pen(ijp, itp) + vh -  &
                        p(itp)*c(ijp, itp)
    enddo

end subroutine
```

with the J budget constraints for $c_{j,s}$ and $a_{j+1,s+1}$ using numerical methods. The function `fzero` from the toolbox helps us here. As before, we compute the optimal consumption path in the subroutine `get_path`, which is shown in Program 7.11. Within this subroutine, we call the subroutine `fzero`. Note that the input variable `x` to this routine is an array with a flexible length, depending on the current age `ij` of the household. We define the communication variables `it_com` and `ij_com`, which we need in function `foc` that defines the non-linear equation system. If `fzero` can solve the system, `x` contains the optimal future consumption path for the household aged `ij` in period `it`. Given initial assets `a(ij, it)`, we can compute the path of future assets from the periodic budget constraints.

Module 7.11m shows the function `foc` that defines the non-linear equation system. Note again that `cons` and `assets` have a flexible array structure. Given a guess for the consumption path from `fzero` and the initial assets `assets(ij)`, we compute the resulting path of future assets and define the non-linear equations `foc(ijp-ij+1)` from

Module 7.11m Non-linear equation system with bequest motives

```
function foc(x)

    implicit none
    real*8, intent(in) :: x(:)
    real*8 ::  foc(size(x, 1))
    real*8 :: vh, cons(ij_com:JJ), assets(ij_com:JJ+1)
    integer :: ij, itp, itm, ijp, it

    ! copy communication variable
    it = it_com
    ij = ij_com
    [......]

    ! get assets
    if(ij == 1)then
        assets(1) = 0d0
    else
        assets(ij) = a(ij, it)
    endif

    ! get consumption and assets
    do ijp = ij, JJ

        itp = year(it, ij, ijp)
        cons(ijp) = x(ijp-ij+1)
        assets(ijp+1) = Rn(itp)*assets(ijp) + wn(itp)*h(ijp)+&
                        beq(ijp, itp) + pen(ijp, itp) + vh -  &
                        p(itp)*cons(ijp)
    enddo

    ! set up focs
    do ijp = ij, JJ
        [......]
    enddo

end function
```

the optimality conditions. Note that the optimality condition in the last period of life J is different, since there is no future consumption. Compared to the model in Exercise 7.10, the model with a bequest motive can be simulated with more parameter combinations. Households now have an intrinsic incentive to save, meaning to leave bequests, so that stability problems such as in Exercise 7.10 are much less likely. Only when the bequest motive becomes very weak will there be problems with finding an equilibrium.

(c) Households receive utility from leaving bequests, meaning that they are not altruistic in the sense that they care for their descendants. Consequently, as in the model without a bequest motive, they reduce savings after the introduction of the pay-as-you-go pension system. This reduces bequest, which hurts future cohorts. If they were truly altruistic towards their descendants, current households would increase bequests in order to neutralize the intergenerational redistribution induced by an increase in pension benefits.

8 Introduction to dynamic programming

Exercise 8.1

In this exercise, we show that *Bellman's Principle of Optimality* holds in our cake-eating problem. Hence, an optimal policy has the property that, no matter what the decisions $\{c_v\}_{v=0}^{t-1}$ prior to a date t have been, the remaining decisions $\{c_v\}_{v=t}^{\infty}$ must constitute an optimal policy with regard to the state a_t resulting from the previous decisions.

For the maximization problem:

$$\max_{\{c_v\}_{v=t}^{\infty}} \; U_t = \sum_{v=t}^{\infty} \beta^{v-t} u(c_v) \quad \text{s.t.} \quad \sum_{v=t}^{\infty} c_v = a_t \tag{8.1}$$

we write the Lagrangean as:

$$\mathcal{L} = \sum_{v=t}^{\infty} \beta^{v-t} u(c_v) + \lambda \left[a_t - \sum_{v=t}^{\infty} c_v \right]$$

in order to obtain the first-order conditions:

$$\beta^{v-t} u'(c_v) = \lambda \quad \Rightarrow \quad \beta^{v-t} u'(c_v) = u'(c_t).$$

Consequently, the solution $\{c_v^*\}_{v=t}^{\infty}$ to this problem is fully described by:

$$\beta^{v-t} u'(c_v^*) = u'(c_t^*) \quad \text{together with} \quad a_t = \sum_{v=t}^{\infty} c_v^*.$$

Now let us take a look at the optimization problem:

$$\max_{c_t, a_{t+1}} \; u(c_t) + \beta \max_{\{c_v\}_{v=t+1}^{\infty}} U_{t+1}$$
$$\text{s.t.} \; a_{t+1} = a_t - c_t \; \text{and} \; \sum_{v=t+1}^{\infty} c_v = a_{t+1}. \tag{8.2}$$

From the above discussion, we know that the solution to:

$$\max_{\{c_v\}_{v=t+1}^{\infty}} U_{t+1} \quad \text{s.t.} \quad \sum_{v=t+1}^{\infty} c_v = a_{t+1}$$

has the property:

$$\beta^{v-(t+1)} u'(c_v^*) = u'(c_{t+1}^*) \quad \text{with} \quad a_{t+1} = \sum_{v=t+1}^{\infty} c_v^*.$$

The total differential of the budget constraint reads:

$$da_{t+1} = \sum_{v=t+1}^{\infty} dc_v^* \quad \Leftrightarrow \quad \sum_{v=t+1}^{\infty} \frac{dc_v^*}{da_{t+1}} = 1.$$

Let us now plug the optimal solution $\{c_v^*\}_{v=t+1}^{\infty}$ as well as the constraint $c_t = a_t - a_{t+1}$ into the optimization problem (8.2) and write:

$$\max_{a_{t+1}} \quad u(a_t - a_{t+1}) + \beta \sum_{v=t+1}^{\infty} \beta^{v-(t+1)} u(c_v^*).$$

Differentiating with respect to a_{t+1} and setting to zero yields:

$$\begin{aligned}
& -u'(c_t^*) + \beta \sum_{v=t+1}^{\infty} \beta^{v-(t+1)} u'(c_v^*) \cdot \frac{dc_v^*}{da_{t+1}^*} = 0 \\
\Leftrightarrow \quad & -u'(c_t^*) + \beta u'(c_{t+1}^*) \cdot \underbrace{\sum_{v=t+1}^{\infty} \frac{dc_v^*}{da_{t+1}}}_{=1} = 0 \\
\Leftrightarrow \quad & u'(c_t) = \beta u'(c_{t+1}).
\end{aligned}$$

So obviously, the solution to (8.2) has the property:

$$\beta^{v-t} u'(c_v^*) = u'(c_t^*) \quad \text{together with} \quad a_t = c_t^* + a_{t+1} = \sum_{v=t}^{\infty} c_v^*.$$

Therefore, the solutions to (8.1) and (8.2) are identical.

Exercise 8.2

We set up the Lagrangean of the problem as:

$$\mathcal{L} = \sum_{t=0}^{\infty} \beta^t \frac{c_t^{1-\frac{1}{\gamma}}}{1-\frac{1}{\gamma}} + \lambda \left[\sum_{t=0}^{\infty} \frac{w}{(1+r)^t} - \sum_{t=0}^{\infty} \frac{c_t}{(1+r)^t} \right].$$

The first-order conditions are:

$$\frac{\partial \mathcal{L}}{\partial c_t} = \beta^t \cdot c_t^{-\frac{1}{\gamma}} - \frac{\lambda}{(1+r)^t} = 0 \quad \text{for all } t = 0, 1, 2, \ldots, \infty.$$

Using these first-order conditions, we find that:

$$[\beta(1+r)]^t c_t^{-\frac{1}{\gamma}} = [\beta(1+r)]^{t-1} c_{t-1}^{-\frac{1}{\gamma}} = \ldots = c_0^{-\frac{1}{\gamma}}$$

$$\Leftrightarrow \quad c_t = [\beta(1+r)]^{\gamma} c_{t-1} = \ldots = [\beta(1+r)]^{t\gamma} c_0.$$

We can substitute this into the constraint and immediately obtain:

$$\sum_{t=0}^{\infty} \frac{w}{(1+r)^t} = \frac{w(1+r)}{r} = \sum_{t=0}^{\infty} \frac{[\beta(1+r)]^{t\gamma} c_0}{(1+r)^t}$$

$$= c_0 \cdot \sum_{t=0}^{\infty} \left(\beta^{\gamma}(1+r)^{\gamma-1}\right)^t = \frac{c_0}{1-\beta^{\gamma}(1+r)^{\gamma-1}}.$$

Note that, in order to be able to use the convergence properties of the geometric series, we require:

$$r > 0 \quad \text{and} \quad 0 \leq \beta^{\gamma}(1+r)^{\gamma-1} < 1 \quad \Leftrightarrow \quad 0 \leq [\beta(1+r)]^{\gamma} < 1 + r.$$

Consequently, the optimal solution to the dynamic optimization problem is given by:

$$c_t = [\beta(1+r)]^{t\gamma} \cdot \left[1 + r - [\beta(1+r)]^{\gamma}\right] \cdot \frac{w}{r}.$$

In the special case of $\beta(1+r) = 1$, we obtain $c_t = w$.

Exercise 8.3

In order to determine what the value function looks like, a useful starting point is to ask at which wealth level a consumption converges to zero. Looking at the periodical budget constraint:

$$(1+r)a + w = c + a^+,$$

we see that for a constant wealth level $a = a^+$ we have $c = ra + w$. Consequently, setting $c = 0$ yields $a = -\frac{w}{r}$.

Two things follow from this:

(i) The individual level of wealth a can never be smaller than $-\frac{w}{r}$ (negative a means that the household is indebted), as otherwise the household wouldn't be able to repay his debt anymore.

(ii) As a approaches $-\frac{w}{r}$, c will have to converge to 0, since the agent is running out of resources.

As a result, the value function should converge to $-\infty$, as a approaches $-\frac{w}{r}$. One candidate that exhibits this behaviour is:

$$V(a) = B \cdot \frac{\left[a + \frac{w}{r}\right]^{1-\frac{1}{\gamma}}}{1-\frac{1}{\gamma}}.$$

We can now apply the same guess-and-verify strategy as in the book. We therefore first solve the maximization problem:

$$V(a) = \max_{c,a^+} \frac{c^{1-\frac{1}{\gamma}}}{1-\frac{1}{\gamma}} + \beta B \cdot \frac{\left[a^+ + \frac{w}{r}\right]^{1-\frac{1}{\gamma}}}{1-\frac{1}{\gamma}} \quad \text{s.t.} \quad (1+r)a + w = c + a^+.$$

The first-order conditions lead us directly to:

$$c = (\beta B)^{-\gamma}\left[a^+ + \frac{w}{r}\right].$$

Plugging this into the budget constraint yields:

$$\begin{aligned}(1+r)a + w &= (\beta B)^{-\gamma}\left[a^+ + \frac{w}{r}\right] + a^+ \\ &= (\beta B)^{-\gamma}\left[a^+ + \frac{w}{r}\right] + a^+ + \frac{w}{r} - \frac{w}{r} \\ \Leftrightarrow \quad (1+r)a + w + \frac{w}{r} &= \left[1 + (\beta B)^{-\gamma}\right]\left[a^+ + \frac{w}{r}\right]\end{aligned}$$

$$
\begin{aligned}
\Leftrightarrow \quad & (1+r)\left[a+\frac{w}{r}\right] = \left[1+(\beta B)^{-\gamma}\right]\left[a^{+}+\frac{w}{r}\right] \\
\Leftrightarrow \quad & \left[a^{+}+\frac{w}{r}\right] = \frac{(1+r)\left[a+\frac{w}{r}\right]}{1+(\beta B)^{-\gamma}} \\
& = \frac{(\beta B)^{\gamma}(1+r)\left[a+\frac{w}{r}\right]}{1+(\beta B)^{\gamma}}.
\end{aligned}
$$

Consequently, we have:

$$
c = \frac{(1+r)\left[a+\frac{w}{r}\right]}{1+(\beta B)^{\gamma}}.
$$

We can plug this into the value function and obtain:

$$
\begin{aligned}
V(a) &= \left\{\left[\frac{(1+r)}{1+(\beta B)^{\gamma}}\right]^{1-\frac{1}{\gamma}} + \beta B \cdot \left[\frac{(\beta B)^{\gamma}(1+r)}{1+(\beta B)^{\gamma}}\right]^{1-\frac{1}{\gamma}}\right\} \cdot \frac{\left[a+\frac{w}{r}\right]^{1-\frac{1}{\gamma}}}{1-\frac{1}{\gamma}} \\
&= (1+r)^{1-\frac{1}{\gamma}} \cdot \left[\frac{1+(\beta B)^{\gamma}}{\left[1+(\beta B)^{\gamma}\right]^{1-\frac{1}{\gamma}}}\right] \cdot \frac{\left[a+\frac{w}{r}\right]^{1-\frac{1}{\gamma}}}{1-\frac{1}{\gamma}} \\
&= (1+r)^{1-\frac{1}{\gamma}} \cdot \left[1+(\beta B)^{\gamma}\right]^{\frac{1}{\gamma}} \cdot \frac{\left[a+\frac{w}{r}\right]^{1-\frac{1}{\gamma}}}{1-\frac{1}{\gamma}} \stackrel{!}{=} B \cdot \frac{\left[a+\frac{w}{r}\right]^{1-\frac{1}{\gamma}}}{1-\frac{1}{\gamma}}.
\end{aligned}
$$

Comparing this with the above guess for the value function, we find that:

$$
\begin{aligned}
& B = (1+r)^{1-\frac{1}{\gamma}} \cdot \left[1+(\beta B)^{\gamma}\right]^{\frac{1}{\gamma}} \\
\Leftrightarrow \quad & B^{\gamma} = (1+r)^{\gamma-1} \cdot \left[1+(\beta B)^{\gamma}\right] \\
\Leftrightarrow \quad & B^{\gamma} = (1+r)^{\gamma-1} + (1+r)^{\gamma-1}(\beta B)^{\gamma} \\
\Leftrightarrow \quad & B^{\gamma} \cdot \left[1-(1+r)^{\gamma-1}\beta^{\gamma}\right] = (1+r)^{\gamma-1} \\
\Leftrightarrow \quad & B^{\gamma} = \frac{(1+r)^{\gamma-1}}{1-(1+r)^{\gamma-1}\beta^{\gamma}} \\
\Leftrightarrow \quad & B^{\gamma} = \frac{1}{(1+r)^{1-\gamma}-\beta^{\gamma}} \\
\Leftrightarrow \quad & B = \left[(1+r)^{1-\gamma}-\beta^{\gamma}\right]^{-\frac{1}{\gamma}}.
\end{aligned}
$$

This directly leads us to:

$$
V(a) = \left[(1+r)^{1-\gamma}-\beta^{\gamma}\right]^{-\frac{1}{\gamma}} \cdot \frac{\left[a+\frac{w}{r}\right]^{1-\frac{1}{\gamma}}}{1-\frac{1}{\gamma}}
$$

and:

$$
\begin{aligned}
c(a) &= \frac{(1+r)\left[a+\frac{w}{r}\right]}{1+\beta^{\gamma}\cdot\left[(1+r)^{1-\gamma}-\beta^{\gamma}\right]^{-1}} \\
&= \frac{\left[(1+r)^{1-\gamma}-\beta^{\gamma}\right]\cdot(1+r)\left[a+\frac{w}{r}\right]}{(1+r)^{1-\gamma}-\beta^{\gamma}+\beta^{\gamma}} \\
&= \frac{\left[(1+r)^{1-\gamma}-\beta^{\gamma}\right]\cdot(1+r)\left[a+\frac{w}{r}\right]}{(1+r)^{1-\gamma}} \\
&= \left[(1+r)^{1-\gamma}-\beta^{\gamma}\right]\cdot(1+r)^{\gamma}\cdot\left[a+\frac{w}{r}\right] \\
&= \left[1+r-[\beta(1+r)]^{\gamma}\right]\cdot\left[a+\frac{w}{r}\right].
\end{aligned}
$$

Finally, substituting $c(a)$ in the budget constraint yields:

$$
\begin{aligned}
a^{+}(a) &= (1+r)a+w-\left[1+r-[\beta(1+r)]^{\gamma}\right]\cdot\left[a+\frac{w}{r}\right] \\
a^{+}(a)+\frac{w}{r} &= (1+r)a+w+\frac{w}{r}-\left[1+r-[\beta(1+r)]^{\gamma}\right]\cdot\left[a+\frac{w}{r}\right] \\
a^{+}(a)+\frac{w}{r} &= (1+r)\left[a+\frac{w}{r}\right]-\left[1+r-[\beta(1+r)]^{\gamma}\right]\cdot\left[a+\frac{w}{r}\right] \\
a^{+}(a) &= [\beta(1+r)]^{\gamma}\cdot\left[a+\frac{w}{r}\right]-\frac{w}{r}.
\end{aligned}
$$

Exercise 8.4

The solution to this exercise builds upon program `prog08_05` from the book. The problem in this exercise differs from the simple cake-eating problem in that it now features a periodical wage income w and an interest rate r that is paid on savings, so that the dynamic programming problem is given by:

$$
V(a) = \max_{c,a^{+}} \frac{c^{1-\frac{1}{\gamma}}}{1-\frac{1}{\gamma}} + \beta V(a^{+}) \quad \text{s.t.} \quad (1+r)a+w = c+a^{+}.
$$

Solving this problem is slightly more complicated than before. In particular, we have to think more carefully about the lower bound a_l and the upper bound a_u of the interval we choose to discretize the asset state space.

If an individual's preferences imply a decreasing consumption path over time, meaning $\beta > \frac{1}{(1+r)}$ like in the initial parameterization with $\beta = 0.975$ and $r = 0.02$, setting the lower bound is straightforward: individuals need to have positive consumption throughout their entire life, so that they are constrained not to take out loans higher than the discounted sum of their future income stream. The lower bound of the asset grid is thus given by $a_l = -\frac{w}{r}$. For the upper bound of our grid, things are less clear cut. Note that we set $r = 0.03$ in our sensitivity analysis, implying an increasing consumption path over time. However, as there is no actual upper limit for the savings an individual accumulates in this case, we will face approximation errors at the upper end of the asset grid when computing the policy functions for any a_u we might set. In what follows, we therefore set up the grid symmetrically and choose $a_u = \frac{w}{r}$.

As in our baseline program `prog08_05` from the book, we initialize all relevant parameters in the module `globals`. We discretize our asset state variable using the subroutine `grid_Cons_Equi` from the toolbox and store this grid $\mathcal{A} = \{\hat{a}_0, \hat{a}_1, \ldots, \hat{a}_n\}$ in the array `a`. Afterwards, the arrays for the value function `v`, the coefficients of the spline function `coeff_v`, and the consumption policy function `c` are initialized.

In the main Program 8.4, we set up the loop for value function iteration to iterate up to a maximum of `itermax = 5000` steps and nest the loop to step through our discretized asset state space in it. Similar to program `prog08_05` in the book, we treat the gridpoint at the lower bound of the asset state separately and manually assign a high negative utility level to it. At any other gridpoint $\hat{a}_v \in \mathcal{A}$, we use the subroutine `fminsearch` to find the optimal division of available wealth $(1 + r)\hat{a}_v + w$ into current consumption $c^*(\hat{a}_v)$ and savings $a^{+,*}(\hat{a}_v)$ that maximizes an individual's value function $V(\hat{a}_v)$. We let `fminsearch` iterate over the optimal level of savings a^+, and set its lower bound to a_l and the upper bound to $\min[(1 + r)\hat{a}_v + w - a^+, a_u]$ in order to obtain only optimal levels of $a^{+,*}$ that lie within our asset grid, ie $a^+ \in [a_l, a_u]$.

Note that we rewrite our value function as illustrated in Module 8.4m to:

$$V(\hat{a}_v) = \begin{cases} u(c) + \beta V(a^+) & c \geq 1^{-10} \\ \frac{(1^{-10})^{1-\frac{1}{\gamma}}}{1-\frac{1}{\gamma}}(1 + |c|) & \text{otherwise.} \end{cases}$$

The penalty in the form of an increasing negative utility for consumption levels $c < 1^{-10}$ ensures that `fminsearch` will only return values of $a^{+,*}$ that imply positive consumption and that suffice the budget constraint. We again re-transform:

$$\frac{S(a^+)^{1-\frac{1}{\gamma}}}{1 - \frac{1}{\gamma}}$$

the spline that interpolates the future value function, as we again interpolate a transformed value function. After having determined the optimal decisions over current consumption and savings at any gridpoint, we transform the individual's value function and use the subroutine `spline_interp` in order to compute the coefficients of the spline we use for interpolation between two gridpoints. Finally, we check whether our value

Program 8.4 Solution with minimization and interpolation

```
! iterate until value function converges
do iter = 1, itermax

    ! policy and value function at a = -w/r manually
    c(0) = 0d0
    V_new(0) = 1d-10**egam/egam

    ! calculate optimal decision for every gridpoint
    do ia = 1, NA

        ! initialize starting value and
        ! communicate resource level
        x_in = a(ia)*(1d0+r) + w - c(ia)
        ia_com = ia

        call fminsearch(x_in, fret, a_l, &
                        min((1d0+r)*a(ia)+w,a_u), utility)

        ! get optimal consumption and value function
        c(ia) = a(ia)*(1d0+r) + w - x_in
        V_new(ia) = -fret

    enddo

    ! interpolate coefficients
    call spline_interp((egam*V_new)**(1d0/egam), coeff_V)

    ! get convergence level
    con_lev = maxval(abs(V_new(:) - V(:))/&
                    max(abs(V(:)), 1d-10))
    write(*,'(i5,2x,f20.7)')iter, con_lev

    ! check for convergence
    if(con_lev < sig)then
        call output()
    endif

    V = V_new
enddo
```

function meets the convergence criterion and stop the iteration procedure if this is the case. We then proceed to printing the output to the screen.

Figure 8.1 shows the decreasing consumption path for 500 periods in the case of $\beta = 0.975$ and $r = 0.02$ when individuals have a preference for immediate consumption starting with $a_0 = 0$. In this case, the numerically approximated policy and value functions come close to the analytical results from Exercise 8.3, as the borders of the grid we chose to discretize our asset space do not restrict the individual's optimal decisions. Computing the Euler equation error thus gives results in the range of 10^{-4}.

However, for an increasing consumption and savings path in the case of $\beta = 0.975$ and $r = 0.03$, our grid restricts the maximum assets an individual is able to accumulate and therefore the policy function a^+ to be smaller than a_u. The left part of Figure 8.2 shows that with an upper bound of $a_u = \frac{w}{r}$, we are able to approximate the consumption path accurately only for 360 periods. The right part of Figure 8.2 illustrates that the

Module 8.4m The value function that should be optimized

```
function utility(x_in)
    [......]
    ! calculate consumption
    cons = (1d0+r)*a(ia_com) + w - x_in

    ! calculate future utility
    vplus = max(spline_eval(x_in, coeff_V, &
                    a_l, a_u), 1d-10)**egam/egam

    ! get utility function
    if(cons < 1d-10)then
        utility = -1d-10**egam/egam*(1d0+abs(cons))
    else
        utility = - (cons**egam/egam + beta*vplus)
    endif

end function
```

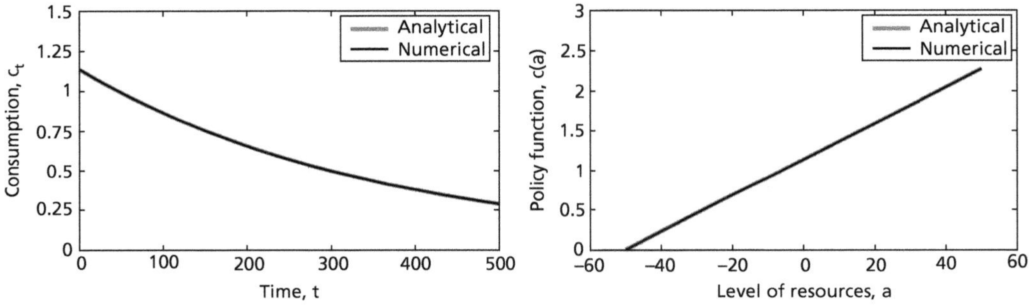

Figure 8.1 Consumption path and policy function ($\beta = 0.975$ and $r = 0.02$)

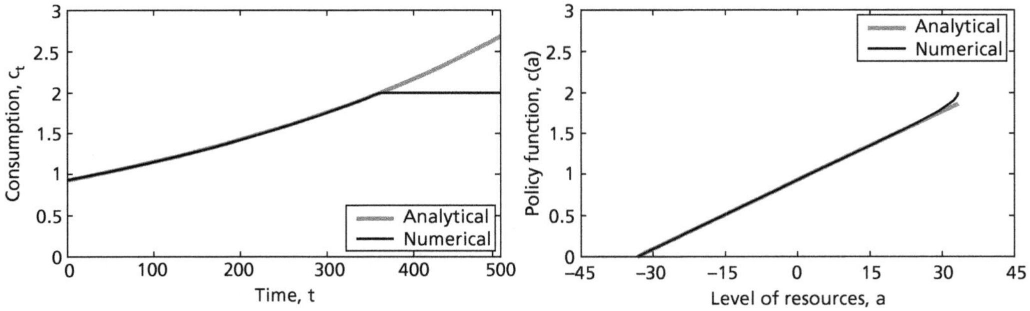

Figure 8.2 Consumption path and policy function ($\beta = 0.975$ and $r = 0.03$)

approximation error resulting from the restriction of the policy functions $a^+(\hat{a}_v)$ occurs for high levels of available resources $\hat{a}_v$. Consumption in our numerical approximation is then too high compared to the analytical solution, as the individual is forced to consume such that her assets don't increase beyond a_u. This also explains a higher Euler equation error in the range of 10^{-2}.

Exercise 8.5

In order to use root-finding and interpolation to solve our optimization problem, we first of all need to derive the first-order condition that needs to hold at any state a of the dynamic programming problem. Similar to Section 8.1.3 in the book, this is done by setting up the Lagrangean:

$$\mathcal{L} = u(c) + \beta V(a^+) + \lambda[(1+r)a + w - c - a^+],$$

which yields the first-order conditions:

$$\frac{\partial \mathcal{L}}{\partial c} = u'(c) - \lambda = 0 \quad \text{and} \quad \frac{\partial \mathcal{L}}{\partial a^+} = \beta V'(a^+) - \lambda = 0.$$

Combining both equations gives:

$$u'(c) = \beta V'(a^+)$$

as the optimal intertemporal allocation.[1] Using Bellman's principle of optimality and rewriting $V(a^+)$ as:

$$V(a^+) = \max_{a^{++}} \; u((1+r)a^+ + w - a^{++}) + \beta V(a^{++}),$$

we obtain an explicit form for the first-order condition:

$$\begin{aligned} u'(c) &= \beta(1+r)u'(c^+) \\ \Leftrightarrow \quad [\beta(1+r)]^{-\gamma}c^+(a^+) - c(a) &= 0. \end{aligned}$$

It implies that marginal utility from consumption today has to be equal to the discounted marginal utility from consumption tomorrow.

For the numerical implementation in Program 8.5, we again discretize the asset state into a finite set of gridpoints $\mathcal{A} = \{\hat{a}_0, \hat{a}_1, \ldots, \hat{a}_n\}$ using the subroutine `grid_cons_Equi`. We use the parameters as in Exercise 8.4 and, hence, set the same interval borders to $a_l = -\frac{w}{r}$ and $a_u = \frac{w}{r}$. We let the loop for our policy function iteration run up to a maximum of `itermax = 5000` steps, treat the gridpoint $\hat{a}_0$ separately by assigning consumption $c(\hat{a}_0) = 0$ to it, and require at any other gridpoint $\hat{a}_v \in \mathcal{A}$ of our discretized state space that the first-order condition holds.

[1] As the optimization problem is nicely behaved in the sense that the utility function $u(c)$ is smooth and strictly concave for non-negative consumption, this first-order condition is sufficient to identify the unique and global optimum of the value function at a certain state a. See Exercise 8.8 for a more detailed discussion.

Program 8.5 Solution with root-finding and interpolation

```
! iterate until policy function converges
do iter = 1, itermax

    c_new(0) = 0d0

    ! calculate optimal decision for every gridpoint
    do ia = 1, NA

        ! initialize starting value and communicate
        ! resource level
        x_in = a(ia)*(1d0+r) + w - c(ia)
        ia_com = ia

        call fzero(x_in, foc, check)

        ! get optimal consumption and value function
        c_new(ia) = a(ia)*(1d0+r) + w - x_in

    enddo

    ! interpolate coefficients
    call spline_interp(c_new, coeff_c)

    ! get convergence level
    con_lev = maxval(abs(c_new(:) - c(:))/&
                    max(abs(c(:)), 1d-10))
    write(*,'(i5,2x,f20.7)')iter, con_lev

    ! check for convergence
    if(con_lev < sig)then
       call output()
    endif

    c = c_new
enddo
```

The first-order condition is stored in the function `foc`, which is shown in Module 8.5m. Note that we rearranged our budget constraint for c and plugged it into the first-order condition, so that we obtain:

$$(1+r)\hat{a}_\nu + w - a^+ - [\beta(1+r)]^{-\gamma} c^+(a^+) = 0.$$

The subroutine `fzero`, hence, solves for the optimal level of future savings a^+ at any state $\hat{a}_\nu$. For any level of future savings a^+, we evaluate the spline $S(a^+)$ that interpolates the future consumption policy function between any two gridpoints on the asset grid. However, as the spline $S(a)$ is only defined on the interval $[a_l, a_u]$, we extrapolate our consumption policy function linearly beyond a_u in the form:

$$c(a^+) = S(a^+) + (a^+ - a_u)\frac{c(\hat{a}_n) - c(\hat{a}_{n-1})}{\hat{a}_n - \hat{a}_{n-1}}.$$

Module 8.5m First-order condition

```
function foc(x_in)
    [......]
    ! calculate right hand side of foc
    cplus = spline_eval(min(x_in, a_u), coeff_c, a_l, a_u)

    ! extrapolate if x_in goes beyond a_u
    if(x_in > a_u)then
        cplus = cplus + (x_in-a_u)*(c(NA)-c(NA-1))/&
                        (a(NA)-a(NA-1))
    endif

    ! get foc
    foc = (1d0+r)*a(ia_com) + w - x_in &
                - (beta*(1d0+r))**(-gamma)*cplus

end function
```

After we computed the optimal level of future savings with `fzero` for any state $\hat{a}_v$, we update the coefficients of our interpolating spline function using the subroutine `spline_interp` from the toolbox. Note that it is not necessary to transform our policy function in this exercise, as the consumption policy function is a function without curvature. In any iteration step, we again check whether our updated policy function meets convergence criteria and proceed to calling the subroutine `output` if this is the case.

Note that policy function iteration with root-finding and interpolation performs much faster than value function iteration with maximization and interpolation. This is because the root-finding subroutine `fzero` uses Newton's method to solve a non-linear equation, which is numerically considerably less costly than searching for a minimum with `fminsearch`. With respect to precision, the implementation of policy function iteration with our root-finding method yields an approximation error in the range of 10^{-5} for both the decreasing ($r = 0.02$) as well as the increasing ($r = 0.03$) consumption path. The lower Euler equation error in the case of an increasing consumption path is a

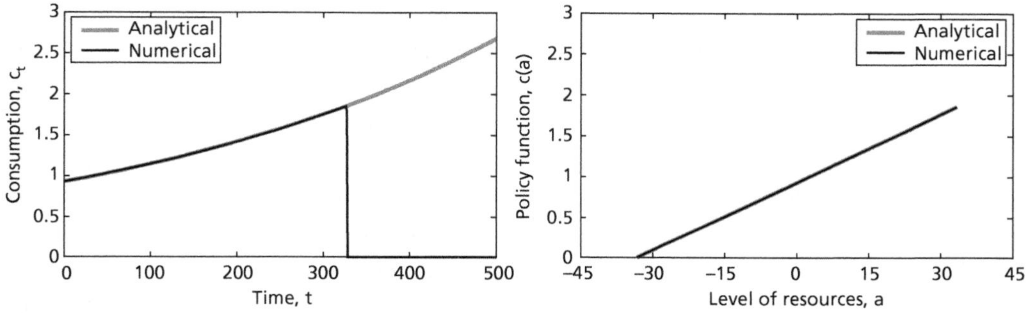

Figure 8.3 Consumption path and policy function ($\beta = 0.975$ and $r = 0.03$)

result of the extrapolation of the first-order condition for values $a^+ > a_u$. As the savings an individual can build up over time are bounded at the upper end by a_u of our asset grid, we can once again approximate the consumption path only for a limited number of periods. In contrast to Exercise 8.4, this is now only possible for 325 instead of 360 periods, as we are no longer overestimating the consumption policy function $c(a)$ for high levels of available resources a (see right part of Figure 8.3) and thus reach the upper bound a_u of our asset grid earlier.

Exercise 8.6

As in root-finding and interpolation, the endogenous gridpoint method makes use of the first-order condition we derived above and carries out the iteration on the policy function. Its crucial advantage is that we do not need to call a root-finding routine when solving the optimization problem at a gridpoint of our discretized state space. This makes it numerically a very efficient method. Instead of asking what is the optimal amount of future assets a^+ given the assets $\hat{a}_v$ available today, the method of endogenous gridpoints looks at the first-order condition the other way round: given that we save $\hat{a}_v$ to the next period, what is the corresponding consumption $c(\tilde{a}_v)$ today. According to the first-order condition, it is given by:

$$c = [\beta(1+r)]^{-\gamma} c^+(\hat{a}_v).$$

This allows us to derive the endogenous gridpoints from the dynamic resource constraint as:

$$\tilde{a}_v = \frac{\hat{a}_v + c - w}{1+r}.$$

The set of endogenous points $\{\tilde{a}_v\}_{v=0}^n$ are used together with the respective consumption values $\{c(\tilde{a}_v)\}_{v=0}^n$ to obtain the values of our consumption policy function at our exogenous grid. We do this by linearly interpolating the consumption policy function between our endogenous asset gridpoints with the subroutine `linint_Gen` from the toolbox. This subroutine is able to deal with an arbitrary set of gridpoints.

The code in Program 8.6 is very similar to regular policy function iteration. In each iteration step, we verify whether we reached convergence. If this is the case, we proceed to plot graphs to the screen and compute the Euler equation error in the output. The Euler equation error is again in the range of 10^{-5}. However, the endogenous gridpoint method now only takes a fraction of the time that policy function iteration with root-finding would need to solve the same optimization problem.

Program 8.6 Solution with endogenous gridpoints

```
! iterate until policy function converges
do iter = 1, itermax

    ! set a = 0 manually
    a_endog(0) = a_l
    c_endog(0) = 0d0

    ! calculate optimal decision for every gridpoint
    do ia = 1, NA

        ! calculate endogenous gridpoint
        ! and consumption at this point
        c_endog(ia) = c(ia)*(beta*(1d0+r))**(-gamma)
        a_endog(ia) = (a(ia) + c_endog(ia) - w)/(1d0+r)

    enddo

    ! stretch out to exogenous grid again
    do ia = 0, NA
        c_new(ia) = linint_Gen(a(ia), a_endog, c_endog, ia)
    enddo

    ! get convergence level
    con_lev = maxval(abs(c_new(:) - c(:))/&
                max(abs(c(:)), 1d-10))
    write(*,'(i5,2x,f20.7)')iter, con_lev

    ! check for convergence
    if(con_lev < sig)then
        call output()
    endif

    c = c_new
enddo
```

Exercise 8.7

The implementation of a borrowing constraint is extremely simple in the case of value function iteration with minimization and interpolation. We only have to initialize the parameter `a_borrow` in the module `globals`, restrict the grid we use to discretize our asset state, as shown in Program 8.7, and no longer assign a penalty in the form of high negative utility to the lowest gridpoint $\hat{a}_0$. The rest of our code is the same as in `sol_prog08_04`. It should be clear that the borrowing constraint only binds in the case of $\beta = 0.975$ and $r = 0.02$, ie when individuals prefer a decreasing consumption path over time and accumulate debt.

As illustrated in Figure 8.4, the borrowing constraint $\bar{a} = 5$ has an enormous impact on an individual's optimal consumption path (for $\beta = 0.975$ and $r = 0.02$), as it prevents individuals from transferring future income streams to earlier periods of their life. Forward-looking individuals that maximize their lifetime utility under this constraint are thus forced to allocate consumption from earlier to later periods of their life. Knowing

Program 8.7 Borrowing constraint with minimization and interpolation

```
! get lower and upper bound of grid
a_l = max(-w/r, -a_borrow)
a_u = w/r

! initialize a, c and value function
call grid_Cons_Equi(a, a_l, a_u)
```

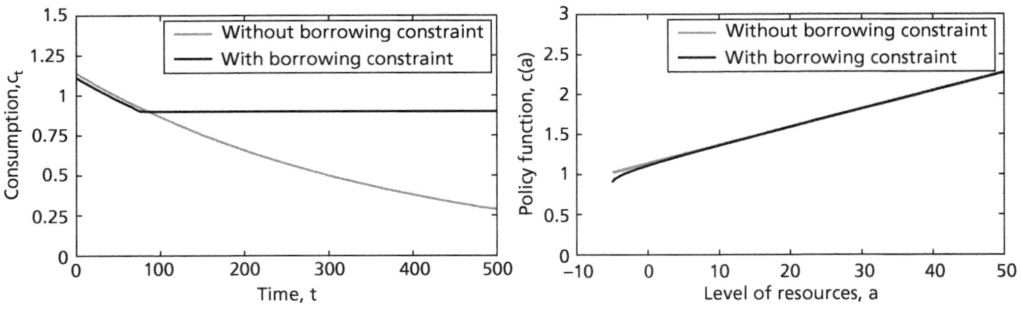

Figure 8.4 Consumption path and policy function with borrowing constraint

that the borrowing constraint will bind in the future, individuals reduce consumption immediately in order to make the budget constraint bind later and postpone utility losses from sub-optimal intertemporal allocation. Intuitively, relaxing the borrowing constraint will yield a result closer to the unconstrained consumption path over time.

Exercise 8.8

The implementation of a borrowing constraint with policy function iteration is slightly different. While the subroutine `fminsearch` allowed us to simply restrict the interval we iterate over to find the optimal a^+ in the presence of a borrowing constraint $\bar{a}$, this is not possible when using a root-finding algorithm. However, we know that our optimization problem is nicely behaved in the sense that our value and utility function are smooth and follow the standard assumptions of positive but decreasing marginal utility of consumption. With these properties at hand, it is possible to show that, as soon as the borrowing constraint is binding and the optimality condition:

$$u'(c) = \beta V(a^+)$$

does not hold anymore, the individual cannot do any better than taking out the maximum debt possible and staying at this debt level forever. In the numerical implementation in

Program 8.8 Borrowing constraint with root-finding and interpolation

```
call fzero(x_in, foc, check)
if(x_in < -a_borrow)x_in = -a_borrow
```

Program 8.8, it is thus sufficient to check whether the optimal a^+ that maximizes the first-order condition is below the level of the borrowing constraint and to choose $a^+ = -\bar{a}$ if this is the case. Once the borrowing constraint is hit, the individual consumes $c = w - r\bar{a}$ in all following periods.

Similar to Exercise 8.7, we do not treat the point $\hat{a}_0$ separately from the other points on our grid any longer and restrict the grid to be bound below by the maximum debt level $\bar{a}$ individuals are allowed to take out. The output we generate in program `sol_prog08_08` is identical to that of Figure 8.4. Again, the borrowing constraint is only binding for a decreasing consumption path over time ($\beta = 0.975$ and $r = 0.02$).

Exercise 8.9

The implementation of the endogenous gridpoint method with a borrowing constraint $\bar{a}$ is very similar to Exercise 8.6. We again start with initializing a set of exogenous gridpoints $\mathcal{A} = \{\hat{a}_0, \hat{a}_1, \ldots, \hat{a}_n\}$ to discretize our asset state, however set the lower bound of this grid to the maximum amount of debt $-\bar{a}$ individuals are allowed to take out. For any amount of assets $\hat{a}_v$ we save to the next period, we use the first-order condition:

$$c = [\beta(1+r)]^{-\gamma} c^+(\hat{a}_v)$$

to determine the corresponding consumption c today and the budget constraint to derive the respective endogenous gridpoint $\tilde{a}_v$. In order to account for the borrowing constraint, we use the result that it is optimal for an individual to take out the maximum debt possible as soon as the borrowing constraint binds. The endogenous gridpoint and the corresponding consumption level in the presence of a borrowing constraint is then given by:

$$\tilde{a}_{-1} = -\bar{a} \quad \text{and} \quad \tilde{c}_{-1} = -r\bar{a} + w.$$

We store this additional gridpoint combination in the entry `-1` of our arrays `a_endog` and `c_endog`. Before we proceed to interpolation in order to obtain our policy function $c(\hat{a}_v)$ at the exogenous gridpoints, we make sure that we only use endogenous gridpoints that lie above the borrowing constraint $\bar{a}$. This is particularly relevant for the case of an increasing consumption path over time, as the endogenous gridpoints will lie below exogenous gridpoints in this case (ie $\tilde{a}_v < \hat{a}_v$).

Program 8.9 Borrowing constraint with endogenous gridpoints

```
! choose gridpoints for interpolation
do ia = NA, -1, -1

    ! find the first endogenous gridpoint
    ! with binding constraint
    if(a_endog(ia) <= -a_borrow)then
        ia_low = ia
        exit
    endif

enddo

! stretch out to exogenous grid again
do ia = 0, NA
    c_new(ia) = linint_Gen(a(ia), &
                    a_endog(ia_low:NA), c_endog(ia_low:NA), ia)
enddo
```

Program 8.9 shows how we identify the endogenous gridpoints for which the constraint holds by walking backwards through our grid. As soon as the constraint binds, we assign the index of this endogenous gridpoint `ia` to the variable `ia_low`. When using the subroutine `linint_Gen` to interpolate our new policy function, we only use the entries from `ia_low` up to `NA`. The other parts of our numerical implementation remain the same. We iterate and update our policy function in each iteration step until convergence is reached. As soon as this is the case, we proceed to plot our output to the screen. The output is the same as in Figure 8.4 and shows how it is optimal in the presence of a borrowing constraint to postpone part of consumption to later periods in life.

9 Dynamic macro I: Infinite horizon models

Exercise 9.1

When we have population growth such that $N_{t+1} = (1 + n_p)N_t$, we have to measure variables in per capita terms of the current population. Hence, we normalize:

$$c = \frac{C_t}{N_t}, \quad k = \frac{K_t}{N_t} \quad \text{and} \quad k^+ = \frac{K_{t+1}}{N_{t+1}} = \frac{N_t}{N_{t+1}} \cdot \frac{K_{t+1}}{N_t}.$$

The problem of the social planner then changes to:

$$V(k) = \max_c \; u(c) + \beta(1 + n_p)V(k^+)$$
$$\text{s.t.} \quad (1 - \delta)k + f(k) = c + (1 + n_p)k^+.$$

Since the social planner takes into account the rising number of future households and since k^+ is measured in per capita of *future* households, the first-order condition remains unchanged, so that:

$$u'(c) = \beta[1 - \delta + f'(k^+)]u'(c^+).$$

(a) The steady state is now determined by:

$$f'(\bar{k}) = \theta + \delta \quad \text{and} \quad \bar{c} = f(\bar{k}) - (\delta + n_p)\bar{k}.$$

Under a Cobb-Douglas technology, we consequently have:

$$\bar{k} = \left[\frac{\alpha}{\delta + \theta}\right]^{\frac{1}{1-\alpha}} \quad \text{and}$$
$$\bar{c} = \left[\frac{\alpha}{\delta + \theta}\right]^{\frac{\alpha}{1-\alpha}} - (\delta + n_p)\left[\frac{\alpha}{\delta + \theta}\right]^{\frac{1}{1-\alpha}}.$$

The equilibrium capital stock does not change with the introduction of population growth, as it still is determined such that the marginal product of capital is equal to the time discount rate plus depreciation. Yet, consumption per capita declines, since additional resources are needed in order to keep the capital stock constant per capita.

(b) Compared to the implementation of policy function iteration in `prog09_01` of the book, there are hardly any changes. The only adjustment we need to make is to introduce population growth when we derive k^+ in the function `foc` and when we compute the evolution of the (per capita) capital stock over time. An increasing population growth rate leads to a downward shift in consumption over time, while setting $n_p = 0$ yields exactly the same result as the implementation of the basic Ramsey model in `prog09_01` of the book.

(c) The implementation of value function iteration shown in Program 9.1 builds upon the algorithms of Chapter 8 in the book. We use the same equidistant grid as in Part (b)

Program 9.1 Ramsey model ($n_p > 0$) and value function iteration

```
! initialize grid, policy and value function
c = k**alpha - (delta+n_p)*k
V = 0d0
coeff_v = 0d0

! iterate until value function converges
do iter = 1, itermax

    ! calculate optimal decision for every gridpoint
    do ik = 0, NK

        ! initialize starting value
        ! and communicate resource level
        x_in = ((1d0-delta)*k(ik)+k(ik)**alpha - &
                c(ik))/(1d0+n_p)
        k_com = k(ik)

        call fminsearch(x_in, fret, k_l, min((1d0-delta)* &
            k(ik)+ k(ik)**alpha, k_u), utility)

        ! get optimal consumption and value function
        c(ik) = (1d0-delta)*k(ik)+k(ik)**alpha&
                - (1d0+n_p)*x_in
        V_new(ik) = -fret

    enddo

    ! interpolate coefficients
    call spline_interp((egam*V_new)**(1d0/egam), coeff_V)

    ! get convergence level
    con_lev = maxval(abs(V_new(:) - V(:))&
                /max(abs(V(:)), 1d-10))
    write(*,'(i5,2x,f20.7)')iter, con_lev

    ! check for convergence
    if(con_lev < sig)then
        call output()
        stop
    endif

    V = V_new
enddo
```

to discretize the capital state space and initialize the arrays for our policy, as well as our value function and the coefficients of the spline we use for interpolation. In each iteration step of the fixed-point iteration, we nest a loop to step through our capital grid and the subroutine `fminsearch` use at any gridpoint to iterate over the next period capital stock k^+. The optimization problem of the social planner is given by:

$$V(\hat{k}_v) = \max_{k^+} \ u\left((1-\delta)\hat{k}_v + \hat{k}_v^\alpha - (1+n_p)k^+\right) + \beta(1+n_p)V(k^+)$$

for any $\hat{k}_v \in \mathcal{K}$. As this optimization problem is very similar to Chapter 8, the solution to the value function will again be of the form $V(k) = B \cdot \frac{k^{1-\frac{1}{\gamma}}}{1-\frac{1}{\gamma}}$. We can thus use our transformation of the value function to increase the numerical accuracy of the interpolation routine. Hence, we evaluate the spline in order to determine $V(k^+)$ in the function `utility` as:

$$V(k^+) = \frac{S\left(k^+\right)^{1-\frac{1}{\gamma}}}{1-\frac{1}{\gamma}}.$$

Note that we are again using a penalty function to ensure non-negative consumption and that setting the lower and upper bound for our grid appropriately can speed up the iteration process considerably (see Module 9.1m). After the new value function is derived for all gridpoints, we can update the spline coefficients using the subroutine `spline_interp` and check for convergence. If convergence is not reached yet, we update the value function and proceed to the next iteration step.

When we introduced value function iteration in Chapter 8 of the book, we raised the point that the convergence speed of our value function iteration procedure is closely tied

Module 9.1m The optimization problem of the social planner

```
function utility(x_in)
   [......]
   ! calculate consumption
   cons = (1d0-delta)*k_com + k_com**alpha - (1d0+n_p)*x_in

   ! calculate future utility
   vplus = max(spline_eval(x_in, coeff_V, &
                             k_l, k_u), 1d-10)**egam/egam

   ! get utility function
   if(cons < 1d-10)then
      utility = -1d-10**egam/egam*(1d0+abs(cons))
   else
      utility = - (cons**egam/egam + beta*(1d0+n_p)*vplus)
   endif

end function
```

to the discount factor for the next period's value function and that values of β close to one would result in slow convergence. Taking this one step further, it is possible to show that a discount factor of $\beta(1+n_p) > 1$, in this exercise would keep our value function iteration procedure from actually converging at all. Chapter 3 of Stokey and Lucas (1989) provides a more detailed discussion of this problem. Otherwise, the results are the same as in Part (b).

Exercise 9.2

(a) We now set $u(c) = \ln c$ and $\delta = 1$. Consequently, we have:

$$V(k) = \max_{c} \;\ln c + \beta V(k^+) \quad \text{s.t.} \quad k^\alpha = c + k^+.$$

A guess for the value function is $V(k) = A + B \ln k$. From the first-order condition, we get:

$$\frac{1}{c} = \frac{\beta B}{k^+} \quad \text{or} \quad c = \frac{k^+}{\beta B}.$$

Substituting this into the resource constraint yields, after rearranging:

$$k^+ = \frac{\beta B}{1+\beta B} \cdot k^\alpha \qquad \text{and} \qquad c = \frac{1}{1+\beta B} \cdot k^\alpha.$$

Plugging these optimal values into the value function, we obtain:

$$\begin{aligned} A + B \ln k &= \ln\left[\frac{1}{1+\beta B} k^\alpha\right] + \beta\left[A + B \ln\left(\frac{\beta B}{1+\beta B} k^\alpha\right)\right] \\ &= \underbrace{\ln\left[\frac{1}{1+\beta B}\right] + \beta\left[A + B \ln\left(\frac{\beta B}{1+\beta B}\right)\right]}_{A} + \underbrace{(\alpha + \beta B \alpha)}_{B} \ln k. \end{aligned}$$

Consequently, we have $B = \alpha + \beta B \alpha$ and therefore $B = \frac{\alpha}{1-\beta\alpha}$. Substituting this result into the definition of A, we get:

$$A = \frac{1}{1-\beta}\left[\ln(1-\beta\alpha) + \frac{\beta\alpha}{1-\beta\alpha} \ln(\beta\alpha)\right].$$

Plugging the definition of B into the policy functions finally yields:

$$k^+ = \beta\alpha k^\alpha \quad \text{and} \quad c = (1-\beta\alpha) k^\alpha.$$

Module 9.2m The numerical implementation of the first-order condition

```
function foc(x_in)
    [......]
    ! future capital
    kplus = k_com**alpha - x_in

    ! calculate future consumption
    cplus = spline_eval(kplus, coeff_c, k_l, k_u)

    ! get first-order condition
    foc = 1d0/x_in - beta*alpha*kplus**(alpha-1d0)/cplus

end function
```

(b) Implementing the simplified growth model with policy function iteration is straightforward. The new first-order condition reads:

$$\frac{1}{c} = \beta\alpha k^{\alpha-1}\frac{1}{c^+}.$$

We then use the subroutine `fzero` to search for the optimal level of consumption c^* at any gridpoint $\hat{k}_v$. The first-order condition `foc` is shown in Module 9.2m. To interpolate our policy function between two gridpoints on the capital grid, we use the coefficients of our spline, which are stored in the array `coeff_c`. These coefficients are updated in each iteration step of our policy function iteration procedure. As soon as convergence is reached, we stop iterating and print the output to the screen.

(c) For value function iteration, we now determine a spline function that satisfies:

$$S(\hat{k}_v) = V(\hat{k}_v) \quad \text{for all } v = 0, \ldots, n,$$

so that the optimization problem now reads:

$$V_{new}(\hat{k}_v) = \max_{k^+} \ \ln\left(\hat{k}_v^{\alpha} - k^+\right) + \beta S\left(k^+\right).$$

The actual numerical implementation follows the same concept as in Exercise 9.1. The difference is in particular the simpler intertemporal budget constraint and that we no longer need to account for population growth in our value function. However, note that we still assign a penalty on negative consumption valued (see Module 9.2m.a). The computation of the Euler equation error is shown in Program 9.2.a. We set up a very dense grid with `n_err=10000` and then derive the maximum error of the spline approximation compared to the analytical solution. For both policy and value function iteration, the Euler equation error is in the range of 10^{-5}, whereas policy function iteration is a lot faster than value function iteration.

Module 9.2m.a The value function which is optimized

```
function utility(x_in)
    [......]
    ! calculate consumption
    cons = k_com**alpha - x_in

    ! calculate future utility
    vplus = spline_eval(x_in, coeff_V, k_l, k_u)

    ! get utility function
    if(cons < 1d-10)then
        utility = 1d10*(1d0+abs(cons))
    else
        utility = - (log(cons) + beta*vplus)
    endif

end function
```

Program 9.2.a Computing the Euler equation error

```
! calculate euler equation error
err = 0d0
do ik = 0, n_err
    k_com = k_l + (k_u-k_l)*dble(ik)/dble(n_err)
    c_err = spline_eval(k_com, coeff_c, k_l, k_u)
    err_temp = abs(foc(c_err)/c_err)
    if(err_temp > err)err = err_temp
enddo
write(*,'(a, es15.7)')'Euler equation error:',err
```

Exercise 9.3

(a) We can write this problem in dynamic programming form as:

$$V(k) = \max_{k_c, k^+} \frac{[(k_c)^{\alpha_c}]^{1-\frac{1}{\gamma}}}{1-\frac{1}{\gamma}} + \beta V(k^+) \quad \text{s.t.} \quad k^+ = (1-\delta)k + (k-k_c)^{\alpha_i}.$$

The Lagrangean of the problem reads:

$$\mathcal{L} = \frac{[(k_c)^{\alpha_c}]^{1-\frac{1}{\gamma}}}{1-\frac{1}{\gamma}} + \beta V(k^+) + \lambda\Big[(1-\delta)k + (k-k_c)^{\alpha_i} - k^+\Big].$$

Taking first derivatives yields:

$$\begin{aligned}
\frac{\partial \mathcal{L}}{\partial k_c} &= (k_c)^{-\frac{\alpha_c}{\gamma}} \cdot \alpha_c (k_c)^{\alpha_c - 1} - \lambda \left[\alpha_i (k-k_c)^{\alpha_i - 1}\right] = 0 \\
\frac{\partial \mathcal{L}}{\partial k^+} &= \beta V'(k^+) - \lambda = 0,
\end{aligned}$$

so that we get:

$$(k_c)^{-\frac{\alpha_c}{\gamma}} \cdot \frac{\alpha_c}{\alpha_i} \cdot \frac{(k_c)^{\alpha_c-1}}{(k-k_c)^{\alpha_i-1}} = \lambda = \beta V'(k^+)$$

as optimality condition. The envelope theorem tells us that:

$$\begin{aligned} V'(k^+) &= \Big[1-\delta+\alpha_i(k^+-k_c^+)^{\alpha_i-1}\Big]\lambda^+ \\ &= \Big[1-\delta+\alpha_i(k^+-k_c^+)^{\alpha_i-1}\Big]\cdot (k_c^+)^{-\frac{\alpha_c}{\gamma}} \cdot \frac{\alpha_c}{\alpha_i} \cdot \frac{(k_c^+)^{\alpha_c-1}}{(k^+-k_c^+)^{\alpha_i-1}}. \end{aligned}$$

This finally yields the first-order condition:

$$k_c = \left\{\beta\Big[1-\delta+\alpha_i(k^+-k_c^+)^{\alpha_i-1}\Big]\left(\frac{k_c}{k_c^+}\right)^{1-\alpha_c}\left(\frac{k^+-k_c^+}{k-k_c}\right)^{1-\alpha_i}\right\}^{-\frac{\gamma}{\alpha_c}} \cdot k_c^+,$$

which needs to be solved under the law of motion for capital:

$$k^+ = (1-\delta)k + (k-k_c)^{\alpha_i}.$$

In the steady state, we need to have $\delta k = k_i^{\alpha_i}$ and $k = k_c + k_i$ as well as:

$$1 = \left\{\beta\Big[1-\delta+\alpha_i(k-k_c)^{\alpha_i-1}\Big]\right\}^{-\frac{\gamma}{\alpha_c}}.$$

Program 9.3 Policy function iteration with two sectors

```
! iterate until policy function converges
do iter = 1, itermax

    call spline_interp(kc, coeff_kc)

    ! calculate optimal decision for every gridpoint
    do ik = 0, NK

        ! initialize starting value
        ! and communicate resource level
        x_in = kc(ik)
        k_com = k(ik)

        ! find the optimal consumption level
        call fzero(x_in, foc, check)
        if(check)write(*,*)'ERROR IN ROOTFINDING PROCESS'

        ! get optimal consumption and value function
        kc_new(ik) = x_in

    enddo
    [......]
    kc = kc_new

enddo
```

The last equation can be simplified to $k_i = \left(\frac{\alpha_i}{1/\beta-1+\delta}\right)^{\frac{1}{1-\alpha_i}}$. Given k_i, we can derive the capital stocks k and k_c as well as c and i.

(b) We use policy function iteration in order to calculate the optimal amount of capital $k_c(k)$ the social planner should allocate to the production of the consumption good in our economy (see Program 9.3). In the main program, we start with initializing the capital grid that is stored in the array `k` and setting up an initial guess for the policy function in the array `kc`. Owing to the higher complexity of this optimization problem, providing intelligent parameterizations for both is crucial for the convergence properties of our iteration procedure. The boundaries k_l and k_u should be chosen to guarantee that both the starting value k_0 and the new steady-state $\bar{k}$ lie within the interval bounds. It proves useful to use the steady-state values as initial guess for all gridpoints. Each iteration step starts with the computation of the spline coefficients we use to interpolate our policy function. At each gridpoint $\hat{k}_v \in \mathcal{K}$, we then use the subroutine `fzero` to find the root of the first-order condition from above that is stored in the function `foc` (see Module 9.3m). Within this function, we first make sure that $0 < k_c < k$ holds. We then compute k^+ from the budget constraint of the economy and compute $k_c^+(k^+)$ from the spline function. For k_c^+, we once again ensure that the restriction $0 < k_c^+ < k^+$ holds. With k_c and k_c^+, we calculate the residual of the first-order condition.

After we have obtained the optimal values of $k_c(\hat{k}_v)$ at all gridpoints and stored them in the array `kc_new`, we proceed to check for convergence and continue with plotting our results if this is the case. Otherwise, we update `kc` and move on to the next iteration step. For generating output, we now define the new arrays `kc_t(0:TT)` and `ki_t(0:TT)` for the two capital inputs k_c and k_i. The left part of Figure 9.1 shows the convergence of

Module 9.3m The function carrying the first-order condition

```
function foc(x_in)
    [......]
    ! limit current consumption capital
    kc = max(x_in, 1d-10)
    kc = min(kc, k_com-1d-10)

    ! future capital
    kplus = (1d0-delta)*k_com + (k_com-kc)**alpha_i

    ! calculate future consumption
    kcplus = spline_eval(kplus, coeff_kc, k_l, k_u)
    kcplus = max(kcplus, 1d-10)
    kcplus = min(kcplus, kplus-1d-10)

    ! get first-order condition
    foc = kc - (beta*(1d0-delta+alpha_i*(kplus-kcplus)&
            **(alpha_i-1d0))*(kc/kcplus)**(1d0-alpha_c)&
            *((kplus-kcplus)/(k_com-kc))**(1d0-alpha_i))&
            **(-gamma/alpha_c)*kcplus

end function
```

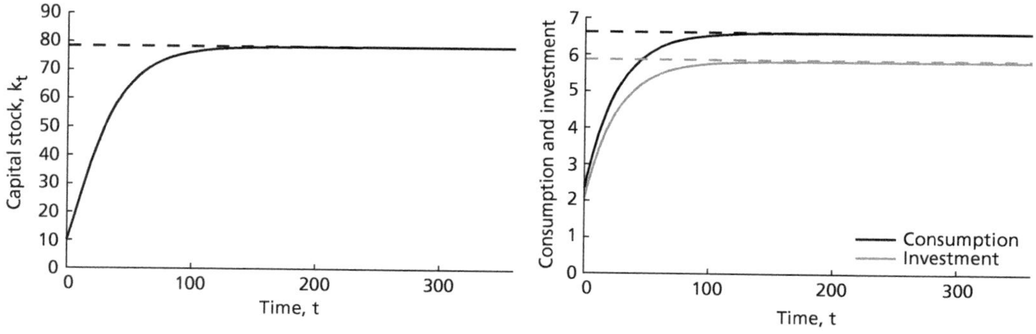

Figure 9.1 Convergence of k, c, and i to the steady state

the capital stock k to the steady-state capital stock $\bar{k}$ and the right part the convergence of consumption c and investment i to steady-state values. The results of a sensitivity analysis are intuitive. A higher α_c leads to a higher steady-state consumption $\bar{c}$, while a higher α_i leads to a higher steady-state investment $\bar{i}$.

Exercise 9.4

(a) We can write this problem in dynamic programming form as:

$$V(k) = \max_{c,l,k^+} \quad u(c, 1-l) + \beta V(k^+) \text{ s.t. } k^+ = (1-\delta)k + k^\alpha l^{1-\alpha} - c$$

with:

$$u(c, 1-l) = \frac{\left[c^\nu (1-l)^{1-\nu}\right]^{1-\frac{1}{\gamma}}}{1-\frac{1}{\gamma}}.$$

The Lagrangean of the problem reads:

$$\mathcal{L} = u(c, 1-l) + \beta V(k^+) + \lambda \Big[(1-\delta)k + k^\alpha l^{1-\alpha} - c - k^+ \Big].$$

The first-order conditions are:

$$\frac{\partial \mathcal{L}}{\partial c} = \frac{\nu}{c} \cdot \left[c^\nu (1-l)^{1-\nu}\right]^{1-\frac{1}{\gamma}} - \lambda = 0$$

$$\frac{\partial \mathcal{L}}{\partial l} = \frac{1-\nu}{1-l} \cdot \left[c^\nu (1-l)^{1-\nu}\right]^{1-\frac{1}{\gamma}} - \lambda(1-\alpha)\left(\frac{k}{l}\right)^\alpha = 0$$

$$\frac{\partial \mathcal{L}}{\partial k^+} = \beta V'(k^+) - \lambda = 0$$

with:

$$V'(k^+) = \left[1 + \alpha\left(\frac{k^+}{l^+}\right)^{\alpha-1} - \delta\right]\frac{\nu \cdot \left[(c^+)^\nu(1-l^+)^{1-\nu}\right]^{1-\frac{1}{\gamma}}}{c^+}.$$

We therefore get:

$$\frac{\nu \cdot \left[c^\nu(1-l)^{1-\nu}\right]^{1-\frac{1}{\gamma}}}{c} = \beta V'(k^+)$$

$$c = \frac{\nu}{1-\nu}\cdot(1-l)\cdot(1-\alpha)\left(\frac{k}{l}\right)^\alpha.$$

(b) In the steady state, the two optimality conditions and the resource constraint are:

$$1 = \beta\left[1 + \alpha\left(\frac{k}{l}\right)^{\alpha-1} - \delta\right]$$

$$c = \frac{\nu}{1-\nu}\cdot(1-l)\cdot(1-\alpha)\left(\frac{k}{l}\right)^\alpha$$

$$c = k^\alpha l^{1-\alpha} - \delta k.$$

From there we can derive:

$$\frac{l}{k} = \left\{\left(\frac{1}{\beta} - 1 + \delta\right)\alpha^{-1}\right\}^{\frac{1}{1-\alpha}} \qquad (I)$$

$$\frac{c}{k} = \left(\frac{l}{k}\right)^{1-\alpha} - \delta \qquad (II)$$

$$k = \left\{\frac{c}{k}\left(\frac{l}{k}\right)^\alpha \frac{1-\nu}{\nu(1-\alpha)} + \frac{l}{k}\right\}^{-1} \qquad (III).$$

Plugging (*I*) and (*II*) into (*III*) yields the steady-state capital stock $\bar{k}$, from which we can compute steady-state labour supply $\bar{l}$ and steady-state consumption $\bar{c}$ (see Program 9.4).

Program 9.4 Computation of the steady state

```
! analytical solution
lk = ((1d0/beta-1d0+delta)/alpha)**(1d0/(1d0-alpha))
ck = lk**(1d0-alpha) - delta
k_stat = (ck*(1d0-nu)*lk**alpha/(nu*(1d0-alpha)) + lk)**(-1d0)
l_stat = lk*k_stat
c_stat = ck*k_stat
y_stat = k_stat**alpha*l_stat**(1d0-alpha)
```

Module 9.4m The function carrying the first-order condition

```
function focs(x_in)
    [......]
    k_temp = x_in(1)
    l_temp = max(min(x_in(2), 1d0-1d-10), 1d-10)

    focs(1) = nu/(1d0-nu)*(1d0-l_temp)/k_temp*(1d0-alpha) &
              - l_temp/k_temp &
              + delta*(l_temp/k_temp)**alpha
    focs(2) = 1d0 - beta*(1d0+alpha* &
              (k_temp/l_temp)**(alpha-1d0)-delta)

end function
```

To compute the steady-state numerically, we plug the budget constraint into the first-order condition and use `fzero` to find the equilibrium labour supply $\bar{l}$ and capital stock $\bar{k}$. To do so, we provide the first-order conditions:

$$\frac{\nu(1-\alpha)}{1-\nu}\frac{1-l}{k} - \frac{l}{k} + \delta\left(\frac{l}{k}\right)^{\alpha} = 0 \quad \text{and}$$

$$1 - \beta\left(1 + \alpha\left(\frac{k}{l}\right)^{\alpha-1} - \delta\right) = 0$$

in the function `focs`, together with an array of initial guesses `x_in` to the subroutine `fzero`. The function `focs` is shown in Module 9.4m.

(c) For a value function iteration procedure, we again use a transformed spline interpolation between two gridpoints, so that:

$$S(\hat{k}_\nu) = \left[\left(1-\frac{1}{\gamma}\right)V(\hat{k}_\nu)\right]^{\frac{1}{1-\frac{1}{\gamma}}}$$

for all $\nu = 0, \ldots, n$. At each gridpoint $\hat{k}_\nu$, we then apply the subroutine `fminsearch` and iterate over the optimal labour supply l to solve the optimization problem of the social planner, which is given by:

$$V(\hat{k}_\nu) = \max_{l}\ u(c, 1-l) + \beta\frac{S(k^+)^{1-\frac{1}{\gamma}}}{1-\frac{1}{\gamma}} \quad \text{s.t.}$$

$$l \in [0, 1]$$

$$c = \frac{\nu}{1-\nu}\cdot(1-l)\cdot(1-\alpha)\left(\frac{\hat{k}_\nu}{l}\right)^{\alpha} \quad \text{and}$$

$$k^+ = (1-\delta)\hat{k}_\nu + (\hat{k}_\nu)^{\alpha} l^{1-\alpha} - c.$$

The first constraint captures that individuals cannot supply negative labour or more than their time-endowment permits, the second constraint is the first-order condition

Module 9.4m.a The optimization problem

```
function utility(x_in)
    [......]
    ! labor supply must be between 0 and 1
    lab = max(min(x_in, 1d0-1d-10), 1d-10)

    ! calculate current consumption
    cons = nu/(1d0-nu)*(1d0-lab)*(1d0-alpha)* &
                    (k_com/lab)**alpha
    cons_lim = max(cons, 1d-10)

    ! calculate future capital
    kplus = (1d0-delta)*k_com + k_com**alpha* &
                    lab**(1d0-alpha) - cons
    kplus_lim = max(min(kplus, k_u), k_l)

    ! calculate future utility
    vplus = max(spline_eval(kplus_lim, coeff_V, &
                    k_l, k_u), 1d-10)**egam/egam

    ! get utility function
    utility = -((cons**nu*(1d0-lab)**(1d0-nu))&
                    **egam/egam + beta*vplus)

    ! penalty for negtive consumption
    ! and kplus outside of [k_l, k_u]
    utility = utility &
              + abs(cons-cons_lim) + abs(kplus-kplus_lim)

end function
```

to derive the corresponding consumption level, and finally k^+ is determined from the intertemporal budget constraint of the social planner. In the function that should be optimized (see Module 9.4m.a), we restrict k^+ to lie in the interval $[k_l, k_u]$ and consumption to be non-negative. The method we use here differs from the penalty we used before with value function iteration in that we simply restrict our variables with **min** and **max** commands and assign a penalty to our value function in the form of the absolute value of the difference to the unrestricted solution. This has the advantage that the penalty no longer induces a discontinuity, but instead only a kink. The remaining set up of the value function iteration procedure is left unchanged. In any iteration step, we update the coefficients `coeff_V` for spline interpolation with the help of the subroutine `spline_interp` and check for convergence. Once this is the case, we proceed to plotting the output to the screen.

Exercise 9.5

(a) We can write the optimization problem of the household in dynamic programming form as:

$$V(k) = \max_{c,l,k^+} \quad u(c, 1-l) + \beta V(k^+) \quad \text{s.t.}$$

$$k^+ + c = (1-\tau^w)wl + [1+(1-\tau^r)r]k.$$

The Lagrangean of the problem reads:

$$\mathcal{L} = u(c, 1-l) + \beta V(k^+) + \lambda \Big[[1 + (1-\tau^r)r]k + (1-\tau^w)wl - c - k^+ \Big].$$

The first-order conditions are:

$$\begin{aligned}
\frac{\partial \mathcal{L}}{\partial c} &= \frac{\nu}{c} \cdot \left[c^\nu (1-l)^{1-\nu}\right]^{1-\frac{1}{\gamma}} - \lambda = 0 \\
\frac{\partial \mathcal{L}}{\partial l} &= \frac{1-\nu}{1-l} \cdot \left[c^\nu (1-l)^{1-\nu}\right]^{1-\frac{1}{\gamma}} - \lambda(1-\tau^w)w = 0 \\
\frac{\partial \mathcal{L}}{\partial k^+} &= \beta V'(k^+) - \lambda = 0.
\end{aligned}$$

With the help of the envelope theorem, we get:

$$\begin{aligned}
V'(k^+) &= \left[\, 1 + (1-\tau^{r+})r^+ \,\right] \lambda^+ \\
&= [1 + (1-\tau^{r+})r^+] \frac{\nu}{c^+} \cdot \left[(c^+)^\nu (1-l^+)^{1-\nu}\right]^{1-\frac{1}{\gamma}}.
\end{aligned}$$

Profit maximization of firms yields:

$$w = (1-\alpha)\left(\frac{k}{l}\right)^\alpha \quad \text{and} \quad r = \alpha \left(\frac{k}{l}\right)^{\alpha-1} - \delta.$$

Integrating the budget constraint of the government:

$$g = \tau^w wl + \tau^r rk$$

and the household budget constraint, the optimal solution is:

$$\begin{aligned}
c &= \frac{\nu}{1-\nu} \cdot (1-\tau^w)(1-\alpha)\left(\frac{k}{l}\right)^\alpha (1-l) \\
\frac{\nu}{c}\left[c^\nu (1-l)^{1-\nu}\right]^{1-\frac{1}{\gamma}} &= \beta \left[1 + (1-\tau^{r+}) \left(\alpha \left(\frac{k^+}{l^+}\right)^{\alpha-1} - \delta \right) \right] \\
&\quad \cdot \frac{\nu}{c^+}\left[(c^+)^\nu (1-l^+)^{1-\nu}\right]^{1-\frac{1}{\gamma}} \\
f(k,l) + (1-\delta)k &= c + g + k^+.
\end{aligned}$$

(b) We first compute the steady-state analytically, as described in the previous exercise. We then introduce the tax system by setting government expenses as a fraction of output to $g_y = 0.1$ and specifying alternative exogenous levels for τ^r. For this, we compute a new steady state and the endogenous government budget-balancing tax rate τ^w numerically. Plugging the resource constraint into the first-order condition and considering the government budget constraint, the steady state is characterized by the following set of equations:

$$\frac{\nu}{1-\nu}\cdot(1-\tau^w)(1-\alpha)\left(\frac{\bar{k}}{\bar{l}}\right)^{\alpha}(1-\bar{l})-\bar{k}^{\alpha}\bar{l}^{1-\alpha}+\delta\bar{k}+\bar{g}=0$$

$$1-\beta\left[1+(1-\tau^r)\left(\alpha\left(\frac{\bar{k}}{\bar{l}}\right)^{\alpha-1}-\delta\right)\right]=0$$

$$\bar{g}-\tau^w\left((1-\alpha)\left(\frac{\bar{k}}{\bar{l}}\right)^{\alpha}\right)\bar{l}+\tau^r\left(\alpha\left(\frac{\bar{k}}{\bar{l}}\right)^{\alpha-1}-\delta\right)\bar{k}=0.$$

We use the subroutine `fzero` from the toolbox and let it iterate over the optimal steady-state capital stock $\bar{k}$, labour supply $\bar{l}$, and the endogenous tax rate τ^w. Module 9.5m shows an excerpt of the function `foc_ss` we use to determine the steady-state variables. Note the restrictions we impose on l and τ^w. Individuals can only provide a fraction between 0 and 1 of their total time-endowment on the labour market, and τ^w is restricted to not be higher than 100 per cent and not below -100 per cent. Negative values of τ^w would imply that the government subsidizes labour supply. Table 9.1 shows the simulation results for alternative combinations of (τ^r, τ^w). The utility of the representative household is maximized with zero capital income taxation, which is in line with findings from the economic literature.

Module 9.5m Restrict labour supply and endogenous budget constraint

```
function foc_ss(x_in)
    [......]
    ! restrict input variables
    x_in_temp(1) = x_in(1)
    x_in_temp(2) = max(min(x_in(2), 1d0-1d-10), 1d-10)
    x_in_temp(3) = max(min(x_in(3), 1d0-1d-10), &
        -1d0+1d-10)
    [......]
end function
```

Table 9.1 Steady state equilibria for alternative tax combinations

τ^r	τ^w	k	l	c	V_{ss}
0.00	**0.17**	**24.09**	**0.31**	**1.11**	**−121.42**
0.10	0.15	22.83	0.31	1.11	−121.88
0.20	0.12	21.39	0.31	1.10	−122.51
0.30	0.10	19.72	0.32	1.09	−123.37
0.40	0.06	17.79	0.32	1.08	−124.57

(c) In order to perform policy function iteration, we determine a spline function that satisfies:

$$S(\hat{k}_\nu) = \left\{\beta\left[1 + (1-\tau^r)\left(\alpha\left(\frac{\hat{k}_\nu}{l}\right)^{\alpha-1} - \delta\right)\right]\frac{\nu}{c}\left[c^\nu(1-l)^{1-\nu}\right]^{1-\frac{1}{\gamma}}\right\}^{-\gamma}$$

for all $\nu = 0, \ldots, n$ in each iteration step. Note the $-\gamma < 1$ in the exponent that is used to avoid the first-order condition diverging to infinity, but instead making it converge to zero for small levels of capital. The set of first-order conditions that needs to hold at any gridpoint now reads:

$$c = \frac{\nu}{1-\nu}(1-\tau^w)(1-\alpha)\left(\frac{\hat{k}_\nu}{l}\right)^\alpha (1-l)$$

$$k^+ = (1-\delta)\hat{k}_\nu + (\hat{k}_\nu)^\alpha l^{1-\alpha} - c - g$$

and:

$$\frac{\nu}{c}\left[c^\nu(1-l)^{1-\nu}\right]^{1-\frac{1}{\gamma}} - S(k^+)^{-\frac{1}{\gamma}} = 0.$$

The policy function iteration procedure is conceptually identical to the previous exercises. In each iteration step, we use `fzero` to numerically solve the first-order conditions at each gridpoint, update the coefficients of the spline interpolation procedure, and check for convergence. However, it is again very important to provide the policy function iteration procedure with good initial guesses to ensure convergence. Keep in mind that the existence of a solution might already be excluded in advance for certain combinations of τ^r, τ^w, and g_y.[1]

Exercise 9.6

(a) We compute the unconditional stationary distribution of the autocorrelated process η_t with the same iterative procedure as in Section 9.4.4 of the book, where the direct computation of the stationary distribution in a heterogeneous agent model is discussed. However, the iteration we implement here is simpler in the sense that we do not need to deal with interpolation of the savings policy functions a^+. After discretizing the shock process with the subroutine `discretize_AR` from the toolbox, we initialize an arbitrary

[1] For instance, with $g_y = 0.3$, $\tau^r = 0$, and τ^w as endogenous tax rate.

Table 9.2 Unconditional distribution for $n = 5, 10, 20, 50$ iteration steps

σ_ϵ^2	ρ	n	$\hat{\mu}_u$	$\hat{\sigma}_u^2$	$\hat{\rho}$	Convergence
1.0	0.5	5	0.000	1.332	0.500	0.02077079
		10	0.000	1.333	0.500	0.00002003
		20	0.000	1.333	0.500	0.00000000
		50	0.000	1.333	0.500	0.00000000

distribution $\hat{\phi}_g$ and use the discretized shocks $\hat{\eta}_g$, as well as the transition matrix $\hat{\pi}_{gg^+}$ to compute the updated distribution:

$$\hat{\phi}_{g^+} = \sum_{g=1}^{m} \hat{\pi}_{gg^+}\hat{\phi}_g \qquad \forall \ \ g^+ = 1, \ldots, m$$

in each iteration step. We then iterate up to a maximum number of iterations `itermax`, or until convergence is reached. The underlying idea of the algorithm is to converge to the unconditional distribution of the autocorrelated process η by simply iterating long enough.[2] As soon as we stop iterating, we call the subroutine `output` where we compute:

$$\hat{\mu}_u = \sum_{g=1}^{m} \hat{\phi}_g \hat{\eta}_g$$

$$\hat{\sigma}_u^2 = \sum_{g=1}^{m} \hat{\phi}_g (\hat{\eta}_g - \hat{\mu}_u)^2$$

$$\hat{\rho} = \sum_{g=1}^{m} \sum_{g^+=1}^{m} \frac{\hat{\phi}_g \hat{\pi}_{gg^+} (\hat{\eta}_g - \hat{\mu}_u)(\hat{\eta}_{g^+} - \hat{\mu}_u)}{\hat{\sigma}_u^2}$$

from our approximated unconditional distribution $\hat{\phi}_g$. Table 9.2 summarizes the results for $n = 5, 10, 20, 50$ iteration steps and shows that twenty iteration steps are already enough to meet a convergence criterion of 10^{-6} for the distribution.

(b) Table 9.3 summarizes the results for $\rho = 0.9$. Compared to the initial parametrization in Part (a), convergence is now considerably slower. It takes sixty-eight iterations until we meet the convergence criterion of 10^{-6}.

(c) A higher autocorrelation ρ implies a higher persistence in the stochastic process:

$$\eta_t = \rho\eta_{t-1} + \epsilon_t \quad \text{with} \quad \epsilon_t \sim N(0, \sigma_\epsilon^2) \quad \text{and} \quad 0 \le |\rho| < 1.$$

[2] Similar to Section 9.4.4 in the book, we refer the reader to more advanced macroeconomic textbooks such as Ljungqvist and Sargent (2004, 569f.) or Miao (2014, 70f.) for a more detailed discussion of why this iterative procedure actually converges.

Table 9.3 Unconditional distribution for $n = 5, 10, 20, 50$ iteration steps

σ_ϵ^2	ρ	n	$\hat{\mu}_u$	$\hat{\sigma}_u^2$	$\hat{\rho}$	Convergence
1.0	0.9	5	0.000	1.332	0.500	1.55821505
		10	0.000	1.333	0.500	0.25989134
		20	0.000	1.333	0.500	0.02498441
		50	0.000	1.333	0.500	0.00004362
		68	0.000	1.333	0.500	0.00000098

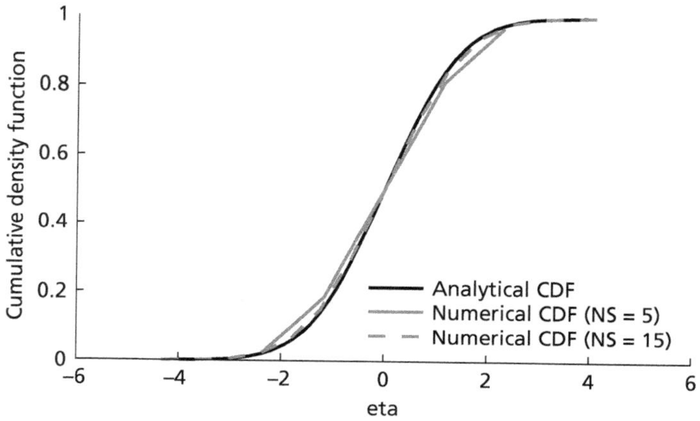

Figure 9.2 Numerical approximation of the stochastic process η_t

The closer we set ρ to 1, the longer will η_t keep information on its initial distribution, and only slowly incorporate the draws of the innovation term ϵ_t during the iteration procedure. In the limit $\rho = 1$, the information of the initial distribution and each draw of the innovation term will persist forever. We then call the stochastic process η_t a *random walk*, which has an unconditional stationary distribution *without a finite variance*. Hence, no matter how long we iterate, the stochastic process would never converge to a stationary distribution. Only as long as $\rho < 1$, does there exist an unconditional distribution, which is a normal distribution with:

$$\mu_u = 0 \quad \text{and} \quad \sigma_u^2 = \frac{\sigma_\epsilon^2}{1 - \rho^2}.$$

In the case of $\rho = 0$, the stochastic process η_t would not remember any of its previous states and hence immediately converges to the unconditional distribution.

(d) Figure 9.2 plots the numerical approximation of the stochastic process η_t. While `NS = 5` only allows for a very vague approximation of the analytical cumulative distribution function of the unconditional distribution, the numerical approximation with `NS = 15` already comes very close.

Exercise 9.7

(a) The optimization problem of the social planner in the stochastic growth model has two state variables and is given by:

$$V(k,\eta) = \max_{c}\ u(c) + \beta E\big[V(k^+,\eta^+)\big|\eta\big] \quad \text{s.t.}$$
$$c = (1-\delta)\hat{k} + \exp(\eta)f(k) - k^+ \quad \text{and}$$
$$\eta^+ = \rho\eta + \epsilon^+ \quad \text{with} \quad \epsilon^+ \sim N(0,\sigma_\epsilon^2)$$

We discretize the capital state as usual by setting up a finite grid and use the subroutine `discretize_AR` for the discretization of the autoregressive shock. In each iteration step of the value function iteration procedure, we determine a spline function:

$$S(\hat{k}_v,\hat{\eta}_g) = \left[\left(1-\frac{1}{\gamma}\right)\sum_{g^+=1}^{m}\pi_{gg^+}V(\hat{k}_v,\hat{\eta}_{g^+})\right]^{\frac{1}{1-\frac{1}{\gamma}}}$$

for all $v = 0,\ldots,n$ and $g = 1,\ldots,m$, so that we are able to interpolate the expected next period value function between any two gridpoints in the capital dimension of our discretized state space.[3] We thus rewrite the optimization problem as:

$$V(\hat{k}_v,\hat{\eta}_g) = \max_{k^+}\ u(c) + \beta\frac{S(k^+,\hat{\eta}_g)^{1-\frac{1}{\gamma}}}{1-\frac{1}{\gamma}} \quad \text{s.t.} \quad c = (1-\delta)\hat{k}_v + \exp(\hat{\eta}_g)(\hat{k}_v)^\alpha - k^+,$$

or better:

$$V(\hat{k}_v,\hat{\eta}_g) = \max_{k^+}\ u(c) + \beta\frac{S(k^+,\hat{\eta}_g)^{1-\frac{1}{\gamma}}}{1-\frac{1}{\gamma}}$$
$$\text{s.t.} \quad c = \hat{X}_v - k^+ \quad \text{with} \quad \hat{X}_v = (1-\delta)\hat{k}_v + \exp(\hat{\eta}_g)(\hat{k}_v)^\alpha.$$

where we define $\hat{X}_v$ as the planner's 'cash-on-hand'. We use the subroutine `fminsearch` to compute the optimal value of the next period capital stock k^+ that maximizes the current value function at each gridpoint (see Program 9.7). The numerical implementation differs from previous exercises in that we pass the social planner's 'cash-on-hand' to the function `utility` through the communication variable `X_com`. This strategy leads to a computational improvement over computing the social planner's available wealth in any iteration step of our value function iteration procedure. In Part (b), we will show how introducing

[3] Keep in mind that we are using our usual transformation strategy for a precise approximation of the steep part of the value function.

Program 9.7 Stochastic growth model with value function iteration

```
! iterate until value function converges
do iter = 1, itermax

    ! calculate optimal decision for every gridpoint
    do ik = 0, NK
        do is = 1, NS

            ! initialize starting value and communicate
            ! cash-on-hand
            X_com = (1d0-delta)*k(ik) &
                    + exp(eta(is))*k(ik)**alpha
            x_in = X_com - c(ik, is)
            is_com = is

            ! find the optimal future capital
            call fminsearch(x_in, fret, k_l, &
                            min(X_com, k_u), utility)

            ! get optimal consumption function
            c(ik, is) = X_com - x_in
            V_new(ik, is) = -fret

        enddo
    enddo

    ! interpolate coefficients
    call interpolate()
    [......]
enddo
```

Module 9.7m Function to be optimized with 'cash-on-hand' notation

```
function utility(x_in)
    [......]
    ! calculate tomorrows capital
    kplus = max(min(x_in, k_u), k_l)

    ! calculate consumption
    cons = max(X_com - kplus, 1d-10)

    ! calculate future utility
    evplus = max(spline_eval(kplus, coeff_EV(:, is_com), &
                k_l, k_u), 1d-10)**egam/egam

    ! get utility function
    utility = - (cons**egam/egam + beta*evplus)

end function
```

a 'cash-on-hand' state variable proves useful when solving this model with endogenous gridpoints and value function iteration (see Barillas and Fernandez-Villaverde, 2007). The corresponding function utility is shown in Module 9.7m. After we computed the optimal policy functions c and k^{+} for all gridpoints by minimizing `utility`, we call the subroutine `interpolate`, and compute the expected value functions for all states and update the spline coefficients until convergence is reached (see Program 9.7). The policy functions we plot in the output are identical to those in the output of `prog09_03` of the book. Note that it is hard to compare the time-paths for capital, consumption, and shocks, as they vary with each run of the program.

(b) The description of the algorithm is closely related to the description provided in the paper of Barillas and Fernandez-Villaverde (2007). Given the two state variables k and η, we begin with again defining 'cash-on-hand' as:

$$X = (1 - \delta)k + \exp(\eta)f(k) = c + k^+.$$

Consequently, the problem can be written recursively as:

$$\mathcal{V}(X, \eta) = \max_{k^+} \frac{(X - k^+)^{1-\frac{1}{\gamma}}}{1 - \frac{1}{\gamma}} + \beta E\left[\, \mathcal{V}(X^+, \eta^+) \,\right]$$
$$\text{s.t.} \quad X = c + k^+ \quad \text{and} \quad \eta^+ = \rho\eta + \epsilon^+.$$

Since X^+ is only a function of k^+ and η^+, we can write the expectation term in the above Bellman equation as:

$$V(k^+, \eta) = E\left[\, \mathcal{V}(X^+, \eta^+) \,\right].$$

Substituting this formulation into the above problem, consumption is now defined through the new first-order condition:

$$c = (u')^{-1}\left[\, \beta V_{k^+}(k^+, \eta) \,\right]$$

endogenously for each value of k^+ and η. Given current consumption c and the future capital stock k^+, current 'cash-on-hand' is obtained from $X = c + k^+$ and the value function is updated by:

$$\mathcal{V}(X, \eta) = \frac{c^{1-\frac{1}{\gamma}}}{1 - \frac{1}{\gamma}} + \beta V(k^+, \eta),$$

where the max-operator can be dropped, since the optimal value of consumption is already used.

In the following, we show how to establish the link between the two different notations of the next period's value function $\mathcal{V}$ and V numerically and how this iteration procedure no longer requires a numerical solution to the above first-order condition. We first discretize the state space for future values of capital k^+ to $\{\hat{k}_v\}_{v=0}^{n}$ and define a discrete grid of shock realizations $\hat{\eta}_g$, as well as the corresponding transition matrix as before. We set up a grid of next-period 'cash-on-hand' implied by $\hat{k}_v$ and $\hat{\eta}_g$ through:

$$\hat{X}_{v,g} = (1 - \delta)\hat{k}_v + \exp(\hat{\eta}_g)f(\hat{k}_v)$$

and initialize the value function for simplicity as:

$$V(\hat{k}_v, \hat{\eta}_g) = \frac{(\hat{X}_{v,g} - \hat{k}_v)^{1-\frac{1}{\gamma}}}{1-\frac{1}{\gamma}}$$

$$= \frac{[\exp(\hat{\eta}_g) f(\hat{k}_v) - \delta\hat{k}_v]^{1-\frac{1}{\gamma}}}{1-\frac{1}{\gamma}}.$$

The underlying idea of the algorithm proposed by Barillas and Fernandez-Villaverde (2007) is now to nest the endogenous gridpoint method into the usual value function iteration. In any iteration step, we proceed as follows:

1. Compute the derivative $V_k(\hat{k}_v, \hat{\eta}_g)$ at every gridpoint using the average of the slopes of the linearly interpolated value functions:

$$V_k(\hat{k}_v, \hat{\eta}_g) = 0.5 \times \left[\frac{V(\hat{k}_{v+1}, \hat{\eta}_g) - V(\hat{k}_v, \hat{\eta}_g)}{\hat{k}_{v+1} - \hat{k}_v} + \frac{V(\hat{k}_v, \hat{\eta}_g) - V(\hat{k}_{v-1}, \hat{\eta}_g)}{\hat{k}_v - \hat{k}_{v-1}}\right].$$

2. Derive optimal endogenous consumption from:

$$\tilde{c}_{v,g} = \left[\beta \sum_{g^+=1}^{m} \hat{\pi}_{gg^+} V_k(\hat{k}_v, \hat{\eta}_{g^+})\right]^{-\gamma}.$$

   Given optimal current consumption, we can calculate 'cash-on-hand' as:

$$\widetilde{X}_{v,g} = \tilde{c}_{v,g} + \hat{k}_v.$$

3. Update the value function as follows:

$$\mathcal{V}(\widetilde{X}_{v,g}, \hat{\eta}_g) = \frac{(\tilde{c}_{v,g})^{1-\frac{1}{\gamma}}}{1-\frac{1}{\gamma}} + \beta V(\hat{k}_v, \hat{\eta}_g).$$

4. Derive a new guess $\mathcal{V}(\hat{X}_{v,g}, \hat{\eta}_g)$ for the value function (on the exogenous grid) by interpolating on the endogenous grid for market resources $\mathcal{V}(\widetilde{X}_{v,g}, \hat{\eta}_g)$ using subroutine `linint_Gen()` from the toolbox.
5. Next, derive a new guess for the value function defined on the capital stock from:

$$V_{new}(\hat{k}_v, \hat{\eta}_g) = \sum_{g^+=1}^{m} \hat{\pi}_{g,g^+} \mathcal{V}(\hat{X}_{v,g}, \hat{\eta}_{g^+}).$$

6. If $|V_{new}(\hat{k}_v, \hat{\eta}_g) - V(\hat{k}_v, \hat{\eta}_g)| < 10^{-6}$ (ie the convergence criterion is met), then exit the iteration. Otherwise, set $V(\cdot) = V_{new}(\cdot)$ and start again in step 1.

Program 9.7.a Solving the model with endogenous gridpoints

```
do iter = 1, itermax

    ! 1. compute derivative of value function
    [......]

    ! 2. determine endogenous consumption function,
    !    cash-on-hand and respective value function
    c_endog = 0d0
    do ik = 0, NK
        do is = 1, NS
            do is_p = 1, NS
                c_endog(ik, is) = c_endog(ik,is) + pi(is, is_p)&
                                                   *dV(ik, is_p)
            enddo
            c_endog(ik, is) = (beta*c_endog(ik, is))**(-gamma)
            X_endog(ik, is) = c_endog(ik, is) + k(ik)
            VX_endog(ik, is) = c_endog(ik, is)**egam/egam +  &
                                                 beta*V(ik, is)
        enddo
    enddo

    ! 4. update value function on resources by interpolation
    do ik = 0, NK
        do is = 1, NS
            VX(ik, is)= linint_Gen(X(ik, is), X_endog(:, is),&
                                         VX_endog(:, is), ik)
        enddo
    enddo

    ! 5. update value function on capital
    V_new = 0d0
    do is = 1, NS
        do is_p = 1, NS
            V_new(:, is)=V_new(:, is) + pi(is, is_p)*VX(:,is_p)
        enddo
    enddo
    [......]

    V = V_new
enddo
```

The numerical implementation is laid out in Program 9.7.a. As soon as the value function has converged, it is possible to retrieve the endogenous current capital $\tilde{k}_{v,g}$ from the 'cash-on-hand' definition $\widetilde{X}_{v,g}$ using subroutine `fzero` (Program 9.7.b). Finally, the policy function $c(\hat{k}_v, \hat{\eta}_g)$ on the exogenous grid can be derived by linear interpolation of the endogenous policy function $\tilde{c}_{v,g}$ on the endogenous capital stock grid.

(c) Value function iteration with endogenous gridpoints takes only half the time of the traditional value function iteration under the same parameterization, even if it requires slightly more iteration steps (1,170 instead of 925). The main shortcoming of the algorithm we implemented is, however, that the quality of our numerical approximation depends heavily on the number of gridpoints we use to discretize the state space. This is because of the numerical approximation of the derivative V_k we compute in each iteration step. In consequence, the Euler equation error rises under the initial parameterization

Program 9.7.b Backward projection from 'cash-on-hand' to capital

```
! calculate endogenous capital for every shock level
do ik = 0, NK
    do is = 1, NS

        ! set starting value and communicate resource level
        x_in = k(ik)
        X_com = X_endog(ik, is)
        is_com = is
        call fzero(x_in, fkend, check)
        if(check)write(*, *)'ERROR IN ROOTFINDING PROCESS'

        ! get endogenous capital stock
        k_endog(ik, is) = x_in
    enddo
enddo

! compute policy function by interpolation
do ik = 0, NK
    do is = 1, NS
        c(ik, is) = linint_Gen(k(ik), k_endog(:, is), &
                               c_endog(:, is), ik)
    enddo
enddo
```

from `4.0E-07` with traditional value function iteration to `1.2E-03` in the algorithm with endogenous gridpoints.

Exercise 9.8

(a) The optimization problem of the social planner in dynamic programming form is given by:

$$
\begin{aligned}
V(k,\eta) &= \max_{c,l}\ u(c, 1-l) + \beta E\big[V(k^+,\eta^+)\big|\eta\big] \\
\text{s.t.}\quad & (1-\delta)k + \exp(\eta)f(k,l) = c + k^+ \quad \text{and} \\
& \eta^+ = \rho\eta + \epsilon^+ \quad \text{with} \quad \epsilon^+ \sim N(0,\sigma_\epsilon^2).
\end{aligned}
$$

As before, we discretize our state space with a finite grid over capital and with the subroutine `discretize_AR` for the autoregressive productivity state. Setting up a spline for the interpolation of the expected value function in each iteration step and using the intratemporal optimality condition:

$$c = \frac{\nu}{1-\nu}\cdot(1-l)\cdot\exp(\hat{\eta}_g)(1-\alpha)\left(\frac{k}{l}\right)^{\alpha}$$

of our optimization problem allows us to rewrite the dynamic programming problem as:

$$V(\hat{k}_v, \hat{\eta}_g) = \max_{l} \quad u(c, 1-l) + \beta \frac{S(k^+, \hat{\eta}_g)^{1-\frac{1}{\gamma}}}{1-\frac{1}{\gamma}}$$

$$\text{with} \quad c = \frac{\nu}{1-\nu} \cdot (1-l) \cdot \exp(\hat{\eta}_g)(1-\alpha)\left(\frac{\hat{k}_v}{l}\right)^{\alpha}$$

$$\text{and} \quad k^+ = (1-\delta)\hat{k}_v + \exp(\hat{\eta}_g)(\hat{k}_v)^{\alpha} l^{1-\alpha} - c.$$

At any gridpoint we let `fminsearch` iterate to find the optimal amount l of labour supplied to maximize the current value function subject to the constraints. We restrict the interval `fminsearch` is searching on to be $[0, 1]$, so that individuals can supply their whole time-endowment on the labour market at the maximum and need to have non-negative labour supply on the other hand. Within the function `utility`, we then derive the optimal level of consumption c from the intratemporal optimality condition and the next period capital stock k^+ from the intertemporal budget constraint of the social planner for any level of supplied labour l (see Module 9.8m). Note that we assign a penalty to all realizations of k^+ that lie outside of the interval we chose to discretize our asset state on. The value function iteration algorithm itself is implemented in the main program in `sol_prog09_08` and is similar to before. At convergence, we obtain the same business cycle statistics as in program `prog09_05` from the book. The policy functions we show in Figure 9.3 yield the

Module 9.8m Utility in RBC model with value function iteration

```
function utility(x_in)
    [......]
    ! labor supply must be between 0 and 1
    lab = max(min(x_in, 1d0-1d-10), 1d-10)

    ! calculate current consumption
    cons = max((nu/(1d0-nu))*(1d0-lab)*exp(eta(is_com))* &
                (1d0-alpha)*(k_com/lab)**alpha, 1d-10)

    ! calculate future capital
    kplus =  (1d0-delta)*k_com + exp(eta(is_com))* &
               k_com**alpha*lab**(1d0-alpha)  - cons
    kplus_lim = max(min(kplus,k_u),k_l)

    ! calculate future utility
    evplus = max(spline_eval(kplus_lim, coeff_ev(:, is_com), &
                   k_l, k_u), 1d-10)**egam/egam

    ! get utility function
    utility = -((cons**nu*(1d0-lab)**(1d0-nu))**egam/egam + &
                   beta*evplus)

    ! penalize for kplus values outside of (k_l, k_u)
    utility = utility + 100d0*abs(kplus-kplus_lim)

end function
```

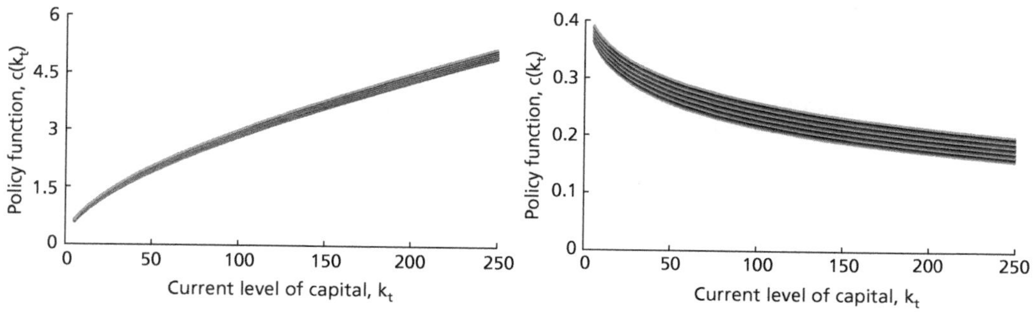

Figure 9.3 Policy functions $c(k_t)$ and $l(k_t)$ for different shock realizations

intuitive result that a higher productivity shock leads to higher labour supply and higher consumption.

(b) The only difference compared to the numerical implementation in program `prog09_05` from the book is that the subroutine `fzero` now receives an array `y_in` of length two with initial guesses for the optimal labour supply and optimal consumption as input. Given guesses for $c(\hat{k}_v, \hat{\eta}_g)$ and $l(\hat{k}_v, \hat{\eta}_g)$, we now derive k^+ from the resource constraint:

$$k^+ = (1-\delta)\hat{k}_v + \exp(\hat{\eta}_g)(\hat{k}_v)^\alpha l(\hat{k}_v, \hat{\eta}_g)^{1-\alpha} - c(\hat{k}_v, \hat{\eta}_g).$$

We compute the intra- and intertemporal optimality conditions by setting up the Lagrangen for the initial dynamic programming problem from above at a certain state and obtain:

$$c(\hat{k}_v, \hat{\eta}_g) - \frac{\nu}{1-\nu} \cdot (1 - l(\hat{k}_v, \hat{\eta}_g)) \cdot \exp(\hat{\eta}_g)(1-\alpha)\left(\frac{\hat{k}_v}{l(\hat{k}_v, \hat{\eta}_g)}\right)^\alpha = 0$$

$$\frac{\nu \cdot \left[c(\hat{k}_v, \hat{\eta}_g)^\nu (1 - l(\hat{k}_v, \hat{\eta}_g))^{1-\nu}\right]^{1-\frac{1}{\gamma}}}{c(\hat{k}_v, \hat{\eta}_g)} - S(k^+, \hat{\eta}_g)^{-\frac{1}{\gamma}} = 0.$$

We interpolate the marginal utility of the next period's value function with a spline function that satisfies:

$$S(\hat{k}_v, \hat{\eta}_g) = \left\{\beta \sum_{g^+=1}^{m} \pi_{gg^+} V_k(\hat{k}_v, \hat{\eta}_{g^+})\right\}^{-\gamma}$$

for all $v = 0, \ldots, n$ and $g = 1, \ldots, m$. The remainder of the code, and in particular the policy function iteration algorithm, is left unchanged. Note that two-dimensional rootfinding is slightly slower (speed increases from 5.5 to 8.1 seconds) and also less accurate than the one-dimensional approach, which tells us that it is advisable to use any analytical solution possible before resorting to numerical approaches.

Exercise 9.9

(a) The problem in dynamic programming form is given by:

$$V(\hat{k},\hat{\eta}_g) = \max_{c,\kappa} \quad u(c,\kappa) + \beta \sum_{g^+=1}^{m} \pi_{gg^+} V(k^+,\hat{\eta}_{g^+})$$
$$\text{s.t.} \quad k^+ = (1-\delta)k + \exp(\hat{\eta}_g)k^\alpha(\kappa h_0)^{1-\alpha} - c.$$

We set up the following Lagrangean:

$$\mathcal{L} = \log c + A\kappa \log(1-h_0) + \beta \sum_{g^+=1}^{m} \pi_{gg^+} V(k^+,\hat{\eta}_{g^+}) +$$
$$\lambda\Big[(1-\delta)k + \exp(\hat{\eta}_g)k^\alpha(\kappa h_0)^{1-\alpha} - c - k^+\Big]$$

in order to obtain the first-order conditions:

$$\frac{\partial \mathcal{L}}{\partial c} = \frac{1}{c} - \lambda = 0 \qquad (I)$$

$$\frac{\partial \mathcal{L}}{\partial \kappa} = A\log(1-h_0) + \lambda(1-\alpha)\exp(\hat{\eta}_g)\left(\frac{k}{\kappa h_0}\right)^\alpha h_0 = 0 \qquad (II)$$

$$\frac{\partial \mathcal{L}}{\partial k^+} = \beta \sum_{g^+=1}^{m} \pi_{gg^+} V_{k^+}(k^+,\hat{\eta}_{g^+}) - \lambda = 0. \qquad (III)$$

We then get:

$$c = -\frac{(1-\alpha)\exp(\hat{\eta}_g)\left(\frac{k}{\kappa h_0}\right)^\alpha h_0}{A\log(1-h_0)}$$

as intratemporal optimality condition from (*I*) and (*II*). With the envelope theorem, we obtain:

$$V_{k^+}(k^+,\hat{\eta}_{g^+}) = \left[1-\delta+\alpha\exp(\hat{\eta}_{g^+})\left(\frac{k^+}{\kappa^+ h_0}\right)^{\alpha-1}\right]\lambda^+$$
$$= \left[1-\delta+\alpha\exp(\hat{\eta}_{g^+})\left(\frac{k^+}{\kappa^+ h_0}\right)^{\alpha-1}\right]\frac{1}{c^+},$$

which yields, after substituting this into the above first-order conditions and setting (*I*) = (*III*):

$$\frac{1}{c} = \beta \sum_{g^+=1}^{m} \pi_{gg^+}\left[1-\delta+\alpha\exp(\hat{\eta}_{g^+})\left(\frac{k^+}{\kappa^+ h_0}\right)^{\alpha-1}\right]\frac{1}{c^+}$$

for intertemporal optimality.

(b) In any iteration step of our policy function iteration we solve the intertemporal optimality condition:

$$c^{-1} = S(k^+, \hat{\eta}_g)$$
$$\text{s.t.} \quad c = \frac{(1-\alpha)\exp(\hat{\eta}_g)\left(\frac{k}{\kappa h_0}\right)^\alpha h_0}{A\log(1-h_0)}$$
$$\text{and} \quad k^+ = (1-\delta)\hat{k}_v + \exp(\hat{\eta}_g)(\hat{k}_v)^\alpha(\kappa h_0)^{1-\alpha} - c$$

at each gridpoint by letting `fzero` iterate over the optimal fraction κ of working households. $S(k^+, \hat{\eta}_g)$ is a spline function that interpolates the right-hand side of our intertemporal first-order condition between any two gridpoints in the capital dimension. It is defined so that it satisfies:

$$S(\hat{k}_v, \hat{\eta}_g) = \beta \sum_{g^+=1}^{m} \pi_{gg^+}\left[1 - \delta + \alpha\exp(\hat{\eta}_{g^+})\left(\frac{\hat{k}_v}{\kappa(\hat{k}_v, \hat{\eta}_{g^+})h_0}\right)^{\alpha-1}\right]\frac{1}{c(\hat{k}_v, \hat{\eta}_{g^+})}$$

for all $v = 0, \ldots, n$ and $g = 0, \ldots, m$. The coefficients we use for spline interpolation are stored in the array `coeff_r` and are updated in each iteration step. As soon as convergence is reached, we stop iterating and plot the decision variables over time and the policy functions. The results are very similar to those of the previous exercise: a higher productivity shock leads to higher consumption c and to a higher fraction of people working κ.

Exercise 9.10

Given the specific form of the utility function $u(c, 1-l)$ in the book, we at first calculate the derivatives:

$$u_c = \frac{\nu}{c}\left[c^\nu(1-l)^{1-\nu}\right]^{1-\frac{1}{\gamma}},$$
$$u_{c,c} = \left[c^\nu(1-l)^{1-\nu}\right]^{1-\frac{1}{\gamma}}\left\{\nu^2\left(1-\frac{1}{\gamma}\right) - \nu\right\}\frac{1}{c^2},$$
$$u_{1-l} = \frac{1-\nu}{1-l}\left[c^\nu(1-l)^{1-\nu}\right]^{1-\frac{1}{\gamma}},$$
$$u_{1-l,1-l} = \left[c^\nu(1-l)^{1-\nu}\right]^{1-\frac{1}{\gamma}}\left\{(1-\nu)^2\left(1-\frac{1}{\gamma}\right) - (1-\nu)\right\}\frac{1}{(1-l)^2}$$
$$u_{c,1-l} = \left[c^\nu(1-l)^{1-\nu}\right]^{1-\frac{1}{\gamma}}\left\{\nu(1-\nu)\left(1-\frac{1}{\gamma}\right)\right\}\frac{1}{c(1-l)}.$$

Using them and plugging them into:

$$\Delta = \frac{u(\mu_c, 1-\mu_l) - u(c^*, 1-l^*)}{u_c(c^*, 1-l^*) \cdot c^*} + \frac{1}{2} \cdot \left\{ \frac{u_{c,c}(\mu_c, 1-\mu_l) \cdot (\mu_c)^2}{u_c(c^*, 1-l^*) \cdot c^*} \cdot CV[c]^2 \right.$$
$$+ \frac{u_{1-l,1-l}(\mu_c, 1-\mu_l) \cdot (1-\mu_l)^2}{u_c(c^*, 1-l^*) \cdot c^*} \cdot CV[1-l]^2$$
$$\left. \frac{u_{c,1-l}(\mu_c, 1-\mu_l) \cdot \mu_c \cdot (1-\mu_l)}{u_c(c^*, 1-l^*) \cdot c^*} \cdot \rho[c, 1-l] \cdot CV[c] \cdot CV[1-l] \right\}$$

yields with the definition $\hat{u} = \frac{u(\mu_c, 1-\mu_l)}{u(c^*, 1-l^*)}$ that:

$$\Delta = \frac{\hat{u}-1}{\nu\left(1-\frac{1}{\gamma}\right)} + \frac{1}{2}\left\{ \hat{u}\frac{\nu^2\left(1-\frac{1}{\gamma}\right)-\nu}{\nu} \cdot CV[c]^2 + \right.$$
$$\hat{u}\frac{(1-\nu)^2\left(1-\frac{1}{\gamma}\right)-(1-\nu)}{\nu} \cdot CV[1-l]^2 +$$
$$\left. 2\hat{u}(1-\nu)\left(1-\frac{1}{\gamma}\right) \cdot \rho[c, 1-l] \cdot CV[c] \cdot CV[1-l] \right\}$$
$$= \frac{\hat{u}-1}{\nu\left(1-\frac{1}{\gamma}\right)} - \frac{\hat{u}}{2\nu\gamma}\left\{ [-\nu^2(\gamma-1)+\nu\gamma] \cdot CV[c]^2 + \right.$$
$$(1-\nu)[\gamma-(1-\nu)(\gamma-1)] \cdot CV[1-l]^2 -$$
$$\left. 2(1-\nu)(\gamma-1)\nu \cdot \rho[c, 1-l] \cdot CV[c] \cdot CV[1-l] \right\}$$
$$= \frac{\hat{u}-1}{\nu\left(1-\frac{1}{\gamma}\right)} - \frac{\hat{u}}{2\nu\gamma}\left\{ [\nu^2+(1-\nu)\nu\gamma] \cdot CV[c]^2 + \right.$$
$$[(1-\nu)^2+(1-\nu)\nu\gamma] \cdot CV[1-l]^2 +$$
$$\left. 2[(1-\nu)\nu-(1-\nu)\nu\gamma] \cdot \rho[c, 1-l] \cdot CV[c] \cdot CV[1-l] \right\},$$

which with $\bar{\nu} = (1-\nu)\nu\gamma$ is equivalent to (9.16) from the book.

In order to derive the formula for the welfare change (9.17), we need to know by how many per cent Δ consumption has to change in scenario 1 so as to make households as well off as in scenario 2, ie

$$E_0\left[\sum_{t=0}^{\infty} \beta^t u((1+\Delta)c_{1t}, 1-l_{1,t})\right] = E_0\left[\sum_{t=0}^{\infty} \beta^t u(c_{2t}, 1-l_{2,t})\right].$$

Using the approximation:

$$E_0\left[\sum_{t=0}^{\infty}\beta^t u(c_{it}, 1-l_{i,t})\right] \approx \frac{1}{1-\beta}\Big\{u(\mu_{c_i}, 1-\mu_{l_i})+$$
$$\frac{1}{2}\cdot u_{cc}(\mu_{c_i}, 1-\mu_{l_i})(\mu_{c_i})^2\cdot CV_i[c]^2+\ldots\Big\}$$

for $i = 1, 2$ from the book as well as a first-order Taylor expansion, we get:

$$u(\mu_{c_1}, 1-\mu_{l_1}) + u_c(\mu_{c_1}, 1-\mu_{l_1})\Delta c_1 + \frac{1}{2}\cdot u_{cc}(\mu_{c_1}, 1-\mu_{l_1})(\mu_{c_1})^2\cdot CV_1[c]^2$$
$$+\cdots \stackrel{!}{=} u(\mu_{c_2}, 1-\mu_{l_2}) + \frac{1}{2}\cdot u_{cc}(\mu_{c_2}, 1-\mu_{l_2})(\mu_{c_2})^2\cdot CV_2[c]^2+$$
$$\frac{1}{2}\cdot u_{1-l,1-l}(\mu_{c_2}, 1-\mu_{l_2})(1-\mu_{l_2})^2\cdot CV_2[1-l]^2+\ldots$$

Rearranging for the welfare change Δ yields:

$$\Delta = \frac{u(\mu_{c_2}, 1-\mu_{l_2}) - u(\mu_{c_1}, 1-\mu_{l_1})}{u_c(\mu_{c_1}, 1-\mu_{l_1})\mu_{c_1}} + \frac{1}{2}\frac{u_{cc}(\mu_{c_2}, 1-\mu_{l_2})(\mu_{c_2})^2}{u_c(\mu_{c_1}, 1-\mu_{l_1})\mu_{c_1}}CV_2[c]^2$$
$$+\cdots - \frac{1}{2}\frac{u_{cc}(\mu_{c_1}, 1-\mu_{l_1})(\mu_{c_1})^2}{u_c(\mu_{c_1}, 1-\mu_{l_1})\mu_{c_1}}CV_1[c]^2$$
$$-\frac{1}{2}\frac{u_{1-l,1-l}(\mu_{c_1}, 1-\mu_{l_1})(1-\mu_{l_1})^2}{u_c(\mu_{c_1}, 1-\mu_{l_1})\mu_{c_1}}CV_1[1-l]^2\ldots$$

Plugging in the above derivatives, setting $\hat{u} = \frac{u(\mu_{c_2},1-\mu_{l_2})}{u(\mu_{c_1},1-\mu_{l_1})}$, and using $\bar{\nu}$ from above yields equation (9.17) from the book, ie

$$\Delta = \hat{u}\cdot W_2 - W_1,$$

with:

$$W_i = \frac{1}{\nu\left(1-\frac{1}{\gamma}\right)} - \frac{1}{2\nu\gamma}\cdot\Big\{[\nu^2+\bar{\nu}]\cdot CV_i[c]^2 + [(1-\nu))]^2+\bar{\nu}]\cdot CV_i[1-l]^2$$
$$+2\cdot[\nu(1-\nu)-\bar{\nu}]\cdot\rho_i[c, 1-l]\cdot CV_i[c]\cdot CV_i[1-l]\Big\}.$$

Exercise 9.11

Instead of taking the perspective of a social planner as in the previous exercises, we look at our real business-cycle model from the perspective of a perfectly competitive, decentralized economy. Introducing government policy with distortive taxation in such a setting is straightforward. The government's budget constraint reads:

$$g = \tau^w wl,$$

where g denotes government consumption and τ_w labour income tax. We abstract from public debt or other taxes, so that labour income taxation is the only source of revenue for the government and, hence, needs to balance the budget constraint. Since in our set-up labour taxes are only levied on the household side, the firms profit maximization problem remains unchanged, which results in factor prices:

$$r = \exp(\eta)\alpha\left(\frac{k}{l}\right)^{\alpha-1} - \delta \quad \text{and} \quad w = \exp(\eta)(1-\alpha)\left(\frac{k}{l}\right)^{\alpha}.$$

Yet, the household optimization problem changes as the household's new dynamic budget constraint accounts for taxes on labour income and is now given by:

$$k^+ + c = (1+r)k + (1-\tau^w)wl.$$

The household's optimization problem in dynamic programming form then reads:

$$\begin{aligned} V(k,\eta) = \max_{c,l,k^+} \; & u(c, 1-l) + \beta E\big[V(k^+,\eta^+)\big] \\ \text{s.t.} \quad & k^+ + c = (1-\tau^w)wl + (1+r)k \\ \text{and} \quad & \eta^+ = \rho\eta + \epsilon^+ \quad \text{with} \quad \epsilon^+ \sim N(0,\sigma_\epsilon^2), \end{aligned}$$

where we have already substituted the capital market equilibrium condition $a = k$ and implicitly assumed that the labour market is in equilibrium. From the corresponding Lagrangean, we can then derive:

$$c = \frac{\nu}{1-\nu} \cdot (1-l) \cdot (1-\tau^w)\exp(\hat{\eta}_g)(1-\alpha)\left(\frac{\hat{k}_v}{l}\right)^{\alpha}$$

as intratemporal optimality condition and:

$$\frac{\nu \cdot \left[c^\nu (1-l)^{1-\nu}\right]^{1-\frac{1}{\gamma}}}{c} = \beta E\big[V_k(k^+,\eta^+)|\eta\big]$$

for intertemporal optimality, with:

$$\begin{aligned} E\big[V_k(k^+,\eta^+)|\eta\big] = E\Bigg\{ & \left[1 + \exp(\eta^+)\alpha\left(\frac{k^+}{l^+}\right)^{\alpha-1} - \delta\right] \\ & \cdot \left.\frac{\nu \cdot \left[(c^+)^\nu (1-l^+)^{1-\nu}\right]^{1-\frac{1}{\gamma}}}{c^+}\right|\eta\Bigg\} \end{aligned}$$

Table 9.4 Constant vs pro-cyclical government expenditure with labour tax

	c	g	i	k	l	τ^w	y
Scenario 1: Pro-cyclical government expenditure							
Average (in %)	58.88	15.00	26.12	343.73	30.06	25.00	
CV (in %)	2.64	3.87	7.68	3.62	1.32	0.00	3.87
Corr. with GDP	0.90	1.00	0.94	0.73	0.79	0.00	
Scenario 2: Constant government expenditure							
Average (in %)	58.86	15.00	26.14	343.94	30.05	25.05	
CV (in %)	4.06	0.00	9.86	4.88	2.00	4.64	4.63
Corr. with GDP	0.93	0.00	0.94	0.76	0.85	−1.00	

from the envelope theorem. Given the equilibria on the capital and labour market, we know from Walras' law that the goods market will also clear. The assumption of perfectly competitive markets thus facilitates our problem significantly, as the dynamics of our economy are completely characterized by the above equations.

In order to solve the model numerically with policy function iteration, we again discretize our state space. We set up a spline function that satisfies:

$$S(\hat{k}_v, \hat{\eta}_g) = \left\{ \beta \sum_{g^+=1}^{m} \pi_{gg^+} \cdot \left[1 + \exp(\hat{\eta}_{g^+})\alpha \left(\frac{\hat{k}_v}{l^+}\right)^{\alpha-1} - \delta \right] \cdot \frac{\nu \cdot \left[(c^+)^\nu (1-l^+)^{1-\nu}\right]^{1-\frac{1}{\gamma}}}{c^+} \right\}^{-\gamma}$$

in order to evaluate the right-hand side of the intertemporal optimality condition between two gridpoints on the capital grid. At each state, we then use `fzero` to solve:

$$\frac{\nu \cdot \left[c^\nu (1-l)^{1-\nu}\right]^{1-\frac{1}{\gamma}}}{c} = S(k^+, \hat{\eta}_g)^{-\frac{1}{\gamma}}$$

$$\text{s.t.} \quad \tau_w = \frac{g}{wl},$$

$$c = \frac{\nu}{1-\nu} \cdot (1-l) \cdot (1-\tau^w) \exp(\hat{\eta}_g)(1-\alpha) \left(\frac{\hat{k}_v}{l}\right)^\alpha, \quad \text{and}$$

$$k^+ = (1-\delta)\hat{k}_v + \exp(\hat{\eta}_g)(\hat{k}_v)^\alpha l^{1-\alpha} - c - g.$$

We start with an initial guess for labour supply l. As long as we do not reach convergence, we continue updating the coefficients of our spline $S(\hat{k}_v, \hat{\eta}_g)$ in each iteration step. Once convergence is achieved, we print the output to the screen, which is summarized in Tables 9.4 and 9.5.

Table 9.5 Welfare with procyclical vs constant government consumption

	Level	CV(c)	CV(1 − l)	ρ(c, 1 − l)	Total
Values scenario 1	−1.24972	0.02642	0.00567	−0.44085	
Values scenario 2	−1.24960	0.04060	0.00859	−0.58495	
Approx. cost (in %)	0.02636	−0.06462	−0.00608	0.00884	−0.03550

The main difference to the lump-sum taxation scenario of Table 9.4 from the book is that labour supply distortions resulting from taxation reduce labour input on the production side from 36 per cent to 30 per cent of output. Pro-cyclical government expenditure in scenario 1 implies that the tax rate will not vary over time and, hence, is uncorrelated with output. In scenario 2, on the other hand, constant government expenditure comes with a positive coefficient of variation for the tax rate τ_w and a perfectly negative correlation with output. A positive aggregate output shock leads to an increase in the tax base, as more labour is employed in the production process. As a result, a lower tax rate τ_w is sufficient to finance government consumption. The same logic holds vice versa for a negative aggregate output shock. On the one hand, this means that labour supply distortions are reduced in the most productive periods, which leads to a boost in average output in the case of constant government expenditure. On the other hand, output (and therefore consumption) volatility also increases compared to Table 9.4 from the book. Table 9.5 shows that the higher volatility of macro variables lets the welfare cost of constant government expenditures compared to pro-cyclical expenditures rise to 0.03550 and is therefore about three times higher than in Table 9.5 from the book.

Exercise 9.12

The derivation of the optimality conditions in the case of a general income tax is equivalent to Exercise 9.11. In each iteration, we now require at any state the following first-order condition to hold:

$$\frac{\nu \cdot \left[c^{\nu}(1-l)^{1-\nu}\right]^{1-\frac{1}{\gamma}}}{c} = S(k^{+}, \hat{\eta}_g)^{-\frac{1}{\gamma}}$$

$$\text{s.t.} \quad \tau^{y} = \frac{g}{wl + rk},$$

$$c = \frac{\nu}{1-\nu} \cdot (1-l) \cdot (1-\tau^{w}-\tau^{y}) \exp(\hat{\eta}_g)(1-\alpha)\left(\frac{\hat{k}_v}{l}\right)^{\alpha}, \quad \text{and}$$

$$k^{+} = (1-\delta)\hat{k}_v + \exp(\hat{\eta}_g)(\hat{k}_v)^{\alpha} l^{1-\alpha} - c - g,$$

where we interpolated the right-hand side of the intertemporal optimality condition again with a spline that now has to satisfy:

Table 9.6 Pro-cyclical government expenditure with labour vs income tax

	c	g	i	k	l	τ^w/τ^y	y
Scenario 1: Pro-cyclical government expenditure with labour tax							
Average (in %)	58.88	15.00	26.12	343.73	30.06	25.00	
CV (in %)	2.64	3.87	7.68	3.62	1.32	0.00	3.87
Corr. with GDP	0.90	1.00	0.94	0.73	0.79	0.00	
Scenario 2: Pro-cyclical government expenditure with general income tax							
Average (in %)	60.93	15.00	24.07	316.75	30.76	19.76	
CV (in %)	2.73	4.00	8.30	3.93	1.43	0.92	4.00
Corr. with GDP	0.91	1.00	0.94	0.73	0.77	−0.38	

Table 9.7 Welfare effects with labour tax vs general income tax

	Level	CV(c)	CV(1 − l)	ρ(c, 1 − l)	Total
Values scenario 1	−1.24986	0.02663	0.00565	−0.43978	
Values scenario 2	−1.25668	0.02748	0.00632	−0.44151	
Approx. cost (in %)	−1.51452	−0.00340	−0.00120	0.00070	−1.51842

$$S(\hat{k}_v, \hat{\eta}_g) = \left\{ \beta \sum_{g^+=1}^{m} \pi_{gg^+} \cdot \left[1 + (1-\tau^y)\exp(\hat{\eta}_{g^+})\alpha \left(\frac{\hat{k}_v}{l^+}\right)^{\alpha-1} - \delta \right] \cdot \frac{\nu \cdot \left[(c^+)^\nu (1-l^+)^{1-\nu}\right]^{1-\frac{1}{\gamma}}}{c^+} \right\}^{-\gamma}$$

for all $v = 0, \ldots, n$ and $g = 1, \ldots, m$. While a pure labour income taxation only changes the intratemporal optimality condition, a general income tax τ^y now distorts the intertemporal optimality condition as well.

As the tax base increases with the introduction of a general income tax, the tax rate τ^y falls to 19.7 per cent on average. The crowding out of capital decreases the capital–output ratio and the investment ratio. In addition, the volatility of macro variables in Table 9.6 rises compared to Table 9.4, which is a direct effect of the distortion of intertemporal choices. Note that, in contrast to the labour tax rate τ^w, the income tax rate τ^y is no longer constant in a pro-cyclical government expenditure regime. Instead, it is negatively correlated with output. Owing to the distortion of capital accumulation, there is now a strong negative level effect on welfare, which declines by 1.5 per cent when we introduce income taxation compared to labour taxation (see Table 9.7). This is the same effect that we already saw in the case of a capital tax in Exercise 9.5.

Exercise 9.13

The optimality condition of the heterogenous agent model with fixed labour supply is:

$$c(a,\eta) = \left\{\beta(1+r)E\left[\, c^{+}(a^{+},\eta^{+})^{-\frac{1}{\gamma}}|\eta \,\right]\right\}^{-\gamma},$$

with $a^{+} = (1+r)a+w\cdot\exp(\eta)-c$, $a^{+} \geq 0$ and $\eta^{+} = \rho\eta+\epsilon^{+}$, with $\epsilon^{+} \sim N(0,\sigma_{\epsilon}^{2})$. Given the discretization of the state space $\hat{a}_v$, the household's policy function $c(a,\hat{\eta}_g)$ is updated in each step of the iteration procedure as follows. For each future asset level $a^{+} = \hat{a}_v$ and each today's shock level $\hat{\eta}_g$ we calculate the endogenous consumption level:

$$\tilde{c}(\hat{a}_v,\hat{\eta}_g) = \left[\beta(1+r)\sum_{g^{+}=1}^{m}\pi_{gg^{+}}\cdot c(\hat{a}_v,\hat{\eta}_{g^{+}})^{-\frac{1}{\gamma}}\right]^{-\gamma}$$

using the policy function from the previous iteration step. For numerical stability reasons, we separately control for the case in which any of the future consumption levels might be very close to zero. The budget constraint then delivers the respective endogenous gridpoint:

$$\tilde{a}(\hat{a}_v,\hat{\eta}_g) = \frac{\hat{a}_v + \tilde{c}(\hat{a}_v,\hat{\eta}_g) - w\cdot\exp(\hat{\eta}_g)}{1+r}.$$

Note that there is one additional step to be made here, which arises because of the non-negativity constraint on individual wealth. Specifically, this step is necessary if $\tilde{a}(0,\hat{\eta}_g) > 0$. If this lowest endogenous gridpoint is actually positive for some level of the labour productivity shock $\hat{\eta}_g$, it means that a household which currently has a wealth of $\tilde{a}(0,\hat{\eta}_g) > 0$ and faces a labour productivity level $\exp(\hat{\eta}_g)$ would actually like to save exactly an amount of 0 into the next period. Obviously, any individual with a current asset level smaller than $\tilde{a}(0,\hat{\eta}_g)$ would then potentially like to save less then an amount of 0, meaning that she would like to run into debt. This is, however, forbidden by assumption, since the minimum asset level possible is $a = 0$. To account for this restriction, we add another endogenous gridpoint to our original set of points which is equal to $\tilde{a}(0_{-},\hat{\eta}_g) = 0$ and features a consumption level of $\tilde{c}(0_{-},\hat{\eta}_g) = w\cdot\exp(\hat{\eta}_g)$. In the program, we store these values in the array entries indexed -1. By doing this, we acknowledge the fact that the individual with zero assets in the current period and a labour productivity of $\hat{\eta}_g$ will save nothing into the future but only consumes her income that is available in the current period (see also Exercise 8.9). Using a linear interpolation routine this in fact implies that any household with a current asset level between 0 and $\tilde{a}(0,\hat{\eta}_g) > 0$ will save nothing into the future and just consume all resources they have,

Module 9.13m Borrowing constraint in an additional gridpoint in entry −1

```
! set the borrowing limit
do is = 1, NS
    if(a_endog(0, is) >= a_l)then
        a_endog(-1, is) = a_l
        c_endog(-1, is) = w*eta(is)
    else
        a_endog(-1, is) = a_endog(0, is)
        c_endog(-1, is) = c_endog(0, is)
    endif
enddo
```

Program 9.13 Computing the Euler equation error

```
! calculate euler equation error
call interpolate()
err = 0d0
do ia = 0, n_err
    a_com = a_l + (a_u-a_l)*dble(ia)/dble(n_err)
    call linint_Grow(a_com, a_l, a_u, a_grow, NA, &
            ial, iar, varphi)
    do is = 1, NS
        c_err = varphi*c(ial, is) + (1d0-varphi)*c(iar, is)
        is_com = is
        err_temp = abs(foc(c_err)/c_err)
        if(err_temp > err .and. ((1d0+r)*a_com + &
                        w*eta(is_com) - c_err) > 1d-6)then
            err = err_temp
        endif
    enddo
enddo
write(*, '(a,f15.7)')'Euler equation error:', err
```

ie their labour income plus the remaining assets. Only when their asset level exceeds $\tilde{a}(0, \hat{\eta}_g)$ will they leave some resources for future periods. In the case that $\tilde{a}(0, \hat{\eta}_g) \leq 0$, such an adjustment of the policy function is not necessary and we store the same values in the array entries indexed 0 and −1 (see Module 9.13m).

Having specified the set of endogenous gridpoints $\tilde{a}(\hat{a}_v, \hat{\eta}_g)$ and respective consumption values $\tilde{c}(\hat{a}_v, \hat{\eta}_g)$, we can update the consumption function as described before using the linear interpolation scheme in subroutine `lininit_Gen`. After that, we need to make one additional adjustment, which is related to the upper bound of the capital grid. Specifically, we do not want the household to save more than the maximum wealth level on our grid. We can ensure that the household asset level will not exceed the maximum gridpoint a_u by adjusting the policy function in a suitable way. The remaining parts of the code and the resulting output is the same as in `prog09_09` of the book.

The computation of the Euler equation error (EEE) is shown in Program 9.13 and depends on the asset grid specification. Given a specific number of gridpoints, there is always an optimal growth rate which minimizes the EEE. In the current specification of $NA = 1,000$ asset gridpoints this is a growth rate of `a_grow = 0.01`.

Exercise 9.14

(a) We can write this problem in dynamic programming form as:

$$\begin{aligned} V(a,\eta) = \max_{c,l,a^+} \quad & u(c,1-l) + \beta E\big[V(a^+,\eta^+)\big] \\ \text{s.t.} \quad & a^+ = (1+r)a + w \cdot \exp(\eta) \cdot l - c \end{aligned}$$

with:

$$u(c,1-l) = \frac{\big[c^\nu (1-l)^{1-\nu}\big]^{1-\frac{1}{\gamma}}}{1-\frac{1}{\gamma}}.$$

Using the discretization $\hat{a}_v$ and $\hat{\eta}_g$, the Lagrangean of the problem reads:

$$\begin{aligned} \mathcal{L} = {} & u(c,1-l) + \beta \sum_{g^+=1}^{m} \pi_{gg^+} V(a^+,\hat{\eta}_{g^+}) \\ & + \lambda\big[(1+r)\hat{a}_v + w\exp(\hat{\eta}_g)l - c - a^+\big]. \end{aligned}$$

The first-order conditions are:

$$\begin{aligned} \frac{\partial \mathcal{L}}{\partial c} &= \frac{\nu}{c} \cdot \big[c^\nu (1-l)^{1-\nu}\big]^{1-\frac{1}{\gamma}} - \lambda = 0 \\ \frac{\partial \mathcal{L}}{\partial l} &= -\frac{1-\nu}{1-l} \cdot \big[c^\nu (1-l)^{1-\nu}\big]^{1-\frac{1}{\gamma}} + \lambda w \exp(\hat{\eta}_g) = 0 \\ \frac{\partial \mathcal{L}}{\partial a^+} &= \beta \sum_{g^+=1}^{m} \pi_{gg^+} V_a(a^+,\hat{\eta}_{g^+}) - \lambda = 0, \end{aligned}$$

with:

$$V_a(a^+,\hat{\eta}_{g^+}) = (1+r)\frac{\nu \cdot \big[(c^+)^\nu (1-l^+)^{1-\nu}\big]^{1-\frac{1}{\gamma}}}{c^+}.$$

We therefore get:

$$\begin{aligned} l &= 1 - \frac{1-\nu}{\nu} \cdot \frac{c}{w\exp(\hat{\eta}_g)} \\ \frac{\nu \cdot \big[c^\nu (1-l)^{1-\nu}\big]^{1-\frac{1}{\gamma}}}{c} &= \beta \sum_{g^+=1}^{m} \pi_{gg^+} V_a(a^+,\hat{\eta}_{g^+}), \end{aligned}$$

with $a^+ = (1+r)\hat{a}_v + w\exp(\eta)l - c$, $a^+ \geq 0$, and $\eta^+ = \rho\eta + \epsilon^+$ with $\epsilon^+ \sim N(0,\sigma_\epsilon^2)$.

Table 9.8 Heterogeneous agent model with variable labour supply

Aggregate quantities and prices:		
Capital-to-output ratio (in %)	K/Y	302.71
Interest rate (in %)	r	3.89
Consumption (in % of output)	C/Y	75.78
Investment (in % of output)	I/Y	24.22
Distributional measures:		
CV of labour earnings (in %)	Std(exp(η))/L	50.48
CV of consumption (in %)	Std(c)/C	11.72
CV of wealth (in %)	Std(a)/A	78.38

(b) In order to perform a policy function iteration, we determine a spline function that satisfies:

$$S(\hat{a}_v, \hat{\eta}_g) = \left\{ \beta \sum_{g^+=1}^{m} \pi_{gg^+}(1+r) \frac{\nu \left[c(\hat{a}_v, \hat{\eta}_{g^+})^\nu (1 - l(\hat{a}_v, \hat{\eta}_{g^+}))^{1-\nu}\right]^{1-\frac{1}{\gamma}}}{c(\hat{a}_v, \hat{\eta}_{g^+})} \right\}^{-\gamma}$$

for all $v = 0, \ldots, n$ and $g = 0, \ldots, m$. The set of optimality conditions now reads:

$$l(\hat{a}_v, \hat{\eta}_g) = \max\left[1 - \frac{1-\nu}{\nu} \cdot \frac{c(\hat{a}_v, \hat{\eta}_g)}{w\exp(\hat{\eta}_g)}, 0\right]$$

$$\left[\frac{\nu \cdot \left[c(\hat{a}_v, \hat{\eta}_g)^\nu (1 - l(\hat{a}_v, \hat{\eta}_g))^{1-\nu}\right]^{1-\frac{1}{\gamma}}}{c(\hat{a}_v, \hat{\eta}_g)}\right]^{-\gamma} - S(a^+, \hat{\eta}_g) = 0$$

and $a^+ = (1+r)\hat{a}_v + w\exp(\hat{\eta}_g)l(\hat{a}_v, \hat{\eta}_g) - c(\hat{a}_v, \hat{\eta}_g)$, $a^+ \geq 0$.

We still need to make sure that $a^+ \geq 0$. If this is not the case, we solve the intratemporal first-order condition for c and plug it into the budget constraint with $a^+ = 0$ in order to obtain:

$$l(\hat{a}_v, \hat{\eta}_g) = \max\left[\nu - \frac{(1-\nu)(1+r)\hat{a}_v}{w\exp(\hat{\eta}_g)}, 0\right]$$

and use the budget constraint to calculate:

$$c(\hat{a}_v, \hat{\eta}_g) = (1+r)\hat{a}_v + w\hat{\eta}_g l(\hat{a}_v, \hat{\eta}_g).$$

The remainder of the program is very similar to the standard heterogeneous agent model of program `prog09_09` of the book. Table 9.8 shows the results for the steady-state simulation. In principle, the values are not so different compared to the model with fixed labour supply shown in Table 9.6 of the book. The main difference is the relative volatility of labour earnings, which is now much higher.

10 Life-cycle choices and risk

Exercise 10.1

(a) With the new definition of labour productivity, the dynamic programming problem of the household reads:

$$V(j, a, \theta, \eta, \zeta) = \max_{c, a^+} u(c) + \beta\psi_{j+1}E\big[V(j+1, a^+, \theta, \eta^+, \zeta^+)\big|\eta\big]$$

$$\text{s.t.} \quad a^+ = (1+r)a + wh + pen - c, \quad a^+ \geq \underline{a}(j+1, \theta),$$

$$\eta^+ = \rho\eta + \epsilon^+ \quad \text{with} \quad \epsilon^+ \sim N(0, \sigma_\epsilon^2) \quad \text{and} \quad \zeta^+ \sim N(0, \sigma_\zeta^2).$$

We define the state vector $z = (j, a, \theta, \eta, \zeta)$ and discretize the white noise component into shock levels $\hat{\zeta}_u$ and respective probabilities π_u with $u = 1, \ldots, m_u$ using the subroutine `normal_discrete` from the toolbox. The Euler equation is identical to the baseline model and is given by:

$$c = \left(\beta\psi_{j+1}(1+r) \cdot E\left[c(z^+)^{-\frac{1}{\gamma}}\Big|\eta\right]\right)^{-\gamma}.$$

In the program `sol_prog10_01`, expectations regarding next period's marginal utility of consumption have to be formed with respect to the autoregressive productivity shock, but also with respect to the realization of the white noise shock component. We compute the right-hand side of the Euler equation from:

$$RHS(j, \hat{a}_v, \hat{\theta}_i, \hat{\eta}_g) = \left[\beta\psi_j(1+r)\sum_{g^+=1}^{m_g}\sum_{u^+=1}^{m_u}\pi_{gg^+}\pi_{u^+}c(j, \hat{a}_v, \hat{\theta}_i, \hat{\eta}_{g^+}, \hat{\zeta}_{u^+})^{-\frac{1}{\gamma}}\right]^{-\gamma}.$$

As the white noise shock is not autoregressive but independent across periods, expectations are independent from today's realization. At each gridpoint of the discretized state space, the solution of the Euler equation is computed in the same way as in the baseline model using subroutine `fzero`. Within the subroutine `get_distribution`, we incorporate the white noise component into the distribution at age $j = 1$ by distributing households according to the probability distribution π_u across the different realizations of the white noise shock $\hat{\zeta}_u$:

$$\phi(1, \hat{a}_v, \hat{\theta}_i, \hat{\eta}_g, \hat{\xi}_u) = \begin{cases} \varphi \cdot \pi_i^\theta \cdot \pi_u, & \text{if } v = l \text{ and } g = \frac{m_g+1}{2} \\ (1-\varphi) \cdot \pi_i^\theta \cdot \pi_u, & \text{if } v = r \text{ and } g = \frac{m_g+1}{2} \\ 0, & \text{otherwise.} \end{cases}$$

We still let households start with the median autoregressive productivity level η. The weights φ and $(1-\varphi)$ are derived from linear interpolation of $\tilde{a} = -\underline{a}(1, \hat{\theta}_i)$ with:

$$\tilde{a} = \varphi \cdot \hat{a}_l + (1-\varphi) \cdot \hat{a}_r$$

in order to identify an asset level of $a = 0$ on the asset grid. Given the initial distribution at age one, the distributions $\phi(z)$ for higher ages $j = 2, \ldots, J$ can be computed directly using the policy functions as:

$$\phi(j+1, \hat{a}_v, \hat{\theta}_i, \hat{\eta}_{g^+}, \hat{\xi}_u) = \begin{cases} \phi(z_{j+1}) + \varphi \pi_{gg^+} \pi_u \phi(z_j) & \text{if } v = l, \\ \phi(z_{j+1}) + (1-\varphi) \pi_{gg^+} \pi_u \phi(z_j) & \text{if } v = r. \end{cases}$$

Note that we again account for the discretized white noise shock using the probability distribution π_u. The remainder of the code is the same as in program `prog10_01` of the book.

(b) Setting $\sigma_\zeta = 0$, ie eliminating any risk from a white noise term, makes us end up in the baseline life-cycle model. When the model is simulated with white noise variance of $\sigma_\zeta = 0.057$ and $a_u = 600$, the highest gridpoint is reached in some cohorts just before retirement. This makes it necessary to increase the upper limit of the asset grid to $a_u = 1000$. Yet, the results are only slightly affected by relaxing the upper bound of the asset grid, as the mass of individuals at the upper bound is very small anyway.

(c) When the model is simulated with $\sigma_\zeta = 0.057$, the number of borrowing-constrained households at the beginning of the life cycle is reduced considerably. At the same time, the coefficient of variation for income rises slightly, while the coefficient of variation for consumption remains unchanged. The economic logic behind this is the following: the white noise component increases income uncertainty during working years, which lets households build up more precautionary savings at the beginning of the life cycle. This smooths consumption volatility, so that it remains unchanged compared to the setting with $\sigma_\zeta = 0$ in the baseline model.

Exercise 10.2

(a) The dynamic programming problem of a household with a bequest motive reads:

$$
\begin{aligned}
V(z) = \max_{c,a^+} \ & u(c) + \beta \left\{ \psi_{j+1} E\big[V(z^+)\big|\eta\big] + (1-\psi_{j+1})\mathcal{B}(Ra^+) \right\} \\
\text{s.t.} \quad a^+ &= (1+r)a + wh + pen - c, \quad a^+ \geq 0, \\
\eta^+ &= \rho\eta + \epsilon^+ \quad \text{with} \quad \epsilon^+ \sim N(0, \sigma_\epsilon^2),
\end{aligned}
$$

where $z = (j, a, \theta, \eta)$ and the bequest motive is given by:

$$
\mathcal{B}(Ra^+) = \nu_j \cdot \frac{\left(1 + \frac{Ra^+}{\chi}\right)^{1-\frac{1}{\gamma}}}{1 - \frac{1}{\gamma}}.
$$

We define $R = (1 + r)$ as the accumulation factor, which implies that heirs receive interest payments on their bequest. Beside that, we follow De Nardi (2004) and require individuals to hold non-negative savings in order to rule out the possibility of leaving debt to the descendants. Consequently, the intertemporal first-order condition is given as:

$$
\begin{aligned}
c(z) &= \left\{\beta\left[\psi_{j+1}E\left[V_a(z^+)\middle|\,\eta\right] + (1-\psi_{j+1})\mathcal{B}_a(Ra^+)\right]\right\}^{-\gamma} \\
&= \left\{\beta(1+r)\left[\psi_{j+1}E\left[c(z^+)^{-\frac{1}{\gamma}}\middle|\,\eta\right] + (1-\psi_{j+1})\frac{\nu_{j+1}}{\chi}\left(1+\frac{Ra^+}{\chi}\right)^{-\frac{1}{\gamma}}\right]\right\}^{-\gamma}.
\end{aligned}
$$

Even in the last period of life, ie when $\psi_{J+1} = 0$, the individual now has a positive marginal utility from one additional unit of savings as long as $\nu_{J+1} > 0$. If, however, $\nu_{J+1} = 0$, then it is optimal again for the individual to consume the entire wealth in the last period J of the life cycle. Taking this into account, we define the arrays `RHS`, `EV`, and `aplus` with `JJ+1` elements and distinguish these two cases regarding ν_{J+1} in our numerical implementation with an if-statement as shown, in Program 10.2. In the subroutine `interpolate` we are now treating age $J+1$ separately from all other ages and calculate the right-hand side of the first-order condition in the last period of the life cycle J as:

$$
RHS(J+1, \hat{a}_v, \hat{\theta}_i, \hat{\eta}_g) = \left(\beta\frac{\nu_{J+1}R}{\chi}\right)^{-\gamma}\left(1 + \frac{R\hat{a}_v}{\chi}\right),
$$

and obtain for the expected value function from leaving a bequest:

$$
EV(J+1, \hat{a}_v, \hat{\theta}_i, \hat{\eta}_g) = \beta\nu_{J+1}^{\frac{1}{1-\frac{1}{\gamma}}}\left(1 + \frac{R\hat{a}_v}{\chi}\right),
$$

where we already normalized using the transformation $\left[\left(1-\frac{1}{\gamma}\right)(\cdot)\right]^{\frac{1}{1-\frac{1}{\gamma}}}$. The remaining parts of the code are the same as in program `prog10_01`, with the slight

Program 10.2 Distinguish $\nu_{J+1} > 0$ and $\nu_{J+1} = 0$ in the last period

```
subroutine solve_household()
    [......]
    if(nu(JJ+1) == 0d0)then

        ! get decision in the last period of life
        do ia = 0, NA
            aplus(JJ, ia, :, :) = 0d0
            [......]
        enddo
        call interpolate(JJ)
        JX = JJ-1

    else

        call interpolate(JJ+1)
        JX = JJ

    endif

    do ij = JX, 1, -1

        ! check about how many is to iterate
        [......]
        ! interpolate individual RHS
        call interpolate(ij)

        write(*,'(a,i3,a)')'Age: ',ij,' DONE!'
    enddo

end subroutine
```

difference that the borrowing constraint $a \geq 0$ is now implicitly defined by the lower bound of our asset grid and no longer stored in a separate array a_bor.

(b) When bequests are not luxury goods, that is $\chi = 1.0$, and households exhibit no altruism to their descendants before retiring, meaning $\nu_j = 0$ for $j < j_r$, they do not change their saving behaviour significantly at young ages compared to the baseline model (see Figure 10.1). Households are, hence, still borrowing-constrained at young ages. However, when the bequest motive is present during retirement (ie $\nu_j = 10$ for $j > j_r$), households build up savings and even die with positive assets at the maximum age. This leads to rising consumption and consumption volatility at high ages, but reduces the number of borrowing-constrained households.

(c) When a bequest motive is also present at young ages, meaning $\nu_j > 0$ for $j < j_r$, the number of borrowing-constrained households also falls during working ages. When bequests are considered to be luxury goods (ie $\chi = 10.0$), richer households in particular leave additional bequest at old ages, so that the amount of savings rises further during retirement (see Figure 10.2). By varying the parameters ν and χ, we are able to model the asset accumulation over the life cycle very flexibly, both along the age dimension as well as in the cross-section of households.

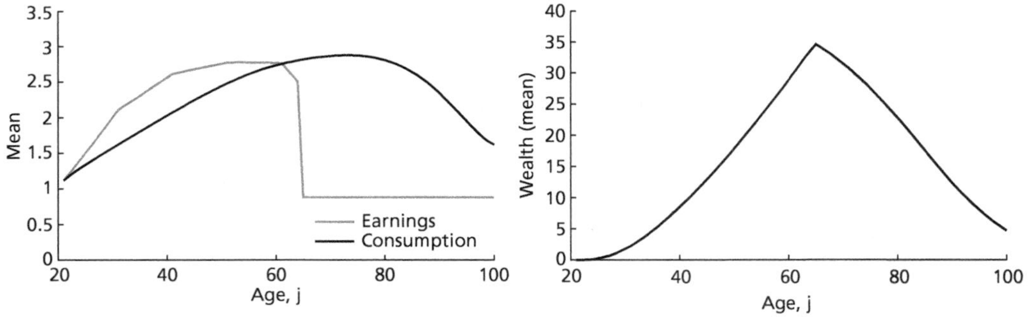

Figure 10.1 Life-cycle consumption and asset accumulation with bequests

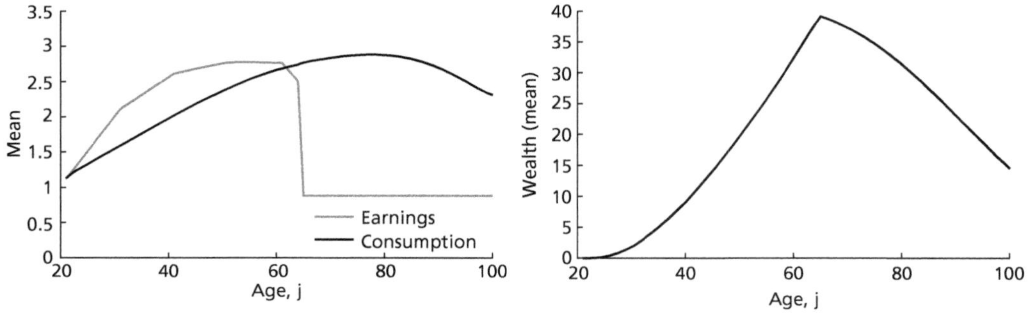

Figure 10.2 Rising wealth accumualtion with bequests as luxury goods

Exercise 10.3

We follow the notation from the exercise in the book to denote the household's actual behaviour by $c(z^+), a(z^+)$, and $V(z^+)$, while we use the $\hat{a}(z^+), \hat{c}(z^+)$, and $\hat{V}(z^+)$ as notation for the agent's beliefs. The first-order condition for the hyperbolic agent with time-inconsistent preferences then reads:

$$c(z) = \left(\hat{\delta}\beta\psi_{j+1}(1+r)\cdot E\left[\hat{c}(z^+)^{-\frac{1}{\gamma}}|\eta\right]\right)^{-\gamma}.$$

Agents in our set-up are *naive* in the sense that they are assumed to behave in a time-consistent way in the future, despite the fact that they violated their preferences previously. The first-order condition, hence, requires that the marginal utility of consumption today has to be equal to the marginal utility of consumption of a rationally acting household in the future, discounted with the interest rate, the survival probability, the standard discount factor β, and, most importantly, the additional discount factor $\hat{\delta}$. To compute the choices of a time-inconsistent agent, we therefore also need to trace the optimal decisions of a time-consistent household in the numerical model. The first-order condition for time-consistent behaviour is equal to the first-order condition in the baseline life-cycle model in Section 10.1.1 of the book and given by:

$$c(z) = \left(\beta\psi_{j+1}(1+r)\cdot E\left[c(z^+)^{-\frac{1}{\gamma}}|\eta\right]\right)^{-\gamma}.$$

In this case the actual beliefs are consistent with the individual's decisions. We distinguish these two cases in the numerical implementation by adding an additional dimension `ih` to the household-level arrays. In the entries with `ih = 0`, we store the time-consistent policy and value function. In entries with `ih = 1`, we store the time-inconsistent counterparts.

In the subroutine `interpolate`, we now separate the computation of the right-hand side of the first-order condition from the computation of the expected value function (see Program 10.3). We compute the expected value function for both the time-consistent and time-inconsistent agent. Yet, we only need to consider the time-consistent case when deriving the right-hand side of the first-order condition, as the naive household is believed to be perfectly rational in the future.

We use the same parameterization as in the baseline model in order to compare hyperbolic ($\hat{\delta} = 0.8$) to rational consumers. Hyperbolic agents consume more at younger ages and build up fewer savings, as illustrated in Figure 10.3. Hence, the fraction of borrowing-constrained households at young ages increases, which results in lower consumption during retirement. As the decisions of hyperbolic agents deviates from optimality, they

Program 10.3 Restructuring of the subroutine `interpolate`

```
subroutine interpolate(ij)
    [......]
    ! get RHS of first order condition
    [......]
    do is = 1, NS
        RHS(ij, ia, ip, is) = 0d0
        do is_p = 1, NS
            chelp = max(c(ij, ia, ip, is_p, 0), 1d-10)
            RHS(ij, ia, ip, is) = RHS(ij, ia, ip, is) + &
                                  pi(is, is_p)*margu(chelp)
        enddo
        RHS(ij, ia, ip, is) = ((1d0+r)*beta*psi(ij)* &
                              RHS(ij, ia, ip, is))**(-gamma)
    enddo
    [......]
    ! get expected value functions
    [......]
    do is = 1, NS
        EV(ij, ia, ip, is, ih) = 0d0
        do is_p = 1, NS
            EV(ij, ia, ip, is, ih) = EV(ij, ia, ip, is, ih) +&
                            pi(is, is_p)*V(ij, ia, ip, is_p, ih)
        enddo
        EV(ij, ia, ip, is, ih) =(egam*EV(ij, ia, ip, is, ih))&
                                                    **(1d0/egam)
    enddo

end subroutine
```

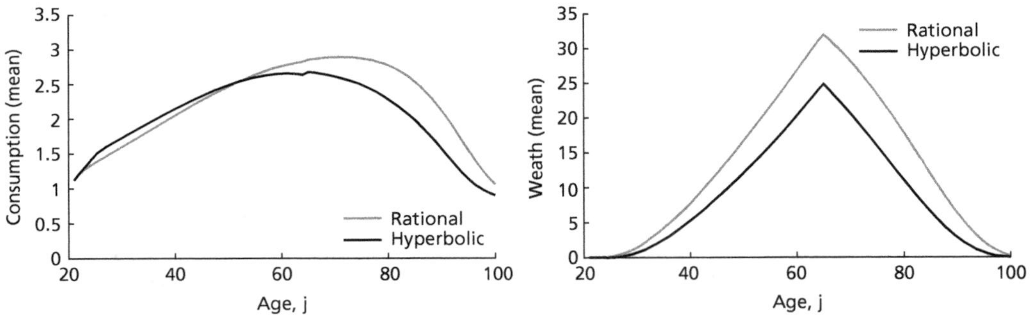

Figure 10.3 Decisions of hyperbolic agents

face utility losses. The life-cycle utility of individuals falls from $V(z_0) = -26.004$ in the case of rational to $\hat{V}(z_0) = -26.235$ in the case of hyperbolic consumers.

Exercise 10.4

(a) The dynamic optimization problem of an individual in the presence of health risk is given by:

$$\begin{aligned} V(z) &= \max_{c,a^+} \; u_m(c) + \beta\psi_{j+1}(m)E\big[V(z^+)\big|m,\eta\big] \\ \text{s.t.} \quad a^+ &= (1+r)a + wh + pen - c, \qquad a^+ \geq 0, \\ \eta^+ &= \rho\eta + \epsilon^+ \quad \text{with} \quad \epsilon^+ \sim N(0,\sigma_\epsilon^2) \\ \pi_{j,m,m^+} &= Pr(m_{j+1} = m^+\big|m_j = m) \quad \text{with} \quad m, m^+ \in \{0,1\}, \end{aligned}$$

where we define the state vector as $z = (j, a, \theta, m, \eta)$. With the definition of the instantaneous utility function $u_m(c)$ from the book, the corresponding Lagrangian yields the first-order condition:

$$c = \left(\beta\psi_{j+1}(m)(1+r)\delta(m)^{-1} \cdot E\left[\delta(m^+)c(z^+)^{-\frac{1}{\gamma}}\middle|\, m,\eta\right]\right)^{-\gamma},$$

where we use the notation $z^+ = (j+1, a^+, \theta, m^+, \eta^+)$. In addition to the current productivity shock realization η, the expected marginal utility of future consumption is also conditional on the current health status m. In each period, the transition between health states is determined through the age-dependent transition matrix π_{j,m,m^+}. The immediate utility of individuals in bad health is scaled by a parameter $\delta(m)$ and their survival probability is subject to a discount factor χ. Note that a bad health state only induces a shock on the survival probability as long as it persists. It disappears again with the transition to a good health state.

In the numerical implementation, we first set the initial distribution of individuals over the states 'good health' and 'bad health' and set up the transition probabilities between these two states. The additional state variable m translates into an additional do-loop whenever we are iterating through our state space. The expected right-hand side of the first-order condition that has to hold at any state of our discretized state space is computed in the subroutine `interpolate` as:

$$RHS(j, \hat{a}_v, \hat{\theta}_i, m, \hat{\eta}_g) = \Bigg[\beta\psi_j(m)(1+r)\delta(m)^{-1} \sum_{g^+=1}^{m_g}\sum_{m^+=1}^{m_m} \pi_{gg^+}\pi_{j,m,m^+}\delta(m^+)c(j, \hat{a}_v, \hat{\theta}_i, m^+, \hat{\eta}_{g^+})^{-\frac{1}{\gamma}}\Bigg]^{-\gamma}.$$

Program 10.4 shows that, in the subroutine `aggregation`, we proceed slightly differently than before. We first compute the conditional cohort averages for households being in good health and in bad health. In a second step, we recover the unconditional cohort averages by weighting the conditional ones with the respective share `frac_phi(ij, im)`

Program 10.4 Conditional and unconditional cohort averages

```
subroutine aggregation()

    ! calculate fraction of good vs. bad health households
    do ij = 1, JJ
        do im = 0, NM
            frac_phi(ij, im) = sum(phi(ij, :, :, im, :))
        enddo
    enddo
    [......]
    ! calculate conditional cohort averages
    [......]
    do ij = 1, JJ
        [......]
        do is = 1, NS

            c_coh(ij, im) = c_coh(ij, im) + &
                         c(ij, ia, ip, im, is) &
            *phi(ij, ia, ip, im, is)/frac_phi(ij, im)
             [......]
        enddo
        [......]
    enddo

    ! recover unconditional cohort averages
    do ij = 1, JJ
        do im = 0, NM
            c_coh(ij, NM+1) = c_coh(ij, NM+1) &
                           + c_coh(ij, im)*frac_phi(ij, im)
             [......]
        enddo
    enddo

end subroutine
```

of good health and bad health agents in the population at age j. We store the unconditional cohort averages in the additional entry NM+1 of the health dimension in our arrays.

In our first parameterization, we do not allow for transition between health states, so that we obtain $Pr(m_{j+1} = m|m_j = m) = 1$ and $Pr(m_{j+1} \neq m|m_j = m) = 0$. The distribution of individuals over the different health states will thus remain unchanged over the entire life cycle. Besides, we abstract from an effect of the health status on mortality (ie $\chi = 1$), so that the only difference between individuals in good and bad health is the scaling factor $\delta(m)$ in the instantaneous utility function. Yet, as this factor cancels out of the first-order condition in the absence of uncertainty on future health status, meaning:

$$c = \left(\beta\psi_{j+1}(m)(1+r) \cdot E\left[c(z^+)^{-\frac{1}{\gamma}} \Big| \eta\right]\right)^{-\gamma},$$

the individual's actual decision remains unaffected by their health status. Consequently, varying the parameter δ obviously does not change the results. Setting $\chi < 1$ implies that individuals in bad health die earlier than those in good health and makes them allocate more consumption to earlier periods of the life cycle (see Figure 10.4). They reduce their savings as the increased mortality leads to a lower expected marginal utility of future consumption. This effect gets more pronounced with decreasing values of χ.

(b) In the following, we return to setting $\chi = 1$. Moreover, we let the probability of moving from a good health to a bad health state next period increase linearly over time on the interval $[0.1, 0.4]$. In addition, we let the probability of remaining in the bad health state increase linearly over time on the interval $[0.6, 0.9]$. With increasing age, the transition from good health to bad health thus gets more likely, while the probability of recovery declines. In the presence of uncertainty on the next period's health status, the scaling factor $\delta(m)$ no longer cancels out the first-order condition and thus has an impact on an individual's optimal decision. Individuals in bad health have an incentive to consume less today, as they might recover to positive health in the future and thus can achieve utility gains from postponing consumption to later periods (see Figure 10.5). Vice versa, individuals in good health have an incentive for immediate consumption as

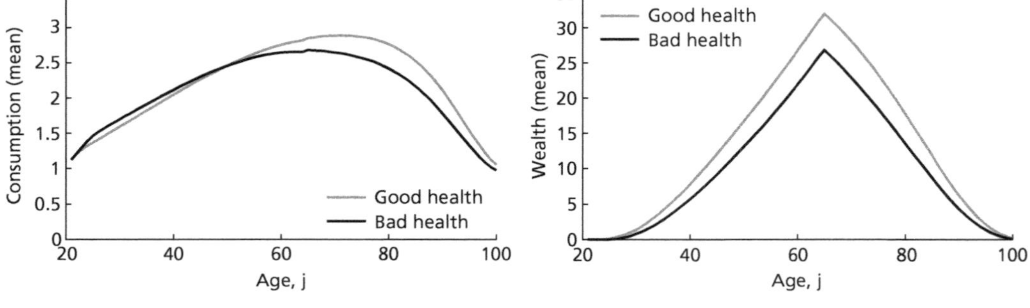

Figure 10.4 Reduced life expectancy and permanent health shocks

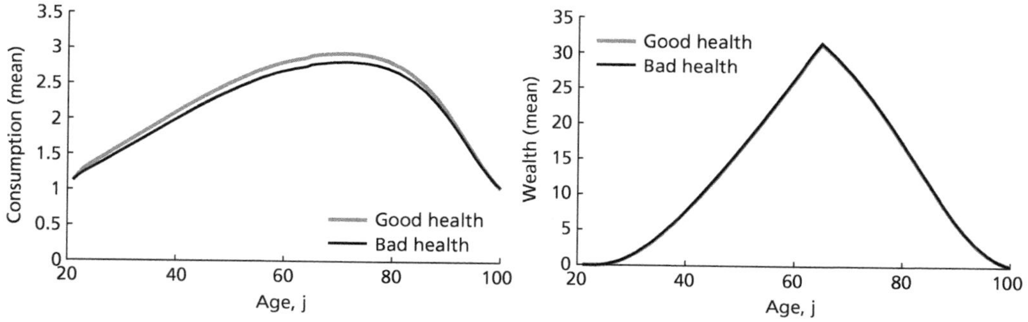

Figure 10.5 Reduced life-expectancy and transitory health shocks

utility losses from a bad health shock might occur in future periods. As the transition probabilities between health states decline with age, this effect gets smaller and the consumption, as well as the savings path of individuals in good and bad health, approach each other. Wealth accumulation is marginally higher for individuals in bad health than for individuals in good health. Obviously, for a scaling factor $\delta(m_j) > 1$ as it is implied with $\delta = -0.1$, the same line of argument would hold the other way round. Such a paramterization might be justified in the sense that particular goods, like a wheelchair, become particularly valuable in the presence of bad health shocks.

Exercise 10.5

(a) The numerical implementation of skill-dependent transition probabilities between health states is nothing more than adding another dimension to the array that stores the transition matrix `pi_m`. Along the additional dimension, we can assign different transition probabilities from good health to bad health for each skill level (see Program 10.5). To take into account that health depends on skill in this set-up, we start with computing the cohort averages over the life cycle conditional on both the skill level and the health status of individuals in the subroutine `aggregation`. Similar to before, we then take these conditional cohort averages to compute the unconditional averages and the cohort averages that are either conditional on health status or on skill level, respectively.

Program 10.5 Initializing new transition probabilities

```
subroutine initialize()
    [......]
    ! probability of bad health when current health is good
    call grid_Cons_Equi(pi_m(:, 1, 0, 1), 0.1d0, 0.4d0)
    call grid_Cons_Equi(pi_m(:, 2, 0, 1), 0.0d0, 0.2d0)
    pi_m(:, :, 0, 0) = 1d0 - pi_m(:, :, 0, 1)
    [......]
end subroutine
```

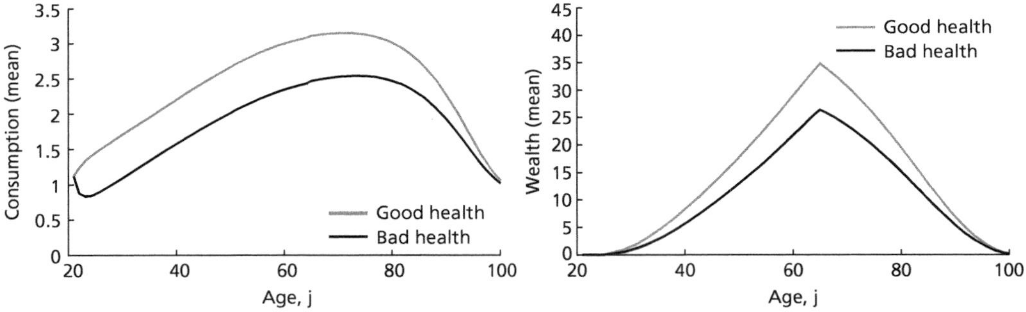

Figure 10.6 Skill-dependent transition probabilities for bad health

Compared to the initial calibration in Exercise 10.4, the difference in life-cycle asset accumulation and consumption of individuals in bad and in good health is now more pronounced, as shown in Figure 10.6. This is mostly owing to a selection effect, meaning that it is more likely that a bad-health individual is also a low-income person and a good-health individual has a high labour productivity. When taking a deeper look into the skill-specific output of the program, the results we observe are in line with our intuition. Conditional on having a certain skill level, individuals in good health consume more than individuals in bad health and the share of individuals in bad health is higher among low-skilled individuals than among the high skilled.

(b) The numerical implementation of a health-dependent labour productivity is very similar to the skill-dependent transition probabilities between health states in Part (a). We initialize a new array `varrho_m` that carries the skill-dependent effect of an adverse health shock on labour productivity and multiply it to labour productivity everywhere in the program where human capital h_j of an individual is needed (see Program 10.5.a).

A negative impact of health status on individual labour productivity first of all implies an income effect. The discounted expected life-time income of a household is now lower than in Part (a) and, hence, results in a lower life-cycle asset and consumption path over time. Making the effect on labour productivity skill-dependent by setting a higher ϱ_θ for low-skilled individuals than for high-skilled individuals leads to a further divergence

Program 10.5.a Initializing new transition probabilities

```
subroutine initialize()
    [......]
    ! initialize impact of shock on
    varrho(1) = 0.2d0
    varrho(2) = 0.1d0
    do ip = 1, NP
        do im = 0, NM
            varrho_m(ip, im) = exp(-varrho(ip)*dble(im))
        enddo
    enddo
    [......]
end subroutine
```

of the life-cycle asset and consumption paths conditional on health status (compare Figure 10.7).

(c) In order to incorporate additional stochastic out-of-pocket expenses for individuals in bad health, we discretize the normal distribution for the stochastic component ζ with the subroutine `normal_discrete` and define the actual out-of-pocket expenses in an array `hc` (see Program 10.5.b). The additional state variable ζ translates into an additional do-loop when iterating over the discretized state space. In each state with a bad current health status (ie $m = 1$), the individual is exposed to out-of-pocket expenses hc.

The effect of out-of-pocket expenses is illustrated in Figure 10.8. Individuals build up precautionary savings to insure against adverse out-of-pocket expenditure shocks.

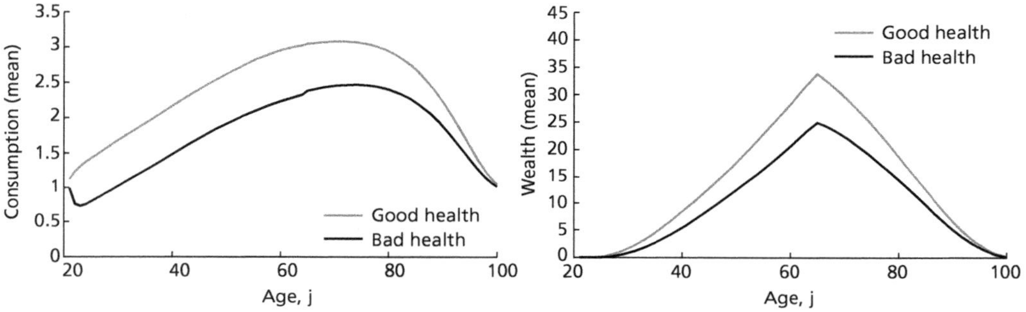

Figure 10.7 Effect of health status on labour productivity.

Program 10.5.b Initializing out-of-pocket expenses from health shock

```
! normally distributed stochastic term
call normal_discrete(zeta, dist_zeta, 0d0, sigma_zeta)
zeta = exp(zeta)

! out of pocket expenses
do ij = 1, JJ
   hc(ij, :) = k(ij)*zeta
enddo
```

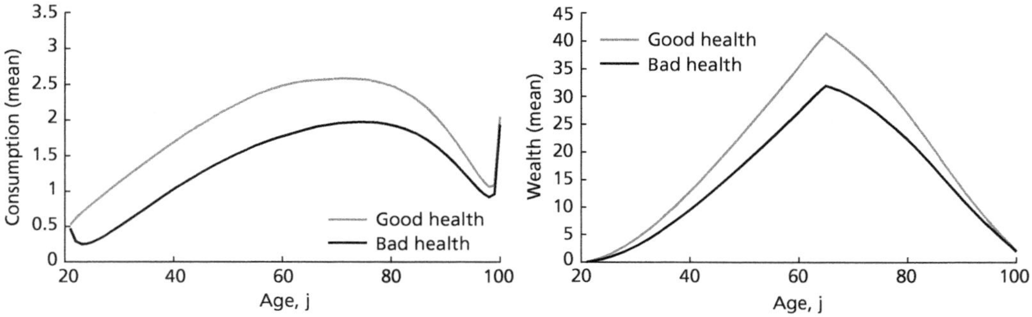

Figure 10.8 Out-of-pocket expenses increase precautionary savings

Consequently, asset accumulation increases substantially and a significantly lower fraction of individuals is borrowing-constrained throughout the life cycle. The government transfer b is necessary to ensure that individuals do not end up in negative consumption owing to out-of-pocket shocks that exceed their wealth and income.

Exercise 10.6

(a) In this exercise we no longer account for different skill classes, but introduce infertility shocks as well as the additional choice to have children, aside from the usual consumption–savings problem. Raising children provides utility, but comes at the expense of lower income, owing to a reduced labour supply. We can write the optimization problem of a fertile household in dynamic programming form as:

$$\begin{aligned}
V(j,a,n^c,\eta,F) = & \max_{c,a^+,k\in\{0,1\}} \quad u(c,n^c) + \\
& \qquad \beta\psi_{j+1}E\big[V(j+1,a^+,n^{c,+},\eta^+,f^+)\big|\eta,n^c,F\big] \\
\text{s.t.} \quad a^+ &= (1+r)a + wh(1-(n^c)^\nu l_c) + pen - c, \quad a^+ \geq 0, \\
\eta^+ &= \rho\eta + \epsilon^+ \quad \text{with} \quad \epsilon^+ \sim N(0,\sigma_\epsilon^2), \\
n^{c,+} &= B(n^c + k, p) \quad \text{and} \\
f^+ &= \begin{cases} I & \text{with probability } p_f^+ \text{ and} \\ F & \text{with probability } 1 - p_f^+. \end{cases}
\end{aligned}$$

In our numerical implementation, we capture the transition between fertile and infertile states by means of a transition matrix, similar to the way we model health shocks in Exercise 10.4. The only difference is that the 'bad' state (ie infertility) is now an absorbing state in the sense that the probability to become fertile again is equal to zero. We store this transition matrix in the array `pf`, where the first dimension of this array captures age-dependency, the second entry the current fertility state, and the third entry the potential future fertility state. Distinguishing between fertile and infertile states is crucial for the numerical solution of the model: if the household is infertile, there is no need to decide about whether to have additional children or not, and the optimization problem reduces to a standard consumption–savings decision. The dynamic programming problem of an infertile household thus simplifies to:

$$\begin{aligned}
V(j,a,n^c,\eta,I) &= \max_{c,a^+} \; u(c,n^c) + \beta\psi_{j+1}E\big[V(j+1,a^+,n^{c,+},\eta^+,I)\big|\eta,n^c\big] \\
\text{s.t.} \quad a^+ &= (1+r)a + wh(1-(n^c)^\nu l_c) + pen - c, \quad a^+ \geq 0, \\
n^{c,+} &= B(n^c,p) \quad \text{and} \quad \eta^+ = \rho\eta + \epsilon^+ \text{ with } \epsilon^+ \sim N(0,\sigma_\epsilon^2).
\end{aligned}$$

The household remains in the infertile state I for the remainder of the household's life time.

Fertile households need to decide whether to have a child or not. As the decision to have a (further) child is discrete, we determine it by directly comparing the respective value functions of the two alternatives, having a child or not. In our numerical implementation, we store the optimal policy function from these two optimization problems in arrays that come with the additional flag `temp`. Depending on which of the two alternatives yields the higher utility, we assign the optimal decisions to the actual arrays that carry the value and policy functions at a certain state of our discretized state space. This is very similar to the model with female labour supply in the book, where we compared the decisions of whether to participate in the labour force or not. Note that we are using the fact that all households are infertile during retirement to treat fertility in a similar way to the autoregressive productivity shock. We only compute the optimal decisions for infertile states and copy them to the respective fertile counterparts.

For a fertile couple, the first-order condition we need to solve at each of our gridpoints is a similar one in the baseline life-cycle model, but conditional on the fertility decision k:

$$c(z,k) = \left(\beta\psi_{j+1}(1+r)\cdot E\left[\, c(z^+)^{-\frac{1}{\gamma}} \,\middle|\, \eta, n^c, f\right]\right)^{-\gamma},$$

where we used $z = (j, a, n^c, \eta, f)$ and $n^{c,+} = B(n^c + k, p)$. We use the subroutine `fzero` from the toolbox to find the optimal level a^+, which ensures that the first-order condition holds. The function `foc` we hand over to `fzero` is almost identical to the one in `prog10_01`, with the difference that we now need to account for the decision whether to give birth to a further child, the reduced income from already existing children, and the infertility shock. Similar to Section 10.1.3 of the book, where female labour supply was a discrete choice, the discrete decision whether to give birth to a child induces a discontinuity in the form of a jump in the first-order condition. We again decide to accept the mistake we make by using linear interpolation and refrain from introducing a more complex interpolation algorithm. In fact, we are even reducing the number of gridpoints on the asset grid to `NA = 50` to lower the computational time.

The computation of the right-hand-side of the first-order condition together with the computation of the expected value function is again carried out in the subroutine `interpolate`, which is shown in Program 10.6. This is where we account for the uncertainty resulting from fertility f, the number of children living at home next period $n^{c,+}$, and the autoregressive productivity shock η. Note that we use the additive separability of the utility function and calculate expected discounted utility from consumption and children in separate arrays. This allows us to use different transformations on these functions in order to improve the results from linear interpolation.

Finally, setting up the distribution over our discretized state space in `get_distribution` is straightforward. At each gridpoint, we need to account for the optimal next period savings a^+ and the decision k whether to have a child or not, in order to set up

Program 10.6 Right-hand-side of first-order condition and value function

```
subroutine interpolate(ij)
    [......]
    RHS(ij, ia, in, is, ift) = 0d0
    EVC(ij, ia, in, is, ift) = 0d0
    EVN(ij, ia, in, is, ift) = 0d0
    do in_p = 0, in
        do is_p = 1, NS
            do ift_p = 0, NF
                chelp = max(c(ij,ia,in_p,is_p,ift_p), 1d-10)
                RHS(ij, ia, in, is, ift) = &
                    RHS(ij, ia, in, is, ift) + &
                    pi(is, is_p)*pf(ij, ift, ift_p)* &
                    binomialPDF(in_p, in, p)*margu(chelp)

                EVC(ij, ia, in, is, ift) = &
                    EVC(ij, ia, in, is, ift) + &
                    pi(is, is_p)*pf(ij, ift, ift_p)* &
                    binomialPDF(in_p, in, p)* &
                    VC(ij, ia, in_p, is_p, ift_p)
                EVN(ij, ia, in, is, ift) = &
                    EVN(ij, ia, in, is, ift) + &
                    pi(is, is_p)*pf(ij, ift, ift_p)* &
                    binomialPDF(in_p, in, p)* &
                    VN(ij, ia, in_p, is_p, ift_p)
            enddo
        enddo
    enddo
    RHS(ij, ia, in, is, ift) = ((1d0+r)*beta*psi(ij)* &
        RHS(ij, ia, in, is, ift))**(-gamma)
    EVC(ij, ia, in, is, ift) = &
        (egam*EVC(ij, ia, in, is, ift))**(1d0/egam)
    EVN(ij, ia, in, is, ift) = &
        (echi*EVN(ij, ia, in, is, ift))**(1d0/echi)
    [......]
end subroutine
```

the distribution of individuals over the next period's gridpoints. In the subroutine `aggregation`, we use this distribution together with the policy functions we obtained in `solve_household` to compute cohort averages. We compute the number of children living at home, the number of children born at any household age and the age at which the n-th child is born.

Figure 10.9 shows the number of children living at home and the number of newborns over the life cycle, while the first row of Table 10.1 summarizes the results.

(b) We report the numbers of the sensitivity analysis in the second to the last row in Table 10.1. The baseline parameterization generates an average number of children per household of 2.13, where the first child is born on average around age twenty-four and the second one at age thirty-two. At age thirty-seven, only about one child remains in the household. A higher autocorrelation parameter ρ induces more uncertainty. Consequently, households have fewer children and particularly postpone the birth of the second child to a higher age, where more uncertainty has already been revealed. Decreasing the growth rate of infertility shocks lets the probability of becoming infertile rise faster over the life cycle. Consequently, as reported in the third row of the table,

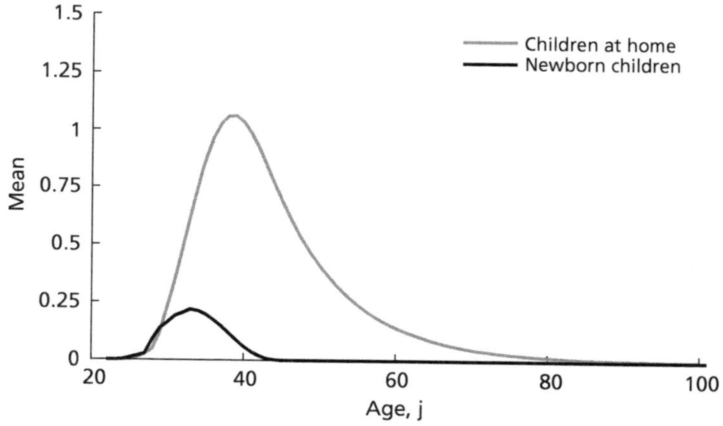

Figure 10.9 Number of children at home and number of newborns

Table 10.1 Results of the sensitivity analysis

	No. of births		Av. age of		
	age 30	age 45	first child	Second child	No. of children at home at age 37
Baseline	0.64	2.13	24.33	31.98	1.06
$\rho = 0.99$	0.56	1.92	24.39	32.56	0.91
$u_f = 0.1$	0.57	1.90	23.85	31.97	0.94
$\kappa = 0.4$	0.69	2.18	24.27	31.79	1.08

households have fewer children and give birth to the first child earlier than in the baseline scenario. Finally, higher pension benefits at old age (without an adaption of the contribution rate) reduce the need for old age savings, so that more resources are available for additional children and consumption. The fertility rate of the population consequently rises.

Exercise 10.7

(a) Implementing value function iteration into `prog10_02` from the book is conceptually equivalent to similar exercises from Chapter 8 and Chapter 9. At each state at a certain age, we use minimization and interpolation to find the optimal individual decisions that maximize the value function. We start from the terminal condition in the last period, for which we know that it is optimal to consume all remaining wealth in the form of accumulated assets as well as pension income. In all prior periods, we hand the function `valuefunc` to the subroutine `fminsearch` and iterate over the optimal level of savings a^+.

The function `valuefunc` takes a future asset level a^+ as input and derives the endogenous labour supply decision from:

$$l = l(a^+) = \min\left\{\max\left[\nu + \frac{1-\nu}{wh}\left(a^+ - (1+r)a - pen\right), 0\right], 1\right\},$$

as shown in Section 10.1.2 in the book. With $l(a^+)$ at hand, we are able to calculate current consumption $c(a^+)$, and together with the interpolated next period value function $V(z^+)$, we can calculate the utility level arising from the savings choice. Note that we introduce a penalty on negative consumption to increase the numerical stability of our algorithm. This penalty is set up similarly to Exercise 9.8 and comes with a kink in our value function at $c = 0$. The subroutines `get_distribution` and `aggregation` do not need to be modified when switching from a policy function iteration algorithm to value function iteration.

(b) In order to compute Euler equation errors, we first need to take a look at the first-order condition of the household optimization problem. Starting from equation (10.17) in the book, we can reformulate the Euler equation in consumption terms as:

$$c(a^+) - \frac{\nu\left[c(a^+)^\nu(1-l(a^+))^{1-\nu}\right]^{1-\frac{1}{\gamma}}}{\beta\psi_{j+1}(1+r)E\left[\frac{\nu\left[c(z^+)^\nu(1-l(z^+))^{1-\nu}\right]^{1-\frac{1}{\gamma}}}{c(z^+)}\right]} = 0.$$

In relative consumption terms, that is dividing by $c(a^+)$, we can hence write the Euler equation residual for a certain current asset level a and savings decision a^+ as:

$$EER(a, a^+) = \left|1 - \frac{\frac{\nu\left[c(a^+)^\nu(1-l(a^+))^{1-\nu}\right]^{1-\frac{1}{\gamma}}}{c(a^+)}}{\beta\psi_{j+1}(1+r)E\left[\frac{\nu\left[c(z^+)^\nu(1-l(z^+))^{1-\nu}\right]^{1-\frac{1}{\gamma}}}{c(z^+)}\right]}\right|.$$

To calculate this residual and the corresponding Euler equation error, we iterate through the discretized state space and evaluate the Euler equation residual on a very dense asset grid with `n_err = 10,000` gridpoints. We store this asset grid in the array `a_err`. At each age, productivity state, and asset level, we obtain the optimal savings decisions by linearly interpolating the policy function `aplus` between the gridpoints on the original asset state space. We store the corresponding Euler equation residual in the variable `err_temp`. This algorithm is illustrated in Program 10.7. Note that, when calculating the Euler equation error, we need to take into account that the Euler equation only holds for households who are not liquidity-constrained. Hence, we only update the Euler equation error if the future savings level a^+ is above a threshold of 10^{-6}.

Program 10.7 Computing the Euler equation error

```
! calculate euler equation error
err = 0d0
do ij = 1, JJ-1
    do ia = 0, n_err

        ! obtain interpolation weights
        call linint_Grow(a_err(ia), a_l, a_u, a_grow, NA, &
            ial, iar, varphi)

        do ip = 1, NP
            do is = 1, NS

                ! set up communication variables
                ij_com = ij
                ip_com = ip
                is_com = is

                ! compute policy function and eer
                a_plus = varphi*aplus(ij, ial, ip, is) + &
                    (1d0-varphi)*aplus(ij, iar, ip, is)
                err_temp = abs(eer(a_err(ia), a_plus))

                ! check whether to update eer
                if(err_temp > err .and. a_plus > 1d-6) &
                    err = err_temp
            enddo
        enddo
    enddo
enddo
write(*,'(a,es15.7)')'Euler equation error:',err
```

The Euler equation residual is computed in the function `eer`, which receives both the current asset level `a_err` and the optimal policy `a_plus` as an input (see Module 10.7m). This function operates in a very similar way to the first-order condition in the baseline model `sol_prog10_02` of the book. The only difference is that it allows for an arbitrary current wealth level a. As the baseline version of program `sol_prog10_02` does not compute the Euler equation error, we incorporate the same lines of code into this program as well. The Euler equation error in the program with value function iteration of `4.19E-02` is slightly higher than in the case of policy function iteration `1.09E-02`. Beside that, policy function iteration is faster in computation than value function iteration.

Exercise 10.8

(a) In this exercise, we introduce variable labour supply into the model with health shocks and account for the effect of these shocks on an individual's time-endowment. However, we no longer consider different skill classes, so that the optimization problem of the household in dynamic programming form is given by:

Module 10.7m The function eer storing the Euler equation error

```
function eer(a_err, a_plus)
    [......]
    ! calculate the wage rate
    wage = w*eff(ij_com)*theta(ip_com)*eta(is_com)

    ! calculate available resources
    available = (1d0+r)*a_err + pen(ij_com)

    ! determine labor
    if(ij_com < JR)then
        lab = min(max(nu + (1d0-nu)*(a_plus-available)/ &
            wage, 0d0), 1d0-1d-10)
    else
        lab = 0d0
    endif

    ! calculate consumption
    cons = available + wage*lab - a_plus
    cons = max(cons, 1d-10)

    ! get interpolation weights
    call linint_Grow(a_plus, a_l, a_u, a_grow, NA, &
        ial, iar, varphi)

    tomorrow = varphi*RHS(ij_com+1, ial, ip_com, is_com) + &
        (1d0-varphi)*RHS(ij_com+1, iar, ip_com, is_com)
    tomorrow = tomorrow**(-1d0/gamma)

    ! calculate Euler equation residual (eer)
    eer = 1d0 - margu(cons, lab)/tomorrow

end function
```

$$V(j,a,m,\eta) = \max_{c,l,a^+} \; u(c, 1-l, m) + \beta\psi_{j+1}(m)E\big[V(j+1, a^+, m^+, \eta^+)\big|\eta, m\big]$$

$$\text{s.t.} \quad a^+ = (1+r)a + whl + pen - c, \qquad a^+ \geq 0,$$

$$\eta^+ = \rho\eta + \epsilon^+ \quad \text{with} \quad \epsilon^+ \sim N(0, \sigma_\epsilon^2)$$

$$\pi_{j,m,m^+} = Pr(m_{j+1} = m^+\big|m_j = m) \quad \text{with} \quad m, m^+ \in \{0,1\}.$$

Deriving the optimality conditions follows the same logic as in Section 10.1.2. in the book: we start with setting up the Lagrangean to solve the household optimization problem at a state $z = (j, a, m, \eta)$. Taking derivatives yields:

$$l(a^+, m) = \min\left\{\max\left[\frac{1-\nu}{wh}\left(a^+ - (1+r)a - pen\right) + \nu(1-\phi_l m), 0\right], 1 - \phi_l m\right\}$$

for optimal labour supply from the intratemporal optimality condition. We restrict labour supply again to be non-negative and let it not exceed the maximum time-endowment of the household. Yet, in contrast to previous models, the maximum time-endowment is no longer constant. Instead, it is reduced by ϕ_l in the presence of an adverse health shock $m = 1$. Plugging $l(a^+, m)$ into the intertemporal budget constraint:

$$c(a^+, m) = (1 + r)a + whl(a^+, m) + pen_j - a^+,$$

yields the optimal current consumption as a function of future savings and the current health shock. Using this, we ultimately obtain:

$$\frac{\nu\left[c(a^+, m)^\nu(1 - l(a^+, m) - \phi_l m)^{1-\nu}\right]^{1-\frac{1}{\gamma}}}{c(a^+, m)} =$$

$$\beta\psi_{j+1}(1 + r) \cdot E_j\left[\frac{\nu\left[c(z^+)^\nu(1 - l(z^+) - \phi_l m^+)^{1-\nu}\right]^{1-\frac{1}{\gamma}}}{c(z^+)}\middle| m, \eta\right]$$

for the intertemporal first-order condition.

In program `sol_prog10_08`, we again use the subroutine `fzero` to search for the optimal savings level a^+ that makes the intertemporal first-order condition hold. The function `foc` that is handed over to the subroutine `fzero` is shown in Module 10.8m and is conceptually similar to its equivalent in program `prog10_02` of the book. The function `margu` computes the left-hand side of the first-order condition, ie today's marginal utility for a given level of consumption, labour, and current health. Note that we apply the transformation $[\cdot]^{-\gamma}$ to both sides of the first-order condition to increase the numerical stability of the algorithm. Similar to Section 10.2.1. of the book, we have

Module 10.8m The function `foc` storing the Euler equation

```
function foc(x_in)
    [......]
    ! determine labor
    if(ij_com < JR)then
      lab_com = min(max((1d0-nu)*(a_plus-available) &
                       /wage + nu*(1d0-phi_l*dble(im_com)), &
                       1d-10), 1d0-phi_l*dble(im_com)-1d-10)
    else
        lab_com = 0d0
    endif

    ! calculate consumption
    cons_com = max(available + wage*lab_com - a_plus, 1d-10)

    ! calculate linear interpolation for future part of foc
    a_plus = max(a_plus, a_l)
    call linint_Grow(a_plus, a_l, a_u, a_grow, NA, &
        ial, iar, varphi)

    tomorrow = varphi*RHS(ij_com+1, ial, im_com, is_com) + &
         (1d0-varphi)*RHS(ij_com+1, iar, im_com, is_com)

    ! calculate first-order condition for consumption
    foc = margu(cons_com, lab_com, im_com)**(-gamma) &
                                            - tomorrow

end function
```

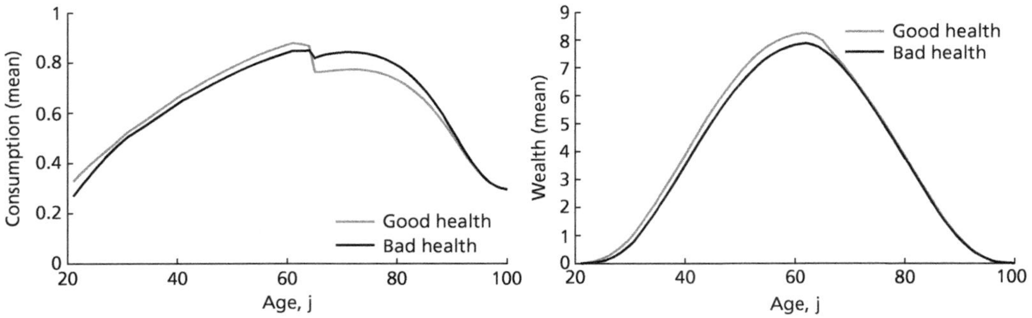

Figure 10.10 Life-cycle profiles with reduced time-endowment in bad health

already performed this transformation for the right-hand side of the Euler equation in the subroutine `interpolate`. In the output subroutine, we at first compute cohort averages conditional on health status. We then recover the unconditional cohort averages. Note that reducing the state space by one dimension, ie abstracting from permanent productivity differences, results in a reduced execution time of our program.

Choosing $\phi_l = 0.2$, so that the maximum time-endowment of individuals in bad health is reduced by 20 per cent, induces individuals in bad health to supply less labour than healthy individuals during working life. Consequently, this results in lower cohort average labour income, consumption, and asset holdings for working-age individuals in bad health. Throughout retirement, however, we observe that individuals in bad health have a higher consumption than individuals in good health, which is somewhat surprising (see Figure 10.10). Yet, this behaviour results from intertemporal consumption-smoothing. It is driven by the fact that, during retirement, the marginal utility of current consumption of an individual in bad health is greater than that of an individual in good health, owing to the reduced time-endowment $1 - \phi_l$, ie

$$\frac{\nu \left[c^{\nu}(1-\phi_l)^{1-\nu}\right]^{1-\frac{1}{\gamma}}}{c} > \frac{\nu \left[c^{\nu}\right]^{1-\frac{1}{\gamma}}}{c}.$$

As long as there is a positive transition probability from bad health to good health, it is thus optimal for individuals in bad health to consume more than individuals in good health.

Like in Exercise 10.4, setting $\chi = 0.8$ leads to a negative effect of health status on survival probabilities. This makes individuals allocate more consumption to earlier periods of their life cycle. Figure 10.11 illustrates that individuals hardly build up any savings, and particularly those households in bad heath are borrowing-constrained, as they already face a considerable risk of dying early in their life.

(b) The numerical implementation of a negative effect of health status on an individual's productivity is almost identical to Part (b) of Exercise 10.5. In the subroutine

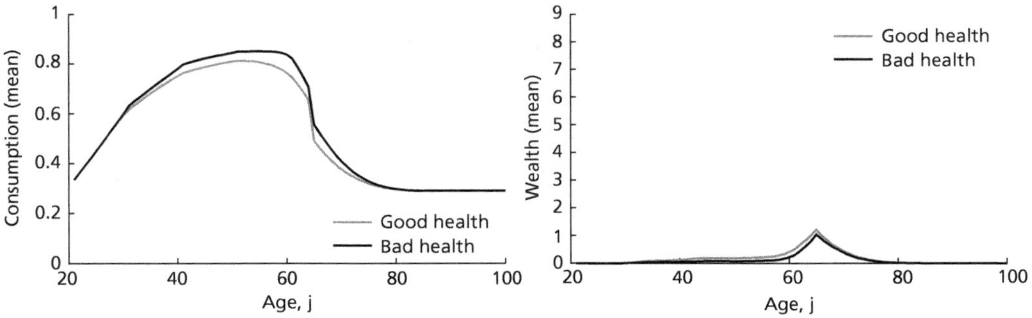

Figure 10.11 Bad health and reduced survival

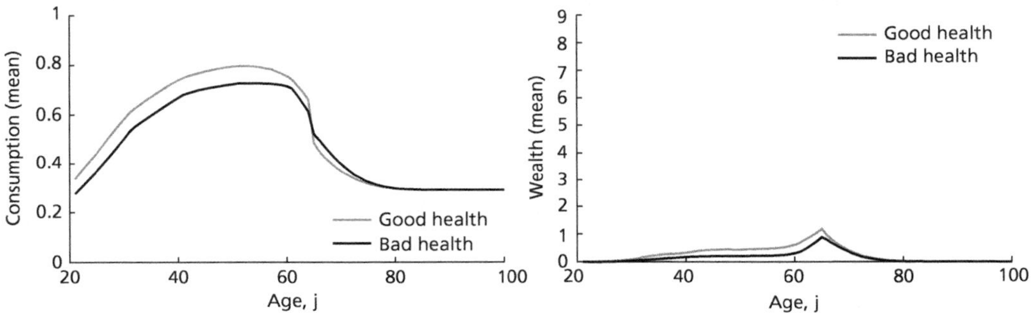

Figure 10.12 Lower productivity in bad health

`initialize` at the beginning of the program, we initialize the array `varrho_m` with the productivity loss ϱ in the bad-health state ($m = 1$) and leave productivity unchanged for individuals in good health ($m = 0$). Setting $\varrho = 0.2$ and $\phi_l = 0.2$ in the case of a bad-health shock leads to a larger difference in the life-cycle consumption and asset profiles between individuals in good health and in bad health (see Figure 10.12).

Exercise 10.9

(a) Writing the life-cycle model with endogenous labour supply and additively separable preferences in dynamic programming form yields:

$$V(z) = \max_{c,l,a^+} \frac{c^{1-\frac{1}{\gamma}}}{1-\frac{1}{\gamma}} - \nu\frac{l^{1+\frac{1}{\chi}}}{1+\frac{1}{\chi}} + \beta\psi_{j+1}E\big[V(z^+)\big|\eta\big]$$

$$\text{s.t.} \quad a^+ + c = (1+r)a + whl + pen, \quad a^+ \geq 0, \quad l \geq 0,$$

$$\text{and} \quad \eta^+ = \rho\eta + \epsilon^+ \quad \text{with} \quad \epsilon^+ \sim N(0, \sigma_\epsilon^2).$$

Compared to the life-cycle model with endogenous labour supply from Section 10.1.2. of the book, households no longer draw utility from leisure, but instead face a disutility from working. Solving the problem with policy function iteration requires us to set up the Lagrangean and take derivatives in order to obtain the inter- and intratemporal first-order conditions:

$$c = \left[(1+r)\beta\psi_{j+1}E\left[c(z^+)^{-\frac{1}{\gamma}}\right]\right]^{-\gamma} \quad \text{and} \quad c = \left[\frac{\nu}{wh}\cdot l^{\frac{1}{\chi}}\right]^{-\gamma}.$$

We again solve the Euler equation using the subroutine `fzero` from the toolbox. However, instead of searching for the optimal level of savings a^+, we now iterate over current consumption c. The reason for this is that it allows us to directly solve the intratemporal optimality condition and derive current labour supply as:

$$l(c) = \max\left[\left(\frac{wh}{\nu}\right)^{\chi}\cdot c^{-\frac{\chi}{\gamma}}, 0\right]$$

in the function `foc` that is handed over to `fzero`. With $l(c)$ at hand, we obtain savings into the next period as:

$$a^+ = (1+r)a + whl(c) + pen - c,$$

which allows us to evaluate the right-hand side of the Euler equation.

Note that, whenever the household is liquidity-constrained ($a^+ < 0$) and still of working age, we determine optimal consumption and labour supply by setting $a^+ = 0$ and using `fzero` to solve for optimal consumption c through the equation:

$$(1+r)a + pen + whl(c) - c = 0,$$

which is stored in function `foc_liq`. For a retired household, on the other hand, the optimal decision simply is to consume all available wealth, as there is no longer a trade-off between utility from consumption and disutility from working. The numerical implementation of these two cases is illustrated in Program 10.9. The remaining code of program `sol_prog10_09` is identical to the numerical implementation of the life-cycle model with endogenous labour supply in program `prog10_02` of the book. The only difference is in the subroutine `interpolate`, where we exploit the additive separability of the utility function to implement a separate interpolation for each of the two parts of the value function. In Exercise 10.6 we followed a similar strategy.

The life-cycle profiles are shown in Figure 10.13. The individual's asset accumulation exhibits the well-known hump shape used to smooth consumption over the life cycle. With increasing age, individuals reduce their labour supply due to a reduced productivity and an increased wealth. The lower we set ν and χ, the lower is the disutility from

Program 10.9 Borrowing constraint for retired vs working households

```
if(a_plus_com < 0d0)then

    if(ij >= JR)then
        a_plus_com = a_l
        lab_com = 0d0
        x_in = (1d0+r)*a(ia) + pen(ij)
    else
        a_plus_com = a_l

        ! solve the household problem using rootfinding
        call fzero(x_in, foc_liq, check)

        ! write screen output in case of a problem
        if(check)write(*,'(a, 4i4)') &
            'ERROR IN ROOTFINDING : ',ij, ia, ip, is
    endif
endif
```

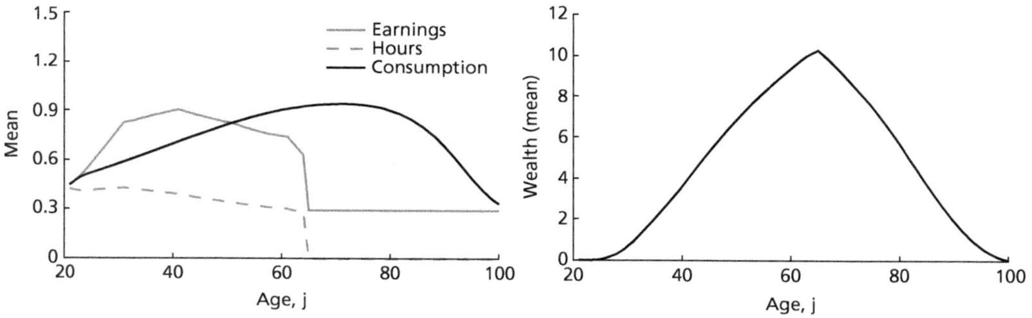

Figure 10.13 Additively separable preferences

working, which translates into higher labour supply and labour income. Individuals then consume more and build up a larger savings stock over the life cycle.

(b) Using the endogenous gridpoint method to solve the above household optimization problem is similar to the implementation of this method in the previous exercises and chapters. The algorithm implemented in subroutine `solve_household_endogenous` consists of the following four steps:

1. For a given level of tomorrow's savings a^+ on the exogenous asset grid, use the first-order condition to determine current consumption endogenously as:

$$c_{end} = \left\{(1+r)\beta\psi_{j+1}E\left[c(z^+)^{-\frac{1}{\gamma}}\right]\right\}^{-\gamma}.$$

2. Use the intratemporal first-order condition to derive the labour supply level that corresponds to c_{end} as:

$$l_{end} = \max\left[\left(\frac{wh}{\nu}\right)^{\chi} \cdot c_{end}^{-\frac{\chi}{\gamma}}, 0\right].$$

3. The endogenous gridpoint then reads:

$$a_{end} = \frac{a^+ + c_{end} - whl_{end} - pen}{1+r}.$$

4. Apply the subroutine `linint_Gen` from the toolbox to determine the optimal policy functions on the exogenous asset grid by using the interpolation data:

$$\{a_{end,i}, c_{end,i}\} \quad \text{and} \quad \{a_{end,i}, l_{end,i}\}.$$

Note that, whenever the exogenous gridpoint a_0 is smaller than the lowest endogenous gridpoint $a_{end,0}$, the agent is borrowing-constrained. We then determine the consumption and labour supply choices from exactly the same first-order condition as in Program 10.9 by using the subroutine `fzero` from the toolbox. We illustrate these two cases in Program 10.9.a.

The results and their interpretation with the endogenous gridpoint method are the same as in Part (a), where we used policy function iteration. Both solutions are implemented in program `sol_prog10_09`. After we initialized the required numerical parameters at the very beginning of the code, we set up a do-loop with two iteration steps. In the first iteration, we solve the model using policy function iteration, while in the second iteration the endogenous gridpoint method is used.

Exercise 10.10

(a) In dynamic programming form, the optimization problem that includes a labour–income tax function is given by:

$$V(z) = \max_{c,l,a^+} \frac{c^{1-\frac{1}{\gamma}}}{1-\frac{1}{\gamma}} - \nu\frac{l^{1+\frac{1}{\chi}}}{1+\frac{1}{\chi}} + \beta\psi_{j+1}E\big[V(z^+)\big|\eta\big]$$

$$\text{s.t.} \quad a^+ + c = (1+r)a + (1-\tau)\,(whl)^{\varrho} + pen, \; a^+ \geq 0, \; l \geq 0$$

$$\text{and} \quad \eta^+ = \rho\eta + \epsilon^+ \quad \text{with} \quad \epsilon^+ \sim N(0, \sigma_\epsilon^2).$$

In the budget constraint, we now account for the progressive taxation of labour income. After taking derivatives, optimal labour supply $l(c)$ is determined by:

$$l(c) = \max\left[\left((1-\tau)\varrho\frac{(wh)^{\varrho}}{\nu}c^{-\frac{1}{\gamma}}\right)^{\frac{1}{1+1/\chi-\varrho}}, 0\right].$$

Program 10.9.a Borrowing constraint with endogenous gridpoints

```
if(a(ia) <= a_endo(0))then

    if(ij >= JR)then
        c(ij, ia, ip, is) = (1d0+r)*a(ia) + pen(ij)
        l(ij, ia, ip, is) = 0d0
        aplus(ij, ia, ip, is) = 0d0
    else

        ! solve FOC under borrowing constriant
        ij_com = ij
        ia_com = ia
        ip_com = ip
        is_com = is

        x_in = c_endo(0)

        ! solve the household problem using rootfinding
        call fzero(x_in, foc_liq, check)

        ! write screen output in case of a problem
        if(check)write(*,'(a, 4i4)') &
        'ERROR IN ROOTFINDING : ',ij, ia, ip, is

        c(ij, ia, ip, is) = x_in
        l(ij, ia, ip, is) = lab_com
        aplus(ij, ia, ip, is) = 0d0
    endif

else

    c(ij, ia, ip, is) = linint_Gen(a(ia), a_endo, c_endo, ia)
    if(ij >= JR)then
        l(ij, ia, ip, is) = 0d0
    else
        l(ij, ia, ip, is) = &
            linint_Gen(a(ia), a_endo, l_endo, ia)
    endif
    aplus(ij, ia, ip, is) = (1d0+r)*a(ia) + &
        wage*l(ij, ia, ip, is) + pen(ij) - c(ij, ia, ip, is)

endif
```

Building up on the numerical implementation in Exercise 10.9, we only need to adapt the equation used for the computation of optimal labour supply as well as the budget constraint. In the case of policy function iteration, this requires us to only adapt the codes in the functions `foc` and `foc_liq`. The adaptions in function `foc` are shown in Module 10.10m. In the case of the endogenous gridpoint method, we need to modify the first-order condition when deriving the optimal endogenous labour supply level l_{end} as well as the budget constraint we use to compute the endogenous gridpoint a_{end}. Moreover, we also account for tax payments when calculating the optimal a^+ on our exogenous asset grid. The modifications in function `foc_liq` are the same as in Module 10.10m.

(b) The accumulated tax burden of 7.79 is slightly higher for households under a progressive tax scheme compared to 6.87 under a proportional scheme. Distortions of labour supply are higher under progressive taxation, too. This results from the fact

Module 10.10m Updating `foc` and `foc_liq` for labour–income taxes

```
function foc(x_in)
    [......]
    ! get exponent
    expo = 1d0/(1d0+1d0/chi-varrho)

    ! get labor supply
    lab_com = max(((1d0-tau)*varrho*wage**varrho/nu)**expo*&
    max(cons, 1d-10)**(-expo/gamma), 0d0)

    ! calculate tomorrows assets
    a_plus_com = (1d0+r)*a(ia_com) + pen(ij_com) + (1d0-tau)*&
    (wage*lab_com)**varrho - cons
    [......]
end function
```

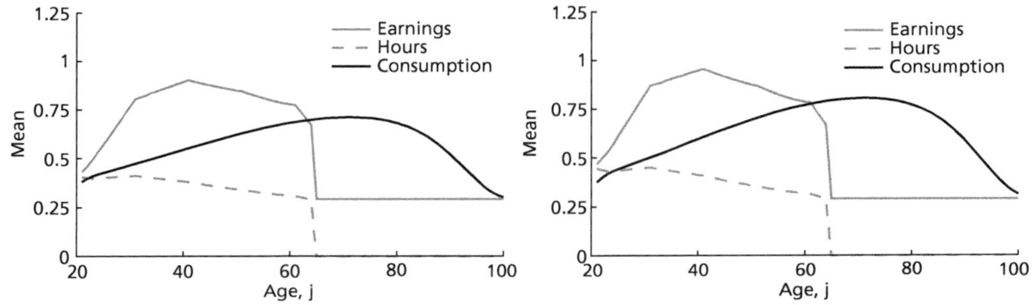

Figure 10.14 Progressive vs proportional labour–income taxation

that with progressive taxation, supplying an additional marginal unit of labour gets increasingly unattractive. The effects on labour hours, income, and consumption over the life cycle are shown in Figure 10.14. Individuals accumulate fewer assets and consume less over the life cycle compared to the case of no labour income taxation in Figure 10.13. This effect is more pronounced in the presence of progressive taxation than in the case of a proportional tax code.

Exercise 10.11

The only thing we need to adapt when we want to introduce a new utility function into the model with female labour-force participation is the first-order condition. We follow the same two-step solution procedure as described in Section 10.1.3 in the book:

1. *Consumption–savings choice*: given the assumption that the household already made a choice on female labour supply l, the decision on how much to consume and save can be derived from the optimization problem:

$$\tilde{V}(z,l) = \max_{c,a^+} \frac{1}{1-\frac{1}{\gamma}}\left[\frac{c}{\sqrt{2+n_j}}\right]^{1-\frac{1}{\gamma}} \exp(\nu_1 \cdot l) - \nu_2 \cdot l + \beta\psi_{j+1}E\big[V(z^+)\big|\eta_f,\eta_m\big]$$

$$s.t.\ a^+ + c = (1+r)a + y_m + y_f + pen - p_j \cdot l, \quad a^+ \geq 0.$$

Setting up the Lagangean, taking derivatives, and using the envelope theorem yields the intertemporal first-order condition

$$\frac{c \cdot \exp(\nu_1 \cdot l)^{-\gamma}}{\left[\sqrt{2+n_j}\right]^{1-\gamma}} = \left\{\beta\psi_{j+1}(1+r)\cdot E\left[\frac{c(z^+)^{-\frac{1}{\gamma}}\exp(\nu_1\cdot l^+)}{\left[\sqrt{2+n_{j+1}}\right]^{1-\frac{1}{\gamma}}}\middle|\eta_f,\eta_m\right]\right\}^{-\gamma}.$$

2. *Labour-force participation*: with the utilities $\tilde{V}(z,l)$ for both labour-supply decisions at hand, we can again identify whether it is optimal for the female partner to participate in the labour force by comparing utility levels and setting:

$$l(z) = \begin{cases} 1 & \text{if } \tilde{V}(z,1) \geq \tilde{V}(z,0) \text{ and} \\ 0 & \text{otherwise.} \end{cases}$$

The respective optimal consumption and savings decisions are then determined by:

$$c(z) = \tilde{c}(z,l(z)) \quad \text{and} \quad a(z) = \tilde{a}(z,l(z)).$$

In the numerical implementation, we thus only need to adapt the function `foc` using the lines of code shown in Module 10.11m. The remainder of program `sol_prog10_11` is equivalent to `prog10_03` in the book.

The introduction of a shift factor $\exp(\nu_1 \cdot l)$ into the utility function reduces utility from consumption with $\nu_1 > 0$. Women will thus supply less labour over the life cycle to minimize these utility losses. Figure 10.15 shows how this leads to a lower family income through two channels: first, non-participation will directly reduce income and, second, it makes female human capital depreciate. The latter leads to lower income in the future and makes working less attractive for older women.

Module 10.11m New first-order condition in function `foc`

```
function foc(x_in)
    [......]
    ! calculate first-order condition for consumption
    foc = cons_com/sqrt(2d0+ &
              dble(nchild(ij_com)))**(1d0-gamma) &
              *(exp(nu_1*dble(il_com)))**(-gamma) - tomorrow

end function
```

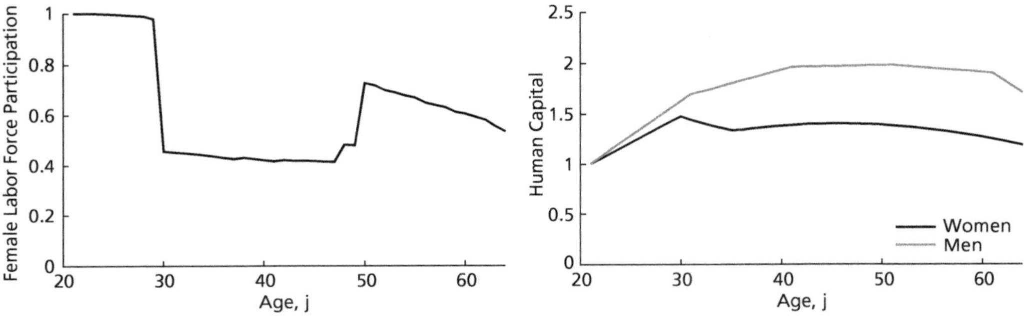

Figure 10.15 Labour force participation and human capital

Exercise 10.12

Introducing value function iteration to solve the model with female labour supply decision from Section 10.1.3. of the book is very similar to applying value function iteration to solve the life-cycle model with endogenous labour supply in Exercise 10.7. The majority of the code is left unchanged. Only in the subroutine `solve_household` the subroutine `fminsearch` is used to find the optimal savings policy a^+ by maximizing the utility function at each state, instead of applying `fzero` to solve the first-order condition. The lower bound for `fminsearch` is set to the lower end of the asset grid a_l, while the upper bound is defined as the minimum of a_u and the savings level `aplus_max` that would lead a household to consume nothing in the current period (see Program 10.12). The great advantage of using `fminsearch` is that we don't have to impose an extra check for whether the borrowing constraint is satisfied. Instead, by setting the lower optimization bound to `a_l`, this constraint is respected automatically. After having computed the optimal solution for both labour-force participation decisions, we again compare value functions and choose the alternative that yields the highest utility.

The function `valuefunc`, which is passed on to `fminsearch`, is structured in a very similar way to Exercise 10.7. It is shown in Module 10.12m. At first, we compute the available income at a certain state and derive current consumption for a given level of savings a^+ into the next period. We store the corresponding level of consumption in the variables `cons_com` and `cons_lim`. We constrain `cons_lim` to be non-negative in order to assign a penalty to the value function for negative consumption choices. This makes such choices very unappealing. In the unconstrained case, the current value function is

Program 10.12 Use `fminsearch` to solve household optimization problem

```
! calculate maximum possible savings
aplus_max = (1d0+r)*a(ia) + w_m*eff(ij)*theta(ip)*eta(ism) + &
    w_f*dble(il)*(exp(h(ih))*theta(ip)*eta(isf) &
        - pchild(ij)) + pen(ij)

! maximize value function
call fminsearch(x_in, fret, a_l, min(aplus_max, a_u), &
                                        valuefunc)
```

Module 10.12m The utility function to be minimized

```
function valuefunc(x_in)
    [......]
    ! calculate consumption
    cons_com = available - a_plus
    cons_lim = max(cons_com, 1d-10)

    ! get interpolation weights
    call linint_Grow(a_plus, a_l, a_u, a_grow, &
              NA, ial, iar, varphi)

    ! calculate future utility
    vplus = (varphi*EV(ial, ih_com, ip_com, ism_com, &
        isf_com, il_com) + (1d0-varphi)*EV(iar, ih_com, &
        ip_com, ism_com, isf_com, il_com))**egam/egam

    ! get value function
    valuefunc = -((cons_com/sqrt(2d0+ &
                 dble(nchild(ij_com))) &
                 **egam/egam - nu*dble(il_com) &
                 + beta*psi(ij_com+1)*vplus)

    ! penalty for negative consumption
    valuefunc = valuefunc + 100d0*abs(cons_com-cons_lim)

end function
```

computed as the sum of current utility and the interpolated expected next-period value function. We use the usual transformation after interpolation.

The results and the economic interpretations are the same as in Section 10.1.3 in the book. The major difference to the implementation with policy function iteration is that the value function iteration algorithm exhibits a higher numerical stability; however, it comes at the cost of a higher computational time.

Exercise 10.13

(a) If the two members of the family have independent survival probabilities, we distinguish the household state vectors:

$$z = (j, a, h_f, \theta, \eta_m, \eta_f)\ ,\ z_f = (j, a, h_f, \theta, 0, \eta_f) \text{ and } z_m = (j, a, 0, \theta, \eta_m, 0),$$

which define the states where both members, only the female, or only the male member are alive, respectively. The dynamic programming problem then depends on the household composition. If only the male partner is alive, he solves:

$$V(z_m) = \max_{c, a^+}\ u(c) + \beta\psi_{j+1} E\big[V(z_m^+)\big|\eta_m\big]$$

$$\text{s.t. } a^+ + c = (1+r)a + y_m + 0.5pen, \quad a^+ \geq 0,$$

$$\eta_m^+ = \rho\eta_m + \epsilon_m^+ \quad \text{with} \quad \epsilon_m^+ \sim N(0, \sigma_\epsilon^2),$$

where the instantaneous utility function is:

$$u(c) = \frac{1}{1-\frac{1}{\gamma}}\left[\frac{c}{\sqrt{1+n}}\right]^{1-\frac{1}{\gamma}}.$$

The Euler equation changes to:

$$\frac{c(z_m)}{\left[\sqrt{1+n_j}\right]^{1-\gamma}} = \left\{\beta(1+r)\psi_{j+1}E\left[\frac{c(z_m^+)^{-\frac{1}{\gamma}}}{\left[\sqrt{1+n_{j+1}}\right]^{1-\frac{1}{\gamma}}}\middle|\eta_m\right]\right\}^{-\gamma}.$$

If only the female partner is alive, she solves:

$$\begin{aligned}
V(z_f) &= \max_{c,l,a^+}\ u(c,l) + \beta\psi_{j+1}E\big[V(z_f^+)\big|\eta_f\big]\\
\text{s.t. } a^+ + c &= (1+r)a + y_f + 0.5pen, \quad a^+ \geq 0,\\
\log(h_f^+) &= \max\big[\log(h_f) + (\xi_1 + \xi_2\cdot j)l - \delta_h(1-l),\ \log(h_{f,1})\big],\\
\eta_f^+ &= \rho\eta_f + \epsilon_f^+ \quad \text{with} \quad \epsilon_f^+ \sim N(0,\sigma_\epsilon^2),
\end{aligned}$$

with the instantaneous utility function being:

$$u(c,l) = \frac{1}{1-\frac{1}{\gamma}}\left[\frac{c}{\sqrt{1+n}}\right]^{1-\frac{1}{\gamma}} - \nu\cdot l.$$

This implies for the Euler equation:

$$\frac{c(z_f)}{\left[\sqrt{1+n_j}\right]^{1-\gamma}} = \left\{\beta(1+r)\psi_{j+1}E\left[\frac{c(z_f^+)^{-\frac{1}{\gamma}}}{\left[\sqrt{1+n_{j+1}}\right]^{1-\frac{1}{\gamma}}}\middle|\eta_f\right]\right\}^{-\gamma}.$$

Finally, the joint couple solves:

$$\begin{aligned}
V(z) &= \max_{c,l,a^+}\ u(c,l) + \beta\psi_{j+1}\Big\{\psi_{j+1}E\big[V(z^+)\big|\eta_m,\eta_f\big] +\\
&\qquad (1-\psi_{j+1})E\big[V(z_m^+)\big|\eta_m\big] + (1-\psi_{j+1})E\big[V(z_f^+)\big|\eta_f\big]\Big\}\\
\text{s.t. } a^+ + c &= (1+r)a + y_m + y_f + pen - p\cdot l, \quad a^+ \geq 0,\\
\log(h_f^+) &= \max\big[\log(h_f) + (\xi_1 + \xi_2\cdot j)l - \delta_h(1-l),\ \log(h_{f,1})\big],\\
\eta_m^+ &= \rho\eta_m + \epsilon_m^+ \quad \text{with} \quad \epsilon_m^+ \sim N(0,\sigma_\epsilon^2),\\
\eta_f^+ &= \rho\eta_f + \epsilon_f^+ \quad \text{with} \quad \epsilon_f^+ \sim N(0,\sigma_\epsilon^2).
\end{aligned}$$

We, hence, end up with the first-order condition:

$$\frac{c}{[\sqrt{2+n_j}]^{1-\gamma}} = \Bigg\{\beta(1+r)\psi_{j+1}\Bigg(\psi_{j+1}E\left[\frac{c(z^+)^{-\frac{1}{\gamma}}}{[\sqrt{2+n_{j+1}}]^{1-\frac{1}{\gamma}}}\middle|\eta_f,\eta_m\right]$$
$$+(1-\psi_{j+1})E\left[\frac{c(z_m^+)^{-\frac{1}{\gamma}}}{[\sqrt{1+n_{j+1}}]^{1-\frac{1}{\gamma}}}\middle|\eta_m\right]$$
$$+(1-\psi_{j+1})E\left[\frac{c(z_f^+)^{-\frac{1}{\gamma}}}{[\sqrt{1+n_{j+1}}]^{1-\frac{1}{\gamma}}}\middle|\eta_f\right]\Bigg)\Bigg\}^{-\gamma}.$$

Whenever the female partner is still alive, the household decides on female labour-force participation by comparing the temporary value functions of both participation states.

The numerical implementation is a bit tedious, as we have to clearly identify the states z, z_m, and z_f and solve different optimization problems in each of the three possible cases. We separate them through if-statements. Module 10.13m, for instance, shows how we have to adapt the function `foc` that is handed over to `fzero` in order to find the optimal policy functions. Further adjustments are implemented in the subroutines `interpolate` and `get_distribution`. For households in which both spouses are still alive, we have to distinguish the case that both spouses survive to the next period from the scenario that only one of the spouses survives. For households in which only one spouse is present, the numerical implementation is equivalent to that of `prog10_03` in the book. Finally, computing cohort averages and printing output to the screen is done in the same way as in the baseline version of the model with endogenous female labour-force participation.

Module 10.13m Function `foc` with different survival risk

```
function foc(x_in)
    [......]
    ! calculate consumption
    if(ism_com > 0 .and. isf_com > 0)then
        wage_f = w_f*dble(il_com)*(exp(h(ih_com))* &
                 theta(ip_com)*eta(isf_com) - pchild(ij_com))
        cons_com = (1d0+r)*a(ia_com) + pen(ij_com) &
                   + wage_f + wage_m - a_plus
    elseif(isf_com == 0)then
        cons_com = (1d0+r)*a(ia_com) + 0.5d0*pen(ij_com) &
                   + wage_m - a_plus
    elseif(ism_com == 0)then
        wage_f = w_f*dble(il_com)*exp(h(ih_com)) &
                *theta(ip_com)*eta(isf_com)
        cons_com = (1d0+r)*a(ia_com) + 0.5d0*pen(ij_com) &
                 + wage_f - a_plus
    endif
    [......]
end function
```

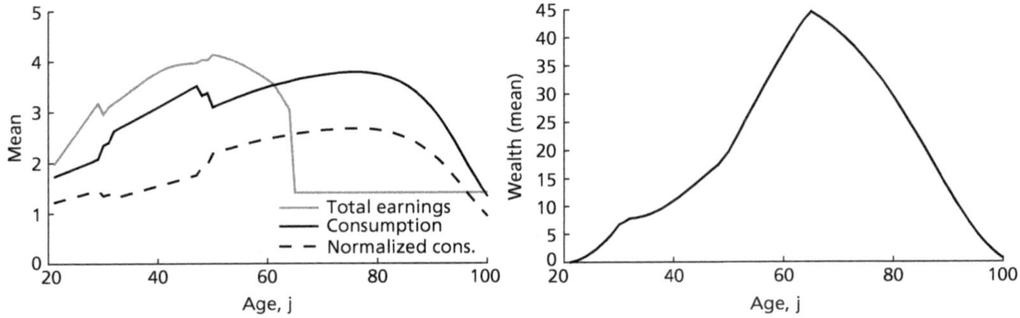

Figure 10.16 Precautionary savings lead to increasing asset accumulation

(b) When survival probabilities are independent, the household accumulates more assets, particularly during young ages. There, survival probabilities are still high and the household can save for precautionary reasons in order to insure against the early death of one of the spouses (see Figure 10.16). As a consequence, savings are much higher at retirement and the fraction of borrowing-constrained households is much lower during retirement compared to the benchmark model. The differences in labour market participation and human capital accumulation are more difficult to identify. On the one hand, the government pays for all costs resulting from child care if one of the spouses dies. On the other hand, the early death of one spouse reduces the pension by 50 per cent. The labour force participation decision is shaped by these two counteracting forces.

Exercise 10.14

The household optimization problem in dynamic programming form reads:

$$V(z) = \max_{c,l,a^+} u(c,l) + \beta\psi_{j+1}E\big[V(z^+|\eta_f,\eta_m)\big]$$

$$\text{s.t.} \quad a^+ + c = (1+r)a + y_m + y_f + pen_{m,j} + pen_{f,j,q} - p_j\cdot l, \quad a^+ \geq 0$$

$$\log(h_f^+) = \max\big[\log(h_f) + (\xi_1 + \xi_2\cdot j)l - \delta_h(1-l), \log(h_{f,1})\big],$$

$$\eta_m^+ = \rho\eta_m + \epsilon_m^+ \quad \text{with} \quad \epsilon_m^+ \sim N(0,\sigma_\epsilon^2)$$

$$\eta_f^+ = \rho\eta_f + \epsilon_f^+ \quad \text{with} \quad \epsilon_f^+ \sim N(0,\sigma_\epsilon^2),$$

with $z = (j, a, h_f, \theta, \eta_m, \eta_f)$. The optimization problem is the same as in the baseline version of the life-cycle model with female labour supply. However, the budget constraint differs in that there are separate pension payments for men and women. In the numerical implementation, we again follow the two-step solution procedure applied in `prog10_03` of the book. Yet, we can no longer ignore the level of female human capital during retirement, meaning that we can not only compute the optimal solution for one level of female human capital and copy the optimal policy functions to all other levels of human

Program 10.14 Pensions and female human capital during retirement

```
! old age transfers wife
pen_f = 0d0
do ih = 0, NH
    pen_f(JR:JJ, ih) = chi*w_f*h(ih)
enddo
```

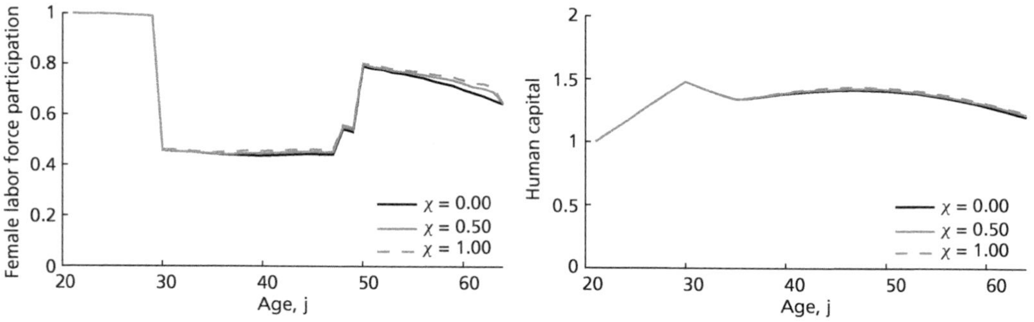

Figure 10.17 Life-cycle profiles with $\kappa = 0.4$ and $\chi = 0.0$

capital. This is because female pensions now depend on the amount of accumulated human capital. To account for the pension of the female spouse, we define an array `pen_f`, as shown in Program 10.14. We include the term `pen_f` into the budget constraint of the household in the function `foc`.

When we set the replacement rate to $\kappa = 0.4$ for the husband and $\chi = 0.0$ for the wife, respectively, the household receives a lower pension compared to the baseline scenario in Section 10.1.3 of the book. Figure 10.17 shows how this makes individuals build up more savings to finance consumption during retirement and how the consumption level over the life cycle decreases. As a result, female labour supply rises slightly in order to compensate the household income losses from the lower pension of the husband.

Holding $\kappa = 0.4$ constant and raising the replacement rate for the wife's pension to $\chi = 0.5$ reduces savings and leads to a small increase in female labour supply and consumption. Female labour force participation now gets increasingly attractive, as accumulating more human capital translates into higher pension payments for the wife. As a result, households need to accumulate fewer savings in order to maintain their consumption standard throughout retirement. Letting the replacement rate for female pensions increase further to $\chi = 1$ leads to even lower savings of the household and a further increase in female labour supply as well as consumption. The underlying mechanism is, of course, the same.

Exercise 10.15

(a) The Solution to this exercise is based on the simple portfolio choice model that is discussed in Section 10.2.1 of the book (see also `prog10_04`). The solution to the

Program 10.15 Compute the share with more than 50% wealth in stocks

```
subroutine calculate_quantiles()
    [......]
    ! copy portfolio choice into one-dimensional array
    ic = 1
    do ie = 0, NE
        do ia = 0, NA
            if(phi_a(ij-1, ia)*phi_e(ij, ie) > 1d-12)then
                a_sort(ic) = a(ia)*eta(ij, ie)
                a_dist(ic) = phi_a(ij-1, ia)*phi_e(ij, ie)
                if(omega_plus(ij-1, ia) > stocks_min)then
                    omega_min(ic) = phi_a(ij-1, ia) &
                                    *phi_e(ij, ie)
                endif
                omega_cur(ic) = omega_plus(ij-1, ia)
                ic = ic + 1
            endif
        enddo
    enddo
    [......]
    ! fraction that invests more than 50% of wealth in stocks
    frac_stocks_min(ij) = sum(omega_min)/sum(a_dist)
    [......]
end subroutine
```

household optimization problem is left unchanged. Only the code for the calculation of quantile statistics in the subroutine `calculate_quantiles` needs to be modified. Specifically, we compute two additional variables at each gridpoint combination `ia` and `ie` for each age $j = 2, \ldots, J$ (see Program 10.15). On the one hand, whenever an investor's portfolio share of risky assets is greater than a threshold `stocks_min`, we store her population share $\phi_a(j-1, \hat{a}_v) \cdot \phi_e(j, \hat{\eta}_{j,q})$ in the one-dimensional array `omega_min`. Otherwise, the entry in `omega_min` will amount to zero. On the other hand, we record each investor's portfolio share in an array `omega_cur`, in order to be able to calculate quantile-specific portfolio shares later on.

The share of investors in a cohort $j \in \{2, \ldots, J\}$ that hold more than 50 per cent of their wealth in stocks is given by:

$$\Phi_{j,\omega>0.5} = \frac{\sum_{q=1}^{n_e} \sum_{v=1}^{n_a} \mathbb{1}_{\omega>0.5} \cdot \phi_a(j-1, \hat{a}_v) \cdot \phi_e(j, \hat{\eta}_{j,q})}{\sum_{q=1}^{n_e} \sum_{v=1}^{n_a} \phi_a(j-1, \hat{a}_v) \cdot \phi_e(j, \hat{\eta}_{j,q})}.$$

Since the individual population shares are stored in the array `a_dist` and we recorded the population shares of investors with at least a 50 per cent risk asset share in the array `omega_min`, we can simply calculate the respective overall cohort share by dividing the sum of the two arrays by each other (see the last line of Program 10.15). In line with the life-cycle profiles we have already computed in `prog10_04` of the book, we observe that almost all households hold more than 50 per cent of their wealth in stocks at the beginning of the life cycle (see Figure 10.18). This share falls steadily until age sixty, but increases from there on until the end of the life cycle.

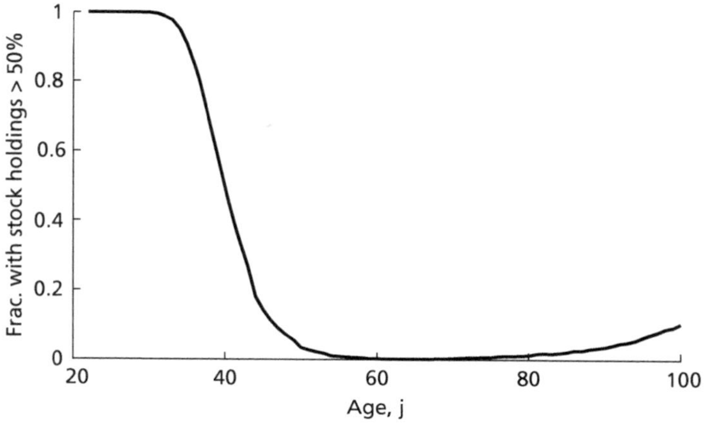

Figure 10.18 Fraction of investors with more than 50% wealth in stocks

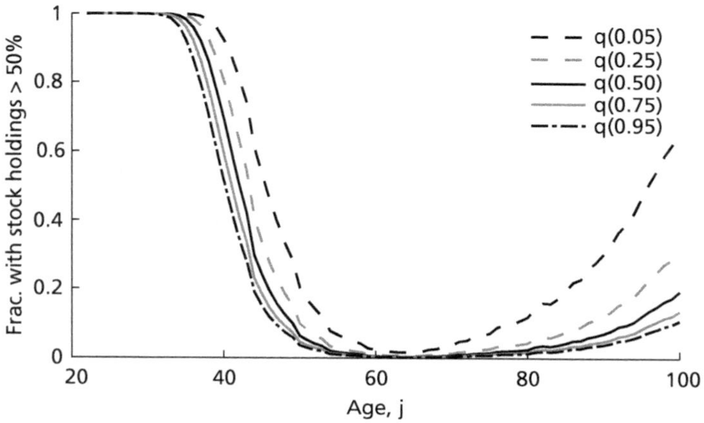

Figure 10.19 Risky investors by wealth quantile

(b) In order to compute the fraction of households with stock holdings greater than 50 per cent for each quantile of the wealth distribution, we proceed in a very similar way to computing average asset holdings for each quantile. We use the array `a_cdist` that carries the individual population shares in increasing order of wealth holdings in order to identify the different wealth quantile thresholds. For each quantile, we compute the share of households that hold more than 50 per cent of their wealth in equity, summing up the information in the array `omega_min` and using the order information in `iorder`. We divide this number by the total mass of households in the respective quantile stored in `a_cdist`.

The fraction of households that hold more than 50 per cent of their wealth in risky assets is smaller for higher quantiles (see Figure 10.19). With constant relative risk aversion, individuals want to keep their overall risk exposure in human capital and financial assets constant over the life cycle. As the average asset holding relative to human

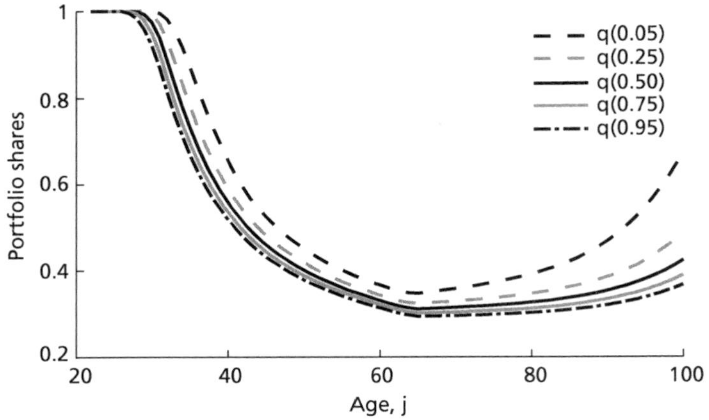

Figure 10.20 Portfolio shares by wealth quantile

capital is small for lower quantiles, this requires individuals in low quantiles to make more risky investments in their financial asset portfolio in order to ensure a constant overall risk exposure.

(c) Computing average portfolio shares for each wealth quantile is very similar to what we did in Part (b). Yet, we now sum up the share of stocks stored in the array `omega_cur` and need to multiply it with the respective population share in the array `a_dist`. Figure 10.20 shows that the average share of wealth invested in equity is again higher in lower quantiles.

Exercise 10.16

The starting point is the normalized version of the life-cycle optimization problem with portfolio choice as shown in equation (10.22) of the book. We again separate the dynamic-programming problem into two sub-problems. In the first step, we determine the optimal investment structure $\omega^+(j, \widetilde{a}^+)$ for each level of future savings $\widetilde{a}^+$ by solving:

$$\widetilde{Q}(j, \widetilde{a}^+) = \max_{0 \leq \omega^+ \leq 1} E\left[\exp(\epsilon^+)^{1-\frac{1}{\gamma}} \widetilde{V}(j+1, \widetilde{X}^+)\right]$$

$$\text{s.t. } \widetilde{X}^+ = R_p(\omega^+, \varphi^+) \cdot \frac{\widetilde{a}^+}{\exp(\epsilon^+)} + w\widetilde{h}^+ + \widetilde{pen}^+.$$

In the second step, given the optimal portfolio composition $\omega^+(j, \widetilde{a}^+)$, the optimal consumption-savings choice is derived by maximizing:

Program 10.16 Solving the portfolio problem with `fminsearch`

```
subroutine solve_portfolio(ij, ia)
    [......]
    ! set up communication variables
    ij_com = ij
    ia_com = ia

    ! initialize starting value
    x_in = omega_plus(ij+1, ia)

    ! find optimal portfolio share
    call fminsearch(x_in, fret, 0d0, 1d0, value_port)

    ! copy decision
    omega_plus(ij, ia) = x_in
    Q(ij, ia) = (-egam*fret)**(1d0/egam)

end subroutine
```

$$\widetilde{V}(j,\widetilde{X}) = \max_{\widetilde{c},\widetilde{a}^+} \; u(\widetilde{c}) + \beta\psi_{j+1}\widetilde{Q}(j,\widetilde{a}^+) \quad \text{s.t.} \quad \widetilde{X} = \widetilde{c} + \widetilde{a}^+.$$

We no longer use first-order conditions to solve the optimization problems, but instead directly apply `fminsearch` to find the optimal policy that maximizes the respective utility functions in the two optimization steps. This facilitates the numerical solution procedure considerably compared to `prog10_04` of the book. In particular, we no longer need the subroutine `interpolate` to compute the right-hand side of the Euler equation and do not have to pay attention to the derivatives of the intermediate value function $\widetilde{Q}(j,\tilde{a}^+)$. In the subroutine `solve_portfolio`, it is now enough to let `fminsearch` iterate for a given guess over the interval $[0, 1]$ (see Program 10.16). Note that we again transform the value functions $\widetilde{Q}(j,\tilde{a}^+)$ and $\widetilde{V}(j,\widetilde{X})$ in both steps of our solution algorithm in order to ensure a better interpolation accuracy when using linear interpolation. We do this immediately after `fminsearch` provided us with the optimal values `fret` for the value functions. Note that we again treat the case of zero savings $\hat{a}_0 = 0$ separately in the subroutine `solve_household` and simply copy the optimal portfolio share we computed at $\hat{a}_1$. This time, however, we also need to compute the corresponding value function at this gridpoint. Module 10.16m shows an excerpt from the function `value_port` we use to derive the optimal portfolio shares. This function looks very similar to the function `foc_port` in the original solution in program `prog10_04` of the book. Yet, we now interpolate the value function stored in the array `V` instead of the policy function `c`.

The results and their economic interpretation are identical to those of Section 10.2.1 of the book. Note that the simplicity of the numerical implementation with value function iteration comes at the cost of an increased computational time. Solving the model with value function iteration now takes three times as long as the policy function iteration method.

Module 10.16m Utility from portfolio choice

```
function value_port(p)
    [......]
    ! store portfolio share
    omega_p = p

    value_port = 0d0
    if(ij_com+1 >= JR)then
        [......]
    else
        do iw = 1, NW
            do isr = 1, NSR

                ! get return on the portfolio
                R_port = 1d0 + r_f + &
                    omega_p*(mu_r + vtheta(isr))

                ! derive labor earnings
                income = w*eff(ij_com+1)*zeta(iw)

                ! get tomorrow's cash on hand
                X_p = R_port*a(ia_com)/eps(isr) + income

                ! derive interpolation weights
                call linint_Grow(X_p, X_l, X_u, X_grow, &
                                        NX, ixl, ixr, varphi)

                ! get distributional weight
                dist = dist_zeta(iw)*dist_epsvtheta(isr)

                ! calculate the future value function
                V_p = max(varphi*V(ij_com+1, ixl) + &
                    (1d0-varphi)*V(ij_com+1, ixr), 1d-10)
                value_port = value_port + &
                            dist*(eps(isr)*V_p)**egam/egam

            enddo
        enddo
    endif
    value_port = -value_port

end function
```

Exercise 10.17

We have already discussed stock market entry cost in Exercise 5.4, but now we consider entry cost in a dynamic programming problem. Fixed costs upon stock market entry require us to consider another state variable f in our optimization problem. This state variable is an indicator variable that takes the value $f = 1$ if the individual has already paid the fixed entry cost and participates in the stock market. In this case, the optimization problem of the household is identical to the one in program `prog10_04` of the book. In case the individual has not yet participated in the stock market, ie $f = 0$, the optimization problem differs from the baseline portfolio-choice model. In this case, we have to compute optimal choices for two scenarios: the scenario in which the household pays the fixed cost today to enter the stock market, and the case where the individual does not want to participate and only saves in risk-free assets. Having computed choices for these two alternatives, we can calculate the associated utility levels and compare them in order to solve for the optimal discrete choice $f^+ \in \{0, 1\}$ of the household, which is very similar to the decision on female labour-force participation in program `prog10_03` of the book.

In the subroutine `solve_consumption`, we thus declare arrays to store the temporary utility and policy functions for an individual that has not entered the stock market yet. These arrays are marked with a flag `temp`. In the case that the individual had already participated in the stock market prior to an age `ij`, the optimization problem is the same as in `prog10_04` of the book. We store the optimal participation decision in an array `e_plus`. When setting up the distribution of individuals over the asset state space in the subroutine `get_distibution_a`, we have to account for the individual stock market participation choice (see Program 10.17).

Figure 10.21 shows how fixed costs lead to a delay of the stock market entry compared to the baseline model in Section 10.2.1 of the book. In order to compute the share of stock investors for the different asset quantiles, we set up the subroutine

Program 10.17 Stock-market participation in `get_distribution_a`

```
subroutine get_distribution_a(ij)
    [......]
    ! iterate over todays cash on hand
    do ix = 0, NX
        do ip = 0, NP[......]
    [......]
            ! interpolate asset decision
            call linint_Grow(a_plus(ij, ix, ip), a_l, a_u, &
                             a_grow, NA, ial, iar, varphi)

            ! next period participation status
            ip_p = e_plus(ij, ix, ip)

            ! get end of period asset distribution
            phi_a(ij, ial, ip_p) = phi_a(ij, ial, ip_p) + &
                          varphi*phi_X(ij, ix, ip)
            phi_a(ij, iar, ip_p) = phi_a(ij, iar, ip_p) + &
                          (1d0-varphi)*phi_X(ij, ix, ip)

        enddo
    enddo

end subroutine
```

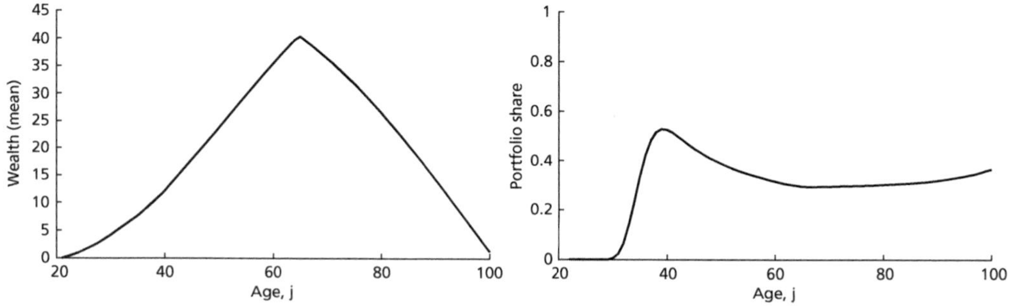

Figure 10.21 Individuals consumption and asset accumulation

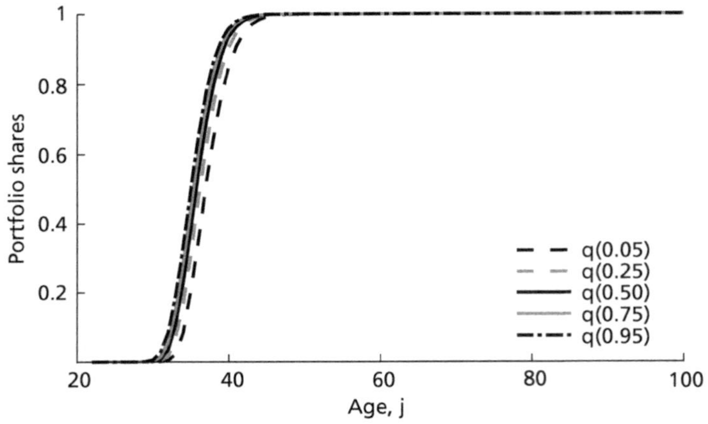

Figure 10.22 Stock market participation with fixed costs

`calculate_quantiles` in the same way as in Exercise 10.15. Figure 10.22 shows that in the presence of fixed costs, stock market participation is increasing for different asset quantiles. Higher fixed costs lead to a further decline in aggregate savings and a delay in the entry into the stock market. Beside that, they increase the difference in stock market participation between wealth quantiles.

Exercise 10.18

This exercise extends the portfolio choice model from Section 10.2.1 of the book in order to distinguish between employment and unemployment phases in periods before retirement. We therefore need to add an additional dimension to the state space which captures the current employment status s.

(a) Given the specific assumptions on unemployment and pension benefits, the normalized version of the optimization problem with unemployment now reads:

$$\widetilde{V}(j, \widetilde{X}, s) = \max_{\widetilde{c}, \widetilde{a}^+, \omega^+} \frac{\widetilde{c}^{1-\frac{1}{\gamma}}}{1-\frac{1}{\gamma}} + \beta\psi_{j+1}E\left[\exp(\epsilon^+)^{1-\frac{1}{\gamma}} \cdot \widetilde{V}(j+1, \widetilde{X}^+, s^+)\right]$$

$$\text{s.t. } \widetilde{X} = \widetilde{c} + \widetilde{a}^+, \quad \widetilde{a}^+ \geq 0,\ 0 \leq \omega^+ \leq 1$$

$$\widetilde{X}^+ = R_p(\omega^+, \vartheta^+)\frac{\widetilde{a}^+}{\exp(\epsilon^+)} + \widetilde{y}^+ + \widetilde{pen}^+$$

$$\widetilde{y}^+ = \begin{cases} w\widetilde{h}^+ & \text{if } s = e \\ \chi_k w e_j & \text{if } s = u_k, k = s, l. \end{cases}$$

$$\widetilde{pen}^+ = \begin{cases} \kappa w e_{j_r-1} & \text{if } s = e \\ \chi_k \kappa w e_{j-r-1} & \text{if } s = u_k, k = s, l \end{cases}$$

$$\text{Prob}(s_{j+1} = s^+ | s_j = s) = \pi_{ss^+} \qquad s, s^+ \in \{e, u_s, u_k\}.$$

Implementing for this new optimization problem the two-step solution as in Section 10.2.1 of the book, we solve the two sub-problems:

1. *Optimal portfolio composition*: for each level of savings $\widetilde{a}^+$ and current employment status s, we can determine the optimal investment structure $\omega^+(j, \widetilde{a}^+, s)$ by solving:

$$\widetilde{Q}(j, \widetilde{a}^+, s) = \max_{0 \le \omega^+ \le 1} E\Big[\exp(\epsilon^+)^{1-\frac{1}{\gamma}} \widetilde{V}(j+1, \widetilde{X}^+, s^+)\Big]$$

$$\text{s.t. } \widetilde{X}^+ = R_p(\omega^+, \vartheta^+) \cdot \frac{\widetilde{a}^+}{\exp(\epsilon^+)} + \widetilde{y}^+ + \widetilde{pen}^+,$$

where the expected value of $\widetilde{V}$ now also depends on the future employment status s^+. Plugging $\widetilde{X}^+$ into the objective function and taking derivatives, we obtain the first-order condition:

$$E[(\mu_r + \vartheta^+)\widetilde{a}^+ \cdot \left(\exp(\epsilon^+) \cdot \widetilde{c}(j+1, \widetilde{X}^+, s^+)\right)^{-\frac{1}{\gamma}}] = 0.$$

The optimal portfolio composition $\omega^+(j, \widetilde{a}^+, s)$ therefore takes into account the future employment risk, which depends on the current employment status.

2. *Consumption–savings choice*: given the optimal portfolio composition $\omega^+(j, \widetilde{a}^+, s)$, the household decides about how much to consume and save by maximizing:

$$\widetilde{V}(j, \widetilde{X}, s) = \max_{\widetilde{c}, \widetilde{a}^+} u(\widetilde{c}) + \beta\psi_{j+1}\widetilde{Q}(j, \widetilde{a}^+, s) \qquad \text{s.t.} \quad \widetilde{X} = \widetilde{c} + \widetilde{a}^+.$$

The respective first-order condition is then:

$$\widetilde{c}(j, \widetilde{X}, s) = \left(\beta\psi_{j+1} \cdot E_j\Big[[1 + r_f + \omega^+(j, \widetilde{a}^+, s)(\mu_r + \vartheta^+)](\exp(\epsilon^+)\widetilde{c}(j+1, \widetilde{X}^+, s^+))^{-\frac{1}{\gamma}}\Big]\right)^{-\gamma}.$$

Again, given the current employment status s, working-age cohorts also form expectations with respect to their future employment risk when they optimize their consumption and saving behaviour.

In our code in program `sol_prog10_18`, we use a matrix `pi` that captures the transition between different employment states and attach values to this matrix in the subroutine `initialize`. Beside that, we need to incorporate an additional element into the state space, which we index by a variable `io` in the program. We use the transition probabilities to form expectations about future employment possibilities in the function `foc_port` when individuals are of working age (see Module 10.18m). This is done by setting up an additional do-loop that captures future employment possibilities `io_p`. The transition probabilities are multiplied to the permanent and transitory productivity shocks in the variable `dist`. Note that we also need to take into account that individuals jump between employment states when we calculate the distribution of households over the state space.

Module 10.18m First-order condition with unemployment risk

```
function foc_port(p)
    [......]
    if(ij_com+1 >= JR)then
        [......]
    else
        do io_p = 1, NO
          do iw = 1, NW
            do isr = 1, NSR

               ! get return on the portfolio
               R_port = 1d0 + r_f + &
                         omega_p*(mu_r + vtheta(isr))

               ! derive labor earnings
               if(io_p == 1)then
                   earnings = w*eff(ij_com+1)*zeta(iw)
               else
                   earnings = w*eff(ij_com+1)*chi(io_p)
               endif

               ! get tomorrow's cash on hand
               X_p = R_port*a(ia_com)/eps(isr) + earnings

               ! derive interpolation weights
               call linint_Grow(X_p, X_l, X_u, X_grow, &
                   NX, ixl, ixr, varphi)

               ! get distributional weight
               dist = dist_zeta(iw)*dist_epsvtheta(isr) &
                       *pi(io_com, io_p)

               ! calculate the RHS of the FOC
               c_p = varphi*c(ij_com+1, ixl, io_p) + &
                     (1d0-varphi)*c(ij_com+1, ixr, io_p)
               c_p = max(c_p, 1d-10)
               foc_port = foc_port + dist*(mu_r + &
                   vtheta(isr))*a(ia_com)*margu(eps(isr)*c_p)
            enddo
          enddo
        enddo
    endif

end function
```

(b) Initializing the diagonal of the transition matrix to a value of one and setting all other values to zero generates the same results as in the baseline model in `prog10_04` of the book when we assume that all households are employed in the initial age. Individuals have no risk to be subject to unemployment and will stay employed throughout their life cycle.

(c) In order to understand the portfolio shares held in the different employment states, it is crucial to keep in mind the constant relative risk aversion property of our utility function. Individuals want to be exposed to the same risk over the whole life cycle and, hence, are now holding fewer wealth in stocks early in life, owing to the additional uncertainty about their employment state (see Figure 10.23). This is particularly so for the long-term unemployed, who face the largest risk of never returning to a full employment

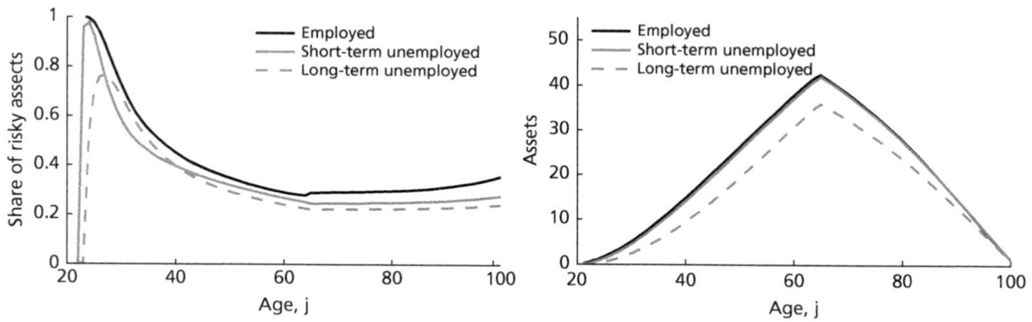

Figure 10.23 Portfolio shares and asset holdings by employment state

state. In addition, the long-term unemployed have the greatest difficulty accumulating wealth, owing to their low transfer income.

Exercise 10.19

(a) The household's maximization problem with endogenous labour supply in dynamic programming form now reads:

$$V(j, a, \omega, \eta, \zeta, \vartheta) = \max_{c,l,a^+\geq 0, 0\leq\omega^+\leq 1} \frac{\left[c^\nu(1-l)^{1-\nu}\right]^{1-\frac{1}{\gamma}}}{1-\frac{1}{\gamma}} + \beta\psi_{j+1}E\left[V(j+1, a^+\omega^+, \eta^+, \zeta^+, \vartheta^+)\right]$$
$$\text{s.t.}\quad R_p(\omega, \vartheta)a + whl + pen = c + a^+.$$

As these preferences imply homotheticity, we can normalize the household optimization problem in a similar way as before. We start with reformulating the problem in 'cash-on-hand' form and summarize $X = R_p(\omega, \vartheta)a + pen$. Note that we exclude the labour productivity component from this variable, as labour hours are an endogenous choice now. We can reformulate the optimization problem to:

$$V(j, X, \eta, \zeta) = \max_{c,l,a^+,\omega^+} u(c, 1-l) + \beta\psi_{j+1}E\left[V(j+1, X^+, \eta^+, \zeta^+)\right]$$
$$\text{s.t. } X + whl = c + a^+,\ a^+ \geq 0,\ 0 \leq \omega^+ \leq 1$$
$$\text{and } X^+ = R_p(\omega^+, \vartheta^+)a^+ + pen^+.$$

Normalization by $\exp(\eta)$ is slightly more complicated than before. It is crucial to recognize that, given our homothetic preferences, the labour supply decision l is independent of the permanent income level shock $\exp(\eta)$. With that in mind, we can write the normalized optimization problem of the household as:

$$\widetilde{V}(j,\widetilde{X},\zeta) = \max_{\widetilde{c},l,\widetilde{a}^+ \geq 0, 0 \leq \omega^+ \leq 1} \frac{\left[\widetilde{c}^{\nu}(1-l)^{1-\nu}\right]^{1-\frac{1}{\gamma}}}{1-\frac{1}{\gamma}} + \beta\psi_{j+1} E\left[\exp(\epsilon^+)^{\nu\left(1-\frac{1}{\gamma}\right)} V(j+1,\widetilde{X}^+,\zeta^+)\right]$$

$$\text{s.t.} \quad \widetilde{X} + we_j \exp(\zeta) l = \widetilde{c} + \widetilde{a}^+$$

$$\text{and:} \quad \widetilde{X}^+ = R_p(\omega^+,\vartheta^+)\frac{\widetilde{a}^+}{\exp(\epsilon^+)} + \widetilde{pen}^+.$$

We can separate the optimization procedure again into two steps. In the first step, we compute the optimal equity exposure in the liquid asset portfolio, and in the second step we derive the optimal choices on consumption, labour supply, and savings.

1. *Optimal portfolio composition*:

$$Q(j,\widetilde{a}^+) = \max_{0 \leq \omega^+ \leq 1} E\left[\exp(\epsilon^+)^{\nu\left(1-\frac{1}{\gamma}\right)} \widetilde{V}(j+1,\widetilde{X}^+,\zeta^+)\right]$$

$$\text{s.t.} \quad \widetilde{X}^+ = R_p(\omega^+,\vartheta^+)\frac{\widetilde{a}^+}{\exp(\epsilon^+)} + \widetilde{pen}^+,$$

   which yields the first-order condition:

$$E\left[(\mu_r + \vartheta^+)\widetilde{a}^+ \cdot \frac{\nu\left[\left(\exp(\epsilon^+)\widetilde{c}^+\right)^{\nu}(1-l^+)^{1-\nu}\right]^{1-\frac{1}{\gamma}}}{\exp(\epsilon^+)\widetilde{c}^+}\right] = 0,$$

   from where we determine $\omega^+(j,\widetilde{a}^+)$.

2. *Consumption–labour-savings choice*:

$$\widetilde{V}(j,\widetilde{X},\zeta) = \max_{\widetilde{c},l,\widetilde{a}^+ \geq 0} \frac{\left[\widetilde{c}^{\nu}(1-l)^{1-\nu}\right]^{1-\frac{1}{\gamma}}}{1-\frac{1}{\gamma}} + \beta\psi_{j+1}Q(j,\widetilde{a}^+)$$

$$\text{s.t.} \quad \widetilde{a}^+ = \widetilde{X} + we_j \exp(\zeta) l - \widetilde{c}.$$

   Labour supply and consumption can be derived from:

$$l = l(\widetilde{a}^+) = \min\left[\max\left[\nu + \frac{1-\nu}{we_j \exp(\zeta)}(\widetilde{a}^+ - \widetilde{X}), 0\right], 1\right]$$

$$\widetilde{c}(\widetilde{a}^+) = \widetilde{X} + we_j \exp(\zeta) l(\widetilde{a}^+) - \widetilde{a}^+$$

(see equations (10.15) and (10.16) in the book), so that the Euler equation is given by:

$$\frac{\nu\left[\widetilde{c}(\widetilde{a}^{+})^{\nu}(1-l(\widetilde{a}^{+}))^{1-\nu}\right]^{1-\frac{1}{\gamma}}}{\widetilde{c}(\widetilde{a}^{+})}$$
$$= \beta\psi_{j+1}E\left[R_p(\omega^{+},\vartheta^{+})\frac{\nu\left[\left(\exp(\epsilon^{+})\widetilde{c}^{+}\right)^{\nu}(1-l^{+})^{1-\nu}\right]^{1-\frac{1}{\gamma}}}{\exp(\epsilon^{+})\widetilde{c}^{+}}\right].$$

Implementing these changes in the numerical model is not overly complicated. Optimal household labour supply can be calculated directly in the function `foc_cons` from the explicit formula. We then need to take into account that labour supply features in the calculation of the marginal utility of consumption, in the same way as in program `prog10_02` of the book. This plays an important role in the function `foc_port`, as well as the subroutine `interpolate`, where we calculate the right-hand side of the Euler equation. Optimal labour supply also features in the calculation of household utility in the function `valuefunc`. Finally, we need to take into account that our definition of the 'cash-on-hand' grid has changed. This means that the lower boundary of the grid should be equal to zero and that all individuals start out their life with zero 'cash-on-hand'.

(b) When labour supply is endogenous, labour can be used to mitigate the consequences of productivity risk. As a result, human capital becomes less risky, which leads to an increase in the risk exposure of households on the asset market. When ν increases from 0.4 to 0.5 (see Figure 10.24), however, leisure has a lower weight in the utility function and consumption gets more important. Consequently, we move back into the direction of a model with less elastic labour supply, which in turn increases the risk exposure in the form of uncertainty about future income. As a result, we observe a reduced share in equity investment.

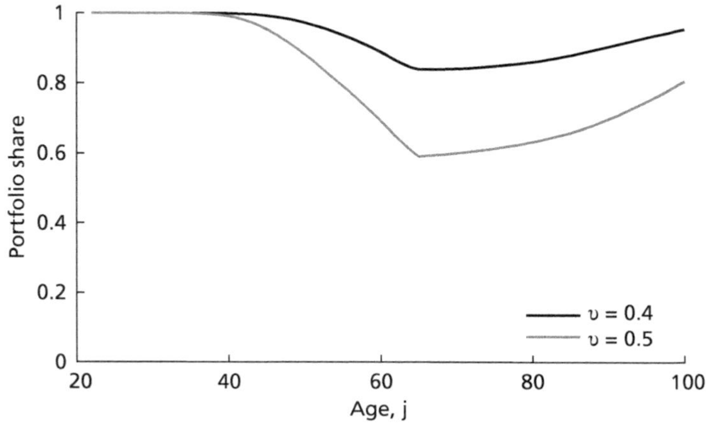

Figure 10.24 Share of risky investment for $\nu = 0.4$ and $\nu = 0.5$

Exercise 10.20

Given the state vector $z = (j, X)$, we formulate the portfolio choice problem with Epstein-Zin preferences as:

$$V(z) = \max_{c,a^+,\omega^+} \left\{ c^{1-\frac{1}{\gamma}} + \beta\psi_{j+1}E\left[\left(\exp(\epsilon^+)V(z^+)\right)^{1-\chi}\right]^{\frac{1-\frac{1}{\gamma}}{1-\chi}} \right\}^{\frac{1}{1-\frac{1}{\gamma}}}$$

$$\text{s.t} \quad X = c + a^+ \ \text{ and } \ X^+ = R_p(\omega^+, \vartheta^+)\frac{a^+}{\exp(\epsilon^+)} + wh^+ + pen^+,$$

where γ is the intertemporal elasticity of substitution and χ is risk aversion. In the following, we consider all variables as already expressed in normalized terms, but omit the $\tilde{\cdot}$ for the sake of clarity. We can separate the optimization problem into the usual two steps of determining the optimal portfolio composition and the consumption-savings choice separately.

1. *Optimal portfolio composition*:

$$Q(j, a^+) = \max_{0\le\omega^+\le 1} E\left\{\left[\exp(\epsilon^+)V(z^+)\right]^{1-\chi}\right\}^{\frac{1}{1-\chi}}$$

$$\text{s.t.} \quad X^+ = R_p(\omega^+, \vartheta^+)\frac{a^+}{\exp(\epsilon^+)} + wh^+ + pen^+.$$

The solution to the problem is:

$$E\left\{\cdot\right\}^{\frac{\chi}{1-\chi}} \cdot E\left[(\mu_r + \vartheta^+)a^+ \cdot [\exp(\cdot)V(z^+)]^{-\chi} V_X(z^+)\right] =$$

$$EV(z^+)^{\chi} \cdot E\left[(\mu_r + \vartheta^+)a^+ \cdot \exp(\epsilon^+)^{-\chi} V(z^+)^{\frac{1}{\gamma}-\chi} c(z^+)^{-\frac{1}{\gamma}}\right] = 0,$$

where we used:

$$V_X(z^+) = \frac{1}{1-\frac{1}{\gamma}}\left\{\cdot\right\}^{\frac{\frac{1}{\gamma}}{1-\frac{1}{\gamma}}} \cdot \left(1 - \frac{1}{\gamma}\right) c(z^+)^{-\frac{1}{\gamma}} = V(z^+)^{\frac{1}{\gamma}} c(z^+)^{-\frac{1}{\gamma}}$$

and:

$$EV(z^+) = E\left[\left[\exp(\epsilon^+)V(z^+)\right]^{1-\chi}\right]^{\frac{1}{1-\chi}}.$$

2. *Consumption–savings choice*:

$$V(z) = \max_{c,a^+\ge 0} \left\{ c^{1-\frac{1}{\gamma}} + \beta\psi_{j+1}Q(j, a^+)^{1-\frac{1}{\gamma}} \right\}^{\frac{1}{1-\frac{1}{\gamma}}} \ \text{s.t} \quad X = c + a^+.$$

The solution is:

$$c(z)^{-\frac{1}{\gamma}} = \beta\psi_{j+1}Q(j,a^+)^{-\frac{1}{\gamma}}Q_a(j,a^+),$$

so that the Euler equation is given by:

$$c(z)^{-\frac{1}{\gamma}} = \beta\psi_{j+1}Q(j,a^+)^{\chi-\frac{1}{\gamma}}E\left[R_p^+\exp(\epsilon^+)^{-\chi}V(z^+)^{\frac{1}{\gamma}-\chi}c(z^+)^{-\frac{1}{\gamma}}\right],$$

or better,

$$c(z) = (\beta\psi_{j+1})^{-\gamma}Q(j,a^+)^{1-\chi\gamma}E\left[R_p^+\exp(\epsilon^+)^{-\chi}V(z^+)^{\frac{1}{\gamma}-\chi}c(z^+)^{-\frac{1}{\gamma}}\right]^{-\gamma},$$

with $R_p^+ = R_p(\omega^+,\vartheta^+)$.

The numerical implementation in program `sol_prog10_20` extends program `prog10_04` in the book. We only have to change the computation of the first-order conditions in `foc_port` as well as `foc_cons` and adapt the value function in `value_func`. Everything else remains unchanged. Module 10.20m shows that we treat the last period separately when calculating the value function. In fact, in the last period of life, where the future is discounted with $\psi_{J+1} = 0$, the value function boils down to $V(z) = c$. This is a result of the Epstein-Zin specification of the utility function. This feature of the value function also tells us that there is no need to transform the value function before and after interpolation as, apparently, the Epstein-Zin specification is linear in consumption anyway.

Module 10.20m Computation of the current value function $V(z)$

```
function valuefunc(a_plus, cons, ij)
    [......]
    ! check whether consumption or leisure are too small
    c_help = max(cons, 1d-10)

    ! calculate tomorrow's part of value function if ij<JJ
    if(ij < JJ)then
        call linint_Grow(a_plus, a_l, a_u, a_grow, &
                                    NA, ial, iar, varphi)

        valuefunc = max(varphi*Q(ij, ial) &
                    + (1d0-varphi)*Q(ij, iar), 1d-10)
        valuefunc = (c_help**egam + beta*psi(ij+1)* &
                    valuefunc**egam)**(1d0/egam)
    else
        valuefunc = c_help
    endif

end function
```

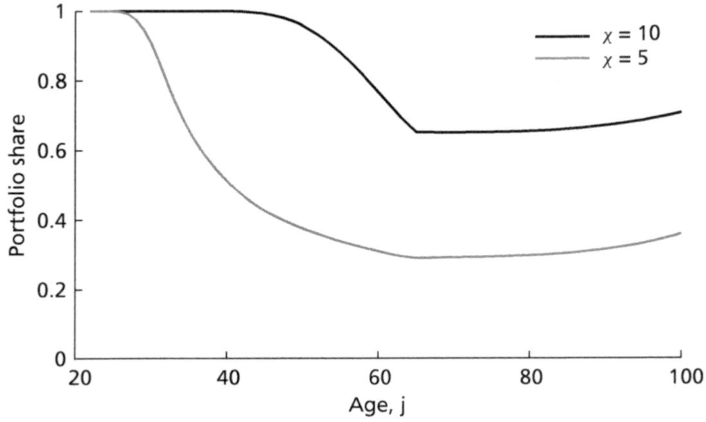

Figure 10.25 Risk exposure and risk aversion ($\chi = 10$ vs $\chi = 5$)

In the baseline parameterization with $\chi = 10.0$, we obtain the same results as with our standard utility function in `prog10_04` of the book (see Figure 10.25). One can in fact show that the Epstein-Zin utility function is equivalent to our usual constant relative risk aversion utility for $\chi = \frac{1}{\gamma}$. Reducing risk aversion to $\chi = 5.0$ will make individuals hold more (risky) equity, so that the equity share increases significantly over the life cycle. Vice versa, a higher risk aversion leads to a decreasing equity share held by individuals.

Exercise 10.21

(a) In order to derive the normalization, we start with the utility function and write it as:

$$U_j = \frac{c_j^{1-\frac{1}{\gamma}}}{1-\frac{1}{\gamma}} + \beta(1-\psi_{j+1})\nu E\left[\frac{\left(R_{p,j+1}a_{l,j+1}\right)^{1-\frac{1}{\gamma}}}{1-\frac{1}{\gamma}}\right]$$

$$+\beta\psi_{j+1}E\Bigg[\sum_{k=j+1}^{J}\beta^{k-(j+1)}\Bigg(\prod_{i=j+2}^{k}\psi_i\Bigg)\Big\{u(c_k)+\beta(1-\psi_{k+1})\mathcal{B}(a_{l,k+1})\Big\}\Bigg]$$

$$= \exp(\eta_j)^{1-\frac{1}{\gamma}}\frac{\tilde{c}_j^{1-\frac{1}{\gamma}}}{1-\frac{1}{\gamma}} + \beta(1-\psi_{j+1})\nu E\left[\exp(\eta_j)^{1-\frac{1}{\gamma}}\frac{\left(R_{p,j+1}\tilde{a}_{l,j+1}\right)^{1-\frac{1}{\gamma}}}{1-\frac{1}{\gamma}}\right]$$

$$+\beta\psi_{j+1}E\Bigg[\sum_{k=j+1}^{J}\exp(\eta_k)^{1-\frac{1}{\gamma}}\beta^{k-(j+1)}\Bigg(\prod_{i=j+2}^{k}\psi_i\Bigg)\Big\{u(\tilde{c}_k)+\beta(1-\psi_{k+1})\mathcal{B}(\tilde{a}_{l,k+1})\Big\}\Bigg].$$

Therefore, the normalized utility function reads:

$$\widetilde{U}_j = \frac{U_j}{\exp(\eta_j)^{1-\frac{1}{\gamma}}} = \frac{\tilde{c}_j^{1-\frac{1}{\gamma}}}{1-\frac{1}{\gamma}} + \beta(1-\psi_{j+1})\nu E\left[\frac{\left(R_{p,j+1}\tilde{a}_{l,j+1}\right)^{1-\frac{1}{\gamma}}}{1-\frac{1}{\gamma}}\right]$$

$$+\beta\psi_{j+1}E\Bigg[\sum_{k=j+1}^{J}\frac{\exp(\eta_k)^{1-\frac{1}{\gamma}}}{\exp(\eta_j)^{1-\frac{1}{\gamma}}}\beta^{k-(j+1)}\left(\prod_{i=j+2}^{k}\psi_i\right)\Big\{u(\tilde{c}_k)+\beta(1-\psi_{k+1})\mathcal{B}(\tilde{a}_{l,k+1})\Big\}\Bigg].$$

After rearranging as in the baseline model, the expected future utility can be written as:

$$E\left[\exp(\epsilon_{j+1})^{1-\frac{1}{\gamma}}\cdot\widetilde{U}_{j+1}\right].$$

In the following, we consider all variables as already expressed in normalized terms, but omit the $\tilde{\cdot}$ for the sake of clarity. At any age j, the household has to decide how to split up resources X into consumption c and total wealth a^+, total wealth into liquid assets $a_l^+ = (1-\omega_r^+)a^+$ and annuity purchases $a_r^+ = \omega_r^+\cdot a^+$, and liquid wealth into stocks $\omega^+ a_l^+$ and bonds $(1-\omega^+)a_l^+$. Annuity purchases generate an annuity stream of $\frac{a_r^+}{p_a}$ starting in the next period, so that the price of an annuity bought at age j is defined by:

$$p_{a,j} = (1+\xi)\sum_{s=j+1}^{J}\frac{\prod_{i=j+1}^{s}\psi_i}{(1+r_f)^{s-j}},$$

where ξ again denotes the load factor. Since households can buy annuities in every period, y_a defines the aggregated annuity stream (from all previous purchases) in a given period. The optimization problem at state $z = (j, X, y_a)$ then reads:

$$V(z) = \max_{c,a^+,\omega^+,\omega_r^+}\frac{c^{1-\frac{1}{\gamma}}}{1-\frac{1}{\gamma}} + \beta\psi_{j+1}E\left[\exp(\epsilon^+)^{1-\frac{1}{\gamma}}V(z^+)\right]$$

$$+\beta(1-\psi_{j+1})\nu E\left[\frac{\left(R_p(\omega^+,\vartheta^+)a_l^+\right)^{1-\frac{1}{\gamma}}}{1-\frac{1}{\gamma}}\right]$$

$$\text{s.t } X = c + a^+,\quad a^+\geq 0,\quad 0\leq\omega^+,\omega_r^+\leq 1$$

$$y_a^+ = \frac{y_a^p}{\exp(\epsilon^+)}\quad\text{with}\quad y_a^p = \left[y_a + \frac{\omega_r(j,a^+,y_a)a^+}{p_{a,j}}\right]\quad\text{and}$$

$$X^+ = R_p(\omega^+,\vartheta^+)\frac{(1-\omega_r(j,a^+,y_a))a^+}{\exp(\epsilon^+)} + wh^+ + pen^+ + y_a^+,$$

with $R_p(\omega^+,\vartheta^+) = 1 + r_f + \omega(j, a_l^+, y_a^p)\cdot(\mu_r+\vartheta^+)$.

In order to solve this problem we proceed backwards in three steps:

1. *Equity exposure in liquid wealth*: given a level of liquid savings a_l^+ and (pre-normalized) annuity income y_a^p, we can solve the household's portfolio optimization problem at age j:

$$Q(j, a_l^+, y_a^p) = \max_{0\leq\omega^+\leq 1} \psi_{j+1} E\left[\, \exp(\epsilon^+)^{1-\frac{1}{\gamma}} V(z^+)\,\right] + \\ (1-\psi_{j+1})\nu E\left[\frac{\left(R_p(\omega^+, \vartheta^+)a_l^+\right)^{1-\frac{1}{\gamma}}}{1-\frac{1}{\gamma}}\right]$$

$$\text{s.t.}\quad y_a^+ = \frac{y_a^p}{\exp(\epsilon^+)}, \quad \text{and } X^+ = R_p(\omega^+, \vartheta^+)\frac{a_l^+}{\exp(\epsilon^+)} + wh^+ + pen^+ + y_a^+.$$

The solution $\omega(j, a_l^+, y_a^p)$ to this problem is defined by the first-order condition:

$$\psi_{j+1} E\left[(\mu_r + \vartheta^+)a_l^+ \left(\exp(\epsilon^+)c(z^+)\right)^{-\frac{1}{\gamma}}\right] + \\ (1-\psi_{j+1})\nu E\left[(\mu_r + \vartheta^+)a_l^+ \left(\, R_p(\omega^+, \vartheta^+)a_l^+\,\right)^{-\frac{1}{\gamma}}\right] = 0.$$

2. *Annuity exposure in total wealth*: the choice of how to split total savings a^+ between liquid assets and annuity purchases requires a separate optimization problem at every age. Given that we already know the optimal equity exposure for a given split of total assets from step 1, we can define the sub-optimization problem:

$$S(j, a^+, y_a) = \max_{\omega_r^+} Q\left(j, (1-\omega_r^+)a^+, y_a^p\right) \text{ s.t. } \; y_a^p = \left[y_a + \frac{\omega_r^+ a^+}{p_{a,j}}\right].$$

Taking the derivative with respect to ω_r^+ immediately yields the first-order condition:

$$Q_{a_l}(j, a_l^+, y_a^p) = \frac{Q_{y_a^p}(j, a_l^+, y_a^p)}{p_{a,j}},$$

where Q_{a_l} and $Q_{y_a^p}$ are the derivatives of Q with respect to liquid assets and (pre-normalized) annuity income, respectively. The first-order condition tells us that the marginal utility of investing one unit of wealth in liquid assets should be equal to the marginal utility of annuity income. Using the envelope theorem, the first derivative is given by:

$$Q_{a_l}(j, a_l^+, y_a^p) = \psi_{j+1} E\left[R_p(\omega^+, \vartheta^+)\left(\exp(\epsilon^+)c(z^+)\right)^{-\frac{1}{\gamma}}\right] \\ +(1-\psi_{j+1})\nu E\left[R_p(\omega^+, \vartheta^+)\left(R_p(\omega^+, \vartheta^+)a_l^+\,\right)^{-\frac{1}{\gamma}}\right],$$

with:

$$R_p(\omega^+, \vartheta^+) = 1 + r_f + \omega(j, a_l^+, y_a^p)\cdot\left(\mu_r + \vartheta^+\right).$$

Using the very same logic, we also obtain:

$$Q_{y_a^p}(j, a_l^+, y_a^p) = \psi_{j+1} E\Big[\big(\exp(\epsilon^+) c(z^+) \big)^{-\frac{1}{\gamma}} + \exp(\epsilon^+)^{-\frac{1}{\gamma}} V_{y_a}(z^+) \Big],$$

where we get from the definition of $V(z)$:

$$V_{y_a}(z) = \beta \psi_{j+1} E\Big[\big(\exp(\epsilon^+) c(z^+) \big)^{-\frac{1}{\gamma}} + \exp(\epsilon^+)^{-\frac{1}{\gamma}} V_{y_a}(z^+) \Big].$$

Given the terminal condition $V_{y_a}(J, X, y_a) = 0$, we can again compute the marginal value function $V_{y_a}(z)$ recursively. Given $\omega_r(j, a^+, y_a)$, we can proceed to the last step.

3. *The consumption–savings decision*: finally, knowing how much wealth to allocate to annuities and how much liquid assets to hold, it is possible to set up the consumption savings problem as:

$$V(j, X, y_a) = \max_{c, a^+} \frac{c^{1-\frac{1}{\gamma}}}{1 - \frac{1}{\gamma}} + \beta S(j, a^+, y_a) \quad \text{s.t.} \quad X = c + a^+,$$

which yields the first-order condition:

$$c = \big[\beta S_a(j, a^+, y_a)\big]^{-\gamma}.$$

From the definition of $S(j, a^+, y_a)$, we immediately see that:

$$S_a(j, a^+, y_a) = (1 - \omega_r^+) \cdot Q_{a_l}(j, a_l^+, y_a^p) + \omega_r^+ \cdot \frac{Q_{y_a^p}(j, a_l^+, y_a^p)}{p_{a,j}}$$

with Q_{a_l}, $Q_{y_a^p}$ and $\omega_r(j, a^+, y_a)$ from step 2.

(b) The solution to this exercise is based on program `prog10_06` of the book. We first rename a couple of variables and routines so as to make them consistent with the wording in this exercise. Specifically, we let the index of the annuity savings grid be `iy` instead of `ir` and we change the names of subroutine `solve_retaccount` and `foc_ret` to `solve_annuities` and `foc_annu`, respectively. We eliminate the tax rate `tau` from the model and change the retirement wealth `ar` to the level of annuity payments `ya`. This means that in the budget constraint of the household, we do not write `ar(ir)/p_a`, but `yi(iy)` instead. Finally, we assume that annuities pay a fixed interest equal to the risk-free rate `r_f`, which is already included in the annuity price.

Program 10.21 Age-dependent annuity prices

```
p_a(JJ) = 0d0
do ij = JJ-1, 1, -1
    p_a(ij) = psi(ij+1)/(1d0+r_f)*(1d0+p_a(ij+1))
enddo
p_a(:) = (1d0+xi)*p_a(:)
```

In the main program, we first have to calculate the age-dependent prices of annuities. We do this using a simple recursive formulation, as shown in Program 10.21. In the optimization problem of the household, we need to incorporate four major changes:

1. Since households in this model have a bequest motive, they might want to leave bequests to their descendants even beyond the final period of their life. This means that in the subroutine `solve_household`, we have to solve for the period `JJ` portfolio composition and consumption choice using the subroutines `solve_portfolio` and `solve_consumption`. The only trivial observation in this period is that household's will not want to buy annuities, as they cannot bequeath such annuities to their children.
2. In the first-order condition that serves to determine the portfolio choice `omega_plus`, we need to incorporate the changes in the portfolio composition change expected value and variance of bequest levels.
3. The annuity purchase decision has to be solved for in each period $j < J$ using the subroutine `solve_annuities`. The subroutine itself, however, hasn't changed compared to the original program `prog10_06` from the book.
4. Finally, we have to change the calculation of `Q_ya`, such that it directly takes into account that, once bought, annuities will directly pay off in the successive period up to the last date of a household's life.

Once we run the program without a bequest motive ($\nu = 0$), we find that, up to the age of forty-five, households do not buy any annuities at all (see the left panel of Figure 10.26). Afterwards, they do use a significant amount of their wealth to buy annuities. Starting from the age of around eighty, they have annuitized almost all of their remaining wealth. Annuities in this set-up have the advantage of insuring the household against longevity risk. However, they pay a low interest rate. Hence, prior to the age of eighty, where survival probabilities are still relatively high, the household holds a significant amount of risky wealth in order to chase high returns. Only when survival probabilities drop is it worthwhile to shift all wealth into annuities. This logic can be seen in the right panel of Figure 10.26, which shows the household's investment behaviour. From the point at which the household holds a substantial amount of wealth in low-yield annuities, it will invest the remaining part of its liquid wealth almost entirely into risky assets to chase high returns and keep risk exposure up.

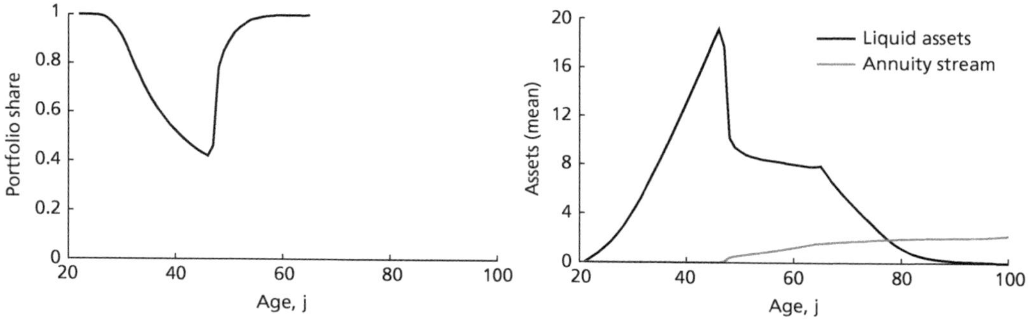

Figure 10.26 Annuity purchases without bequest motive ($\nu = 0$)

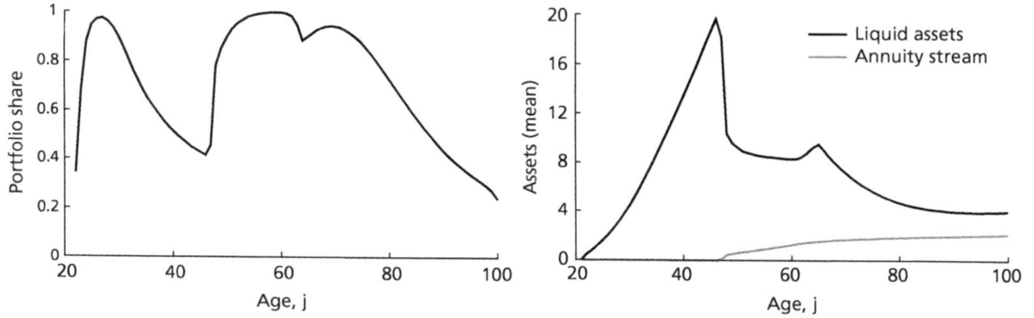

Figure 10.27 Annuity purchases with bequest motive ($\nu = 10$)

(c) Once we introduce a bequest motive into the model ($\nu = 10$), households always hold a chunk of their wealth in the liquid account in order to bequeath it to their descendants (see the left panel of Figure 10.27). We still see that annuity purchases increase over the life cycle. However, relative to total wealth, they are much smaller. Owing to the larger amount of liquid wealth in their portfolio, households reduce risk exposure in their liquid wealth as they age.

Exercise 10.22

This exercise asks us to solve the (normalized) optimization problem:[1]

$$V(z) = \max_{c,a^+,\omega^+,\omega_h^+} \theta \frac{c^{1-\frac{1}{\gamma}}}{1-\frac{1}{\gamma}} + (1-\theta)\frac{a_h^{1-\frac{1}{\gamma}}}{1-\frac{1}{\gamma}}$$
$$+ \beta\psi_{j+1}E\left[\exp(\epsilon^+)V(z^+)\right] + \beta(1-\psi_{j+1})E\left[\nu\frac{(b^+)^{1-\frac{1}{\gamma}}}{1-\frac{1}{\gamma}}\right],$$

[1] In the following, we consider all variables as already expressed in normalized terms, but omit the $\tilde{}$ for the sake of clarity.

subject to the constraints:[2]

$$
\begin{aligned}
X &= c + a^+, \quad b^+ = R_p(\omega^+, \vartheta^+)\hat{a}_l^+ + (1-\delta_h)a_h^+ \\
X^+ &= \frac{R_p(\omega^+, \vartheta^+)\hat{a}_l^+}{\exp(\epsilon^+)} + wh^+ + pen^+ + \frac{(1-\delta_h)a_h^+}{\exp(\epsilon^+)} \\
a_h^+ &= \omega_h^+ a^+ \geq h_{min}, \quad \hat{a}_l^+ = (1-\omega_h^+)a^+ \geq -\xi a_h^+ \\
z^+ &= \left(j+1, X^+, \frac{a_h^+}{\exp(\epsilon^+)}\right), \quad 0 \leq \omega^+, \omega_h^+ \leq 1,
\end{aligned}
$$

as well as the portfolio return:

$$
R_p(\omega^+, \vartheta^+) = \begin{cases} 1 + r_f + \omega^+ \cdot (\mu_r + \vartheta^+) & \text{if } \hat{a}_l^+ \geq 0 \\ 1 + r_f + 0.02 & \text{otherwise.} \end{cases}
$$

We defined b^+ as the amount of the bequest for notational convenience. This dynamic programming problem is a very complicated problem to solve, for mainly three reasons. First, we need to ensure that housing wealth a_h^+ is always greater than or equal to the minimum house size h_{min}. Second, liquid wealth $\hat{a}_l^+$ can now be negative, but needs to be greater than or equal to the collateral constraint $-\xi a_h^+$. Third, the collateral constraint is not a fixed parameter, but is endogenous to the household's choices.

When looking upon this problem, however, there is a way to simplify things and bring the problem into a form that is quite similar to what we solved for so far. We start out with the first problem. In order to deal with the problem of a minimum house size, we simply rephrase the household budget constraint to:

$$
X = c + a^+ + (1-\xi)h_{min} \quad \text{and} \quad a_h^+ = h_{min} + \omega^+ a^+.
$$

By doing so, we force the household in every period of the life cycle to make a housing investment of at least the minimum house size h_{min}. Note that, whenever borrowing against the house is allowed, ie $\xi > 0$, the household only has to make a down payment of $(1-\xi)h_{min}$ in order to acquire a house of size h_{min}. Consequently, the household's future housing wealth is at least h_{min} and $\omega^+ a^+ = (1-\xi)(a_h^+ - h_{min})$ defines the required down payment for the housing investment in excess of the minimum house size.

Next, we need to deal with the problem of an endogenous collateral constraint $\hat{a}_l^+ \geq -\xi a_h^+$. Note, however, that we can simply rephrase this constraint as:

$$
a_l^+ := \hat{a}_l^+ + \xi a_h^+ \geq 0,
$$

[2] Note that we used the notation $\hat{a}_l^+$ on purpose, which deviates from the notation in the book. This is just a notational subtlety, but the reason for it will become clear very quickly.

which is a 'hard' constraint in the sense that the sum of liquid savings plus the borrowing frame obtained form purchasing a house cannot be smaller than zero. In order to exploit this 'hard' and therefore easy-to-manage constraint, we simply define the sum of $\hat{a}_l^+$ and ξa_h^+ to be a_l^+. This allows us to rephrase the dynamic programming problem into an isomorphic problem that has the same value function as above, but the constraints read:

$$
\begin{aligned}
X &= c + a^+ + (1-\xi)h_{min}\\
b^+ &= R_p(\omega^+, \vartheta^+)(a_l^+ - \xi a_h^+) + (1-\delta_h)a_h^+\\
X^+ &= \frac{R_p(\omega^+, \vartheta^+)(a_l^+ - \xi a_h^+)}{\exp(\epsilon^+)} + wh^+ + pen^+ + \frac{(1-\delta_h)a_h^+}{\exp(\epsilon^+)}\\
a_h^+ &= h_{min} + \frac{\omega_h^+ a^+}{1-\xi}, \quad a_l^+ = (1-\omega_h^+)a^+ \geq 0\\
z^+ &= \left(j+1, X^+, \frac{a_h^+}{\exp(\epsilon^+)}\right), \quad 0 \leq \omega^+, \omega_h^+ \leq 1,
\end{aligned}
$$

with the portfolio return being:

$$
R_p(\omega^+, \vartheta^+) = \begin{cases} 1 + r_f + \omega^+ \cdot (\mu_r + \vartheta^+) & \text{if } a_l^+ - \xi a_h^+ \geq 0 \\ 1 + r_f + 0.02 & \text{otherwise.} \end{cases}
$$

Note that this is a much easier problem to solve, as the constraints on savings and portfolio shares are now very simple. We just require that the portfolio shares ω^+ and ω_h^+ range between zero and one and that household (excess) savings a^+ are greater than or equal to zero. Total savings plus minimum housing investments are consequently equal to the sum of housing wealth a_h^+ and (positive or negative) financial wealth, that is:

$$
a^+ + (1-\xi)h_{min} = a_h^+ + (a_l^+ - \xi a_h^+).
$$

Positive financial wealth is split into stocks $\omega^+(a_l^+ - \xi a_h^+)$ and bonds $(1-\omega^+)(a_l^+ - \xi a_h^+)$. Equity investments are not possible with negative financial wealth, meaning when the household holds a mortgage against its house. We therefore require $\omega^+ = 0$ whenever $a_l^+ < \xi a_h^+$. The mortgage interest rate is then equal to $r_f + 0.02$. Finally, we have to make some assumption about the housing stock the agent holds in the very first period of the life cycle. If the agent were to start with a value of $a_h = 0$, then utility would diverge to $-\infty$, which is not desirable. In order to keep things simple, we therefore assume that $a_h = e_1$ at age one, ie the household is endowed with a house the size of which is equal to the permanent productivity at age one. Note that, whenever we want the minimum house size to increase beyond this value, we could also set $a_h = h_{min}$.

(a) The normalization of the household problem works in exactly the same way as in Exercise 10.21. Therefore we will not repeat it at this point. Note, however, that in the non-normalized version of the problem, we have to set the minimum house size as a fraction of the agent's permanent productivity shock, ie $h_{min}\exp(\eta)$, in order for the problem to be tractable.

We can separate the optimization problem into the usual three steps of determining the optimal portfolio composition, the optimal amount of real estate holdings, and finally solving the consumption–savings problem separately.

1. *Equity exposure in liquid wealth*: given a level of liquid savings a_l^+ and housing assets a_h^+, we can solve the household's portfolio optimization problem at age j:

$$Q(j, a_l^+, a_h^+) = \max_{0\leq\omega^+\leq 1} \psi_{j+1} E\left[\exp(\epsilon^+)^{1-\frac{1}{\gamma}} V(z^+)\right] + (1-\psi_{j+1})\nu E\left[\frac{(b^+)^{1-\frac{1}{\gamma}}}{1-\frac{1}{\gamma}}\right],$$

subject to:

$$z^+ = \left(j+1, X^+, \frac{a_h^+}{\exp(\epsilon^+)}\right),$$

$$X^+ = \frac{R_p(\omega^+, \vartheta^+)(a_l^+ - \xi a_h^+)}{\exp(\epsilon^+)} + wh^+ + pen^+ + \frac{(1-\delta_h)a_h^+}{\exp(\epsilon^+)}, \quad \text{and}$$

$$b^+ = R_p(\omega^+, \vartheta^+)(a_l^+ - \xi a_h^+) + (1-\delta_h)a_h^+.$$

For $a_l^+ > \xi a_h^+$, the solution to this problem $\omega^+(j, a_l^+, a_h^+)$ is defined by the first-order condition:

$$E\left[(\mu_r + \vartheta^+)(a_l^+ - \xi a_h^+)\left\{\psi_{j+1}\theta\left(\exp(\epsilon^+)c(z^+)\right)^{-\frac{1}{\gamma}} + (1-\psi_{j+1})\nu(b^+)^{-\frac{1}{\gamma}}\right\}\right] = 0.$$

For $a_l^+ \leq \xi a_h^+$, we simply set $\omega^+(j, a_l^+, a_h^+) = 0$.

2. *Real estate exposure in total wealth*: the choice of how to split total savings a^+ between liquid and housing assets requires a separate optimization problem at every age. Given that we already know the optimal equity exposure for a given split of total assets from step 1, we can define the sub-optimization problem:

$$S(j, a^+) = \max_{\omega_h^+} Q\left(j, (1-\omega_h^+)a^+, h_{min} + \frac{\omega_h^+ a^+}{1-\xi}\right).$$

Note that, in contrast to Exercise 10.21, housing is not a permanent stock of savings, but its size can be freely re-optimized in every period. Consequently, the current housing stock a_h does not need to be an element of the state space of the function S. Taking the derivative with respect to ω_h^+ immediately yields the first-order condition:

$$Q_{a_l}(j, a_l^+, a_h^+) = Q_{a_h}(j, a_l^+, a_h^+)/(1-\xi),$$

where Q_{a_l} and Q_{a_h} are the derivatives of Q with respect to (pre-normalized) savings in liquid and real-estate assets, respectively. The first-order condition tells us that the marginal utility of investing one unit of wealth in liquid assets should be equal to the marginal utility of one unit investment in housing assets. Using the envelope theorem, the first derivative is given by:

$$Q_{a_l}(j, a_l^+, a_h^+) = E\Big[R_p^+\Big\{\psi_{j+1}\theta\left(\exp(\epsilon^+)c(z^+)\right)^{-\frac{1}{\gamma}} \\ +(1-\psi_{j+1})\nu(b^+)^{-\frac{1}{\gamma}}\Big\}\Big],$$

with:

$$R_p^+ = \begin{cases} 1 + r_f + \omega^+(j, a_l^+, a_h^+)\cdot(\mu_r + \vartheta^+) & \text{if } a_l^+ > \xi a_h^+ \\ 1 + r_f + 0.02 & \text{otherwise,} \end{cases}$$

as well as:

$$z^+ = \left(j+1, X^+, \frac{a_h^+}{\exp(\epsilon^+)}\right)$$

$$X^+ = \frac{R_p^+(a_l^+ - \xi a_h^+)}{\exp(\epsilon^+)} + wh^+ + pen^+ + \frac{(1-\delta_h)a_h^+}{\exp(\epsilon^+)} \quad \text{and}$$

$$b^+ = R_p(\omega^+, \vartheta^+)(a_l^+ - \xi a_h^+) + (1-\delta_h)a_h^+.$$

Using the very same logic, we also obtain:

$$Q_{a_h}(j, a_l^+, a_h^+) = E\Big[\psi_{j+1}\exp(\epsilon^+)^{1-\frac{1}{\gamma}}\left(V_X(z^+)X_{a_h} + \frac{V_{a_h}(z^+)}{\exp(\epsilon^+)}\right) \\ + (1-\psi_{j+1})\nu(1-\delta_h-\xi R_p^+)(b^+)^{-\frac{1}{\gamma}}\Big]$$

$$= E\Big[\psi_{j+1}\Big\{(1-\delta_h-\xi R_p^+)\theta\left(\exp(\epsilon^+)c(z^+)\right)^{-\frac{1}{\gamma}} + \\ (1-\theta)\left(\exp(\epsilon^+)a_h^+\right)^{-\frac{1}{\gamma}}\Big\} + \\ (1-\psi_{j+1})\nu(1-\delta_h-\xi R_p^+)(b^+)^{-\frac{1}{\gamma}}\Big].$$

Given the definition $V(j+1, X^+, a_h^+/\exp(\epsilon^+))$ used above, it should be clear that changes in a_h^+ have an indirect impact on the future value function through future 'cash-on-hand' X^+ and a direct impact, as households derive utility from housing assets. Given $\omega_h(j, a^+)$, we can proceed to the last step.

3. *The consumption–savings decision*: finally knowing how much wealth to allocate to real estate and how much liquid assets to hold, it is possible to set up the consumption savings problem as:

$$V(j, X, a_h) = \max_{c, a^+} \theta \frac{c^{1-\frac{1}{\gamma}}}{1-\frac{1}{\gamma}} + (1-\theta)\frac{a_h^{1-\frac{1}{\gamma}}}{1-\frac{1}{\gamma}} + \beta S(j, a^+)$$
$$\text{s.t. } X = c + a^+ + (1-\xi)h_{min},$$

which yields the first-order condition:

$$c = \left[\frac{\beta S_a(j, a^+)}{\theta}\right]^{-\gamma}.$$

Note again that, owing to the additive separability of the instantaneous utility function, this first-order condition is independent of the current housing wealth a_h. Consequently, the consumption policy function is also independent of a_h. From the definition of $S(j, a^+)$ above, we immediately see that:

$$S_a(j, a^+) = (1-\omega_h^+) \cdot Q_{a_l}(j, a_l^+, a_h^+) + \omega_h^+ \cdot \frac{Q_{a_h}(j, a_l^+, a_h^+)}{1-\xi},$$

with Q_{a_l}, Q_{a_h} and $\omega_h(j, a^+)$ from above.

(b) The numerical implementation of this model is almost identical to the one in Exercise 10.21. Hence, we do not repeat code elements at this point. Note that we need to account for the minimum housing size when defining the grid for housing wealth. In addition, we should incorporate the fact that whenever $\xi > 0$, the household only needs to make a down payment of $(1-\xi)a_h$ in order to purchase a house of size a_h. Hence, we specify the upper limit of the housing wealth grid as `ah_u = a_u/(1d0-xi)`. Finally, we also need to take into account that the household is endowed with e_1 units of housing wealth at the beginning of the life cycle. We do this in the subroutine `get_distribution_X` by recognizing that the initial 'cash-on-hand' reads:

$$X = we_1 \exp(\zeta) + (1-\delta_h)e_1$$

(see Program 10.22).

Program 10.22 Initializing the distribution at age 1

```
subroutine get_distribution_X(ij)
    [......]
    ! get initial cash-on-hand
    X_p = w*eff(1)*zeta(iw) + (1d0-delta_h)*eff(1)

    ! derive interpolation weights
    call linint_Grow(X_p, X_l, X_u, X_grow, NX, &
        ixl, ixr, varphi_X)
    call linint_Grow(eff(1), ah_l, ah_u, ah_grow, NAH, &
        ihl, ihr, varphi_h)

    ! get distributional weight
    dist = dist_zeta(iw)
    [......]
end subroutine
```

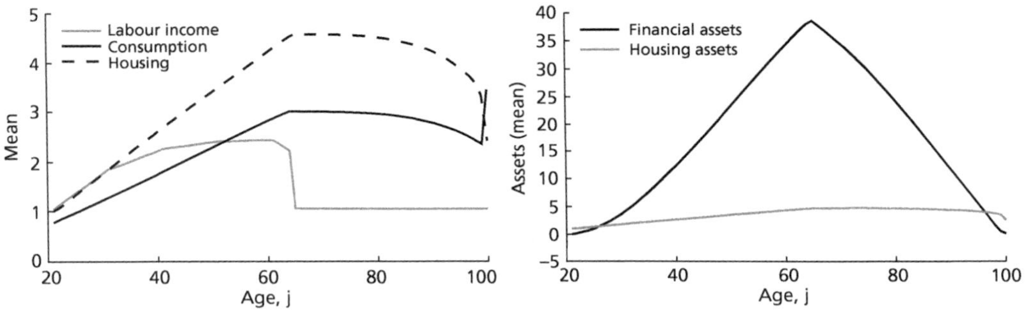

Figure 10.28 Life-cycle without collateralized debt ($\xi = 0$)

Figure 10.28 shows the life-cycle choices when we set $\theta = 0.35$, $\nu = h_{min} = 0$, and assume that the agent is not allowed to borrow against real estate ($\xi = 0$). To understand these pictures, we need to keep in mind that the financial return to real estate is very low in this model. In fact, there is no house price growth and the house depreciates over time at rate δ_h. Consequently, the financial return to housing investments is smaller than one, while the expected return to regular financial wealth is positive. In this set-up, it can therefore never be optimal to hold real estate as financial investment. The only reason agents buy houses is that they directly derive utility from them. When making optimal decisions, the marginal utility from houses should be equal to the marginal utility of regular consumption. Hence, it should not be surprising that the life-cycle path of housing traces the life-cycle path of consumption in the left panel of Figure 10.28. As $\theta = 0.35$, agents value houses relatively more than regular consumption. Consequently, they also spend more on housing than on other consumption. Only in the last period of life does the link between consumption and housing get broken. This happens as there is no future period in which holding a house could provide the household with additional utility. As a result, the household will sell off all real estate in the last period of life, which leads to an 'excessive' amount of consumption. Finally, in the right panel of Figure 10.28

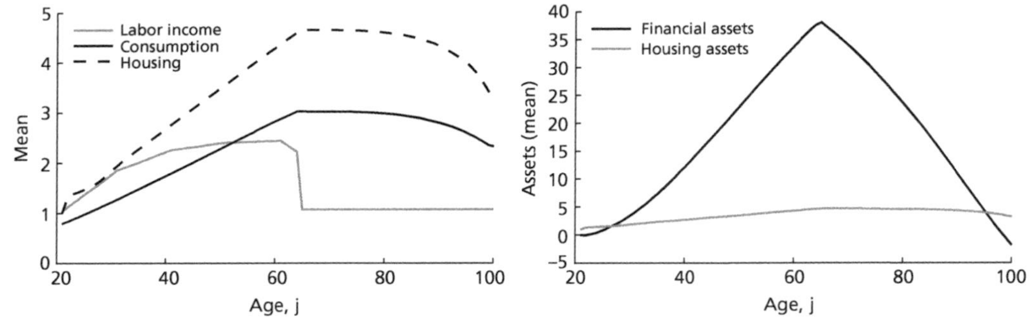

Figure 10.29 Life-cycle with collateralized debt ($\xi = 0.7$)

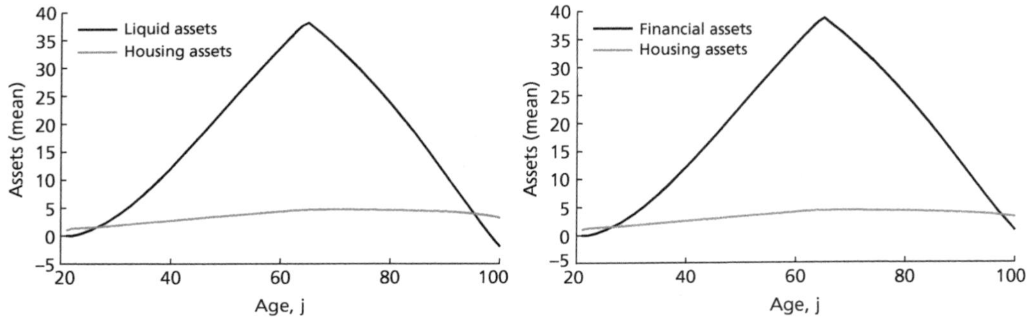

Figure 10.30 Life-cycle with $h_{min} = e_1$ (left) and $\nu = 10$ (right)

that depicts financial and housing wealth, we see that all life-cycle savings of the agent are made in financial investments and not in real estate. Therefore, the financial wealth profile exhibits the usual hump-shape we've seen many times before.

(c) When we loosen liquidity constraints and allow the household to hold collateralized debt, the profiles of consumption and investment change significantly at the beginning and the end of the life cycle (see Figure 10.29). In the first periods of life, households finance additional real estate by mortgages, which explains the discontinuous jump from age twenty-one to age twenty-two. Recall that the agent is endowed with a house of size 1. In the following periods, households repay their mortgages that exhibit higher interest rates than the regular risk-free rate. Consequently, they will be hesitant to buy additional houses. Once they have bought themselves out of debt, the life-cycle profiles looks similar to the situation without collateralized debt until the very end of the life cycle. There, the jump in the consumption profile disappeared, as agents now use reverse mortgaging to smooth the consumption profile over the final periods of life. This means that they run into debt against their real estate, and in the final period of life the returns from selling the house and the amount of outstanding mortgage balance in a way that the amount of consumption the household can afford makes the consumption profile smooth.

(c) The left panel of Figure 10.30 shows the savings profile that results from introducing a minimum house size of $h_{min} = e_1$. As households (at least on average) held amounts of real estate far greater than h_{min} already in Part (b), the life-cycle profiles are hardly affected from such a change in the model set-up.

(d) Finally, introducing a bequest motive makes households save more relative to Part (c) (see the right panel of Figure 10.30). Yet, as all life-cycle savings motives mainly affect financial savings, it is not surprising that the additional desire to save for leaving bequests leads to an increase in financial assets towards the end of the life cycle, but not in real estate holdings.

11 Dynamic macro II: The stochastic OLG model

Exercise 11.1

We can simply implement a model without uncertainty by setting the two variances σ_θ^2 and σ_ϵ^2 to zero. Now, income taxes only distort the labour supply and the savings decision. Yet, they do not provide insurance anymore. Consequently, it is optimal to substitute income taxes entirely with a lump-sum tax Tr, if this instrument is available. Table 11.1 shows that the elimination of labour income taxation generates an efficiency gain of 3.49 per cent of resources, while the full elimination of income taxation generates an efficiency gain of 3.89 per cent of resources. In both cases, the consumption tax rate is not altered. Since the consumption tax also distorts labour supply, it would be optimal to even get rid of this tax and to finance all public expenditures by lump-sum taxation.

If lump-sum taxes are not available, then consumption taxation turns out to be the most efficient source of taxation. The substitution of income taxes by consumption taxes increases the tax rate from 7.5 to 33.7 per cent and generates an efficiency gain of 1.4 per cent of resources in the present case (see the last line of Table 11.1). The efficiency gain results from the fact that consumption taxation implicitly taxes the existing capital stock, which creates no distortions (see the discussion in Auerbach and Kotlikoff (1987, p. 77ff.)).

Exercise 11.2

We explained in Exercise 6.2 how to implement a small, open economy in the overlapping generation model (OLG). The mechanics are identical in the case of a model with

Table 11.1 Optimal tax structure without uncertainty

τ^w	τ^r	τ^c	Tr	Δ^*
0.00	0.2086	0.075	−18.69	3.49
0.00	0.00	0.075	−24.44	3.89
0.00	0.00	0.000	−33.22	4.29
0.00	0.00	0.337	0.00	1.40

uncertainty. In a small, open economy, it is still optimal to tax capital income. However, the supply of capital is much more volatile, and therefore distortions are higher and optimal tax rates are smaller than in the closed economy case.

Table 11.2 starts from the same initial equilibrium as in the closed economy case. When we implement the optimal tax structure from the closed economy (see Table 11.6 in the book), the resulting efficiency gains increase to 0.66 per cent of aggregate resources, instead of 0.33 per cent in the closed economy scenario. A further reduction of the capital income tax rate increases efficiency gains to 0.82 per cent. Finally, the optimal tax structure in the small open economy also requires a reduction of the labour income tax rate.

Exercise 11.3

In order to calculate Euler equation errors in the OLG model, we proceed in a similar way as in the heterogeneous agent model, (see Exercise 9.13). Before we can do this, we need to formulate the first-order condition in consumption terms. The first-order condition of the OLG model reads (in a steady state):

$$\frac{\nu}{p_t} \cdot \frac{\left[c^\nu (1-l)^{1-\nu}\right]^{1-\frac{1}{\gamma}}}{c} = \beta E\left[V_{a^+}(z^+)|\eta\right],$$

which we can immediately write (using the state vector z) as:

$$f(z) = c(z) - \frac{\nu}{p_t} \cdot \frac{\left[c(z)^\nu (1-l(z))^{1-\nu}\right]^{1-\frac{1}{\gamma}}}{\beta E\left[V_{a^+}(z^+)|\eta\right]} = 0.$$

The Euler equation residual is the absolute of the residual of this first-order condition, relative to the current consumption level, meaning:

$$EER(z) = \left|\frac{f(z)}{c(z)}\right| = \left|1 - \frac{\frac{\nu}{p_t} \cdot \frac{\left[c(z)^\nu (1-l(z))^{1-\nu}\right]^{1-\frac{1}{\gamma}}}{c(z)}}{\beta E\left[V_{a^+}(z^+)|\eta\right]}\right|,$$

Table 11.2 Optimal tax structure in smopec

τ^w	τ^r	τ^c	*Tr*	Δ^*
0.15	0.20	0.075	−4.62	0.66
0.15	0.11	0.075	−6.85	0.82
0.13	0.11	0.075	−8.53	0.82

and the Euler equation error is the maximum of this residual along the asset state space:

$$EEE = \max_{a} EER(z).$$

We calculate the $EER(z)$ in the function `foc_EER` in the module `globals` to Program 11.3. We do not show this function here, as it is almost identical to the standard first-order condition. Note that we have to implement one minor change in order to be able to calculate Euler equation residuals for arbitrary levels of current assets a that are not located on the discretized asset grid. To do so, we communicate the actual current asset level `a_com` to the function `foc_EER`, instead of the index `ia_com` of the current asset gridpoint.

The subroutine `euler_equation_errors`, which is shown in Program 11.3, manages the calculation of the Euler equation error. At the beginning of this subroutine, we define for how many asset levels we want to calculate the Euler equation error in a variable `n_err`. We then iterate over the total state space, starting with age `ij` and going over all labour productivity shocks. For each of the specified asset levels, which we directly store in the communication variable `a_com`, we interpolate the savings function `aplus`

Program 11.3 Calculating Euler equation errors

```
subroutine euler_equation_errors()

    implicit none
    integer, parameter :: n_err = 10000
    [......]
    ! calculate euler equation errors for each age ij
    do ij = 1, JJ-1
        [......]
        a_com = a_l + (a_u-a_l)*dble(ia)/dble(n_err)

        ! linearly interpolate the savings function
        call linint_Grow(a_com, a_l, a_u, a_grow, &
                                 NA, ial, iar, varphi)
        a_plus = varphi*aplus(ij, ial, ip, is) &
                    + (1d0-varphi)*aplus(ij, iar, ip, is)

        ! calculate current error
        ij_com = ij
        ip_com = ip
        is_com = is

        err_temp = foc_EER(a_plus)

        ! check for greatest error
        if(err_temp > EEE .and. a_plus > a(1))then
            EEE = err_temp
            EEE_a = a_com
        endif
        [......]
    enddo

end subroutine
```

linearly, specify the remaining communication variables, and evaluate the Euler equation residual. The final if-statement updates the Euler equation error, if this residual is larger than the current error. Note that, similar to the solution in Exercise 9.13, we require that household savings are actually positive (enough), in this case meaning greater than the asset gridpoint a_1. By doing so, we rule out the possibility of the household being liquidity-constrained, in which case the Euler equation should not hold anyway.

We evaluate Euler equation errors by age in the initial equilibrium of the economy. They range at around $2.8 \cdot 10^{-2}$, which is not spectacular, but enough for our purposes. One can easily increase the accuracy of the model by choosing a greater number of asset gridpoints.

Exercise 11.4

In Exercise 10.20, we explained how to numerically implement Epstein-Zin (EZ) preferences in a life-cycle set-up. Since the ordinary preference structure from the benchmark model is only a special case of EZ preferences, it is easy to verify the correctness of the numerical model by setting the risk-aversion parameter to $\chi = 2.0$. Since the intertemporal substitution elasticity in the benchmark is set to $\gamma = 0.5$, the model with EZ preferences should give exactly the same results as the benchmark model with standard CRRA preferences.

In order to analyze the impact of a higher risk aversion χ on the optimal tax structure in the stochastic OLG model, we set $\chi = 4.0$, meaning that we double risk aversion. Note that the initial equilibrium will now change slightly compared to Table 11.2 in the book. When we implement the tax structure that was optimal under $\chi = 2.0$, households incur an efficiency loss of 0.32 per cent of initial resources (see the first line of Table 11.3). Higher labour taxes improve economic efficiency. The optimal tax structure is roughly $\tau^w = 0.19$ and $\tau^r = 0.22$, with a tiny efficiency gain of 0.01 per cent of aggregate resources. Of course, households with higher risk aversion require more insurance provision by the tax system, so that optimal tax rates are higher than in the case of $\chi = 2.0$. For the same reason, the optimal size of the pension system also increases to $\kappa = 0.42$, compared to $\kappa = 0.33$ in the benchmark case.

Table 11.3 Optimal tax structure with higher risk aversion

τ^w	τ^r	τ^c	Tr	κ	Δ^*
0.15	0.20	0.075	−4.57	0.50	−0.32
0.20	0.20	0.075	−0.78	0.50	0.00
0.19	0.22	0.075	−1.13	0.50	0.01
0.20	0.20	0.075	0.00	0.42	0.07

Exercise 11.5

We discussed the implementation of value function iteration in Exercises 10.12 and 10.16 of Chapter 10. The program `sol_prog11_05` has the very same structure, so that we do not need to discuss it again.

Exercise 11.6

Implementing a policy announcement is extremely simple. Instead of starting the policy reform in the first period of the transition, it is delayed for one or several periods. However, since the reform is announced in the first period of the transition, agents change their behaviour, starting in $t = 1$. For example, if the privatization of the pension system is announced one period before implementation, the pension replacement rate is set to `kappa(0:1)=0.5` and `kappa(2:TT)=0.0`. Agents already know in period 1 of the transition that pensions will be eliminated starting from period 2.

Table 11.4 shows that households decrease their consumption considerably in period 1 of the transition and increase their labour supply in order to prepare for their retirement without a public pension system. In the following periods, the adjustment is similar to what we see in Table 11.4 of the book, so that the economy finally ends up in the same long-run equilibrium. The efficiency losses from pension privatization with policy announcement amount to roughly 2 per cent of aggregate resources. They are significantly higher than without announcement (1.16 per cent—see Figure 11.6 in the book), because the announcement introduces additional distortions over the distortions already induced by the pension reform.

Exercise 11.7

Implementing life-span uncertainty should be no major problem, since a household problem with life-span uncertainty was already discussed extensively in Chapter 10. In

Table 11.4 Pension privatization with policy announcement

t	A	K	L	r^*	w	C	τ_w^*	τ_p^*
1	0.00	0.00	0.90	0.06	−0.32	−5.08	0.16	−0.07
2	4.57	5.49	11.46	0.36	−1.96	1.06	−1.70	−12.27
3	14.26	17.11	11.18	−0.33	1.89	5.29	−2.66	−12.27
⋮	⋮	⋮	⋮	⋮	⋮	⋮	⋮	⋮
∞	44.69	53.62	11.55	−1.93	12.21	21.52	−5.15	−12.27

* change in percentage points.

addition, how to determine aggregate bequests and how to distribute them within the group of living households was explained in Section 7.3 of the book.

Compared to the benchmark situation without life-span uncertainty, there are now much fewer pensioners. Consequently, for a given replacement rate, the resulting contribution rate τ^p is much lower than before. Hence, distortions associated with a specific replacement rate are lower, so that the optimal size of the pension system increases compared to what we found in Section 11.3.1 of the book. Given the assumptions with respect to the bequest distribution, the optimal size of the pension system increases to a replacement rate of roughly 43 per cent, compared to 33 per cent in the benchmark scenario of the book.

Exercise 11.8

When pension benefits are a function of the individual earnings history, we need to introduce a new state in which we accumulate the previous earnings or pension contributions. The German pension system defines so-called *earning points* (*ep*) that capture individual gross income relative to economy-wide average income for each contribution year, ie:

$$ep_{j+1} = \left[ep_j \times (j-1) + \left(\lambda + (1-\lambda)\frac{whl_j}{\bar{y}}\right)\right] / j.$$

The parameter λ specifies the *progressivity* of the pension system. Setting $\lambda = 1$ captures the baseline progressive pension system studied in Section 11.3 of the book, where benefits are independent of previous contributions. When $\lambda = 0$, benefits depend entirely on the previous earnings history. After entering the retirement phase $j \geq j_r$, earning points remain constant, and benefits are computed from:

$$pen_j = \kappa_t \times ep_{j_r} \times \bar{y}.$$

We formulate the household's optimization problem as:

$$V(z) = \max_{c,l,a^+,ep^+} \frac{\left[c^\nu (1-l)^{1-\nu}\right]^{1-\frac{1}{\gamma}}}{1-\frac{1}{\gamma}} + \beta E\left[V(z^+)|\eta\right],$$

with a state vector $z = (j, a, ep, \theta, \eta)$. The pension claims ep evolve according to the formula:

$$ep^+ = \begin{cases} \frac{j-1}{j} \cdot ep + \frac{1}{j} \cdot \left[\lambda + (1-\lambda) \cdot \frac{w_t hl}{\bar{y}_t}\right] & \text{if } j < j_r, \text{ and} \\ ep & \text{otherwise.} \end{cases}$$

In line with the previous discussion, the earnings points formula consists of two parts, the accumulation phase ($j < j_r$) and the yield phase ($j \geq j_r$). The household's budget constraint changes to:

$$a^+ + p_t c = (1 + r_t^n)a + w_t^n hl + \mathbb{1}_{j \geq j_r} \kappa_t \bar{y}_t ep.$$

Pension payments are only paid upon reaching the retirement age j_r and are the product of the current replacement rate κ_t, the average income $\bar{y}_t$ as well as the household's accumulated earnings points ep.

The Lagrangean of the household's optimization problem reads:

$$\begin{aligned}
\mathcal{L} = & \frac{\left[c^\nu (1-l)^{1-\nu}\right]^{1-\frac{1}{\gamma}}}{1-\frac{1}{\gamma}} + \beta E\left[V(z^+)|\eta\right] + \\
& + \mu_1 \left[(1+r_t^n)a + w_t^n hl + \mathbb{1}_{j \geq j_r} \kappa_t \bar{y}_t ep - a^+ - p_t c\right] \\
& + \mu_2 \mathbb{1}_{j<j_r} \left[\frac{j-1}{j} \cdot ep + \frac{1}{j} \cdot \left[\lambda + (1-\lambda) \cdot \frac{w_t hl}{\bar{y}_t}\right] - ep^+\right] \\
& + \mu_2 \mathbb{1}_{j \geq j_r} \left[ep - ep^+\right],
\end{aligned}$$

with the first-order conditions at working age being:

$$\frac{\nu}{p_t} \cdot \frac{\left[c^\nu (1-l)^{1-\nu}\right]^{1-\frac{1}{\gamma}}}{c} = \beta E\left[V_{a^+}(z^+)|\eta\right]$$

$$\frac{1-\nu}{\nu} \cdot p_t c = w_t h (1-l) \left\{ 1 - \tau_t^w - \tau_t^p + \frac{1-\lambda}{j \cdot \bar{y}} \cdot \frac{\beta E\left[V_{ep^+}(z^+)|\eta\right]}{\frac{\nu}{p_t} \cdot \frac{\left[c^\nu (1-l)^{1-\nu}\right]^{1-\frac{1}{\gamma}}}{c}} \right\}.$$

Note that for $\lambda = 1$ (ie in case of a flat pension benefit), the second formula collapses to the well-known intratemporal first-order condition.

The envelope theorem yields:

$$V_{a^+}(z^+) = (1 + r_{t+1}^n) \cdot \frac{\nu}{p_{t+1}} \cdot \frac{\left[(c^+)^\nu (1-l^+)^{1-\nu}\right]^{1-\frac{1}{\gamma}}}{c^+}$$

$$\begin{aligned}
V_{ep^+}(z^+) = & \mathbb{1}_{j+1 \geq j_r} \cdot \kappa_{t+1} \bar{y}_{t+1} \cdot \frac{\nu}{p_{t+1}} \cdot \frac{\left[(c^+)^\nu (1-l^+)^{1-\nu}\right]^{1-\frac{1}{\gamma}}}{c^+} \\
& + \left[\mathbb{1}_{j+1<j_r} \cdot \frac{j}{j+1} + \mathbb{1}_{j+1 \geq j_r}\right] \cdot \beta E\left[V_{ep^{++}}(z^{++})|\eta\right].
\end{aligned}$$

Iterating the first optimality condition forward therefore implies:

$$\beta^{i-j}E\left[\frac{\nu}{p_{t+i-j}}\cdot\frac{\left[(c_i)^\nu(1-l_i)^{1-\nu}\right]^{1-\frac{1}{\gamma}}}{c_i}\middle|\eta_j\right] = \frac{\frac{\nu}{p_t}\cdot\frac{\left[(c_j)^\nu(1-l_j)^{1-\nu}\right]^{1-\frac{1}{\gamma}}}{c_j}}{\prod_{k=j+1}^{i}(1+r_{t+k-j})} \qquad (I)$$

for any $i > j$.[1]

For age $j+1 = j_r$ the second envelope equation simplifies to:

$$V_{ep}(z_{j_r}) = \kappa_{t+1}\bar{y}_{t+1}\cdot\frac{\nu}{p_{t+1}}\cdot\frac{\left[(c_{j_r})^\nu(1-l_{j_r})^{1-\nu}\right]^{1-\frac{1}{\gamma}}}{c_{j_r}} + \beta E\left[V_{ep}(z_{j_r+1})|\eta_j\right],$$

where we use the age index j at consumption, labour, the productivity and the state vector for a clearer notation. Plugging in future definitions of V_{ep} into this recursive formulation, we obtain:

$$V_{ep}(z_{j_r}) = \sum_{i=j_r}^{J}\kappa_s\bar{y}_s\cdot\beta^{i-j_r}E\left[\frac{\nu}{p_s}\cdot\frac{\left[(c_i)^\nu(1-l_i)^{1-\nu}\right]^{1-\frac{1}{\gamma}}}{c_i}\middle|\eta_j\right], \qquad (II)$$

with $s = t+1+i-j_r$. Now, for any $j+1 < j_r$, we have:

$$\begin{aligned} V_{ep}(z_{j+1}) &= \frac{j}{j+1}\cdot\beta E\left[V_{ep}(z_{j+2})|\eta_j\right] \\ &= \frac{j}{j+1}\cdot\beta E\left[\frac{j+1}{j+2}\cdot\beta E\left[V_{ep}(z_{j+3})|\eta_j\right]\middle|\eta_j\right] \\ &= \frac{j}{j+2}\cdot\beta^2 E\left[V_{ep}(z_{j+3})|\eta_j\right] = \dots \\ &= \frac{j}{j_r-1}\cdot\beta^{j_r-(j+1)}E\left[V_{ep}(z_{j_r})|\eta_j\right]. \end{aligned}$$

Substituting definition (II) we can write:

$$\beta E\left[V_{ep^+}(z^+)|\eta_j\right] = \frac{j}{j_r-1}\sum_{i=j_r}^{J}\kappa_s\bar{y}_s\cdot\beta^{i-j}E\left[\frac{\nu}{p_s}\cdot\frac{\left[(c_i)^\nu(1-l_i)^{1-\nu}\right]^{1-\frac{1}{\gamma}}}{c_i}\middle|\eta_j\right],$$

[1] Note that we are making one little abstraction here. The Euler equation does not hold for liquidity-constrained households. For the sake of simplicity, however, we use this simplified formulation for all households. If one wants to be even more accurate, one has to explicitly take liquidity constraints into account, which makes the problem vastly more complex.

with $s = t + i - j$. Substituting finally equation (I) from above, we can write:

$$\frac{1-\lambda}{j \cdot \bar{y}_t} \cdot \frac{\beta E\left[V_{ep^+}(z^+)|\eta\right]}{\frac{\nu}{p_t} \cdot \frac{\left[c^\nu(1-l)^{1-\nu}\right]^{1-\frac{1}{\gamma}}}{c}} = \frac{1-\lambda}{(j_r-1) \cdot \bar{y}_t} \cdot \sum_{i=j_r}^{J} \frac{\kappa_s \bar{y}_s}{\prod_{k=j+1}^{i}(1+r_{t+k-j})},$$

with $s = t + i - j$. We consequently define the so-called *implicit tax rate* of the pension system as:

$$\tau_{j,t}^{impl} = \tau_t^p - \frac{1-\lambda}{(j_r-1) \cdot \bar{y}_t} \cdot \sum_{i=j_r}^{J} \frac{\kappa_s \bar{y}_s}{\prod_{k=j+1}^{i}(1+r_{t+k-j})}.$$

The implicit tax rate takes into account that, whenever $\lambda < 1$, pension payments increase with rising labour income and therefore rising pension contributions. Hence, not all of the pension contribution τ_t^p is perceived as a simple tax by the households. With the definition of the implicit tax rate, the household's first-order conditions finally read:

$$\frac{\nu}{p_t} \cdot \frac{\left[c^\nu(1-l)^{1-\nu}\right]^{1-\frac{1}{\gamma}}}{c} = \beta E\left[V_{a^+}(z^+)|\eta\right]$$

$$\frac{1-\nu}{\nu} \cdot p_t c = w_t h(1-l)\left\{1 - \tau_t^w - \tau_{j,t}^{impl}\right\},$$

where we again note that $\tau_{j,t}^{impl} = \tau_t^p$ for $\lambda = 1$, which brings us back to our original model.

We calculate the implicit tax rates using the above formula in a subroutine `implicit_taxes`, shown in Program 11.8. We therefore iterate over all working ages

Program 11.8 Implicit tax rates

```
subroutine implicit_taxes(it)
    [......]
    do ij = 1, JR-1
        itp = year(it, ij, JJ)
        tau_impl(ij, it) = 0d0
        do ijp = JJ, ij+1, -1
            itp = year(it, ij, ijp)
            if(ijp >= JR)then
                tau_impl(ij, it) = tau_impl(ij, it) &
                    + kappa(itp)*INC(itp)
            endif
            tau_impl(ij, it) = tau_impl(ij, it)/(1d0+rn(itp))
        enddo
        tau_impl(ij, it) = taup(it) - (1d0-lambda(it))* &
            tau_impl(ij, it)/(dble(JR-1)*INC(it))
    enddo

end subroutine
```

and calculate the implicit tax rate at each age by discounting the future $\kappa\bar{y}$ products with the respective future interest rates. Within the function `foc` that defines the first-order conditions, we then use the implicit tax rates to calculate optimal labour supply. In addition to this adjustment of the first-order condition, we need to take care of the fact that there is a second continuous state on our state space, the earnings points ep. We therefore define a second set of gridpoints `ep(0:NR)` with lower and upper bounds `ep_l` and `ep_u` and a growth rate between gridpoints `ep_grow`. Future earning points of an individual are captured in the array `epplus`, while pension benefits are now stored in the array `penp(JJ, 0:TT, 0:NR)`. In addition to age and time, pension payments now also depend on the individual's accumulated earning points. Of course, all other individual variables now include the earning points state as well. Within the function `foc`, we then perform a bilinear interpolation on the asset–earnings-points grid to interpolate the values of the future first-order condition.

There are two different kinds of exercises we can conduct in this model. At first, we can replicate our findings from Section 11.3 in the book by setting $\lambda = 1$ and verifying that the optimal pension system still is given by a replacement rate of approximately $\kappa = 0.33$. Next, we set $\lambda = 0$ and investigate reforms of the replacement rate of the pension system, when pension payments are perfectly related to previous labour earnings. In this case, the pension system provides no insurance against income risk at all. It is therefore not overly surprising that the maximum efficiency gain is found for $\kappa = 0.19$, instead of $\kappa = 0.33$, with an efficiency gain of 0.96 per cent of aggregate resources. Finally, we also study the optimal progressivity of the pension system. To this end, we keep the replacement rate at $\kappa = 0.5$ and only vary the progressivity parameter λ along the transition. It turns out that the optimal pension system features a progressivity of $\lambda = 1$, meaning that it is fully flat. In the present set-up, where the tax system is proportional and therefore only provides a small amount of insurance, households value the insurance provision through the pension system a lot and, hence, want it to be as flat as possible.

Exercise 11.9

A flat income tax with a basic allowance is equivalent to a proportional income tax plus a lump-sum tax, ie:

$$T_t(y, a) = \tau_t[y + ra - tr_t] = \tau_t(y + ra) - \tau_t tr_t = \tau_t(y + ra) - Tr_t,$$

if the allowance term tr_t is negative. Consequently, compared to the analysis in Section 11.3.3 of the book, there are two differences: First, we cannot vary the two tax rates for labour and capital income independently any more. Second, optimal lump-sum taxes now not only burden working cohorts, but also pensioners. The first difference will clearly

Program 11.9 Implicit tax rates

```
subroutine prices(it)
    [......]
    rn(it) = r(it)*(1d0-taur(it)-tauy(it))
    wn(it) = w(it)*(1d0-tauw(it)-taup(it)-tauy(it))

end subroutine
```

reduce flexibility, so that we can expect a reduced aggregate efficiency gain compared to the one reported in the first line of Table 11.6 in the book. The broader base of the lump-sum tax will probably work in the opposite direction. Therefore, the optimal tax structure and the resulting aggregate efficiency effects are not so clear.

Implementing the income tax system in program `prog11_02` of the book is straightforward. The new variables `tauy(0:TT)` and `try(0:TT)` define the income tax rate and the allowance term, respectively. The income tax rate is included in the definition of net factor prices in subroutine `prices`, as shown in Program 11.9.

Therefore, we can simulate the initial equilibrium now with an endogenous income tax rate instead of enforcing the equalization of the labour and the capital income tax in subroutine `government`. The tax base for the income tax is derived in variable `YTAX(0:TT)`, which aggregates the cohort-specific tax base `ytax_coh(JJ,0:TT)` in subroutine `aggregation`. Besides that, we only have to add the product `tauy(it)*try(it)` to the budget constraints of all households. For computation of the initial equilibrium shown in Table 11.2 of the book, we simply set `try(0)=0` and derive `tauy(0)` endogenously. Then we set a negative value for `try(1:TT)` and compute the budget-balancing income tax rates on the resulting transition path to the new steady state without and with compensating transfer payments. As it turns out, aggregate efficiency is maximized at 0.32 per cent of aggregate resources with $tr_t = -0.215$ and $\tau_\infty = 0.15$. Lump-sum taxes now amount to -4.19 per cent of average income, but they now apply to all households. Compared to the optimal differentiated tax structure reported in the first line of Table 11.6 in the book, aggregate efficiency gains are now only slightly lower.

Note finally that in practice governments typically do not pay transfers to low income earners, so that the income tax schedule changes to:

$$T_t(y,a) = \begin{cases} \tau_t[y + ra - tr_t] & \text{if } y + ra > tr_t \\ 0 & \text{otherwise.} \end{cases}$$

Modelling this specific income tax system is numerically challenging due to the implied discontinuity in the budget constraint. Agents with an income $y + ra$ close to the allowance tr_t would jump back and forth when the marginal tax rate switches between zero and τ_t. In order to solve the problem for these agents, one needs to compute a 'fictive' marginal income tax rate which 'bridges' the gap between zero and τ_t. This fictive marginal tax generates an income $y + ra = tr_t$ when agents optimize their behaviour.

REFERENCES

Auerbach, A J and L J Kotlikoff. 1987. *Dynamic Fiscal Policy*. Cambridge: Cambridge University Press.

Barillas, F and J Fernandez-Villaverde. 2007. 'A Generalization of the Endogenous Grid Method.' *Journal of Economic Dynamics and Control* 31: 2698–712.

De Nardi, M 2004. 'Wealth Inequality and Intergenerational Links.' *Review of Economic Studies* 71(3): 743–68.

Ljungqvist, L and T J Sargent. 2004. *Recursive Macroeconomic Theory*. 2nd edn. Cambridge: The MIT Press.

Miao, J 2014. *Economic Dynamics in Discrete Time*. Cambridge: The MIT Press.

Stokey, N and R E Lucas. 1989. *Recursive Methods in Economic Dynamics*. Cambridge: Harvard University Press.